D1031818

# Situational Judgment Tests
## Theory, Measurement, and Application

Edited by

**Jeff A. Weekley**
*Kenexa*

**Robert E. Ployhart**
*University of South Carolina*

Holy Family University
Newtown Campus - LRC

**LEA**

LAWRENCE ERLBAUM ASSOCIATES, PUBLISHERS

**2006**   Mahwah, New Jersey                    London

Senior Acquisitions Editor:     Anne Duffy
Editorial Assistant:            Rebecca Larsen
Cover Design:                   Kathryn Houghtaling Lacey
Full-Service Compositor:        TechBooks
Text and Cover Printer:         Hamilton Printing Company

This book was typeset in 10/12 pt. Palatino.
The heads were typeset in Poppl Laudatio, Poppl Laudatio Bold, and Poppl Laudatio Bold Italic.

Lawrence Erlbaum Associates, Inc., Publishers
10 Industrial Avenue
Mahwah, New Jersey 07430
www.erlbaum.com

**Library of Congress Cataloging-in-Publication Data**

Situational judgment tests : theory, measurement and application / edited by
  Jeff A. Weekley, Robert E. Ployhart.
    p.    cm.—(SIOP organizational frontiers series)
    Includes bibliographical references and index.
    ISBN 0-8058-5251-4 (cloth : alk. paper)
    1. Ability–Testing.   2. Prediction of occupational success.   I. Weekley, Jeff A.
II. Ployhart, Robert E., 1970-    III. Organizational frontiers series

  BF431.S54   2006
  153.9′4—dc22                                          2005029199

Books published by Lawrence Erlbaum Associates are printed on
acid-free paper, and their bindings are chosen for strength and
durability.

Printed in the United States of America
10  9  8  7  6  5  4  3  2  1

# The Organizational Frontiers Series

The Organizational Frontiers Series is sponsored by The Society for Industrial and Organizational Psychology (SIOP). Launched in 1983 to make scientific contributions to the field, the series has attempted to publish books on cutting-edge theory, research, and theory-driven practice in industrial/organizational psychology and related organizational science disciplines.

Our overall objective is to inform and to stimulate research for SIOP members (students, practitioners, and researchers) and people in related disciplines including the other subdisciplines of psychology, organizational behavior, human resource management, and labor and industrial relations. The volumes in the Organizational Frontiers Series have the following goals:

1. Focus on research and theory in organizational science, and the implications for practice.
2. Inform readers of significant advances in theory and research in psychology and related disciplines that are relevant to our research and practice.
3. Challenge the research and practice community to develop and adapt new ideas and to conduct research on these developments.
4. Promote the use of scientific knowledge in the solution of public policy issues and increased organizational effectiveness.

The volumes originated in the hope that they would facilitate continuous learning and a continuing research curiosity about organizational phenomena on the part of both scientists and practitioners.

# SIOP Organizational Frontiers Series

# SIOP Organizational Frontiers Series

*Series Editor*
## Robert Pritchard
*University of Central Florida*

**Dipboye/Colella:** (2005) *The Psychological and Organizational Bases of Discrimination at Work.*

**Griffin/O'Leary-Kelly:** (2004) *The Dark Side of Organizational Behavior.*

**Hofmann/Tetrick:** (2003) *Health and Safety in Organizations.*

**Jackson/Hitt/DeNisi:** (2003) *Managing Knowledge for Sustained Competitive Advantage.*

**Barrick/Ryan:** (2003) *Personality and Work: Reconsidering the Role of Personality in Organizations.*

**Lord/Klimoski/Kanfer:** (2002) *Emotions in the Workplace.*

**Drasgow/Schmitt:** (2002) *Measuring and Analyzing Behavior in Organizations: Advances in Measurement and Data Analysis.*

**Feldman:** (2002) *Work Careers: A Developmental Perspective.*

**Zaccaro/Klimoski:** (2001) *The Nature of Organizational Leadership: Understanding the Performance Imperatives Confronting Today's Leaders.*

**Rynes/Gerhart:** (2000) *Compensation in Organizations: Current Research and Practice.*

**Klein/Kozlowski:** (2000) *Multilevel Theory, Research, and Methods in Organizations: Foundations, Extensions, and New Directions.*

**Ilgen/Pulakos:** (1999) *The Changing Nature of Performance: Implications for Staffing, Motivation, and Development.*

**Earley/Erez:** (1997) *New Perspectives on International I-O Psychology.*

**Murphy:** (1996) *Individual Differences and Behavior in Organizations.*

**Guzzo/Salas:** (1995) *Team Effectiveness and Decision Making in Organizations.*

**Howard:** (1995) *The Changing Nature of Work.*

**Schmitt/Borman:** (1993) *Personnel Selection in Organizations.*

**Zedeck:** (1992) *Work, Families and Organizations.*

**Schneider:** (1990) *Organizational Culture and Climate.*

**Goldstein:** (1989) *Training and Development in Organizations.*

**Campbell/Campbell:** (1988) *Productivity in Organizations.*

**Hall:** (1986) *Career Development in Organizations.*

For a complete list of LEA titles, please contact Lawrence Erlbaum Associates, Publishers, at www.erlbaum.com.

For Susie . . . and everything
— Jeff

To Lynn and Matt
— Rob

# Contents

## III Application

# Series Foreword

This is the 23rd book in the Organizational Frontiers Series of books initiated by the Society for Industrial and Organizational Psychology (SIOP). The overall purpose of the volumes in this series is to promote the scientific status of the field. Ray Katzell first edited the series. He was followed by Irwin Goldstein, Sheldon Zedeck, and Neal Schmitt. The topics of the volumes and the volume editors are either chosen by the editorial board or individuals propose volumes to the editorial board. The series editor and the editorial board then work with the volume editor(s) in planning the volume. During the writing of the volume, the series editor often works with the editor and the publisher to bring the manuscript to completion.

The success of this series is evident in the high number of sales (now more than $50,000). Volumes have also received excellent reviews and individual chapters as well as volumes have been cited frequently. A symposium at the SIOP annual meeting examined the impact of the series on research and theory in industrial and organizational psychology. Although such influence is difficult to track and volumes varied in intent and perceived centrality to the discipline, the conclusion of most participants was that the volumes have exerted a significant impact on research and theory in the field and are regarded as being representative of the best the field has to offer.

This volume, edited by Jeff Weekley and Robert Ployhart, reflects new thinking and research in the area of situational judgment testing (SJT). It identifies a large body of research, theory, and practical information about understanding and using SJT. The volume also enlarges our perspective on this type of testing and integrates a large body of information into the SJT framework.

There are several other strengths of this volume. Past work on SJT has largely been atheoretical. This volume changes that with several chapters focusing on basic processes such as perception, judgment and decision making, practical intelligence, and tacit knowledge, with special attention to the psychological processes examinees' use in such tests. The volume also includes a major section on methodological issues, with considerable emphasis on future methodological needs. It also contains a major section on the applications of such testing.

Another major strength of the volume is how it identifies research needs. These are noted in many of the chapters and the concluding chapter discusses specific improvements that future research could make. These include work on the construct validity and how to structure SJTs to target particular constructs; the need for more experimental research in addition to the current correlational research; the need for more theory; and work to expand SJTs to new organizational settings.

The editors and chapter authors deserve our gratitude for clearly communicating the nature, application, and implications of the theory and research described in this book. Production of a volume such as this involves the hard work and cooperative effort of many individuals. The editors, the chapter authors, and the editorial board all played important roles in this endeavor. As all royalties from the series volumes are used to help support SIOP, none of the editors or authors received any remuneration. The editors and authors deserve our appreciation for engaging a difficult task for the sole purpose of furthering our understanding of organizational science. We want to express our gratitude to Anne Duffy, our editor at Lawrence Erlbaum Associates, who has been a great help in the planning and production of the volume.

—Robert D. Pritchard
*University of Central Florida*
*Series Editor, 2003–2008*

# Preface

In our research on situational judgment testing (SJTs) we frequently encountered situations where there were no clear answers and little relevant theory. We struggled with these issues, developing some solutions of our own and relying on the expertise of many colleagues for others. It became apparent that much useful knowledge existed solely in the minds and experiences of our colleagues. At the same time, the empirical database on SJTs continued to develop at an increasing rate. Given the increased interest in SJTs, we felt a book that integrated and summarized cutting-edge SJT research and practice would be extremely useful. We hope you agree.

This volume advances the science and practice of SJTs by promoting a theoretical framework, providing an understanding of best practices, and establishing a research agenda for years to come. Currently, there is no other source that provides such comprehensive treatment of SJT. There are several features of this book that make it relevant for academics, practitioners, and students of human resource, organizational behavior, management, and industrial/organizational psychology. First, the chapters are rich with theoretical insights and future research possibilities. Second, the chapters provide numerous implications for improving the practical application of SJTs. This includes not only SJT development and scoring, but also operational issues affecting test administration and interpretation. Third, the chapters are comprehensive summaries of published and unpublished SJT research. Finally, the chapters address topics that are timely and current, such as issues involving the international application of SJTs and technological considerations.

We would like to express our sincere thanks to many people for their assistance on this project. We'd first like to thank our families for putting up with us while working on this book (particularly for living with the large piles of paper that seemed to spring up overnight!). The time the authors invested was substantial and is reflected in the many insights and ideas they offer. They worked under a very tight schedule yet always rose to the challenge with enthusiasm. Bob Pritchard and the SIOP Frontiers Series board provided much guidance and feedback and were a pleasure to work with. Finally, Anne Duffy and her colleagues at Lawrence Erlbaum Associates have been extremely helpful and walked us through every step of the process, exhibiting patience that remains greatly appreciated (how they do it we'll never know). This book would not exist without the efforts of all these individuals.

—Jeff A. Weekley
—Robert E. Ployhart

# Contributors

**Talya N. Bauer** earned her undergraduate degree in psychology from Humboldt State University in California and a Ph.D. degree in Organizational Behavior and Human Resources from Purdue University in Indiana. She joined the PSU faculty in 1994. Dr. Bauer teaches organizational behavior, human resource management, interpersonal relations, negotiations, as well as training and development at the graduate and undergraduate level. She conducts research about relationships at work. More specifically, she works in the areas of selection, leadership, employee fit, and new employee socialization which have resulted in dozens of journal publications. She acts as a consultant for government, Fortune 1000, and start-up organizations. Dr. Bauer is involved in professional organizations and conferences at the national level such as serving on the Human Resource Management Executive Committee of the Academy of Management and as Membership Chair for SIOP. She is currently on the editorial board for the *Journal of Applied Psychology*, *Personnel Psychology*, and the *Journal of Management*.

**Margaret E. Brooks** received her Ph.D. in 2004 from Bowling Green State University. She is an Assistant Professor in the Industrial/Organizational Area of the Department of Psychology at Wayne State University. Maggie is a member of the Society for Industrial and Organizational Psychology (SIOP) and the Society for Judgment and Decision Making (SJDM). Her research interests are in the areas of employee selection, recruitment, job choice, and organizational image, with emphasis on how people form perceptions of the job and the organization.

**C. Shawn Burke** is a Research Scientist at the Institute for Simulation and Training of the University of Central Florida. Her expertise includes teams and their leadership, team adaptability, team training, measurement, evaluation, and team effectiveness. Dr. Burke has published over 40 journal articles and book chapters related to the above topics and has presented at over 70 peer-reviewed conferences. She is currently investigating team adaptability and its corresponding measurement, issues related to multi-cultural team performance, leadership, and training of such teams, and the impact of stress on team process and performance. Dr. Burke earned her doctorate in Industrial/Organizational Psychology from George Mason University. Dr. Burke serves as an ad-hoc reviewer for *Human Factors, Leadership Quarterly,* and *Quality and Safety in Healthcare.* She is currently co-editing two books, one on adaptability and one on advances in team effectiveness research.

**Michael A. Campion** is a Professor of Management at Purdue University (for the last 19 years). Previous industrial experience includes 8 years at IBM and Weyerhaeuser Company. He has an MS and PhD in industrial and organizational psychology. He has over 85 articles in scientific and professional journals, and has given over 170 presentations at professional meetings, on such topics as interviewing, testing, job analysis, work design, teams, training, turnover, promotion, and motivation. He is among the 10 most published authors in the top journals in his field for both the last two decades. He is past editor of *Personnel Psychology* (a scientific research journal) and past president of the Society for Industrial and Organizational Psychology. He also manages a small consulting firm (Campion Consulting Services) and a small I/O recruiting firm (Campion Recruiting Services).

**David Chan** received his Ph.D. in Industrial and Organizational Psychology from Michigan State University and is currently Professor of Psychology at the Singapore Management University. He has published in the areas of research methodology, personnel selection, longitudinal modeling, and adaptation to changes. He is currently an elected Representative-at-Large Member of the Executive Committee of the Research Methods Division, Academy of Management. David has received several awards including the Distinguished Early Career Contributions Award, William Owens Scholarly Achievement Award, and Edwin Ghiselli Award for Innovative Research Design from SIOP and the Dissertation Research Award from APA. He currently serves as Consulting Editor or editorial board member for seven journals and acts as regular reviewer for several journals and research grant organizations including the National Science Foundation and the Hong Kong Research Grants Council. He is also Consultant to the Prime Minister's Office in Singapore, the Ministry of Defence, the Ministry of Community Development, Youth and Sports, the Singapore Police Force, the Singapore Prison Service, and other public and private sector organizations. David has been appointed by the Singapore Government as a member of the National Council on Problem Gambling, which an independent body that decides on funding applications for preventive and rehabilitative programs and advises the Government on various public education efforts and program evaluation issues related to problem gambling.

**Michael J. Cullen** is a research scientist at Personnel Decisions Research Institutes, where he has participated in a wide variety of large-scale applied research projects with private sector and government clients. His primary research interests are training, personality, selection, and counterproductive workplace behaviors. His research has been published in the *Journal of Applied Psychology* and *American Psychologist*, and he has authored or co-authored several book chapters relating to his research interests. He received his Ph.D. in industrial/organizational psychology from the University of Minnesota.

**Fritz Drasgow** received his Ph.D. from the University of Illinois at Urbana-Champaign where he is currently Professor of Psychology and of Labor and Industrial Relations. Drasgow's research focuses on psychological measurement. He has conducted research designed to identify individuals mismeasured by tests and used multimedia computer technology to assess social and interpersonal skills not easily measured by paper-and-pencil tests. Drasgow has served on a variety of advisory committees and is a member of the editorial review board of eight journals, including *Journal of Applied Psychology* and *Applied Psychological Measurement*. He is the past president of the Society for Industrial and Organizational Psychology (Division 14).

**Barbara A. Fritzsche** is Director of the Ph.D. program in industrial and organizational psychology at the University of Central Florida. Her research interests include job selection, learner control in training, diversity in the workplace, and prosocial personality. Her work has appeared in journals such as the *Journal of Personality and Social Psychology*, *Journal of Occupational and Organizational Psychology*, *Journal of Management*, *Journal of Vocational Behavior*, and *Journal of Applied Social Psychology*.

**Theodore Gessner** received his Ph.D. (1971) in social psychology from the University of Maryland in 1971. He is an associate professor of psychology at George Mason University. His research interests include anxiety, and personality factors in human destructiveness and sense of humor.

**W. Lee Grubb III** is an assistant professor in the Department of Management at East Carolina University. He received his Ph.D. in Management from Virginia Commonwealth University. His research interests include situational judgment tests, emotional intelligence and entrepreneurship.

**Nathan S. Hartman** (Ph.D., Virginia Commonwealth University) is an Assistant Professor of Management at the Boler School of Business at John Carroll University. His research interests include organizational citizenship behaviors, employee selection, situational judgment tests, and research methods.

**Scott Highhouse** received his Ph.D. in 1992 from the University of Missouri at Saint Louis. He is a Professor and former Director of the Industrial-Organizational Area in the Department of Psychology, Bowling Green State University. Scott is Associate Editor of *Organizational Behavior and Human Decision Processes,* and serves of the editorial boards of *Journal of Applied Psychology* and *Journal of Occupational and Organizational Psychology.* He is a member of the Society for Judgment and Decision Making, and was named a fellow of the American Psychological Association and Society for Industrial and Organizational Psychologists. Scott has published numerous studies on decision making in employment contexts. His research interests include organizational image and attraction, employee recruitment and selection, context effects on judgment and choice, and the history of applied psychology.

**Brian C. Holtz** is an assistant professor of psychology at the University of Calgary. He received his M.A. (2003) and Ph.D. (2005) degrees in industrial/organizational psychology from George Mason University. His research interests include personnel selection, applicant reactions, and organizational justice. His research has appeared in several scholarly journals and professional conferences.

**Amy C. Hooper** is a doctoral student in the Industrial/Organizational program at the University of Minnesota. Her research interests include personality measurement, faking on non-cognitive measures, and racial and ethnic diversity. Her research on situational judgment tests has been presented at SIOP and is in press in the *Journal of Applied Psychology.*

**Hannah L. Jackson** is a doctoral candidate in the Industrial/Organizational program at the University of Minnesota. Her research interests include expatriate job performance, group differences in personality, leadership and emotional labor, and counterproductive work behavior. Her research on situational judgment tests has been presented at SIOP and is in press in the Journal of Applied Psychology.

**Richard J. Klimoski** is Dean of the School of Management and Professor Psychology and Management at George Mason University in Fairfax, Virginia. His teaching and research interests revolve around the areas of organizational control systems in the form of performance appraisal and performance feedback programs and team performance. His research has appeared in the Journal of Applied Psychology, Personnel Psychology, Academy of Management Journal, Journal of Management, Administrative Science Quarterly, and Journal of Conflict Resolution. He is coauthor with Neal Schmitt of Research Methods in Human Resource Management (1991) and coeditor with Stephen Zaccaro of The Nature of Organizational Leadership (2001). He is also coeditor with Robert G. Lord and Ruth Kanfer of Emotions in the Work Place (2002). He is on the editorial review board of Human Resource Management Review and Organizational Research Methods.

**Filip Lievens** received his Ph.D from Ghent University, Belgium and is currently Associate Professor at the Department of Personnel Management and Work and Organizational Psychology at the same university. He is the author of over 40 articles in the areas of organizational attractiveness, high-stakes testing, perceptions of staffing practices, and alternative selection procedures including assessment centers, situational judgment tests, and web-based assessment. His works have been published in the *Journal of Applied Psychology, Personnel Psychology, Journal of Organizational Behavior, Journal of Occupational and Organizational Psychology, Applied Psychology: An international Review*, and *International Journal of Selection and Assessment*. He was a past book review editor for the *International Journal of Selection and Assessment* and he currently serves as editorial board member for five journals. He is currently secretary for the Organizational Psychology Division of the International Association for Applied Psychology. Filip has received several awards including the Best Paper Award from the International Personnel Management Association.

**Michael A. McDaniel** received his Ph.D. in industrial/organizational psychology at George Washington University in 1986. He is a professor of Management at Virginia Commonwealth University and President of Work Skills First, Inc. a human resource consulting firm. Dr. McDaniel is nationally recognized for his research and practice in personnel selection system development and validation. Dr. McDaniel has published in several major journals including *the Academy of Management Journal*, the *Journal of Applied Psychology*, and *Personnel Psychology*. Dr. McDaniel is a member of the Academy of Management and a Fellow of the Society of Industrial and Organizational Psychology, Inc. and the American Psychological Society. His current research interests include situational judgment tests, applications of meta-analysis to I/O psychology, publication bias and demographic differences in the workplace.

**Frederick P. Morgeson**, Ph.D. is an Associate Professor of Management in the Eli Broad College of Business at Michigan State University. He received his Ph.D. in Industrial and Organizational Psychology from Purdue University in 1998. Dr. Morgeson conducts research in the areas of work design, job analysis, personnel selection, leadership, and work teams. He has published over 35 articles and book chapters; with 14 of these appearing in the most highly cited referred outlets. In addition, he has presented over 50 papers at professional meetings, and is a member of the *Personnel Psychology* and *Journal of Management* editorial boards. In 2005, he received the American Psychological Association Distinguished Scientific Award for Early Career Contribution to Psychology in Applied Psychology.

**Stephan J. Motowidlo** received his Ph.D. degree from the University of Minnesota (1976) in industrial and organizational psychology. He is now the Herbert S. Autry Professor of Psychology at Rice University. His research interests include work attitudes, ocupational stress, selection interviews, job simulations, situational judgment tests, performance appraisal, and models of the performance domain. Motowidlo serves on the editorial boards of the *Journal of Applied Psychology*, *Human Performance*, and the *Journal of Organizational Behavior*.

**Dr. Troy Mumford** received his Ph.D. in Organizational Behavior and Human Resource Management from the Krannert Graduate School of Management at Purdue University. He currently teaches courses Human Resource Management including compensation, performance management, and organizational behavior. His current research interests include determinants of team member effectiveness, employee choice of flexible benefit options, and multi-level leadership skill requirements. Troy has also been involved in variety of independent consulting and applied research projects for a number of organizations in the biomedical, manufacturing, financial, and airline industries as well as the United States Government. These projects span many HR functions, including: Job Analysis, Selection, Recruiting, Training, Compensation, HR planning, Process Analysis, and Performance Appraisal.

**Nhung T. Nguyen**, assistant professor of management at Towson University, received her Ph.D. degree in organizational behavior/human resource management from Virginia Commonwealth University. Her primary research interests include employee selection, impression management, and performance appraisals. Her methodological interests include the application of meta-analysis and structural equations modeling to organizational research. She has published articles in the *International Journal of Selection and Assessment*, the *Journal of Applied Psychology*, the *Journal of Applied Social Psychology*, *Applied H.R.M. Research* journal, and the *Journal of Higher Education Policy and Management*.

**Julie B. Olson-Buchanan** is a professor and department chair in the Department of Management at the Craig School of Business, California State University, Fresno. Her research interests include the development of technology-based assessments and the antecedents and consequences of experiencing and voicing mistreatment in the workplace. Her work has been published in such journals as the *Journal of Applied Psychology*, *Personnel Psychology*, and the *Academy of Management Journal*. She is the 2006 Program Chair for the Society for Industrial and Organizational Psychology Conference. She received her Ph.D. in industrial/organizational psychology from the University of Illinois, Urbana-Champaign, in 1992.

**Robert E. Ployhart** is an Associate Professor of Management in the Darla Moore School of Business at the University of South Carolina. He received his Ph.D. from Michigan State University (1999) and M.A. from Bowling Green State University (1996), both in Industrial/Organizational Psychology. His research focuses on staffing, personnel selection, recruitment, and applied statistical models such as structural equation, multilevel, and longitudinal modeling. Rob has published over 50 journal articles and chapters on these topics, and his research has received nearly $200,000.00 in external funding. In addition to Situational Judgment Tests, he has coauthored Staffing Organizations with Ben Schneider and Neal Schmitt. Rob serves on the editorial boards of numerous journals and has received several awards from the Society of Industrial and Organizational Psychology and the Human Resource Division of the Academy of Management. He is also an active practitioner, part owner of the consulting firm Human Capital Solutions, Inc., and has consulted with numerous private organizations and government agencies.

**Paul R. Sackett** is a professor of psychology at the University of Minnesota. He received his Ph.D. in Industrial and Organizational Psychology at the Ohio State University in 1979. He served as the editor of *Personnel Psychology* from 1984 to 1990, as president of the Society for Industrial and Organizational Psychology, as co-chair of the Joint Committee on the *Standards for Educational and Psychological Testing*, as a member of the National Research Council's Board on Testing and Assessment, as chair of APA's Committee on Psychological Tests and Assessments, and as chair of APA's Board of Scientific Affairs. His research interests revolve around various aspects of psychological testing and assessment in workplace settings.

**Eduardo Salas,** Ph.D. is Trustee Chair and Professor of Psychology at the University of Central Florida. Also holds an appointment as Program Director for the Human-Systems Integration Department at the Institute for Simulation & Training at UCF. He has co-authored over 300 journal articles and book chapters, has edited 15 books, serves on 10 editorial boards and is Past Editor of *Human Factors* journal. He is a Fellow of Division 14(recipient of the Division's applied research award) and 21(recipient of Division's Taylor award for contributions to the field) (member of Division 19) of APA and a Fellow of the Human Factors and Ergonomics Society. His research interests include team training and performance, training effectiveness, decision-making under stress and training technology.

**Neal Schmitt** obtained his Ph.D. from Purdue University in 1972 in Industrial/Organizational Psychology and is currently University Distinguished Professor of Psychology and Management at Michigan State University. He was editor of *Journal of Applied Psychology* from 1988–1994 and has served on ten editorial boards. He has also been a Fulbright Scholar at the University of Manchester Institute of Science and Technology. He has received the Society for Industrial/Organizational Psychology's Distinguished Scientific Contributions Award (1999) and its Distinguished Service Contributions Award (1998). He served as the Society's President in 1989–90. He was also awarded the Heneman Career Achievement Award from the Human Resources Division of the Academy of Management. He has coauthored three textbooks, *Staffing Organizations* with Ben Schneider and Rob Ployhart, *Research Methods in Human Resource Management* with Richard Klimoski, *Personnel Selection* with David Chan, co-edited *Personnel Selection in Organizations* with Walter Borman and *Measurement and Data Analysis* with Fritz Drasgow and published approximately 150 articles. His current research centers on the effectiveness of organization's selection procedures and the outcomes of these procedures, particularly as they relate to subgroup employment and applicant reactions and behavior. Over the past three years, he has also been working on the development and validation of noncognitive measures for college admissions.

**Kevin C. Stagl** is a doctoral candidate in the Industrial and Organizational Psychology program at the University of Central Florida. Kevin is currently employed as a research assistant at UCF's Institute for Simulation and Training (IST). At IST his theoretical and empirical research addresses the full spectrum of multilevel team effectiveness issues with an emphasis on the promotion of team leadership, distributed team performance, and team adaptation. His research has been featured in dozens of scholarly outlets such as the *Organizational Frontiers Series, International Review of Industrial and Organizational Psychology, International Encyclopedia of Ergonomics and Human Factors,* and *Research in Multi-level Issues.* Prior to joining IST, Kevin spent five years as a member of an organizational consultancy. In his former role, Kevin worked with a global team of experts to provide clientele with customized human resource decision support strategies, systems, and solutions.

**Steven E. Stemler** is an Associate Research Scientist in the Department of Psychology at Yale University. He received his doctorate in Educational Research, Measurement and Evaluation from Boston College, where he worked at the Center for the Study of Testing, Evaluation, and Educational Policy. Steve has also served as a consultant in policy and planning for the Massachusetts Board of Higher Education. His areas of interest include measurement and assessment, especially within the domains of practical intelligence and wisdom.

**Robert J. Sternberg** is Dean of Arts and Sciences at Tufts University. Prior to that, he was IBM Professor of Psychology and Education, Professor of Management, and Director of the Center for the Psychology of Abilities, Competencies, and Expertise at Yale University. His main interests are in intelligence, creativity, wisdom, and leadership. Sternberg received his Ph.D. in 1975 from Stanford and subsequently has received five honorary doctorates.

**Donald M. Truxillo** is a professor of psychology at Portland State University. Earlier, he worked in public sector for several years designing tests, simulations, and assessment centers. His research has focused on the areas of test-taking predispositions and applicant and employee reactions to selection procedures, test score banding, and substance abuse screening. His work has been published in journals such as *Journal of Applied Psychology* and *Personnel Psychology,* and he serves on the editorial board of *Journal of Management.* He has served as program chair and as conference chair for the SIOP conference. He received his Ph.D. in industrial/organizational psychology from Louisiana State University.

**Jeff Weekley** is a principal in the human capital management firm Kenexa, where he has consulted with many of the world's best companies on the development and implementation of employee selection systems, succession planning processes, performance management systems, and employee surveys. He has held several senior human resource management positions, including with Zale Corporation, Southland Corporation, and Greyhound Lines. Dr. Weekley received his Ph.D. in Organizational Behavior from the University of Texas at Dallas and Master of Science in Industrial & Organizational Psychology and Bachelor of Science in Psychology from Texas A&M. He is a member of the American Psychological Association, the Society for Industrial & Organizational Psychology, and the Academy of Management and has authored articles in journals such as the Journal of Applied Psychology, Personnel Psychology, Academy of Management Journal, Human Performance, and Journal of Management.

**Deborah L. Whetzel** received her Ph.D. in industrial/organizational psychology at George Washington University in 1991. She is a principal with Work Skills First, Inc. a human resource consulting firm. She has directed or conducted research on projects dealing with competency model development and job analysis, selection, promotion and assessment, nationally administered test development, and test development, research, and implementation. Dr. Whetzel co-edited a book, *Applied Measurement Methods in Industrial Psychology*, which describes, in laypersons terms, methods for conducting job analysis and for developing various kinds of instruments used to predict and assess performance. The book has received several positive reviews. Her work has been presented at professional conferences and published in peer-reviewed journals.

# Situational Judgment Tests

Theory, Measurement, and Application

# 1

# An Introduction to Situational Judgment Testing

Jeff A. Weekley
*Kenexa*

Robert E. Ployhart
*University of South Carolina*

In selection, testing, and assessment contexts, the fundamental task is to make accurate predictions about a person's current and future job performance based on limited information obtained during the selection/testing process. The more accurate and relevant the information obtained in the selection/testing process, the better this prediction is going to be. The magnitude and consequences of testing in today's world is staggering. From assessments in elementary and high school, to college and graduate admissions, to employment testing and certification, to placement in military occupations, millions of people are affected by testing each year. When done correctly, such testing programs improve the effectiveness of organizations and possibly entire nations. Therefore, the continued search for better and more efficient predictors of performance is critical.

The situational judgment test (SJT) presents one such "new" predictor. Over the past 15 years, SJTs have increased in popularity as a predictor of performance. In the typical SJT, an applicant is presented with a variety of situations he or she would be likely to encounter on the job—these situations are usually gleaned from critical incidents or other job-analytic methods. Accompanying each situation are multiple possible ways to handle or respond to the hypothetical situation. The test taker is then asked to make judgments about the possible courses of action, in either a forced-choice (e.g., "select the course of action you would be most and least likely to perform") or Likert-style format (e.g., "rate the effectiveness of each option on a five-point scale"). Scoring is done by comparing the applicant's choices to a key, which itself can be determined rationally or empirically. Although most SJTs are of the paper–pencil variety, a few have been adapted to video (e.g., Dalessio, 1994; Weekley & Jones, 1997) and more recently to the personal computer (Olson-Buchanan et al., 1998), including Web-based administration (e.g., Ployhart, Weekley, Holtz, & Kemp, 2003). Samples of typical SJT items appear in Table 1.1 (see also chap. 9 for other examples).

Although SJTs have been around for quite some time, research on the subject has until recently, been very sporadic. Publications by Sternberg and colleagues (Sternberg, Wagner, & Okagaki, 1993; Wagner, 1987; Wagner & Sternberg, 1985) on "tacit knowledge" and by Motowidlo, Dunnette, and Carter (1990) on the "low fidelity simulation" stimulated renewed interest in SJT. Since Motowidlo et al.'s (1990) reintroduction of the subject to industrial/organizational psychology, there has been a surge in research directed at understanding SJTs. Consider submissions to the annual conference of the Society for Industrial and Organizational Psychology. Over the past decade, there has been a dramatic surge in the number of papers on the topic presented at the conference. For example, the number of SJT-related papers and presentations more than doubled from 1999 to 2004. Further growth in research on the topic is expected.

This increased popularity of SJTs is undoubtedly due to research showing these tests to have a number of very positive features. First, research indicates that SJTs can have validity approaching that of cognitive ability tests. McDaniel, Morgeson, Finnegan, Campion, and Braverman (2001), for example, accumulated 102 validity coefficients and estimated the mean corrected validity of SJTs to be 0.34. Furthermore, there have been several studies showing SJTs to have incremental validity above and beyond traditional predictors such as cognitive ability and personality (e.g., Clevenger, Pereira, Wiechmann, Schmitt, & Schmidt-Harvey, 2001; Weekley & Ployhart, 2005). These studies suggest that SJTs are capturing something unique, something related to performance that is not captured by other traditional constructs.

Second, mean subgroup differences are typically small to moderate. Importantly, SJTs show smaller racial subgroup differences than those observed for cognitive ability tests (e.g., Motowidlo & Tippins, 1993; Pulakos & Schmitt, 1996; Weekley & Jones, 1999; see Hough, Oswald, & Ployhart, 2001, for a review). Although there is wide variation in the effect sizes found

**TABLE 1.1**

Sample Situation Judgment Items

One of the people who reports to you doesn't think he or she has anywhere near the resources (such as budget, equipment, and so on) required to complete a special task you've assigned. You are this person's manager.

A. Tell him/her how he/she might go about it.
B. Give the assignment to another employee who doesn't have the same objections.
C. Tell the person to "just go do it."
D. Ask the person to think of some alternatives and review them with you.
E. Provide the employee with more resources.

   Which response above do you think is *best*?
   Which response above do you think is *worst*?

You have been trying to get an appointment with a very important prospect for several months, but you can't seem to get past her secretary. The secretary screens all of her boss' calls and mail. Of the following options:

A. Try just dropping in when you are nearby, and say you will wait to meet with her.
B. Diplomatically tell the secretary that her boss, rather than she, should make the decision whether to see you.
C. Write a confidential/private letter to the prospect, explaining the situation.
D. Try to reach the prospect early in the morning or in the evening when the secretary is not there.
E. Try to get the prospect's attention by doing something unusual, such as sending flowers, tickets to something special, or a singing telegram.

Rate each option above using the following scale:
   6 = highly effective
   5 = moderately effective
   4 = slightly effective
   3 = slightly ineffective
   2 = moderately ineffective
   1 = highly ineffective

for race, in almost all cases they are lower than the standardized mean difference of $d = 1.0$ typically reported for cognitive ability tests (Sackett & Wilk, 1994). This is important because the passing of the 1991 Civil Rights Act outlawed the practice of "within-group norming." By making the practice illegal, this legislation ensured that measures of cognitive ability, one of our most predictive constructs, will generate adverse impact in use at even modest cut scores (Bobko, Roth, & Potosky, 1999; Schmitt, Rogers, Chan,

Sheppard, & Jennings, 1997). Consequently, researchers and practitioners began to look for high-validity tests that would produce less adverse impact against minority candidates. The SJTs fit these requirements nicely.

Finally, the face validity inherent in the typical SJT can be an important benefit to selection procedures. Although research has yet to fully examine this question, it seems reasonable to expect SJTs to be readily accepted and explainable to applicants and may even offer the benefit of providing a realistic preview of the job. Thus, SJTs appear to provide validity nearing that of cognitive ability tests, yet produce smaller subgroup differences and possibly more favorable applicant reactions (Clevinger et al., 2001).

Perhaps because the early interest in SJTs was based on addressing these practical issues, research has predominantly focused on showing the relevance of SJTs in predicting job performance with less adverse impact. This work has been valuable in that SJTs have moved from obscurity to an increasingly common predictor method (e.g., in their comprehensive review of predictor validity, Schmidt and Hunter, 1998, do not even list SJTs as a predictor). However, it has proceeded largely without benefit of a theoretical framework and has not addressed the many kinds of practical issues that contribute to effective selection. As a result, it is an appropriate time for researchers and practitioners to take stock of where SJT research has been and to set an agenda for future research and practice. In this book, leading experts have been asked to comment on important issues related to theory of situational judgment, SJT design, and SJT implementation. They address a number of current challenges, offer solutions for better understanding SJTs theoretically and using them practically, and establish a future research agenda. Before considering these chapters, let us first place SJTs in context, both in terms of other similar predictors and the historical development of SJTs.

## SITUATIONAL JUDGMENT TESTS COMPARED TO OTHER ASSESSMENTS

It is instructive to distinguish SJTs from other similarly situation-based assessment methods. The situational interview (Latham & Saari, 1984; Latham, Saari, Pursell, & Campion, 1980), wherein applicants are presented with likely job-related situations and the interviewer rates the effectiveness of responses (often using behaviorally anchored rating scales), is a close cousin of the SJT both in form (e.g., Weekley & Gier, 1987) and validity (e.g., McDaniel, Whetzel, Schmidt, & Maurer, 1994). The primary differences between the situational interview and most SJTs are in how they are presented to examinees (verbally vs. in writing); how examinee responses are given (verbally vs. selecting from among a closed-ended set of options), and how responses are scored (interviewer judgment vs. comparison to some scoring key).

SJT also shares some similarity to other situational-based methods such as work samples (Asher & Sciarrino, 1974) and many assessment center exercises such as in-baskets, role plays, and the like (Thornton & Byham, 1982). Work samples and assessment centers, however, go well beyond the SJT format in that they actually put the examinee "in the situation" as opposed to merely presenting a description of it to the examinee. Ployhart, Schneider, and Schmitt (2005) noted that these simulation methods vary on a continuum of physical fidelity, such that SJTs are low fidelity, assessment centers are higher fidelity, and work samples are the highest fidelity. Thus, these methods measure the ability to do rather than to know (Cascio & Phillips, 1979) and behavior is assessed directly rather than through self-reports of what one would or should do. Finally, as with the situational interview, these methods require "assessors" to assign scores to examinees, whereas SJTs can be scored mechanically. Thus, SJTs share some features of interviews, work samples, and assessment centers, but have a number of important differences. These differences are such that SJTs may be easier to score and implement in large-scale testing programs, making them attractive options for early stages of recruitment and selection. Because of these important differences, the historical review that follows is restricted to SJTs as described earlier.

## THE EARLY DAYS OF SITUATIONAL JUDGMENT TESTING

Although research interest in SJTs has grown quickly in recent years, the notion of measuring human judgment has been around for a very long time. The earliest example of SJT depends, in part, on how an SJT is defined. As reported by DuBois (1970), the first civil service examinations in the United States contained some items of a distinctly situational nature. For example, one such 1873 test for the Examiner of Trade-Marks, Patent Office, contained the following: "A banking company asks protection for a certain device, as a trade-mark, which they propose to put upon their notes. What action would you take on the application?" (DuBois, 1970, p. 148). Other similarly worded items were present on this exam. Later, the 1905 Binet scale (used to assess intelligence in children) included 25 abstract questions such as, "When a person has offended you, and comes to offer his apologies, what should you do?" and "When one asks your opinion of someone whom you know only a little, what ought you to say?" This section of the Binet scale (as translated by Kite, 1916) included instructions that are decidedly situational: "This consists in reading the beginning of a sentence and suspending the voice when one arrives at the point, and repeating, 'What ought one do?'"

Although situations were presented, these early efforts did not include possible ways of handling the situation and it was left up to assessors to evaluate the effectiveness of the open-ended responses. In effect, these items may have been the earliest recorded examples of a situational interview (e.g., Latham et al., 1980). As noted by McDaniel et al. (2001), probably the first widely used SJT, complete with closed-ended response options, was the George Washington Social Intelligence Test (Moss, 1926). World War II saw continued attempts to use SJTs to measure judgment, although the effectiveness of such attempts is unknown (Northrop, 1989). Throughout the 1940s and into the early 1960s, several attempts were made to develop SJTs to assess supervisory and managerial potential (e.g., Bruce, 1965; Bruce & Learner, 1958; Cardall, 1942; File, 1945; Greenberg, 1963; Kirkpatrick & Planty, 1960). This emphasis on predicting supervisory and managerial potential continued into the 1980s (see McDaniel et al., 2001, for an excellent discussion of the history of SJTs).

It is interesting to note the conclusions of most reviewers of these early SJTs. Although these tests were designed to measure "judgment," critics consistently noted that these measures were highly related to general intelligence (e.g., Carrington, 1949; File & Remmers, 1971; Millard, 1952; Taylor, 1949a, 1949b; Thorndike, 1941; Thorndike & Stein, 1937) and often factorially complex (e.g., Northrop, 1989). That the same criticisms exist today (e.g., Schmitt & Chan, chap. 7, this volume) suggests that little progress has been made over the years in terms of improving the measurement characteristics of SJTs. Fortunately, nothing could be further from the truth. As previously mentioned, the recent surge of research on SJTs has generated many new and thought-provoking findings. However, empirical research has run in front of theory development, resulting in many, often fragmented approaches being taken to the study of SJTs. Although this manner of conducting research offers some advantages (e.g., great variety in the topics researched), it does not readily allow for the development of consensus regarding "best practices" for SJT. It does not allow the identification of an underlying theme or convergence toward a coherent theory.

In the spirit of developing such theory, it is hoped that this volume will serve three objectives. The first is as a single source summarization of the extant literature, with an emphasis on what is believed to work best (at least as of the time of this writing). There has been a lot of work on SJTs but there is no single source that reviews this information. The second objective is to encourage more theory-driven effort. The absence of compelling theory in SJT is perhaps its greatest limitation. If SJTs are to contribute meaningfully to organizational science, this lack of theory must be addressed. Finally, it is hoped that a broad agenda for future research might be established. This third objective, if fulfilled, will enable future researchers to methodically plug the "gaps" in our current knowledge — the reader will see throughout this book that there are many such gaps. Consistent with these objectives, it is hoped that both scientists and practitioners will find the volume useful.

## OUTLINE OF THE BOOK

The remainder of this volume is divided into three sections, plus a summary chapter. The first section focuses on theory and SJT. As noted, to date research on SJTs has proceeded in a largely atheoretical fashion. The contributors of these chapters bring some much needed theoretical perspective to SJT. Yet each also brings a unique and different perspective, giving the reader a broad theoretical orientation that offers many directions for research. Gessner and Kilmoski (chap. 2) examine various theories regarding how people perceive situations, the factors that impact these perceptions, and the implications therein for situational judgment. In chapter 3, Brooks and Highhouse consider the literature on judgment and decision making as applied to SJTs, providing another perspective for research on situational judgment tests. In chapter 4, Motowidlo, Brooks, and Jackson integrate a diverse body of literature in the development of a theoretical framework for SJTs, and in doing so provide a much needed rationale for what SJTs measure and why they work. Ployhart (chap. 5), drawing on relevant theories in cognitive psychology and psychometrics, presents a model of the psychological processes examinee's engage in when responding to situational judgment items. Finally, Stemler and Sternberg (chap. 6) review previous theory and research on practical intelligence or tacit knowledge and illustrate the application of their work on practical intelligence in the development of an SJT.

The second section focuses on methodological issues in SJT development and research. Schmitt and Chan (chap. 7) consider evidence for the construct validity of SJTs and offer their insights into what SJTs measure. Weekley, Ployhart, and Holtz (chap. 8) review research on the wide variety of approaches used to develop SJTs, including variations in content determination, response option development, response instructions, determining response option effectiveness, and scoring. McDaniel, Hartman, Nguyen, and Grubb (chap. 9) summarize the empirical research to date on validity of situational judgment tests and consider how the framing of SJT questions impact the constructs captured. Hooper, Cullen, and Sackett (chap. 10) examine operational threats to the use of situational judgment tests, including faking, coaching, and, retesting. Finally chapter 11, Bauer and Truxillo, in drawing on the procedural justice literature, consider applicant reactions to SJTs and the implications of SJT perceptions for issues such as face validity and applicant motivation.

The third section considers four important issues relative to the application of SJTs. Olson-Buchanan and Drasgow (chap. 12) consider the use of alternative media in the presentation of SJTs, the challenges associated with the use of multimedia SJTs, and the implications of varying degrees of fidelity for measurement properties and applicant reactions. Lievens (chap. 13) reviews SJT research from other countries and, within the context of cross-cultural theory, explores the limits of the generalizability of SJT validity across cultural boundaries. Fritzsche, Stagl, Salas, and Burke (chap. 14) explore the underresearched issue of SJTs and training, including the use of SJTs in needs assessment, scenario-based training delivery, and training evaluation. Finally, Mumford, Campion, and Morgeson (chap. 15) consider their research on SJTs as predictors of team staffing and contextual performance.

In the concluding chapter, we (chap. 16) attempt to summarize the major themes of the preceding chapters. By integrating the directions for research offered by the contributing authors, the hope is to provide future researchers with a general road map for the advancement of our understanding of SJT.

## REFERENCES

Asher, J. J., & Sciarrino, J. A. (1974). Realistic work sample tests: A review. *Personnel Psychology*, 27, 519–533.

Binet, A. (1905). New methods for the diagnosis of the intellectual level of subnormals. *L'Année Psychologique*, 12, 191–244.

Bobko, P., Roth, P. L., & Potosky, D. (1999). Derivation and implications of a meta-analytic matrix incorporating cognitive ability, alternative predictors, and job performance. *Personnel Psychology*, 52, 561–589.

Bruce, M. M. (1965). *Examiner's manual: Supervisory practices test* (rev. ed.). Larchmont, NY: Author.

Bruce, M. M., & Learner, D. B. (1958). A supervisory practices test. *Personnel Psychology*, 11, 207–216.

Cardall, A. J. (1942). *Preliminary manual for the test of practical judgment.* Chicago IL: Science Research.

Carrington, D. H. (1949). Note on the Cardall practical judgment test. *Journal of Applied Psychology*, 33, 29–30.

Cascio, W. F., & Phillips, N. F. (1979). Performance testing: A rose among thorns? *Personnel Psychology*, 32, 751–766.

Clevenger, J., Pereira, G. M., Wiechmann, D., Schmitt, N., Schmidt-Harvey, V. (2001). Incremental validity of situational judgment tests. *Journal of Applied Psychology*, 86, 410–417.

Dalessio, A. T. (1994). Predicting insurance agent turnover using a video-based situational judgment test. *Journal of Business and Psychology, 9*, 23–32.

DuBois, P. H. (1970). *A history of psychological testing.* Boston, MA: Allyn & Bacon.

File, Q. W. (1945). The measurement of supervisory quality in industry. *Journal of Applied Psychology, 29*, 381–387.

File, Q. W., & Remmers, H. H. (1971). *How supervise? Manual 1971 revision.* Cleveland OH: Psychological Corp.

Greenberg, S. H. (1963). *Supervisory judgment test manual.* Washington, DC: U. S. Civil Service Commission.

Hough, L. M., Oswald, F. L., & Ployhart, R. E. (2001). Determinants, detection, and amelioration of adverse impact in personnel selection procedures: Issues, evidence, and lessons learned. *Internal Journal of Selection and Assessment, 9*, 152–194.

Kirkpatrick, D. L., & Planty, E. (1960). *Supervisory inventory on human relations.* Chicago, IL: Science Research Associates.

Kite, E. S. (1916). *The development of intelligence in children.* Vineland, NJ: Publications of the Training School at Vineland.

Latham, G. P., & Saari, L. M. (1984). Do people do what they say? Further studies of the situational interview. *Journal of Applied Psychology, 69*, 569–573.

Latham, G. P., Saari, L. M., Pursell, E. D., & Campion, M. A. (1980). The situational interview. *Journal of Applied Psychology, 65*, 422–427.

McDaniel, M. A., Whetzel, D. L., Schmidt, F. L., & Maurer, S. D. (1994). The validity of employment interviews: A comprehensive review and meta-analysis. *Journal of Applied Psychology, 79*, 599–616.

McDaniel, M. A., Morgerson, F. P., Finnegan, E. B., Campion, M. A., & Braverman, E. P. (2001). Use of situational judgment tests to predict job performance: A clarification of the literature. *Journal of Applied Psychology, 80*, 730–740.

Millard, K. A. (1952). Is how supervise? an intelligence test? *Journal of Applied Psychology, 36*, 221–224.

Moss, F. A. (1926). Do you know how to get along with people? Why some people get ahead in the world while others do not. *Scientific American, 135*, 26–27.

Motowidlo, S. J., Dunnette, M. D., & Carter, G. W. (1990). An alternative selection procedure: The low-fidelity simulation. *Journal of Applied Psychology, 75*, 640–647.

Motowidlo, S. J., & Tippins, N. (1993). Further studies of the low-fidelity simulation in the form of a situational inventory. *Journal of Occupational and Organizational Psychology, 66*, 337–344.

Northrop, L. C. (1989). *The psychometric history of selected ability constructs.* Washington, DC: U.S. Office of Personnel Management.

Olson-Buchanan, J. B., Drasgow, F., Moberg, P. J., Mead, A. D., Keenan, P. A., & Donovan, M. A. (1998). Interactive video assessment of conflict resolution skills. *Personnel Psychology, 51*, 1–24.

Ployhart, R. E., Schneider, B., & Schmitt, N. (2005). *Organizational staffing: Contemporary practice and theory.* Mahwah, NJ: Lawrence Erlbaum Associates.

Ployhart, R. E., Weekley, J. A., Holtz, B. C., & Kemp, C. F. (2003). Web-based and paper-and-pencil testing of applicants in a proctored setting: Are personality, biodata, and situational judgment tests comparable? *Personnel Psychology, 56*, 733–752.

Pulakos, E. D., & Schmitt, N. (1996). An evaluation of two strategies for reducing adverse impact and their effects on criterion-related validity. *Human Performance, 9*, 241–258.

Sackett, P. R., & Wilk, S. L. (1994). Within-group norming and other forms of score adjustment in preemployment testing. *American Psychologist, 49*, 929–954.

Schmidt, F. L. & Hunter, J. E. (1998). The validity and utility of selection methods in personnel psychology: Practical and theoretical implications of 85 years of research findings. *Psychological Bulletin, 124,* 262–274.

Schmitt, N., Rogers, W., Chan, D., Sheppard, L., & Jennings, D. (1997). Adverse impact and predictive efficiency of various predictor combinations. *Journal of Applied Psychology, 82,* 719–730.

Sternberg, R. A., Wagner, R. K., & Okagaki, L. (1993). Practical intelligence: The nature and role of tacit knowledge in work and at school. In H. Reese & J. Puckett (Eds.), *Advances in lifespan development* (pp. 205–227)., Hillside, NJ: Lawrence Erlbaum Associates.

Taylor, H. R. (1949a). Social intelligence test: George Washington University series. In O.K. Buros (Ed.), *The third mental measurements yearbook* (pp. xx ). New Brunswick, NJ: Rutgers University Press.

Taylor, H. R. (1949b). Test of practical judgment. In O.K. Buros (Ed.), *The third mental measurements yearbook* (pp. xx). New Brunswick, NJ: Rutgers University Press.

Thorndike, R. L. (1941). Social intelligence test. In O.K. Buros (Ed.), *The 1940 mental measurements yearbook* (pp. xx). Highland Park, NJ: Mental Measurements Yearbook.

Thorndike, R. L., & Stein, S. (1937). An evaluation of attempts to measure social intelligence. *Psychological Bulletin, 34,* 275–285.

Thornton, G. C., & Byham, W. C. (1982). *Assessment centers and managerial performance.* New York: Academic Press.

Wagner, R. K. (1987). Tacit knowledge in everyday intelligent behavior. *Journal of Personality and Social Psychology, 52,* 1236–1247.

Wagner, R. K., & Sternberg, R. J. (1985). Practical intelligence in real world pursuits: The role of tacit knowledge. *Journal of Personality and Social Psychology, 49,* 436–458.

Weekley, J. A., & Gier, J. A. (1987). Reliability and validity of the situational interview for a sales position. *Journal of Applied Psychology, 72,* 484–487.

Weekley, J. A., & Jones, C. (1997). Video-based situational testing. *Personnel Psychology,50,* 25–49.

Weekley, J. A., & Jones, C. (1999). Further studies of situational tests. *Personnel Psychology, 52,* 679–700.

Weekley, J. A., & Ployhart, R. E. (2005). Situational judgment: Antecedents and relationships with performance. *Human Performance, 18,* 81–104.

# I

# Theory

# 2

# Making Sense of Situations

Theodore L. Gessner
Richard J. Klimoski
*George Mason University*

This chapter examines the role of the "situation" as it relates to the design, implementation, and interpretation of the results from situational judgment tests (SJTs). The point of view taken here is that both researchers and practitioners have been all too sanguine about conceptualizing the notion of the *situation*. Hattrup and Jackson (1996) stressed the importance of individual judgments that are caused by an interaction between the situation and individual differences. The individual tries to make sense of the situation and apply the appropriate personal resources to perform in that type of situation. Hattrup and Jackson contended that middle-level constructs (e.g., situational judgments) will provide improved prediction over generalized measures (ability, personality, etc.) when the criterion is tied to specific performance demands.

We note that there is a rich tradition in psychology that offers conceptualizations of the situation as both the stimulus for and context of behavior and performance. The area of social psychology represents a relevant tradition. We focus on the social psychological research and suggest that McGrath's (1984) framework, which builds on the concept of the *behavior setting*, has special merit. It not only describes plausible dynamics promulgated by situations, but provides a basis for the metaphor of the test-taking situation as a "conversation" among stakeholders and can serve as a platform on which to make recommendations for improved SJT design and administration.

## OVERVIEW

This chapter reviews the way that situations have been conceptualized within a selected set of research traditions. Initially, we look at how three groups of stakeholders make sense of SJT. Then we highlight some of the ways that the situation has been modeled in an effort to predict or understand behavior in life situations. We then examine how the situation has been treated by those who are interested in modeling performance in high-stakes assessment contexts and how that influences what we are calling the SJT conversation. The potential for SJT research to expand our understanding of situation by individual difference constructs is discussed. Finally, we examine the role of sense-making as part of the SJT conversation in the design and use of the test platform. In short, we propose the need for a better theory of the test taker.

## HOW STAKEHOLDERS MAKE SENSE OF SJTs

The sense-making perspective we have adopted makes us aware of the fact that different stakeholders in the testing process have different perceptions of the meaning of the SJT. This creates special challenges for the field. For the purposes of this chapter, we focus on three prototypical stakeholders involved in the process of hiring applicants for entry-level positions. The three primary stakeholders are the test designer, the test administrator/user, and the applicant. These three sets of participants have very different lenses through which they view the SJT.

SJT literature usually gives voice to the perspective of the test designer. In fact, the major purpose of this volume is to set out insights relative to the specification of the SJT design process. We assume that the designer is invested in creating a quality measuring instrument that complies with the major demands of testing development. He or she seeks to craft an efficient assessment platform that allows for valid inferences regarding an applicant's knowledge, abilities, and disposition. Furthermore, the rules of the testing situation are quite pragmatic and the designer has the goal of developing a reliable setting that enhances prediction of job performance.

But the test administrator is also a stakeholder with somewhat different goals and needs that should be addressed. Although these may overlap with those of the designers, we propose that the user views the situation associated with the SJT more broadly. For example, the test user desires to have an SJT that is seen as face valid by the general public so as to mitigate against the likelihood of applicant adverse reactions. The user also wants a screening device that allows for simple scoring, one that is efficient and fits easily into the whole recruiting platform. Thus, for users the situation represented by the SJT would include not just the scenarios represented by the items or by the test as a whole. It incorporates an appreciation for the instructional, administrative, and reporting experience. For SJT users, the physical and temporal setting in which the SJT is presented to applicants will have an impact as well (see Bauer & Truxillo, chap. 11, this volume)

Most central to the arguments we present in this chapter, the subjective experience of a testing session will include the interpersonal dimension of test-taking and administrating situation. Is the SJT taken by groups, to be overseen in person by the administrator? Is more than one staff member engaged in the administration and scoring of the SJT? What is their relationship to each other and to their conceptualization of the test? What is the test administrator's responsibility for reporting and defending scores, or for making a recommendation to hire? And importantly, how does the administrator's role, experience, beliefs, and the current social context at work play out vis-à-vis the applicant? As implied, we feel that the administrator's typical engagement with the complete SJT situation will shape his or her behavior. And from the applicant's point of view, the administrator's behavior and beliefs about the SJT as these get projected to the job applicant, will, in effect, be a part of the situation that the latter must face, understand, perform in, and even try to influence.

The thought processes of the applicant who is asked to perform on the SJT are a major theme of this chapter. Clearly, in our view the applicant has an investment in the assessment process (Gilliland, 1993; Ryan & Ployhart, 2000). Most obviously, the applicant wants to perform well in the eyes of the firm, certainly well enough to get a job offer (even if to turn it down later for a better one). Less obvious perhaps, thoughtful applicants often use their experience with the organization's recruitment/selection process as a basis for deciding that they could indeed fit well into the company (Ployhart & Harold, 2004). Based on their experiences with the whole application process (including the taking of an SJT), applicants seek to estimate such things as how well they would perform on the job, how they would get along with their prospective boss and work colleagues, how successful they might be in using the job as a basis for a career, and so on. Applicants want some reassurance that they would be satisfied or fulfilled if they decide to work for the company (e.g., Campbell, Dunnette, Lawler, & Weick, 1970).

Framed this way, we argue that the applicant's conceptualization of the situation associated with the SJT would be very broad. Certainly, it will include the applicant's experience with the particular items of the SJT and the collection of items that are presented in a test. But we feel that the applicant's experience of the SJT situation will be conditioned by his or her exposure to the context of the recruiting and test administration.

The applicant interprets experiences with the SJT with reference to the history of recent contacts with the firm. Reactions to the SJT itself will be conditioned by numerous experiential factors, such as the way the position was described in recruiting materials, by discussions with current and past company employees, and by the treatment given to the applicant by those managing the various parts of the selection program. For example, the situation faced by someone who is taking an SJT online as a first point of contact, would be a very different one compared with someone who has had several encounters with representatives of the firm (e.g., interviews) prior to being asked to complete the SJT. Similarly, the inexperienced applicant who has had no exposure to the SJT in the past will react very differently to the SJT than an experienced applicant. In both of these examples, the latter applicant encounters a different situation in the context of taking the SJT than the former. The test and its items are contextualized.

## UNDERSTANDING SITUATIONS

### The Social Psychological Traditions

Social psychology has been characterized as the study of behavior in mundane social situations, and a primary characteristic of humans is their ability to make sense of these situations. Lewin's (1951) famous formulation stressed that behavior is a function of the person and the environment. His view served to increase psychologists' awareness of human behavior as complex and as the result of both personal and situational causes. In addition, Lewin's concept of life space emphasized the individual's ability to impose meaning on objective situations. However, over the second half of the last century, social psychology became reliant on experimental methods that focused on the manipulation of the situation and dealt with the person side of the equation as error.

The importance and strength of the situation in shaping behavior and cognition has been a primary focus of social psychology. Research often involved standardized experimental paradigms, the goal of which is, in effect, to discern the predictable impact of situations. Thus, the experimental method emphasized the careful contrivance of the situation as the independent variable to measure its impact on behaviors or cognitions. Well-known studies in social psychology, including those by Asch (1956), Milgram (1963) and Zimbardo (1974), have been portrayed as uncovering the potency of the situation. As a result of these studies, we know that strong situational demands severely restrict the impact of individual differences in values, abilities, and goals. Importantly, researchers have learned that they must take a nuanced approach to setting up situations, otherwise they overcome the cognitive, affective, or interpersonal processes that are really of interest.

A major theory of meaning-making or sense-making that arises out of the Lewinian approach is Heider's (1958) theory of attribution dynamics. This theory conceived of humans as naïve-scientists who are attempting to ascertain the intentions of others. According to attribution theory, noticing the behavior of an "actor" and especially behavior with potentially important or extreme outcomes, an "observer" initiates an active search for causal explanations. This process involves searching for the effective environmental forces (the situation) and the effective personal forces (the can and the try) in order to make an assessment of the intentions and dispositions of the actor. Heider pointed out that the advantage of knowing the actor's intention is that it allows the observer to predict the observed individual's future actions. This provides a tactical advantage in social interaction. It is important to note that attribution theorists tended to see the sense-making process through a prescriptive lens. Thus, they presumed that people typically performed certain mental diagnostics (e.g., consistency tests) in their daily lives. But, as often as studies could find evidence for the "detective," they also found that people do not expend such effort under most circumstances in life. It seems that only by apprehending the situation as important, novel or, even dangerous, do individuals invest a lot in situation assessments. But, as we point out later, social interactions in the context of taking an SJT fit into the latter cases.

More recently, sociocognitive psychologists (Fiske & Taylor, 1991) have proposed a more sophisticated approach to social sense-making. They characterized actors as invoking either automatic or controlled mental processes, depending on the circumstances. Each of these can determine their perceptions and actions in social settings. Similarly, an individual's history of experience and learning tends to build up interpretative filters such as schema, scripts, and heuristics that are also thought to govern behavior and performance (Kunda, 1999). In most settings people often operate efficiently by using automatic mental processes that involve surface features of situations and the reactions of others as cues to what they should do. However, when the situation exhibits cues that imply threat, opportunity, or the unexpected, most individuals tend to take a more effortful, planful, and tactical approach. They try to figure out just what the situation really means so that they can act appropriately. As the situation becomes important, careful sense-making becomes more important.

## Interaction Theories

The importance of the situation in evoking active mental processes is evident in both attribution theory and sociocognitive approaches, but their emphasis has been more on the person than on the person's interaction with the situation. However, there are many different approaches to the modeling of the person-by-situation interaction. We focus on two traditions of research in social psychology that have particular relevance to understanding those cognitive and behavioral processes in which the actor engages when he or she encounters situations. The first line of research looks at the person-by-situation interaction at the meso-level. This is based on Barker's (1963) ecological perspective and the modification of this approach to the study of group processes as offered by McGrath (1984). The second line of research is focused on the person-by-situation interaction as it is manifested at a more micro-level. The study of "the social psychology of the experiment" (Rosenthal, 1966) looked at the different demands created by the experimental situation, and how they influenced the inferences made from experiments

The Lewinian perspective is responsible for the genesis of many theories in psychology, but one of the most ignored offspring is Barker's (1963) ecological perspective. This approach took the idea of person-by-situational units seriously and developed methods to observe actions within the natural settings. One of the major concepts that arose from this immense research undertaking was the concept of the *behavior setting*. The behavior setting is conceptualized as involving a standing pattern of behavior where the behavior is surrounded by and congruent with the environment. The behavior setting is a joint product of the environment and the qualities of the person. One of the major insights of Barker's work was that the actions of different individuals in one environment were often more similar than the actions of a single individual across different environments (Barker & Wright, 1954). Within each environment, there are shared expectations about what each type of actor should do and most individuals conform to the expectations. In this approach, the behavior setting is the person-by-situation unit. However, there are many different behavior settings and the series of actions within the situation are complex, and a coherent taxonomy of person-by-situation constructs was never developed.

McGrath's (1984) framework for conceptualizing group interaction was developed using the ecological perspective. His approach differs from other frameworks for the study of group processes because it places considerable emphasis on the situational demands that (a) exist prior to the interaction and (b) shape both the pattern of communication within a group and the behavior of its members.

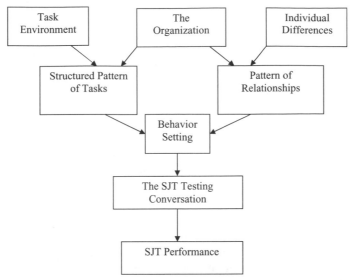

FIG. 2.1. Modification of McGrath's (1984) framework for understanding the role of the behavior setting in SJT performance.

The centerpiece of McGrath's framework is the acting group, which is concerned with the dynamics of group interaction. The group interaction does not occur in a vacuum, but is constantly being shaped and reshaped by its environment. The interaction in any group is a complex phenomenon influenced by both objective task and social factors, and by the social construction of the features and meaning of such factors.

A diagram of this multilevel framework that has been modified as it might be applied to the SJT situation is presented in Fig. 2.1. The testing conversation and SJT performance have been substituted for the acting group. We treat the testing situation as an interaction between the applicant and the representatives of the organization. The most distal level from the testing interaction is the objective environment. It is composed of the personal environment, which includes the biological, social, and psychological properties of the individuals, and the task environment, which includes physical, sociocultural, and technological properties of the task. In our modified framework, we have added reference to the organization because it is clearly salient to the job applicant.

The middle level has two perceptual components that correspond to the aspects of the objective environment, namely, the standing group, and the task/situation. The standing group is the perceived pattern of relationships among the group members. Similarly the task/situation is the perceived

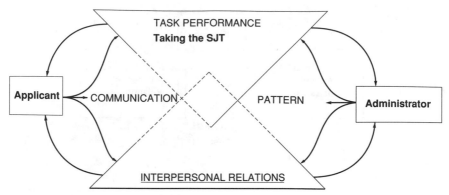

FIG. 2.2. Communication dynamics of the behavior setting associated with the situational Judgment test (after McGrath, 1984).

patterned relationships among task features. Our framework suggests that both the perceptions of the task and the pattern of relationships are also shaped by perceptions of features of the organization (e.g., its motives and goals).

The most immediate determinant of interaction in the group is the behavior setting, which is the sum of the actor's expectations about the relationships between the individuals and the characteristics of the group task. McGrath (1984) modified the concept of the behavior setting and defined it as "A pattern—a fit—between the group as a structured entity (the standing group) and the task/situation as a structured set of requirements/demands/opportunities/ possibilities/constraints" (p. 16). The behavior setting is a direct precursor of group interaction and serves as a continuous background condition for interaction in the group.

McGrath also presents a micro-view of communication within a group. Communication is seen as promoted by a behavior setting and as involving three interwoven processes. A modification of McGrath's view of these processes as applied to the testing situation is presented in Fig. 2.2. The first process is the actual communication that occurs and includes the communication channels, modalities used, and distribution of communication across people and over time. The second is the content of the communication, which involves task or action process that alter perceptions of the task-performance pattern and the attraction process, which results in changes in the perceived interpersonal relationship pattern. The third is the influence process, which results from the combination of the components of the earlier two stages. The influence process is the consequences for the participants in terms of relationships, task performance, and future communication. This dynamic of social influence (especially conformity pressures) highlights the fact that interaction in groups is affected by both the social environment (affective, influence, and sense-making processes) and the task environment.

Our modification of this model to the applicant's response to the task of taking the SJT takes the position that the taking of an SJT involves communication with at least the test administrator. The SJT is not just a thing and it is not the only thing to which the applicant is responding. The test is part of a larger behavior setting, and making sense of that setting depends on the conversation within the test itself and the larger conversation that surrounds the administration of the test. The communication process keeps the applicant aware of the demands of the task and the expectations of others. The quality of the applicant's communication within this situation involves an active and reciprocal exchange with the administrator and other in the behavior setting.

## Social Psychology of Experiments

At a more prescriptive level, Rosenthal (1966) studied the experimental situation as a social context in which the expectations of the subject and the experimenter impact behaviors within the experimental situation, and the validity of the inferences made. We cover this work in our review of the psychology of situations because we feel it is analogous to what is happening while taking an SJT. Rosenthal identified two types of influences in experimental situations: experimenter effects and experimenter expectancy effects. The experimenter effects research is concerned with how the characteristics of the experimenters relative to the characteristics of the subjects impact behavior in the experiment (e.g., do Black and White subjects get different feedback from White experimenters). The experimenter expectancies are concerned with how experimenter's expectations about the desired outcome of an experiment (often automatically) affect both the behaviors of the subjects and the observations of the experimenter.

The work on the social psychology of experiments caused some concern initially about the validity of social experiments (Aronson & Carlsmith, 1968). However, these findings were eventually placed in context. For example, researchers as situation designers learned to conduct pilot work to discover how their contrived settings affected behavior. With this insight, they could try to "control against artifacts." On the more affirmative side, the literature also informed investigators about ways to better design experimental situations that were more construct valid and thus they were able to create both the mundane realism and psychological fidelity in their studies required (Weick, 1969). Another result of this research was that experimenters began paying greater attention to the careful scripting of their experiments to address the probable effects of such things as the "cover" story used for recruiting participants, the features of the task to be performed (e.g., degree of familiarity), the instructions given, the experimenter's own expectations and behavior (e.g., promoting double-blind arrangements), and the potential impact of the behavior of other subjects in the experimental situation (e.g., behavioral contagion, arousal).

## The Social Psychology of Surveys

On the face of it, the relevance of survey design to the SJT might seem limited. However, there is a great deal of insight that has been gained from researchers and practitioners in this arena as they, like SJT designers, have sought to create a "situation" that allows for obtaining valid information.

The survey has been conceptualized as a social exchange (Dillman, 2000) that requires a consideration of those forces that both motivates respondents to be honest and allows respondents to perform at their best (e.g., recall facts, provide true opinions). Thus, such things as the message used to recruit respondents, the instructions, the item-level wording, response options supplied, length and sequencing of items and, especially the perception of the status and legitimacy of the survey organization have all been found to be important. The application of the conversation metaphor to analysis of responses to surveys (Dillman, 2000; Schwarz, 1994, 1999) has also been found valuable. To get more accurate data, investigators have focused on uncovering and then using the general social rules that govern interpersonal communication and shape the micro-situation surrounding written or oral surveys. According to this tradition, the failure to understand how communication processes operate can lead to the faulty attribution that it is the actor rather than the structure of the testing situation that accounts for survey results.

Grice's (1975) communication theory has been used as the basis for characterizing the testing conversation. Communication processes involve active attempts to exchange accurate information about a topic of importance between people who have some level of mutual knowledge. The norms that shape most communications are based on an expectation of cooperation. The speaker is expected to ask about relevant information and the respondent is expected to supply the relevant information in a clear and direct manner. The maxims that Grice used to explain cooperative conversation are concerned with quality, quantity, relation, and manner. The maxim of *quality* is concerned with the truth value of the conversation. It assumes that within the context of conversation individuals will attempt to give information that is most probably true. The maxim of *quantity* says that individuals will focus on information that is relevant to the conversation and not on information that is already known or shared. The maxim of *relation* adds the enjoinder that the conversation should focus only on information that is relevant to the question at hand and should not include information that is misleading or irrelevant to the communication. The maxim of *manner* adds the idea that conversations should be clear, orderly, and direct.

At a more operational level, survey practitioners learned the importance of clearly explaining the "task" of completing surveys. Participants might be explicitly instructed to respond with either the "first thing that comes to mind" or to "take time and reflect." Researchers took pains to answer often *unstated* questions about the meta-tasks surrounding the answering of survey questions (i.e., respondents should be cooperative, helpful, ask for clarification when warranted). Similarly, survey researchers were careful to motivate participation in a manner that did not induce bias. Finally, there was the recognition that even if motivated, the conscientious respondent often needs assistance to do a "good job." Thus, good survey wording or instructions provide clarification of such things as the time frame that shapes the response to the items or even the right perspective (e.g., describe "typical" or "maximum" behavior) to take when answering the questions.

We feel that the rules of conversation should be considered in the design and implementation of not just surveys but of psychological tests generally. Although there are test designers who routinely adopt this view, the lessons from survey design and administration are often overlooked. In fact, errors in surveys (Schwarz, 1994, 1999) and the biases in experimentation (Hilton, 1995) are often the result of the researchers' failure to frame their questions with participants' needs and motives in mind.

## The High-Stakes Setting

Several of the traditions summarized to this point have often been focused on gaining insights as to the nature of human behavior (attribution theory, ecological psychology, experimental methods) or opinions or preferences (surveys). In some ways, the interests of investigators have revolved around uncovering the contemporaneous views of people or the antecedents of their "typical behavior." However, there are additional perspectives that have attempted to model behavior in what have been called *high-stakes* contexts. From the perspective of job applicants, the testing protocol that they experience can be seen as presenting not only a strong situation, but one where behavior has important consequences.

As noted earlier, a number of authors (e.g., Sabini & Silver, 1983; Zimbardo, 1974) have reported that in certain contexts there is low variability across individuals in either their behavior or their performance. This has led to the notion that some situations may be strong in the sense of promoting homogeneity, whereas others would be weak in this regard. To put it differently, depending on context, the performance that one sees may reveal less about the nature of the individual than about the nature of the situation as it exists or is contrived.

There appears to be several plausible bases for situation strength. One might be the cueing properties of the situation and how these are linked (through biology or learning) to patterns of behavior. Thus, in an extreme case, a gunshot almost always promotes a startle response and "freeze" or "flight" behavior, an artifact of biology. But in the same situation, a soldier is trained to respond differently (and ostensibly in a more appropriate way). More commonly, the causes for a strong situation is response tendencies promoted by years of instruction and social development, including the influence of popular culture, all of which may be backed up by the threat of sanctions. Thus, according to attribution theory, observing a person stop a car at a stop sign is not particularly informative to an observer relative to inferring dispositions in as much as most (but not all) people have been socialized to do this. Similarly, manifestations of courtesy or civility (saying "hello") are triggered by many strong situations (e.g., meeting a co-worker for the first time that day).

But a strong situation may also exist because of the anticipation of rewards or because of potential sanctions, including social pressure. Here, we might see similar behavior by most people brought about as a result of shared fears or needs. Thus, the real or presumed presence of others or anticipating a review by others (Frink & Klimoski, 1998) can have similar homogenizing effects. As a final illustration, we might point out a paradox of sorts. A type of strong situation may actually be one that is inherently ambiguous to most people. The literature on social conformity (Asch, 1956; Milgram, 1963) has discovered that most individuals are likely to look to others for guidance under these circumstances, thus promoting conformity and limiting more ideographic (personalized) responses to that situation. This process is known to produce more homogeneous (and extreme) decisions in groups (Moscovici & Zavalloni, 1969)

Research on the dynamics of high-stakes testing as it relates "stereotype threat" (Steele & Aronson, 1995; Steele & Davies, 2003) reveals that testing can be seen not only as a strong situation, but at least for some subgroups, as a means of promoting the activation of group identity. In the testing situation, this can have a detrimental effect on performance when there is a prevailing stereotype that level of performance on the test is related to that group identity (e.g., Blacks perform more poorly on intelligence measures). Although the effect does not seem to be as replicable as initially suggested (Herriot, 2004; Sackett, 2003), there is sufficient evidence that the activation of self-relevant information alters the meaning of the testing conversation. To the extent that the group identity information activates expectations regarding the meaning of the testing situation, it can be predicted that there will be subgroup differences in test performance (e.g., higher test anxiety, lower effort, self-handicapping, choice of performance strategy, etc.). To the extent that this is an unexpected consequence of SJT design or administration, it will be a flawed platform for selection.

## Summary

The cumulative wisdom of these approaches is that the taking of something like an SJT is experienced as the function of the setting. Test-taking is embedded in a larger context, and performance has important consequences for the individual. The tests are seen as systematically presenting important questions that the actor has to answer appropriately. But therein lies the challenge. Using the insights from several lines of research, we view the testing situation less as a uniform experience than as an opportunity for sense-making. In this regard, the applicant is not just involved in test-taking but is actually participating in a meaningful conversation with the goal of ascertaining the best way to meet the expectations of the other stakeholders (the organization, the test administrator, or the hiring official). This shapes the applicant's thoughts and interactions with others in the testing situation. Most significantly, it shapes performance. The challenge is to build on the implications of the conversation metaphor to improve the likelihood that the testing allows for a performance that is a valid indicator of the person's potential.

## THE SITUATIONAL JUDGMENT TEST

### SJT and the Criterion Space

Although the interactionist approach has not been a central focus of industrial organizational psychology, there has been the pragmatic realization that a measurement of both the person and the situation adds value in understanding, modeling, and predicting job performance (Hattrup & Jackson, 1996). This approach implies that systematic measurement and modeling of the situation is needed.

The measurement of individual's responses to job-related situations gained impetus from the study of critical incidents (Flanagan, 1954). Based on the realization that prediction was improved when the situational factors were taken into consideration, work skills and capabilities have routinely been linked to situations with the goal of better understanding worker behavior and performance. Although much has been written relative to the role of capabilities (e.g., mental ability) across situations (e.g., Murphy & Shiarella, 1997; Sackett, Schmitt, Ellingson, & Kabin, 2001) better models of what it takes to be effective can be had by pairing such capacities with job-specific information. Indeed, prevailing practice in personnel work is to use job analyses to do this. All this is to say that practitioners often attempt to understand the factors in the work situation that must be managed by the job incumbent. In doing this, they are, in effect, developing a conceptualization of the situation and what it takes to be effective in it. Moreover, investigators often try to establish if coping with situational ambiguity is part of the criterion performance construct.

The theory of the job situation, once developed, becomes the basis for a firm's selection program. Importantly, designers and administrators must decide just what elements of the job situation need to be captured or embedded in one way or another in the company's selection or screening program. Certainly, if the firm uses such things as assessment centers, inbaskets, job-skill tests, work samples, structured job interviews, or especially the SJT, the fundamental assumption would seem to be that measures that incorporate aspects of specific future demands of the work situation generate data that are potentially better correlates of job performance than those that do not. Because they are designed for screening applicants for specific jobs and the way that they measure relevant capabilities, they will increase prediction.

## Describing the SJT

The SJT has been around for a relatively long period of time, but its potential as a relatively inexpensive and easy-to-administer instrument has lead to an increase in its popularity. The SJT can be defined as a low- to moderate-fidelity simulation or work sample designed to assess preferences for appropriate behaviors in a work situation. The prototypical situations presented in SJT items involve representations of common problems or challenges that might arise within a specific type of job. Potential responses to these specific problems are in a multiple-choice format that presents a range of potential responses. The response formats used most often require the applicant to "choose the best option," "choose the best and worse options," or "rate the appropriateness or effectiveness of each option." The multiple-choice format of SJTs makes them easier to administer and score compared with some other measures included in the category of work-skill measures. The SJT usually contains a set of items that attempts to cover the range of common problems encountered in the work setting. As implied, items are often selected on the basis of job analysis or on the judgments of Subject Matter Experts (SME), and occasionally on the basis of theory. A person's score is calculated as the sum of performance across items. Although it is possible to weigh items in terms of their difficulty or centrality to the job, this is not usually done.

It is fair to assume that the test designer is acutely aware of the need to establish content validity of the SJT. The scenarios offered are abstractions from the job. But although there may be considerable methodological rigor in selecting and constructing SJT items and item clusters, we feel that not much effort has been spent on the articulation of the constructs being measured. This, in conjunction with the emphasis on capturing key aspects of the job context, leads to questions regarding which "situation" is being presented to the applicant and why. Because both content and context affect the test-taking demands placed on the applicant and the traits or qualities that are needed to perform well on the SJT, these are not trivial issues. To the extent that the situation as presented and interpreted by the actor requires similar qualities to those required on the job, there is a greater likelihood that selection decisions made on the basis of SJT performance will be valid. On the other hand, if the demands are not articulated and/or are inappropriate, a mismatch will occur.

Many different types of situations have been represented in the SJT. To illustrate, the following SJT item has been taken from the Army Judgment Test and has been used by McDaniel, Morgeson, Finnegan, Campion, and Braverman (2001) in a review of SJT and by Landy and Conte (2004) in their textbook as an exemplar of a SJT item:

A man on a very urgent mission during a battle finds he must cross a stream about 40 feet wide. A blizzard has been blowing and the stream has frozen over. However, because of the snow, he does not know how thick the ice is. He sees two planks about 10 feet long near the point where he wishes to cross. He also knows that there is a bridge about 2 miles downstream. Under the circumstances he should:

A. Walk to the bridge and cross it
B. Run rapidly across the ice
C. Break a hole in the ice near the edge of the stream to see how deep the stream is
D. Cross with the aid of the planks, pushing one ahead of the other and walking on them
E. Creep slowly across the ice

This illustration serves several purposes. It reveals the typical structure of the SJT. It also shows how a "situation" can be presented and thus serves as the basis for responding. But it also highlights two other points. One is that the description of the situation is an abstraction. Very little information is made available to the test taker. Second it also illustrates the range of the individual differences constructs that could underlie performance on an item.

Is this item a measure of:

A. reasoning ability
B. creativity
C. knowledge of military procedures
D. survival skills
E. skill at "second guessing" the test designer

Importantly, does it matter? For those in the business of personnel assessment and prediction, we think it should.

The methodology that has been used to ensure the psychometric soundness of the SJT is a major theme of this volume. Certainly, careful methodology is important to the SJT enterprise. But there is another truism that there is nothing as practical as a good theory (Lewin, 1951). Although it might be argued that the methods of test development and the process of choosing content by SJT designers represent tacit statements of a theoretical position, this is not enough. The development of meaningful and practical SJT measures can only be accelerated by more explicit statements of a theory of situation-driven performance. Moreover, this theory must include a more complete consideration of the testing situation, one that includes a broader consideration of the alignment of the contexts for test-taking and job performance.

Our concerns with the factors underlying the meaning of SJT scores are related to discussions of content versus construct validity in the design of assessment (Mitchell & Klimoski, 1986; Sackett & Dreher, 1982). Many years ago, this duality was framed as seeking the right emphasis on signs versus samples (Wernimont & Campbell, 1968). Although we concur that there is room for both in personnel work, we feel that the issue has not been worked through in the literature on SJT. Specifically, is the test a situation designed to reveal evidence of performance (a sample) or of potential (a sign)?

## The Meaning of SJT Scores

The purpose of tests is to obtain a valid picture of characteristics that predict job performance. There is agreement at the empirical level that data from SJTs and their close relatives (e.g., work samples, structured interviews) enhance the prediction of job performance over and above that which can be obtained from more general ability or skill measures (Clevenger, Pereira, Wiechmann, Schmitt, & Harvey, 2001; Weekley & Jones, 1999). But why does this occur? Here, there is much less agreement about the exact meaning of SJT scores. At a practical level, the output of an SJT is usually an aggregate score across vignettes. Curiously, the scores are frequently treated like alternative measures of a general ability or trait dimensions such as "g" or conscientiousness, but this is done without much justification.

The cacophony of meanings becomes evident when the variation in scales content and focus are examined. Data from SJTs have been seen as assessing a range of constructs such as social intelligence (Legree, 1995), tacit knowledge (Sternberg, Wagner, Williams, Horvath et al., 1995), interpersonal skills (Motowidlo, Dunnette, & Carter, 1990), pilot judgment (Hunter, 2003), customer service orientation (Weekley & Jones, 1999), or contextual job knowledge (Clevenger et al., 2001 ). Format choices appear to be arbitrary as well. In fact, the communality between these tests that share a format has not been clearly defined. More specifically, there is the need for increased conceptual clarity about the nature of and the appropriateness of the person-by-situation units.

## Promising Too Much

The issue of meaning becomes especially important when we look at the aspirations for SJTs. It is not trivial that these measures are called judgment tests and are often contrasted to job knowledge tests or job samples. Indeed, the potential of these measures (as represented in this volume) is that they have the capacity to measure complex processes of judgment, choice, or decision making. But judgment, choice, and decision making are processes that require the test taker to integrate different types of information. Measures of correct situational-based decision making will have to rely on more complex situations and on scoring schemes than are currently being used. But this, in turn, can only happen if the SJT, its content, and format and the nature of the situation surrounding SJT administration are better conceptualized.

## THE SJT AND THE TESTING CONVERSATION

We conceptualize the taking of an SJT as a conversation embedded within a behavior setting and the total applicant assessment process as a complex behavior setting with a series of interrelated conversations. Most operational assessment programs follow what has been called a *multiple hurdle* plan (Ryan, Sacco, McFarland, & Kriska, 2000). That is, applicants or candidates are screened over time, with assessment tools being used to gain an increasingly accurate picture of the individual's potential as an employee. If the firm is efficient about this (and assuming a favorable selection ratio), it would use assessment tools that are less expensive in the early phases of the process, even if these might be somewhat less accurate, in order to reduce the pool of applicants to a more manageable number. The SJT then might be used at any part of the process, but because of its features it might be used early on in the sequence.

However, relative to the notion of a testing situation as promoting a conversation about sense-making, we would expect that its placement in the sequence of screening hurdles will make a difference. Were it to come at the beginning, the candidate would be far less "informed" than if it came much later. The individual would have to rely much more on his or her "extra-task" capabilities in order to place the situation component of the SJT in its larger context. And clearly, the capacity for a successful conversation would be much greater for an internal job candidate than one from the outside.

The implications of approaching the SJT or other tests from the conversation perspective is that we are forced to look at the testing situation not simply from the perspective of valid content but also from the constructs that are implicated (as a rival hypothesis) in test performance as induced by the particular choice of items, the response format, the medium used for testing, the administration platform (especially the behavior of organizational representatives and the larger recruiting context in which the SJT is but one part).

Throughout this chapter we have implied that there is a major role for individual differences to play in our thinking and models of how the situation will affect people generally, but especially those in high-stakes contexts. It seems clear from our review and from our framing of situation dynamics as involving a conversation that will shape the applicant's sense-making that several classes of individual differences will make a difference. But just how should they?

## Ability Determinants

It seems that individual differences in the amount of past experience with the situation or similar situations will provide both the basis for responding to and/or a meta-context for conversations and sense-making. Thus, in a job interview, what might be a "problem-solving event" to one applicant (i.e., trying to mutually figure out where to fit into the organization as a prospective future employee), might appear to be an opportunity for "bargaining" (i.e., trying to get the highest starting salary) to another. In a related way, levels of subject matter expertise will be a factor in how one approaches the analysis of an SJT scenario that is being offered. The individual who has effectively managed the demands of a situation "like this one" in the past will also see the hypothetical situation differently and perhaps be more effective in responding. Moreover, the expert will certainly have a different expectation for success than the novice. This in turn will affect both the dynamics of self-regulation (e.g., time management, emotional reactions) in the SJT and the actuality of high performance (Ryan et al., 2000). As a final example, one can easily argue that key traits or attributes that facilitate sense-making, even in the absence of experience or expertise, might be relevant. In particular, the well-documented relationship between general mental ability (fluid intelligence) and effective performance in unclear or dynamic situations comes to mind. As the saying goes, "intelligence is what you need when you don't know what to do." Note that these examples of individual difference factors correspond to some of the potential stable components of test-score variability as usually identified by reliability theory.

It is worth pointing out, however, that individual differences can also be thought of as an "emergent" property of a situation. The situation is not just a context for individual differences to play out. It may actually produce variability. This is because of the link between sense-making and individual action. In many ways, the situation as interpreted has reciprocal effects on the situation as it plays out. Thus, a novice applicant who interprets the test situation as "hopeless" responds accordingly. In an interview context, this will have predictable effects on the recruiter. This is analogous to the current thinking of the way personality plays out in much of life. A person's disposition not only inclines his or her choice of situation in which to engage, but once engaged, this same disposition will have predictable effects on situation features, most notably, the behavior of other people with whom there is interaction in that setting.

Relevant to the thesis of this chapter, what is not so obvious is that the situation, if arbitrarily chosen by the SJT assessor or if poorly contrived by the test designer, will have the same potential for inadvertently elevating individual difference factors to causal status. For example, as mentioned, durable individual differences in social identity (and thus context-induced susceptibility to identity cues) may affect the impact of the testing situation on minority applicants. This is felt to shape both applicant behavior (e.g., levels of effort, degree of self-handicapping) and likely performance (Steele & Aronson, 1995; Steele & Davies, 2003). Yet these propensities, according to the model, will not be activated unless identity cues are salient. The question here is whether such cues should be built into the testing situation.

If so, why? To anticipate the point of this section, the appropriateness of such cues of course, depends on the "meaning" of the role of the situation in the theories of performance for both the SJT and for the job as adopted by the test designer or administrator.

## Personality Factors

Those involved in applicant response research have begun to address the role of generalized personality traits. In this literature, it has been found that stable traits (e.g., neuroticism, need for achievement) affect both the individual's approach to recruiting situations (e.g., motivational "press" felt, amount and type of sense-making) and the pattern of self-regulation demonstrated (e.g., levels of effort, focus on self, task and social environment in testing). These are also major drivers of test performance. Although these too can add apparent variability to SJT scores, should they be "allowed" to do so? Of course, it depends on whether these are seen as significant determinants of job performance as well. In another way of stating the issue, process-linked attributes must be carefully reviewed regarding their role in both the testing and job setting to ensure construct validity.

Finally, we have indicated in our review that proximal needs and goals are individual difference factors that will influence the applicant's reaction to situations. Thus, higher levels of motivation cause the individual to shift from a passive or habitual way of engaging in situations to one that is active and effortful. Certainly, the perception that a given situation involves high stakes may cut across individuals. More likely, however, is that individual differences in needs and goals are at work. The applicant who is gainfully employed and exploring a job opportunity has clearly different needs and goals than one who has been out of work or has few job options by virtue of weak credentials. Note, too, that here the anticipated consequences of poor performance or failure in the test situation can have either motivating or de-motivating effects on applicants' test-taking behavior and performance depending on needs and goals. These factors notwithstanding, it is ultimately the conversation at the place of the test-taking that will influence just which needs and goals of the applicant become paramount. Here, the physical setting, the test features, instructions, and the administrator's behavior will play an important role in making certain needs and goals relevant. For example, it seems reasonable to expect applicants being assessed in a group setting to be differentially affected than those who are assessed individually.

## Implications for SJT Research

The followings are implications for SJT research.

1.  Establish the capacity for sense-making as an important worker skill. Normally, identifying worker requirements is done in test development by using job analyses or subject matter experts. Although many jobs are well engineered and thus do not demand much by way of judgment or decision making on the part of the incumbent, this is not always the case. Most service jobs, for example, call for employees to be responsive to ambiguous and often challenging interactions with clients or customers. To the point, should evidence of sense-making competency on the part of applicants be sought through the SJT? Should the capacity for sense-making (with or with out training) be the focus of the SJT? (The former would emphasize a content focus, the latter a construct focus.) Or should it not be part of the SJT rationale? Given the ambiguity inherent in most scenarios presented in SJTs, this is a nontrivial parameter to establish.

2.  Adopt a construct approach. In the long run, the unique contribution of SJTs to the development of a process theory of selection and employment will depend on adopting a construct approach to SJT measurement. If a construct focus is to be taken, it is then necessary to be clear on the nature of those constructs of interest to the SJT designer. In particular, the level of specificity of the construct remains a key detail to be worked out. Although there are those who might argue that it is sufficient to index the most general of traits (e.g., intelligence) through a test like the SJT, others have seen the value of greater specificity (e.g., inductive reasoning, decisiveness, risk propensity). In any event, it is important to establish why the construct is being assessed in the SJT (e.g., as a driver of task performance or of sense-making in the service of this performance). Ideally, we would expect clarification of not only of individual constructs, but evidence of the situational constructs of interest.

3.  Articulate a clear conceptualization of the situation as it is to be experienced in the application process. In our opinion, the test designer must operate differently and, whether taking a content or a construct approach, must articulate the meaning of the situation from the point of view of the applicant. This implies that pilot studies should be done with identifiable subgroups to ascertain how both the test (e.g., modality, instructions, item format, item order, etc.) and the extra test situations (e.g., group vs. individual, group composition, etc.) affect the perceptions of the testing conversation.

4.  Reporting matters. For both researchers and practitioners we would recommend greater attention to documenting the SJT context in greater detail in the reports and publications that are produced. As has become clear to those doing work in meta-analysis and to others who have the task of making sense of when and where a test of procedure might have an effect, complete documentation is important. The empirical record of SJT effects and the meaning of assembled findings can only be understood if authors take care to better describe some of those things that surround the SJT itself. In particular, as we have stressed, authors need to be especially clear about if, when, and where the applicants' interpretation of the situation are expected to alter responses to the SJT. Certainly, the domain or construct mapping of both the predictor and criterion space should be included in the report.

5.  Applicant reactions. Applicant reactions are important at all stages of personnel testing (Hausknecht, Day, & Thomas 2004), but research assessing the role of such things as pretest expectations about recruitment processes and employment testing (Arvey, Strickland, Drauden, & Martin, 1990) and other aspects of how the applicant approaches and reacts to the behavior setting could enhance our effort to understanding applicant responses to SJTs.

## Implications for SJT in Practice

It should be clear by now that we have presented a different view of tests and of the test-taking process. But we feel it is a view that will have value to the field. Based on the way that several research streams have conceptualized the situation and using the conversation metaphor as a description of the dynamics surrounding the applicant as he or she attempts to make sense of the test-taking situation, we offer the following:

1.  Adopt a broader view of the situation in which the SJT instrument is embedded. In this regard, we feel that the whole selection experience matters and will affect test performance. Test administrators need to understand the impact of placement of the SJT within a multistage recruiting program. Is the applicant's capacity to effectively navigate the company's screening process part of the criterion construct space to be captured? Here, such things as the applicant's social skills and capacity for self-regulation should be an advantage in gaining insights about the expectations and can plausibly contribute to a deeper understanding of the meaning of SJT items. But should these capabilities be construed as contributing to true score variance in the SJT? If not, what can be done to control for extrane-

ous and differential effects of screening experience? In this regard, the field should at least be more clear about just where and when in the applicant experience the SJT properly belongs.

2. Sense-making changes with conditions of test administration. In our brief treatment of situation-related concepts we highlighted the importance of the applicant's expectations. One implication for the SJT field is that administrators as well as designers should use people similar to the kind of applicants they will be recruiting in their pilot studies. Similarly, the importance of variations in job-search experience might be explored. In general, it would be good practice to try out initial items and test administration procedures on groups of pilot subjects that represent the range of differences that is characteristic of applicants (e.g., job experience, company experience, race, education, etc.) likely to be screened by the firm once the SJT is operational.

3. Is the SJT performance a necessary hurdle? SJT constructs are not well specified. Thus, it may not add predictive power to measures of individual difference constructs already included in the test platform (e.g., interviews or other types of assessment; Schmidt & Hunter, 1998). Does the inclusion of an SJT add value?

4. Sense-making matters. The issues of who, where, when, and how are important not just for test development, but also for test administration. The SJT administrator is part of the larger conversation. The administrator has to understand and structure the screening experience so as to manage all of the applicants in a consistent manner and to guard against reduced capacity for valid inference.

## CONCLUSION

Despite its popularity, work on the SJT is still in its formative stage. In looking across our set of recommendations, it is clear that we are calling for greater attention on the part of researchers and practitioners to the refinement of a more explicit "theory of the situation" as it impacts the worker and especially, as it gets consciously mapped into the SJT test bed. The emphasis here, as in all of testing, is to be quite certain about the sources of true-score variability. But we are also calling for the development of something that might be considered a "theory of the test taker" as well. In our view, the work of Chan and Schmitt (Chan, Schmitt, Jennings, Clause, & Delbridge, 1998; Chan, Schmitt, Sacco, & DeShon, 1998), Steele (Steele & Aronson, 1995; Steele & Davies, 2003), and others (Hausknecht et al., 2004; Ployhart & Harold, 2004; Truxillo, Steiner, & Gilliland, 2004) represents a good start. But because the situational features (and therefore the experience of) the SJT are somewhat peculiar, we feel that a theory that helps to explain the origin and effects of applicant expectations, test-taking behavior or decisions (and therefore test results) within the SJT context should be the "gold" standard to be worked toward.

## REFERENCES

Aronson, E., & Carlsmith, J. M. (1968). Experimentation in social psychology. In G. Lindsey & E. Aronson (Eds.), *The handbook of social psychology* (Vol. 2, pp. 1–79). Reading MA: Addison-Wesley.

Asch, S. E. (1956). Studies of independence and conformity: A minority of one against a unanimous majority. *Psychological Monographs, 70,* 9 (Whole No. 416).

Arvey, R. D., Strickland, W., Drauden, G., & Martin, C. (1990). Motivational components of test taking. *Personnel Psychology, 43*(4), 695–716.

Barker, R. G. (1963). *The stream of behavior.* East Norwalk, CT: Appleton-Century-Crofts.

Barker, R. G., & Wright, H. F. (1954). *Midwest and its children: The psychological ecology of an American town.* New York: Row, Peterson.

Campbell, J. J., Dunnette, M. D., Lawler, E. E., & Weick, K. E. (1970). *Managerial behavior, performance, and effectiveness.* New York: McGraw-Hill.

Chan, D., Schmitt, N., Jennings, D., Clause, C. S., & Delbridge, K. (1998). Applicant perceptions of test fairness integrating justice and self-serving bias perspectives. *International Journal of Selection & Assessment, 6*(4), 232–239.

Chan, D., Schmitt, N., Sacco, J. M., & DeShon, R. P. (1998). Understanding pretest and posttest reactions to cognitive ability and personality tests. *Journal of Applied Psychology, 83*(3), 471–485.

Clevenger, J., Pereira, G. M., Wiechmann, D., Schmitt, N., & Harvey, V. S. (2001). Incremental validity of situational judgment tests. *Journal of Applied Psychology, 86*(3), 410–417.

Dillman, D. A. (2000). *Mail and internet surveys: The tailored design method* (2nd ed.). New York: Wiley.

Fiske, S. T., & Taylor, S. E. (1991). *Social cognition.* New York: McGraw-Hill.

Flanagan, J. C. (1954). The critical incident technique. *Psychological Bulletin, 41,* 237–258.

Frink, D. D., & Klimoski, R. J. (1998). Toward a theory of accountability in organizations and human resource management. In G. R. Ferris (Ed.), *Research in personnel and human resources management* (Vol. 16, pp. 1–51). US: Elsevier Science/JAI Press.

Gilliland, S. W. (1993). The perceived fairness of selection systems: An organizational justice perspective. *Academy of Management Review, 18*(4), 694–734.

Grice, H. P. (1975). Logic and conversation. In P. Cole & J. L. Morgan (Eds.), *Syntax and semantics 3: Speech acts* (pp. 41–58). San Diego, CA: Academic Press.

Hattrup, K., & Jackson, S. E. (1996). Learning about individual differences by taking situations seriously. In K. R. Murphy (Ed.), *Individual differences and behavior in organizations* (pp. 507–547). San Francisco, CA: Jossey-Bass.

Hausknecht, J. P., Day, D. V., & Thomas, S. C. (2004). Applicant reactions to selection procedures: An updated model and meta-abalysis. *Personnel Psychology, 57,* 639–683.

Heider, F. (1958). *The psychology of interpersonal relations.* New York: Wiley.

Herriot, P. (2004). Social identities and applicant reactions. *International Journal of Selection & Assessment, 12*(1–2), 75–83.

Hilton, D. J. (1995). The social context of reasoning: Conversational inference and rational judgment. *Psychological Bulletin, 118*(2), 248–271.

Hunter, D. R. (2003). Measuring general aviation pilot judgment using a situational judgment technique. *International Journal of Aviation Psychology, 13*(4), 373–386.

Kunda, Z. (1999). *Social cognition: Making sense of people.* Cambridge, MA: MIT Press.

Landy, F. J., & Conte, J. M. (2004). *Work in the 21st century.* Boston MA: McGraw-Hill.

Legree, P. J. (1995). Evidence for an oblique social intelligence factor established with a Likert-based testing procedure. *Intelligence, 21*(3), 247–266.

Lewin, K. (1951). *Field theory in social science: selected theoretical papers* (D Cartwright, ed.). Oxford, England: Harpers.

Lievens, F., & Klimoski, R. (2001). Understanding the assessment center process: Where are we now? In C. L. Cooper & I. T. Robertson (Eds.), *International review of industrial and organizational psychology* (Vol. 16, pp. 245–286). New York: Wiley.

McDaniel, M. A., Morgeson, F. P., Finnegan, E. B., Campion, M. A., & Braverman, E. P. (2001). Use of situational judgment tests to predict job performance: A clarification of the literature. *Journal of Applied Psychology, 86*(4), 730–740.

McGrath, J. E. (1984). *Groups: Interaction and performance.* Englewood Cliffs, NJ: Prentice-Hall.

Milgram, S. (1963). Behavioral studies of obedience. *Journal of Abnornal and Social Psychology, 67,* 371–378.

Mitchell, T. W., & Klimoski, R. J. (1986). Estimating the validity of cross-validity estimation. *Journal of Applied Psychology, 71*(2), 311–317.

Moscovici, S., & Zavalloni, M. (1969). The group as a polarizer of attitudes. *Journal of Personality & Social Psychology, 12*(2), 125–135.

Motowidlo, S. J., Dunnette, M. D., & Carter, G. W. (1990). An alternative selection procedure: The low-fidelity simulation. *Journal of Applied Psychology, 75*(6), 640–647.

Murphy, K. R., & Shiarella, A. H. (1997). Implications of the multidimensional nature of job performance for the validity of selection tests: Multivariate frameworks for studying test validity. *Personnel Psychology, 50*(4), 823–854.

Ployhart, R. E., & Harold, C. M. (2004). The Applicant Attribution-Reaction Theory (AART): An integrative theory of applicant attributional processing. *International Journal of Selection & Assessment, 12*(1–2), 84–98.

Rosenthal, R. (1966). *Experimenter effects in behavioral research*: East Norwalk, CT: Appleton-Century-Crofts.

Ryan, A. M., & Ployhart, R. E. (2000). Applicants' perceptions of selection procedures and decisions: A critical review and agenda for the future. *Journal of Management, 26*(3), 565–606.

Ryan, A. M., Sacco, J. M., McFarland, L. A., & Kriska, S. (2000). Applicant self-selection: Correlates of withdrawal from a multiple hurdle process. *Journal of Applied Psychology, 85*(2), 163–179.

Sabini, J., & Silver, M. (1983). Dispositional vs. situational interpretations of Milgram's obedience experiments: "The fundamental attributional error." *Journal for the Theory of Social Behaviour, 13*(2), 147–154.

Sackett, P. R. (2003). Stereotype threat in applied selection settings: A commentary. *Human Performance, 16*(3), 295–309.

Sackett, P. R., & Dreher, G. F. (1982). Constructs and assessment center dimensions: Some troubling empirical findings. *Journal of Applied Psychology, 67*(4), 401–410.

Sackett, P. R., Schmitt, N., Ellingson, J. E., & Kabin, M. B. (2001). High-stakes testing in employment, credentialing, and higher education: Prospects in a post-affirmative-action world. *American Psychologist, 56*(4), 302–318.

Schmidt, F. L., & Hunter, J. E. (1998). The validity and utility of selection methods in personnel psychology: Practical and theoretical implications of 85 years of research findings. *Psychological Bulletin, 124,* 262–274.

Schwarz, N. (1994). Judgment in a social context: Biases, shortcomings, and the logic of conversation. In M. P. Zanna (Ed.), *Advances in experimental social psychology,* (Vol 26, pp. 123–162). San Diego, CA: Academic Press.

Schwarz, N. (1999). Self-reports: How the questions shape the answers. *American Psychologist, 54*(2), 93–105.

Steele, C. M., & Aronson, J. (1995). Stereotype threat and the intellectual test performance of African Americans. *Journal of Personality & Social Psychology, 69*(5), 797–811.

Steele, C. M., & Davies, P. G. (2003). Stereotype threat and employment testing: A commentary. *Human Performance, 16*(3), 311–326.

Sternberg, R. J., Wagner, R. K., Williams, W. M., & Horvath, J. A. (1995). Testing common sense. *American Psychologist, 50*(11), 912–927.

Truxillo, D. M., Steiner, D. D., & Gilliland, S. W. (2004). The importance of organizational justice in personnel selection: Defining when selection fairness really matters. *International Journal of Selection & Assessment, 12*(1–2), 39–53.

Weekley, J. A., & Jones, C. (1999). Further studies of situational tests. *Personnel Psychology, 52*(3), 679–700.

Weick, K. E. (1969). Social psychology in an era of social change. *American Psychologist, 24*(11), 990–998.

Wernimont, P. F., & Campbell, J. P. (1968). Signs, samples, and criteria. *Journal of Applied Psychology, 52*(5), 372–376.

Zimbardo, P. G. (1974). On "Obedience to authority." *American Psychologist, 29*(7), 566–567.

# 3

# Can Good Judgment be Measured?

Margaret E. Brooks
*Wayne State University*

Scott Highhouse
*Bowling Green State University*

Despite having the word judgment in its very name, there has been no serious discussion in the situational judgment test (SJT) literature about the nature of human judgment and its role in situational judgment testing. Although content varies widely across SJTs, compared with other ability tests, the tests typically require a series of judgments in response to domain-related dilemmas. Consider this example item from the situational judgment portion of the FBI special agent selection process:

> You are shopping when you notice a man robbing the store. What would you do?

1. Leave the store as quickly as possible and call the police.
2. Try to apprehend the robber yourself.
3. Follow the man and call the police as soon as he appears settled somewhere.
4. Nothing, as you do not wished to get involved in the matter.

Note that the special agent candidate is expected to consider the circumstances, weigh the proposed alternatives, and consider possible outcomes.

Hastie and Dawes (2001) defined *judgment* as "the human ability to infer, estimate, and predict the character of events" (p. 48). Clearly, the FBI was interested in assessing the candidate's judgment.

The use of SJTs is based on the assumption—either explicit or implicit—that judgment ability varies across candidates, and that this ability can be measured. We believe that an understanding of SJTs requires an understanding of what judgment ability is, and whether it can be assessed as a domain-specific individual difference. The SJT literature has treated construct validity as though it is something discoverable in the tests themselves. Researchers correlate scores on SJTs with responses to personality and cognitive ability measures and, when correlations are observed, conclude that the tests cannot be measuring judgment. An investigation of the validity of inferences from SJT scores must begin with a theory of situational judgment. Such a theory should be able to specify relations with other constructs, such as personality and cognitive ability, and should specify what future behaviors should be related to SJT scores. The theory must, however, begin with an understanding of what it means to say someone has "good judgment."

This chapter attempts to begin this endeavor by taking a closer look at just what is meant by good judgment, and outlining issues that must be contended with in any attempt to measure it. This is followed by a discussion of hypothesis testing strategies that are needed for validating inferences about scores on SJT items. Along the way, we review judgment and decision making (JDM) research and theory as it relates to the issue of identifying and measuring good judgment.

## WHAT IS GOOD JUDGMENT?

Within the JDM community, the term *judgment* often connotes a program of research based on the early thinking of Egon Brunswik (1952). In a now classic article in *Psychological Review*, Hammond (1955) showed how Brunswik's work on perception was relevant to the task of making inferences from incomplete and fallible cues in the environment. People are seen as intuitive statisticians forced to make probabilistic judgments based on their perceptions of how environmental cues relate to one another. Industrial-organizational (I-O) psychologists are usually only exposed to this work as it relates to deriving decision weights after, for example, examining a large number of interviewer judgments (e.g., Dougherty, Ebert, & Callender, 1986). Indeed, the name Brunswik has become almost synonymous with the policy-capturing method (Aiman-Smith, Scullen, & Barr, 2002).

Brunswik and his followers' contributions, however, go well beyond simply developing a method for identifying the importance of judgment cues. Although it is beyond the scope of this chapter to outline Brunswik's contributions to psychology (see Hammond & Stewart, 2001), the perception analogy to judgment is helpful for gaining a better appreciation of the potentialities of SJT. Brunswik noted that individuals achieve a percept (e.g., recognizing a friend who is some distance away) by taking into account various cues (e.g., build, way of walking, hair color), and weighing these cues in a way that overcomes indecision (Hogarth, 2001). An important characteristic of this perception process is that it is covert, in the sense that one does not have access to the process of recognition, and that one cannot necessarily defend it on logical, step-by-step grounds. Moreover, this process occurs automatically. That is, it happens quickly and with little effort. In the next section, we discuss how Hammond (1996) applied Brunswik's model of perception to the arena of judgment, and how this application offers some hypotheses about the content and nature of SJTs.

## Situational Judgment as Quasi-Rationality

A long-standing dichotomy in cognition has been the distinction between analysis and intuition. Analytical decisions are characterized by logical, step-by-step processes, whereas intuitive decisions often produce choices without logically defensible, methodical processes behind them. In his cognitive continuum theory, Hammond rejected the analysis–intuition dichotomy in favor of a continuum. Hammond proposed that judgment is conducted on a continuum anchored at one pole by intuition and at the other by analysis. He argued that the most common mode of judgment is *quasi-rationality*, which includes elements of both intuition and analysis.

The unusual aspect of Hammond's approach is that it accords intuition the same degree of status as it does analysis. It recognizes that intuition, like analysis, has both strengths and weaknesses. Quasi-rationality, therefore, is a kind of common sense that balances the strengths and weaknesses of both intuition and analysis (Hogarth, 2001). We believe that SJTs may be methods of assessing Hammond's quasi-rationality, or the ability to effectively use intuition and analysis in making good judgments. What really distinguishes SJTs from other commonly used ability measures, we believe, is their potential to get at the intuition component of quasi-rationality.

Carl Jung was one of the early psychologists to view intuition as something more than merely sloppy thinking. In Jung's (1926) theory of personality, intuition referred to the ability to perceive possibilities, implications, and principles without them being weighed down by details. In contrast, Hammond (1996) views intuition much as Brunswik viewed perception—as a cognitive process that produces a solution without the use of conscious procedures. Just as all humans perceive things, all humans have access to intuition. Whereas analytical thinking is done using logically defensible, step-by-step procedures, intuition cannot be reconstructed or justified in a purely logical way. In a comprehensive examination of the philosophical and scientific literature on intuition, Hogarth (2001) defined an *intuitive response* as something that is reached with little effort, and involving little or no conscious deliberation (see also Dijksterhuis, 2004; Wegner, Fuller, & Sparrow, 2003). In addition, Hogarth noted that the term *intuition* suggests certain correlates, most notably speed and confidence.

Just because intuitive responses come quickly and confidently does not mean they are accurate. Consider people asked which alternative (1 or 2) is more likely:

1. An all-out war between the United States and China
2. A situation in which a third country, such as Iran or Pakistan, triggers an all-out war between the United States and China

An overwhelming majority of people given this choice will quickly and confidently choose the second option. Yet, a close analysis of the options reveals that option 2 is a subset of option 1, making it a logical impossibility that it could be the more probable outcome (Highhouse, 2001). Consider the friend who refuses to stay home from the football game during a blizzard because he paid a lot of money for his ticket. Although intuition says that it makes no sense to waste money, an analysis of the problem shows that sunk costs should not factor into the future costs and benefits of risking an automobile accident to suffer through the freezing ball game (Arkes & Blumer, 1985).

Indeed, decades of research comparing the predictions of human judgments with mechanical procedures that mathematically combine numerical cues, have shown that the mechanical procedures consistently outperform the judges (Camerer & Johnson, 1991). This occurs even when the formulas are based on the exact same information used by the human judges.[1] It is the consistency of the mechanical formula that accounts for its accuracy on average. People, knowing that formulas applied across the board are bound to lead to errors in prediction, feel that they are closing their eyes to errors that could otherwise be avoided. Yet, these people are

---

[1]One thing to keep in mind with these results, however, is that many of the *inputs* to these mechanical models are derived from intuition. For example, human judges may assign a score to a subjective process, such as assessing a candidate's interpersonal skills, or reading a resume (Highhouse, 2002).

not considering the even greater number of errors that are being made when they ignore the mechanical rules. As Hogarth (2001) observed, people find it difficult to understand that one must accept error to make less error.

Even within the arena of prediction, however, there are some victories to be found for intuition. Professional financial analysts outpredict novices because the experts can interpret the impact of news events (Johnson, 1988). Combinations of intuitive and mechanical judgments can outperform mechanical judgments alone in environments where one needs to be able to detect change (e.g., Blattberg & Hoch, 1990; Whitecotton, Sanders, & Norris, 1998). Ganzach, Kluger, and Klayman (2000) showed that expert fine-tuning of mechanical combinations of employment interview scores resulted in more accurate predictions than using the mechanically combined scores alone. Thus, human intuition can sometimes allow for the recognition of rare but diagnostic cues (e.g., the job candidate makes off-color jokes at lunch) that could never be incorporated into a purely analytic procedure.

Funder (1987) noted that good judgment is the ability to go beyond the information given, and to rely on one's broader knowledge and past experiences. Wilson and Schooler (1991) presented a series of studies suggesting that people who go about reasoning in a deliberate or methodical fashion can make poorer decisions than people who trust their intuition. The notion is similar to work on automatic versus controlled behavior (Vallacher & Wegner, 1985). Just as an experienced golfer plays worse when he or she thinks through the stroke, decision makers who analyze their reasons for choice make worse consumer choices (McMackin & Slovic, 2000; Wilson & Schooler, 1991), basketball predictions (Halberstadt & Levine, 1999), roommate choices (Dijksterhuis, 2004), and eyewitness identifications (Dunning & Stern, 1994). Add this to research showing that people who always strive to maximize their decisions are more unhappy than those who satisfice (Schwartz et al., 2002), and you have a pretty good argument for relying on your intuition over analysis in many situations.

## Summary

Determining whether SJTs can assess good judgment requires a theory of situational judgment. We have briefly outlined one useful theoretical perspective—one that defines good judgment as the effective balance of analysis and intuition. Later in this chapter, we propose some methods for assessing construct validity, using the quasi-rationality view of situational judgment as a starting point. In the next section, however, we consider some of the barriers to assessing judgment using the SJT paradigm.

Because prediction plays a central role in any definition of judgment, we now outline some issues related to prediction that must be contended with in any attempt to measure judgment.

## SITUATIONAL JUDGMENTS AS PREDICTIONS

Situational judgment items present hypothetical situations one might encounter in the workplace, and ask respondents to evaluate and choose among alternative responses to the dilemma. Although differences in SJT instructions can change the nature of the predictions respondents are asked to make, we argue that all situational judgment items, regardless of their nature, require some kind of estimation or prediction. Determining either what one "would" do or what one "should" do in a hypothetical situation requires the respondent to predict what would result from each potential response to the situation. Consider, for example, the FBI special agent test item presented earlier; were the item to require the respondent to indicate what *should* be done in reaction to the robbery, the applicant would have to imagine the consequences of apprehending the person, doing nothing, and so forth. The applicant would then need to compare the utility of these predicted outcomes and choose the option with the highest expected value. Thus, responding to the "would" version of the FBI item requires predicting one's own future behavior, whereas responding to the "should" version requires predicting $y$ given $x$ response. Ployhart and Ehrhart (2003) found substantive differences between SJT responses to "should do" and "would do" instructions, which is consistent with the idea that these two types of instructions require qualitatively different predictions.

We believe that an understanding of the literature on people's ability to predict their own future behaviors and preferences, along with their ability to predict various outcomes for different responses, is important for understanding the nature of SJTs and for identifying future research needs. In a review of the SJT literature, McDaniel and Nguyen (2001) noted the variety of items across SJTs and urged researchers to look into how item characteristics affect the validity of SJTs. We agree, and believe that research in JDM can help inform research on the implications of item-level differences in SJTs. The following sections are not an argument for any one kind of item or instruction type, but rather an attempt to point out potential implications of research in JDM for different kinds of SJT questions and issues. We begin by examining research on our ability to predict our future states.

## Predictions About Ourselves

One of the most common explanations for why SJTs predict job performance is that SJTs assess intentions to respond in a certain way, and these intentions predict future behavior. SJTs that aim to assess intentions use instructions that ask participants to indicate what they "would" do in a hypothetical situation as opposed to what they "should" do. We have argued that all types of instructions require cognitive work that includes estimation and prediction, but instructions that ask respondents to indicate what they "would" do, or to list the response they would "most likely" perform, clearly require an additional type of prediction. These instructions require respondents to predict their own future behavior. Although we have considerable evidence that intentions predict actions, research in JDM suggests that our predictions about ourselves can be highly context dependent. An understanding of this literature is important for understanding the efficacy of intentional items for predicting job performance.

Research in JDM has demonstrated that we are overconfident in our predictions, and nowhere is this more evident than in the well-documented planning fallacy (Kahneman & Lovallo, 1993). When asked to indicate the amount of time it will take us to complete a task, we tend to base our estimation on the "best-case" scenario, often resulting in an inaccurate prediction (e.g., Buehler, Griffin, & Ross, 1994; Newby-Clark, Ross, Buehler, Koehler, & Griffin, 2000). For example, consider the following situation:

> A student has a paper due in one month. If she hands in the paper one week before the deadline, she can get feedback from the professor, make revisions, and turn in the improved paper by the final due date.

If asked to predict whether she will turn in the paper early, the student is likely to think about all the time she could potentially spend working on it. She is unlikely to consider all of the possible barriers and distractions to writing the paper, including other classes, personal issues, and social events.

Buehler et al. (1994) found that people make more accurate predictions of the future when they consider relevant past experiences, and how these experiences relate to the current prediction. Instead of relying on their past behavior, however, unaided decision makers tend to create overly optimistic intentions. Newby-Clark and Ross (2003) found that people's future intentions were much more positive than would be expected based on their past behaviors, even when they were asked to recall negative events from the past before making future predictions. This suggests that developers of SJTs may be wise to avoid items that require respondents to make predictions about time.

Another potential explanation for our inability to accurately predict our future behavior is that we have a hard time accurately predicting how we will *feel* in the future (Loewenstein & Schkade, 1999). In a study looking at predictions of future preferences, Simonson (1990) gave students six snack choices and told them they could have one snack during each of the next three class sessions. One group was asked to immediately choose a snack for each of the next three sessions, thereby *choosing* a snack for the day, and *predicting* what snack they would want during the second and third class sessions (simultaneous condition). The other group chose a snack each day before the session (sequential condition). Simonson found that those in the simultaneous condition had more variety in their three choices than those in the sequential condition. He interpreted this result to be evidence for a "diversification bias." People predicted that they would want more diversity in their snacks than was revealed in actual choices. In a replication and extension of this study, Read and Lowenstein (1995) found that people in the simultaneous condition regretted choices for variety and, when given the option, were likely to choose to "change snacks" for the second and third session from what they had initially chosen. Other research on predicting future feelings has found that when we are in a cold state (e.g., not aroused, calm, satiated), we have difficulty predicting what our behavior will entail when we are in a hot state (e.g., angry, anxious, hungry). Lowenstein (1996) suggested that such visceral factors as are experienced in a "hot" state have an inordinate influence on our feelings about a given product or situation, and consequently on our decision making. Furthermore, we discount these factors when predicting future states.

Research on predicting future feelings suggests that we may be able to more accurately predict our responses to workplace situations that are not highly affect-laden. One implication for SJTs is that applicants may be better able to predict their responses to items that assess more task-oriented issues, as opposed to items that are more people-oriented. Would the FBI special agent applicant be able to predict his behavior in the high-arousal situation described in the robbery SJT item? Future research should look at the effects of mood states on SJT scores in both hypothetical and actual contexts.

Taken together, the research discussed in this section suggests that our estimations of our own future behavior can be inaccurate, but we do know that in some situations we are more accurate than in others. Future research should explore differences in SJTs that may lead to differential prediction accuracy. Of particular interest are differences in SJT items that may lead to a more positive relationship between intentions and behaviors. There are a number of characteristics of intentions that affect their likelihood of predicting behavior. For example, temporal stability of intentions has been shown to moderate the relationship between intentions and behaviors (Sheeran, Orbell, & Trafimow, 1999). Research could explore items or even domains of items that may be associated with more stable intentions. In general, researchers investigating the psychological mechanisms by which SJTs function should be wary about assuming that intentions translate to behaviors in all domains.

## Estimating *y* Given *x*

Even situational judgment items that do not require respondents to predict their future behavior still require respondents to imagine much of the context within which they must decide on the best response. That is, respondents are charged with the task of making a decision based on limited information in a hypothetical context—an ambiguous task even in the case of well-written items and responses. Decision making research has suggested that decision makers seem not to be bothered by contextual ambiguity when making predictions (Ross, 1987; Ross & Nisbett, 1990). Instead of constructing the many possible alternative representations of an ambiguous situation, people tend to rely on a single construal of the situation to make decisions (e.g., Arkes, Faust, Guilmette, & Hart, 1988; Shaklee, & Fischhoff, 1982). People make confident predictions based on the assumption that their construal of the situation represents the reality of that situation (Griffin, Dunning, & Ross, 1990). Returning to the FBI example, respondents were told only that a man was robbing a store. This situation has considerable ambiguity. Among the many details left to the imagination of the respondent are important issues such as the following: How big is the man? Does he have a weapon? Are there other people around? Different assumptions about key aspects of this situation could certainly result in different responses to this item. There has been little research in the SJT literature on the issue of item elaboration, despite the existence of item-level variability in the amount of ambiguity in SJT items. Particularly in cases of high ambiguity, there could be considerable variance in situational construal. Most worrisome is the possibility of construal differences between those taking the test, and those writing the test. The "answer key" for an SJT is determined by experts, who determine the best choices based on their construal of the situation. The best answer based on one construal may represent poor judgment based on a different set of assumptions.

Another issue that may affect situational construal is temporal distance from the actual event. When temporal distance is greater, temporal construal theory (Liberman & Trope, 1998) predicts that people will construe outcomes or events at a higher level (i.e., in more big-picture terms), and as temporal distance decreases, people will rely more on specific, practical construals. Liberman and Trope asked participants to imagine engaging in an everyday activity (e.g., watching TV) in the near future or in the distant future, and then provide an open-ended description of the activity. They found that those in the near future condition were more likely to focus on specific features of the activity, such as "flipping channels," and those in the distant future condition were more likely to focus on more general features of the activity, such as "being entertained." This theory may suggest that SJT items varying in temporal distance will vary in the degree to which they elicit big-picture, idealistic responses versus more pragmatic, realistic responses. For example, SJT items tapping issues that seem farther removed from the applicant, such as strategic planning, may elicit more idealistic responses than items tapping more immediate task-performance issues.

Research on situational construal suggests several future research directions for those studying SJTs. Item elaboration seems to be one important area for more exploration. Items that are too long may be associated with test-taker fatigue, and research in judgment and decision making has also shown that we often make poorer decisions when we are given too much information (Nisbett, Zukier, & Lemley, 1981); however, making certain that there is enough item elaboration to ensure that assumptions about important aspects of the situation are consistent across people is an important and potentially conflicting concern. In addition, issues of temporal distance should be examined within the context of SJT items. Whether the candidate gives a realistic response or an idealistic one may be influenced by contextual features of the items. Table 3.1 summarizes the judgment limitations presented in this section, and their implications for the development of SJT items.

## Summary

Whether it is making predictions about our own future behavior or predicting the nature of a hypothetical situation, it is clear that—regardless of item type or content—any test of situational judgment requires some kind of prediction. We reviewed research that addresses conditions under which our ability to make accurate predictions is particularly limited. This research is relevant to practical, item-level issues that arise when designing and evaluating the content of SJTs. In the next section, we discuss hypotheses that need to be tested about the relation between SJT test scores and good judgment.

TABLE 3.1

Selected Judgment Limitations and Their Implications for SJT Item Development

| Judgment Limitation | Explanation | Implications for SJT Items |
|---|---|---|
| Planning fallacy | We base predictions of future behavior on the "best case scenario," thereby discounting other, less favorable, scenarios. | Be wary of assuming that intentions predict behavior in all situations. Judgments of duration are especially biased. |
| Diversification bias | We predict that we will prefer variety, but in reality we often prefer consistency. | Espoused preferences may be more diverse than actual behavioral responses. |
| Predicting future feelings | When we are in a "cold" state, we have difficulty predicting our behavior in a "hot" state (and vice versa). | The emotional context of the items may affect the accuracy of predictions. |
| Construal of ambiguous situations | When faced with an ambiguous situation, we form one set of assumptions on which to base our judgment, and discount all others. What constitutes good judgment depends on our assumptions. | The test taker's assumptions may be different than those upon which the "best answer" was based. What is the "best answer" for an SJT item may depend on situational construal. |
| Temporal construal | Temporal distance from an event affects our construal such that when the event is far away we focus on the "big picture," and as it gets closer we become more pragmatic in our concerns. | SJT items tapping issues farther in temporal distance may elicit more idealistic responses than those tapping more immediate issues. |

## THEORY TESTING

It appears possible to create a test containing a number of situational dilemmas, responses that correlate with performance over and above job experience, cognitive ability, and personality (Chan & Schmitt, 2002). What, therefore, is being measured? The implicit or explicit assumption behind most SJT measures is that people vary on judgment, and that this construct can be assessed using situational dilemmas. Defining what good judgment is, and specifying the nomological network of relations to other constructs is a necessary next step in SJT research. Unfortunately, many

**TABLE 3.2**

Characteristics of Analytical and Intuitive Items

| Item Type | Ability to Articulate Reason for Answer | Speed in Responding to the Item | Confidence in the Response |
|---|---|---|---|
| Analytical | High | Slow | Tentative |
| Intuitive | Low | Fast | Bold |

researchers attempt to sidestep this issue by simply referring to the SJT as a "measurement method" that may assess a variety of constructs (e.g., McDaniel, Morgeson, Finnegan, Campion, & Braverman, 2001). We believe that a more productive approach, both theoretically and practically, is to try to hone in on the characteristics of SJTs that allow us to identify good judgment. This will require a better understanding of the judgment construct, and considerable research—some of it laboratory-based—on how to better understand its measurement.

We argued in the earlier section that intuition and analysis both have value, and that knowing when to employ each is an important part of judgment. Moreover, we have suggested that effectively trading off analysis and intuition, what Hammond (1996) referred to as quasi-rationality, may be what SJTs are tapping. If SJTs do indeed measure quasi-rationality (i.e., the balancing of intuition and analysis), should we be surprised to find that they correlate moderately with personality and cognitive ability measures? Certainly, effectively balancing idealism with practicality, or knowing when or when not to obsess over details, involves both intellectual and temperamental components.

If it is the ability to tap intuition that sets SJTs apart from ability and temperament measures, then we should be able to make some predictions about SJT responses. Table 3.2 presents characteristics of analytical and intuitive items that can guide hypotheses. Recall that intuition is characterized by a difficulty in articulating the process, and is correlated with speed and confidence. One might expect, therefore, that those items for which the process of arriving at an answer is more difficult to articulate (i.e., items requiring more intuition) should also be the ones answered more quickly and confidently. Based on Wilson and Schooler's (1991) work, we might also expect that correct answers to SJT items would be made more quickly and confidently than incorrect answers. Test takers should have a harder time describing in a step-by-step fashion how they arrived at an answer to an SJT item, as compared with a cognitive ability test item. Individual differences in use of intuition (e.g., Scott & Bruce, 1995) should correlate more strongly with performance on SJTs than to performance on cognitive ability tests.

Neuropsychological studies have even shown that intuitive-based judgments activate different areas of the brain from evidence-based judgments (Lieberman, Jarcho, & Satpute, 2004). We might even predict that brain-imaging studies will reveal differences for responses to SJT items versus cognitive ability or personality items. The point is that research and theory in JDM can better allow us to elaborate the nomological net within which the judgment ability construct occurs. Careful hypotheses about relations with various criteria are necessary to advance our understanding of what SJTs measure.

Another important component of any theory of good judgment is the ability to predict the nature of events. Indeed, much research on judgmental accuracy is based on predictions of events that can be quantified, such as outcomes of baseball games (Balzer, Doherty, & O'Connor, 1989). We have discussed in this chapter how all situational judgment items require some form of prediction, and we have identified some of the many problems that must be overcome in attempts to assess judgment in terms of prediction. Adding additional complexity to this issue is the fact that respondents to SJTs are not asked to predict quantifiable outcomes such as who will win the Super Bowl, or whether we will see rain in the forecast. Instead, applicants are required to rely on their general intuition and past experiences in similar situations to make a good judgment for each item. How then do we establish the construct validity of a situational judgment item as a measure of good judgment? Funder (1987) advocated two approaches for establishing the accuracy of judgments: agreement with others, and ability to predict behavior. The agreement criterion is most likely used in establishing the scoring key for SJTs, either via job analysis (McDaniel & Nguyen, 2001) or from expert profiles (Wagner & Sternberg, 1985). The ability to predict behavior is the trickier criterion.

We know of only one study that has used the ability to predict behavior as a correlate of judgment. Zalesny and Highhouse (1992) showed groups of student teachers a videotaped mathematics lesson in which a teacher was faced with a series of disorderly behaviors from one unruly student. After the fourth episode (approximately 25 minutes into the session), the videotape was stopped and the student teachers were asked to predict what the target teacher would do next. The student teachers also rated the performance of the target teacher on a number of dimensions. Zalesny and Highhouse found that the accuracy of the student teachers' predictions about the target's behavior were correlated with judgmental accuracy as measured as agreement with expert performance ratings.[2] We

---

[2]Specifically, accuracy in ability to predict the disciplinary behavior was significantly correlated with expert agreement on ratings of classroom management.

could envision similar research being conducted in establishing the construct validity of SJTs. If, indeed, SJTs measure good judgment, then we would expect high scorers, rather than low scorers, to better predict what others would do in work-related circumstances. Other behavioral predictions that might be used for establishing construct validity of SJT items could include predicting responses of counterparts in a competitive negotiation (see Morris, Larrick, & Su, 1999), or predicting an interviewee's profile on the Big Five personality traits (see Barrick, Patton, & Haugland, 2000). The point is, any theory of situational judgment should include predictions concerning how the construct relates to things other than job performance.

## FINAL COMMENTS

This chapter is a call for SJT researchers to take judgment more seriously. We believe that the next generation of SJT research needs to focus on defining good judgment, and developing a theory to guide item development and hypothesis testing. We offered Hammond's quasi-rationality as a possible starting point for such a theory. The advantage of this approach is that it offers some predictions that can be studied in the field and in the lab.

We also believe that JDM research provides a fruitful area for identifying practical concerns associated with SJTs. Research examining our ability to predict future feelings and behaviors suggests that the accuracy of our predictions is affected by numerous variables such as overconfidence, unrealistic optimism, mood states, and situational construal. Understanding the boundary conditions associated with our ability to predict future outcomes may lead to a better understanding of how to develop and improve SJT items.

In summary, JDM research may be one of the keys to clarifying some of the ambiguities in the current conception of situational judgment. As Guion (1998) noted, we can make valid decisions, even without understanding the constructs we are measuring "[But] at this point in the history of employment psychology we should be getting tired of not knowing what we are doing, no matter how carefully we do it" (p. 618). We believe judgment should be a central component of research on the SJT. Indeed, judgment is already central to its name.

## REFERENCES

Aiman-Smith, L., Scullen, S. E., & Barr, S. H. (2002). Conducting studies of decision making in organizational contexts: A tutorial for policy-capturing and other regression-based techniques. *Organizational Research Methods, 5,* 388–414.

Ajzen, I., Brown, T. C., & Carvajl, F. (2004). Explaining the discrepancy between intentions and actions: The case of hypothetical bias in contingent valuation, *Personality and Social Psychology Bulletin, 30*(9), 1008–1121.

Anderson, J. R. (1983). *The architecture of cognition.* Cambridge, MA: Harvard University Press.

Arkes, H., Faust, D., Guilmette, T. J., & Hart, K. (1988). Eliminating the hindsight bias. *Journal of Applied Psychology, 73,* 305–307.

Arkes, H. R., & Blumer, C. (1985) The psychology of sunk cost. *Organizational Behavior and Human Decision Processes, 35,* 122–140.

Balzer, W. K., Doherty, M. E., & O'Connor, R. (1989). Effects of cognitive feedback on performance. *Psychological Bulletin, 106,* 410–433.

Barrick, M. R., Patton, G. K., & Haugland, S. N. (2000). Accuracy of interviewer judgments of job applicant personality traits. *Personnel Psychology, 53,* 925–951.

Blattberg, R. C., & Hoch, S. J. (1990). Database models and managerial intuition: 50% model + 50% intuition, *Managerial Science, 36,* 887–899.

Brunswik, E. (1952). *The conceptual framework of psychology.* Chicago, IL: University of Chicago Press.

Buehler, R., Griffin, D., & Ross, M. (1994). Exploring the "planning fallacy": Why people underestimate their task completion times. *Journal of Personality & Social Psychology, 67*(3), 366–381.

Buehler, R., Griffin, D., & Ross, M. (2002). Inside the planning fallacy: On the causes and consequences of optimistic time predictions. In T. Gilovich, D. Griffin & D. Kahneman (Eds.), *Heuristics and biases: The psychology of intuitive judgment* (pp. 250–270). Cambridge, MA: Cambridge University Press.

Camerer C. F., & Johnson E. J. (1991). The process-performance paradox in expert judgment: How can experts know so much and predict so badly? In K. A. Ericsson, & J. Smith (Eds.), *Toward a general theory of expertise: Prospects and limits* (pp. 195–217). Cambridge: Cambridge University Press.

Chan, D., & Schmitt, N. (2002). Situational judgment and job performance. *Human Performance, 15,* 233–254.

Dijksterhuis, A. (2004). Think different: The merits of unconscious thought in preference development in decision making. *Journal of Personality and Social Psychology, 87,* 586–598.

Dougherty, T. W., Ebert, R. J., & Callender, J. C. (1986). Policy capturing in the employment interview. *Journal of Applied Psychology, 71,* 9–15.

Dunning, D., & Stern, L. B. (1994). Distinguishing accurate from inaccurate eyewitness identifications via inquiries about decision processes. *Journal of Personality and Social Psychology, 67,* 818–835.

Funder, D. C. (1987). Errors and mistakes: Evaluating the accuracy of social judgment. *Psychological Bulletin, 101,* 75–90.

Ganzach, Y., Kluger, A. N., & Klayman, N. (2000). Making decisions from an interview: Expert measurement and mechanical combination, *Personnel Psychology, 53,* 1–20.

Griffin, D. W., Dunning, D., & Ross, L. (1990). The role of construal processes in overconfident predictions about the self and others. *Journal of Personality and Social Psychology, 59*(6), 1128–1139.

Guion, R. M. (1998). *Assessment, measurement, and prediction for personnel decisions.* Mahwah, NJ: Lawrence Erlbaum Associates.

Halberstadt, J. B., & Levine, G. M. (1999). Effects of reasons analysis on the accuracy of predicting basketball games, *Journal of Applied Social Psychology, 29,* 517–530.

Hammond, K. R. (1955). Probabilistic functioning and the clinical method, *Psychological Review, 62,* 255–262.

Hammond, K. R. (1996). *Human judgment and social policy: Irreducible uncertainty, inevitable error, unavoidable injustice.* New York: Oxford University Press.

Hammond, K. R., & Stewart, T. R. (2001). *The essential Brunswik: Beginnings, explications, applications.* London: Oxford University Press.

Hastie, R., & Dawes, R. M. (2001). *Rational choice in an uncertain world: The psychology of judgment and decision making.* Thousand Oaks, CA: Sage Publications.

Highhouse, S. (2001). Judgment and decision making research: Relevance to industrial and organizational psychology. In N. Anderson, D. S. Ones, H. K. Sinangil, & C. Viswesvaran (Eds.), *Handbook of industrial, work and organizational psychology* (pp. 314–332). New York: Sage.

Highhouse, S. (2002). Assessing the candidate as a whole: A historical and critical analysis of individual psychological assessment for personnel decision making. *Personnel Psychology, 55,* 363–396.

Hogarth, R. M. (2001). *Educating intuition.* Chicago, IL:The University of Chicago Press.

Johnson, E. J. (1988). Expertise and decision under uncertainty: Performance and process. In M. T. H. Chi, R. Glaser, & M. J. Farr (Eds.), *The nature of expertise* (pp. 209–228). Hillsdale, NJ: Lawrence Erlbaum Associates.

Jung, C. (1926). *Psychological types* (H. G. Baynes, Trans.) London: Routledge & Kegan Paul.

Kahneman, D., & Lovallo, D. (1993). Timid choices and bold forecasts: A cognitive perspective on risk taking. *Management Science, 39,* 17–31.

Lieberman, M.D., Jarcho, J. M., & Satpute, A. B. (2004). Evidence-based and intuition-based self-knowledge: An fMRI study. *Journal of Personality and Social Psychology, 87,* 421–435.

Liberman, N., & Trope, Y. (1998). The role of feasibility and desirability considerations in near and distant future decisions: A test of temporal construal theory. *Journal of Personality and Social Psychology, 75,* 5–18.

Loewenstein, G. (1996). Out of control: Visceral influences on behavior. *Organizational Behavior and Human Decision Processes, 116,* 75–98.

Loewenstein, G., & Schkade, D. (1999). Wouldn't it be nice? Predicting future feelings. In D. Kahneman, E. Diener, & N. Schwarz (Eds.), *Well-being: The foundations of hedonic psychology* (pp. 85–105). New York: Sage.

McDaniel, M. A., Morgeson, F. P., Finnegan, F. B., Campion, M. A., & Braverman, E. P. (2001). Use of situational judgment tests to predict job performance: A clarification of the literature. *Journal of Applied Psychology, 86,* 730–740.

McDaniel, M. A., & Nguyen, N. T. (2001). Situational judgment tests: A review of practice and constructs assessed. *International Journal of Selection and Assessment, 9,* 103–113.

McMackin, J., & Slovic, P. (2000). When does explicit justification impair decision making? *Journal of Applied Cognitive Psychology, 14,* 527–541.

Morris, M. W., Larrick, R. P., & Su, S. K. (1999). Misperceiving negotiation counterparts: When situationally determined bargaining behaviors are attributed to personality traits. *Journal of Personality & Social Psychology, 77,* 52–67.

Newby-Clark, I. R., & Ross, M. (2003). Conceiving the past and future. *Personality and Social Psychology Bulletin, 29*(7), 807–818.

Newby-Clark, I. R., Ross, M., Buehler, R., Koehler, D. J., & Griffin, D. (2000). People focus on optimistic scenarios and disregard pessimistic scenarios while predicting task completion times. *Journal of Experimental Social Psychology: Applied, 6*(3), 171–182.

Nisbett, R. E., Zukier, H., & Lemley, R. E. (1981). The dilution effect: Nondiagnostic information weakens the implications of diagnostic information. *Cognitive Psychology, 13,* 248–277.

Ployhart, R. E., & Ehrhart, M. G. (2003). Be careful what you ask for: Effects of response instructions on the construct validity and reliability of situational judgment tests. *International Journal of Selection and Assessment, 11*(1), 1–16.

Read, D., & Lowenstein, G. F. (1995). Diversification bias: Explaining the discrepancy in variety-seeking between combined and separated choices. *Journal of Experimental Psychology: Applied, 1*, 34–49.

Ross, M. (1987). The problem of construal in social inference and social psychology. In N. E. Grunberg, R. E. Nisbett, J. Rodin, & J. E. Singer (Eds.), *A distinctive approach to psychological research: The influence of Stanley Schachter* (pp. 118–130). Hillsdale, NJ: Lawrence Erlbaum Associates.

Ross, M., & Newby-Clark, I. R. (1998). Construing the past and future. *Social Cognition, 16*(1), 133–150.

Ross, M., & Nisbett, R. E. (1991). *The person and the situation: Perspectives of social psychology*. New York: McGraw-Hill.

Schwartz, B., Ward, A., Monterosso, J., Lyubomirsky, S., White, K., & Lehman, D. R. (2002). Maximizing versus satisficing: Happiness is a matter of choice. *Journal of Personality and Social Psychology, 83*, 1178–1197.

Scott, S. G., & Bruce, R. A. (1995). Decision making style: The development and assessment of a new measure. *Educational and Psychological Measurement, 55*, 818–831.

Shaklee, H., & Fischhoff, B. (1982). Strategies of information search in causal analysis. *Memory and Cognition, 10*, 520–530.

Sheeran, P., Orbell, S., & Trafimow, D. (1999). Does the temporal stability of behavioral intentions moderate intention-behavior and past behavior-future behavior relations? *Personality and Social Psychology Bulletin, 25*(6), 724–730.

Sternberg, R. J. (1997). *Successful intelligence: How practical and creative intelligence determine success in life*. New York: Plume.

Taylor, S. E., & Schneider, S. K. (1989). Coping and the simulation of events. *Social Cognition, 7*(2), 174–194.

Vallacher, R. R., & Wegner, D. M. (1985). *A theory of action identification*. Hillsdale, NJ: Lawrence Erlbaum Associates.

Wagner, R. K., & Sternberg, R. J. (1985). Practical intelligence in real-world pursuits: The role of tacit knowledge. *Journal of Personality and Social Psychology, 49*, 436–458.

Wegner, D. M., Fuller, V. A., & Sparrow, B. (2003). Clever hands: Uncontrolled intelligence in facilitated communication. *Journal of Personality and Social Psychology, 85*, 5–19.

Whitecotton, S. M., Sanders, D. E., & Norris, K. B. (1998). Improving predictive accuracy with a combination of human intuition and mechanical decision aids. *Organizational Behavior and Human Decision Processes, 76*, 325–348.

Wilson, T. D., & Schooler, J. W. (1991). Thinking too much: Introspection can reduce the quality of preferences and decisions. *Journal of Personality and Social Psychology, 60*, 181–192.

Zalesny, M., & Highhouse, S. (1992). Accuracy in performance evaluations. *Organizational Behavior and Human Decision Processes, 51*, 22–50.

# 4

# A Theoretical Basis for Situational Judgment Tests

Stephan J. Motowidlo
Amy C. Hooper
Hannah L. Jackson
*University of Minnesota*

Starting from the premise that common methods for scoring situational judgment tests (SJTs) produce measures of procedural knowledge, this chapter develops a theory about its causal antecedents in the form of experiential and dispositional variables and its consequences for job performance. The concept of *implicit trait policy* (ITP) plays a central role in this theory. ITPs are implicit beliefs about the effectiveness of different levels of trait expression. The theory explains relations between personality scores and SJT scores by arguing that ITPs mediate relations between personality traits and procedural knowledge. Experiential variables in the theory are presumed to have causal effects on both ITPs and procedural knowledge. This chapter reviews empirical studies that test theoretical predictions that individuals' personality traits are correlated with their ITPs and that ITPs mediate effects of personality traits on procedural knowledge.

This relation between personality traits and ITPs implies that individuals' judgments about the effectiveness of SJT response options carry information about the individuals' personality traits. Therefore, it might be possible to capture useful information about personality traits indirectly or implicitly by asking people to judge the effectiveness of SJT options known to express especially high or low levels of targeted traits. This chapter reviews several studies in which we attempted to develop SJTs specifically to assess ITPs (not procedural knowledge) in this way and examine their convergent validity against explicit (NEO-Five Factor Inventory) trait measures and a behavioral measure of individuals' traits. Results provide preliminary support for the usefulness of ITP measures for predicting behavior and for the hypothesis that they are more resistant to faking than explicit trait measures generated by the NEO.

## SITUATIONAL JUDGMENT TESTS

SJTs are tests that present brief descriptions of problematic situations like those that occur on the job and ask applicants to indicate how they would or should respond to them. The situation can be described orally as in situational interviews (e.g., Latham, Saari, Pursell, & Campion, 1980) in written form (e.g., Motowidlo, Dunnette, & Carter, 1990), or in a video format (e.g., Chan & Schmitt, 1997; Weekley & Jones, 1997). Responses can be open-ended as in the situational interview or based on specified options prepared for each situational stem. Tests that use specified options usually use either of two basic response formats (Nguyen, McDaniel, & Biderman, 2002; Ployhart & Ehrhart, 2004). Some ask people to indicate how they *would* handle the test situations by selecting options they would most likely and least likely perform or by rating their likelihood of performing each option. Others ask people to indicate how they *should* handle the test situations by selecting the best and worst options in each set or by rating the effectiveness of each response. An example of an SJT stem describing a problematic work situation and alternative responses is shown here:

> You and someone from another department are jointly responsible for coordinating a project involving both departments. This other person is not carrying out his share of the responsibilities. You would . . .
> ——— Most Likely ———Least Likely

> a) Discuss the situation with your manager and ask him to take it up with the other person's manager.
> b) Remind him that you need his help and that the project won't be completed effectively without a full team effort from both of you.
> c) Tell him that he is not doing his share of the work, that you will not do it all yourself, and that if he does not start doing more, you'll be forced to take the matter to his manager.
> d) Try to find out why he is not doing his share and explain to him that this creates more work for you and makes it harder to finish the project.
> e) Get someone else from his department to help with the project.

SJTs are often scored by comparing applicants' answers with experts' judgments. Applicants obtain higher scores on tests that ask them to pick the best and worst options or options they would most likely and least likely perform when options they identify as best or as options they would most likely perform are among those that experts believe are relatively effective. They also obtain higher scores when options they identify as the worst or as options they would least likely perform are among those that experts believe are relatively ineffective. Similarly, applicants obtain higher scores on tests that ask for ratings of the likelihood that they would perform each of the options or of the effectiveness of each of the options when their ratings agree with ratings of effectiveness provided by experts.

SJTs that ask applicants how they *should* act and that are scored by comparing applicants' answers with experts' judgments are straightforward measures of applicants' knowledge (Clevenger, Pereira, Wiechmann, Schmitt, & Harvey, 2001; McDaniel & Nguyen, 2001; Motowidlo, Borman, & Schmitt, 1997; Motowidlo, Hanson, & Crafts, 1997; Weekley & Jones, 1999). This premise assumes that experts' judgments about the effectiveness of SJT options are correct, or close to correct, for a particular organizational setting and that applicants really do register their beliefs about the effectiveness of SJT options on these tests. Because this knowledge is about effective and ineffective courses of action in problematic work situations, it is appropriately described as procedural knowledge.

Exactly what applicants really register on SJTs that ask how they *would* act, however, might be open to some question. Applicants might interpret instructions to indicate how they would act essentially as instructions to show whether or not they know how they should act. Or, because they are applying for a job and should therefore be eager to do well on the employment test, they might be likely to indicate that they would do what they believe to be the best thing to do. In fact, Weekley and Jones (1999) offered the opinion that the difference between judgments about what should be done in situations described by SJT items (i.e., judgments about their effectiveness) and statements about what someone would actually do if in the situations described is probably trivial because people are not likely to say they would perform actions in work situations unless they believed they were effective. This suggests that SJT instructions to indicate what applicants would do will elicit the same information as that elicited by instructions to indicate what they should do and SJTs that ask what applicants would do therefore measure procedural knowledge, too.

Another possibility is that when asked what they would do, applicants describe actions they believe they would perform, whether they believe those actions are effective or not. If they are being completely honest and take SJT instructions literally, they might indicate what they think they really would do even if they know that what they would do is not the best thing to do. In that case, scoring the SJT against effectiveness judgments by experts produces a measure of how effective their habitual actions are and this might be different from their procedural knowledge. In support of this possibility, results of two studies suggest that the difference between asking people how they would act and asking people how they should act in SJT items can have implications for fakability and validity. Nguyen et al. (2002) found that when a situational judgment inventory asked for the most and least likely responses (i.e., how people would act), its scores were significantly affected by instructions to fake good. But when the same situational judgment inventory asked for the best and worst responses (i.e., how people should act), its scores were not affected by instructions to fake good. Ployhart and Ehrhart (2004) compared the validity of a situational judgment inventory when it asked for the most and least likely responses with its validity when it asked for the best and worst responses. They found that the validity of the situational judgment inventory was higher under instructions to pick most likely and least likely responses.

On balance, however, because (a) people are probably inclined to put their best foot forward, especially in employment settings, (b) they are likely to interpret instructions to indicate what they would do essentially as instructions to indicate what they should do; and (c) they are generally likely to be inclined to carry out actions they believe to be effective, it seems reasonable at this point to treat statements about what people would do as conceptually the same as their judgments about what they should do. Consequently, the theory described here assumes that both SJT formats that ask what people should do and SJT formats that ask what they would do measure procedural knowledge. Procedural knowledge measured by formats that ask what people would do might be diluted, however, by exceptionally honest or literal responding that introduces variance unrelated to procedural knowledge.

It is important to bear in mind that different SJTs could be measuring different kinds of procedural knowledge. For instance, some SJT items might be measuring knowledge about how to handle interpersonal situations and others might be measuring knowledge about how to handle problem-solving situations, and different types of knowledge measured in SJTs may well have different antecedents and predict different domains of job performance. Thus, correlations between SJT scores and personality traits (Chan & Schmitt, 2002; Clevenger et al., 2001) and between SJT scores and performance dimensions are likely to vary according to the types of situations included in the SJT.

Procedural knowledge should have causal effects on job performance because people who know what they should do in order to be effective are more likely actually to perform effectively on the job. Accordingly, SJT scores should be correlated with measures of job performance. In fact, correlations between SJT scores and measures of job performance generally do support their criterion-related validity (McDaniel, Morgeson, Finnegan, Campion, & Braverman, 2001.

Meta-analytic studies have also shown relations between SJT scores and measures of personality characteristics (McDaniel & Nguyen, 2001). If SJTs measure procedural knowledge, their relations with some personality measures raise questions about their construct validity. In order to interpret these observed relations as evidence for the construct validity of SJTs as measures of procedural knowledge, we need a sound theory that explains why the knowledge construct they measure *should* be related to those personality constructs. The theory described next attempts to do precisely that.

## A THEORY OF PROCEDURAL KNOWLEDGE MEASURED BY SJTs

The theory described in Fig. 4.1 has three main parts. The first part simply stipulates that procedural knowledge as measured by SJTs has causal effects on job performance. Effects of general job knowledge on performance

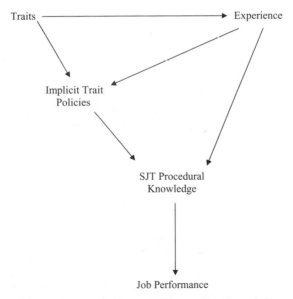

FIG. 4.1. A general theory of SJT procedural knowledge.

are well known (e.g., Hunter, 1983) and results of meta-analyses reported by McDaniel et al. (2001) that support the criterion-related validity of SJTs also support the theoretical contention that the kind of procedural knowledge that is measured by SJTs affects job performance. The second part of the theory is about causal effects of personality traits on SJT procedural knowledge and the third part is about causal effects of experience on SJT procedural knowledge.

Major terms used in the formal development of our theory are defined here:

Personal traits: Our theory makes an important distinction between traits that people possess and traits expressed by behavioral episodes like those described in SJT response options. To stem confusion between these two kinds of trait properties, we use the term personal traits to refer to traits of people. Thus, some people who complete an SJT might be highly agreeable, for instance, and others might be highly disagreeable.

Behavioral traits: We use this term to refer to traits that are expressed by behaviors described in SJT response options. Thus, some response options might describe highly agreeable actions, for instance, and others might describe highly disagreeable actions.

Behavioral effectiveness: We refer to the true effectiveness of a behavior described in an SJT response option as its behavioral effectiveness. This is estimated by combining judgments about the effectiveness of response options provided by subject matter experts.

Judgments of behavioral effectiveness: These are judgments of the effectiveness of response options provided by people who are asked to complete the SJT. They can take various forms, including ratings of the effectiveness of each response option, ratings of the likelihood that an individual would perform each response option, endorsement of response options believed to be the best and the worst, or endorsement of response options that an individual would most likely and least likely carry out.

Procedural knowledge: Procedural knowledge is how much a person knows about effective behavior in situations like those described in an SJT. It is measured as a joint function of behavioral effectiveness and judgments of behavioral effectiveness. Exactly how these two factors combine to produce a measure of procedural knowledge depends on the way judgments of behavioral effectiveness are collected. If judgments of behavioral effectiveness are collected as ratings of the effectiveness of each response options or as ratings of the likelihood that an individual would perform each response option, procedural knowledge can be scored as the correlation between the (true) behavioral effectiveness of each response option and an individual's ratings of its effectiveness or likelihood of performing it. If judgments of behavioral effectiveness are collected as most likely/least likely choices or as best/worst choices, procedural knowledge can be scored as the sum of (true) behavioral effectiveness scores of response items chosen as most likely or best minus the sum of (true) behavioral effectiveness scores of response options chosen as least likely or worst.

*Implicit trait policy*: ITPs are implicit beliefs about the causal effect of traits expressed by various actions on the effectiveness of those actions. They are measured as a joint function of the behavioral traits of response options and individuals' judgments about their behavioral effectiveness. Again, exactly how these factors combine depends on how judgments of behavioral effectiveness are collected. If judgments of behavioral effectiveness are collected as ratings of the effectiveness of each response options or as ratings of the likelihood that an individual would perform each response option, ITP for a particular trait can be scored as the correlation between the behavioral trait score of each response option and an individual's ratings of its effectiveness or likelihood of performing it. If an SJT is constructed specifically to measure ITP for a targeted trait as we recommend later, by developing some response options that express especially high levels and some that express especially low levels of the targeted trait, ITP for that trait can be scored simply by summing effectiveness ratings given to response options that express high trait levels and subtracting effectiveness ratings given to response options that express low trait levels. If judgments of behavioral effectiveness are collected as most likely/least likely choices or as best/worst choices, ITP for a targeted trait can be scored as the sum of behavioral trait scores of response items chosen as most likely or best minus the sum of behavioral trait scores of response options chosen as least likely or worst.

## Effects of Personality Traits on SJT Procedural Knowledge

The theory shown in Fig. 4.1 assigns a central role to the concept of *implicit trait policy* (ITP). The theory assumes there are stable differences between individuals in their implicit beliefs about the importance of various personality traits for determining behavioral effectiveness. Some people harbor ITPs that weigh the level of agreeableness, for instance, expressed by an action relatively strongly when judging its effectiveness. When asked to judge the effectiveness of one agreeable response option and one disagreeable response option for an SJT question, such people are likely to judge the agreeable option as much more effective than the disagreeable option. Other people harbor ITPs that weigh the level of agreeableness expressed by an action less strongly when judging its effectiveness. When asked to judge the effectiveness of one agreeable response option and one disagreeable response for an SJT question, they are likely to judge the agreeable option as only slightly more effective than the disagreeable option. This assumes that the agreeable response option truly is more effective than the disagreeable response option in this case.

The theory predicts that individuals' personality traits have causal effects on their ITPs. Thus, the ITPs of more agreeable people are predicted to place more weight on the agreeableness of an action when judging its effectiveness than are the ITPs of less agreeable people. Consequently, more agreeable people should discriminate more between SJT response options that express high and low levels of agreeableness when judging their effectiveness than less agreeable people do. Highly agreeable people should judge agreeable SJT response options as much more effective than disagreeable response options, while highly disagreeable people should judge agreeable response options as only slightly more effective than disagreeable response options.

When situations described in SJT items truly demand high levels of a particular trait for effective action, people whose ITPs weigh that trait more heavily will judge the effectiveness of the options in those SJT items more accurately and thereby show they have more procedural knowledge. Thus, the causal arrow shown in Fig. 4.1 from ITPs to procedural knowledge assumes that the particular personality trait in question is necessary for effective performance in the situations described by the SJT items.

Which particular personality traits are involved in these relations will depend on the content domain of the SJT. The SJT reported by Motowidlo et al. (1990), for instance, was developed to predict interpersonal and problem-solving performance in managerial, administrative, and professional jobs. Interpersonal performance includes elements of leadership, assertiveness, flexibility, and sensitivity and problem-solving performance includes elements of organization, thoroughness, drive, and resourcefulness. These behavioral patterns appear to reflect personality traits of agreeableness (in flexibility and sensitivity), extraversion (in leadership and assertiveness), and conscientiousness (in organization, thoroughness, and drive). Consequently, we expect that response options in this particular SJT that express higher levels of agreeableness, extraversion, and conscientiousness are likely to be more effective.

To illustrate these issues concretely, we invite readers to imagine an SJT that includes 50 situational problems and 5 response options for each, for a total of 250 response options. Instructions for this test ask applicants to rate the effectiveness of every response option. Imagine also that we have measured the degree to which each response option expresses a particular trait such as agreeableness, for example. When someone completes this SJT, it is possible to compute the correlation, for that person, between the degree to which response options express agreeableness and that individual's ratings of response effectiveness across the (250) response options. That correlation represents the individual's implicit policy about the importance of response agreeableness for determining response effectiveness.

In this case, ITP is conceived as a correlation that reflects the causal effect of a behavioral trait expressed by SJT response options on an individual's judgments of their effectiveness. Consequently, if, as shown in Fig. 4.1, an individual's personal trait is said to have a causal effect on his or her ITP for that trait, that means the individual's personal trait interacts with the behavioral trait expressed by SJT response options to affect the individual's judgments of behavioral effectiveness. Fig. 4.2 shows this theoretically expected interaction effect with agreeableness as the illustrative trait. It shows that individuals who are high in agreeableness judge very agreeable response options in an SJT as much more effective than

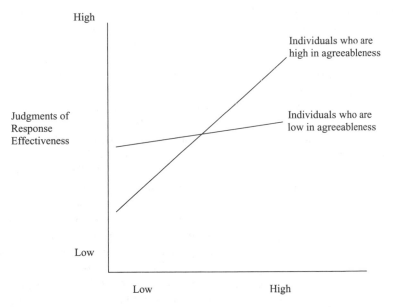

FIG. 4.2. Predicted ITPs for individuals high and low in agreeableness when the SJT format asks for ratings of response effectiveness.

very disagreeable response options, so their ITPs would be represented by relatively strong positive correlations between the behavioral trait of agreeableness expressed by response options and their judgments of behavioral effectiveness. It also shows that individuals who are low in agreeableness judge very agreeable response options as only slightly more effective than very disagreeable response options, so their ITPs would be represented by relatively weak positive correlations between the behavioral trait of agreeableness expressed by response options and their judgments of behavioral effectiveness.

The same logic can be applied to SJTs that ask applicants to pick one response option they would most likely take and one response option they would least likely take, as in the illustrative SJT question provided earlier. Now we invite readers to imagine that our hypothetical SJT with 50 situational problems and 5 response options for each asks applicants to pick one response option they would most likely perform and one they would least likely perform in each situation. If we have measured the level of a trait, such as agreeableness, for example, that each response option expresses, it is possible to compute the sum of the agreeableness scores for all response options a person indicated as most likely choices and the sum of the agreeableness scores for all response options the person indicated as least likely choices. The difference between these two sums represents the extent to which an individual relies on the level of agreeableness expressed by a response option when deciding whether or not he or she would perform a particular action. The larger the algebraic difference (of agreeableness scores for response options chosen as most likely minus agreeableness scores for response options chosen as least likely), the stronger the effect of the level of agreeableness expressed by response options on a person's reported likelihood of performing the actions they describe. Thus, the difference score is analogous to the correlational measure of ITP described in connection with SJTs that ask for ratings of response effectiveness.

Fig. 4.3 shows the interaction between individuals' traits and traits expressed by SJT response options on individuals' judgments about whether or not they would be likely to perform the actions described in the response options, with agreeableness as the illustrative trait. It shows that individuals who are high in agreeableness pick response options as most likely choices that are much more agreeable than the response options they pick as least likely choices, so their ITPs would be represented by relatively large difference scores. Individuals who are low in agreeableness are predicted to pick response options as most likely choices that are only slightly more agreeable than the response options they pick as least likely choices, so their ITPs would be represented by relatively small difference scores.

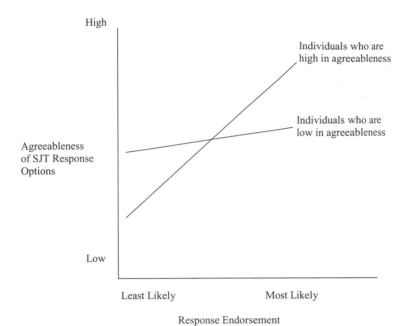

FIG. 4.3. Predicted ITPs for individuals high and low in agreeableness when the SJT format asks for most and least likely choices.

## Effects of Experience on SJT Procedural Knowledge

Effects of experience shown in Fig. 4.1 assume that knowledge can be acquired as people become exposed to situations that provide opportunities for learning. The theory assumes that one type of learning involves very general principles about the social costs and benefits of expressing different kinds of traits. For instance, we expect that fundamental socialization processes instill notions about effective behavior, often encapsulated in aphorisms such as "You can catch more flies with honey than you can with vinegar," which might be interpreted as a plug for agreeable behavior over disagreeable behavior, and the Machiavellian dictum, "It is better to be feared than loved," which might be read as a plug for disagreeable behavior over agreeable behavior. Exactly how people come to acquire these broad beliefs is not clear, however, and the theory is not yet sufficiently developed to suggest specific situational or experiential variables that could be studied as their precursors. At this point, the theory only suggests that this type of broad learning about effective ways to behave is likely to affect ITPs. After people have learned, through whatever means, that agreeable actions are generally effective in sensitive interpersonal situations, they will be more likely to develop beliefs that specific agreeable actions that could be taken in response to sensitive interpersonal situations at work are more effective than alternative actions that express disagreeableness.

Another type of learning implied by effects of experience shown Fig. 4.1 is on procedural knowledge directly. The theory assumes that with exposure to a variety of work situations, people develop a better appreciation for the consequences of their actions in those particular settings. This type of knowledge supplements the broad knowledge represented by ITPs with information about when expressing a particular level of a trait is more effective and when it is less effective. For example, even if someone has firmly learned that agreeable action is generally more effective in sensitive interpersonal situations than disagreeable action, there is still room for learning when disagreeable action might be more effective instead. Also, even if a situation does call for an agreeable response, not all kinds of agreeable responses are equally appropriate. Thus, for example, it may be perfectly appropriate and effective to offer a colleague a warm and sympathetic hearing if he or she is experiencing some personal distress, but if that warm sympathy turns into a sexual overture, it is probably inappropriate and ineffective, although it would still express agreeableness.

Fig. 4.1 also shows a direct effect of traits on experience. One way in which this can happen is by people selecting themselves into situations partly because they offer opportunities to express their traits. Agreeable people are likely to gravitate to social situations that allow them to act agreeably; extraverts are likely to gravitate to social situations that allow them to be outgoing and ascendant, and so on. Then the kinds of experiences that people have will in part reflect and reinforce their traits. Another way this can happen is by people actively creating their situations by expressing their traits. For instance, disagreeable people, who act in a critical and quarrelsome way, are more likely to generate conflict for themselves; unconscientious people who act in an undependable, unreliable, and disorganized way are more likely to create confusion for themselves, and so on.

## EMPIRICAL TESTS OF RELATIONS BETWEEN PERSONALITY TRAITS, ITPS, AND PROCEDURAL KNOWLEDGE

We conducted two studies that tested relations between personality traits, ITPs, and procedural knowledge measured by SJTs developed by Motowidlo et al. (1990) according to relations spelled out in Fig. 4.1 (Motowidlo, Jackson, & Hooper, 2005). The studies tested the hypotheses (a) that individuals' traits of agreeableness, extraversion, and conscientiousness were related to their ITPS for these traits on our SJTs; (b) that ITPs for these traits were related to procedural knowledge as measured by our SJTs; and (c) that these ITPs mediated effects of these traits on procedural knowledge as measured by our SJTs.

## SJT With an Effectiveness Rating Format

The first study used an SJT format that asked undergraduates to rate the effectiveness of all SJT response options. Four hundred and thirty-eight students completed an SJT that was a preliminary version of the test described by Motowidlo et al. (1990). It contained 64 situational stems, each with 5 to 7 response options, for a total of 341 response options. The SJT was developed for entry-level management, administrative, and professional positions in the telecommunications industry and was intended to predict two broad aspects of managerial performance—interpersonal performance (leadership, assertiveness, flexibility, and sensitivity) and problem-solving performance (organization, thoroughness, drive, and resourcefulness). As mentioned, we expect that personality traits of agreeableness, extraversion, and conscientiousness are necessary for effective performance in these areas. Students in our study rated the effectiveness of each response option for each situational stem on a 6-point scale ranging from 1 (*very ineffective*) to 6 (*very effective*).

They also completed the NEO Five-Factor Inventory (Costa & McRae, 1989), which we scored for agreeableness, extraversion, and conscientiousness.

In the original study in which this SJT was developed, its response options had been rated for effectiveness by 33 or 34 managers in the companies that participated in the development and validation of the instrument. The behavioral effectiveness score for each SJT option in this study is the average effectiveness rating given to it by these managers.

We prepared rating scales based on a brief measure of the Big Five traits developed by Gosling, Rentfrow, and Swann (2003) to measure the levels of agreeableness, extraversion, and conscientiousness that the response options expressed. We adapted the scales that Gosling et al. developed by creating a 7-point, bipolar scale for each trait. Six doctoral students rated each of the 341 response alternatives in our SJT on each of these three scales. Reliability estimates of the means of their ratings were .87 for behavioral agreeableness, .88 for behavioral extraversion, and .85 for behavioral conscientiousness. Mean scores across all six judges for each SJT response option served as our measures of behavioral traits expressed by the response options. Thus, *each SJT response option* had three behavioral trait scores computed in this way.

We calculated three ITP scores *for each person* who completed our SJT by correlating the response options' behavioral trait scores for agreeableness, extraversion, and conscientiousness with an individual's judgments of their behavioral effectiveness. For example, ITP for agreeableness was calculated as the correlation between response options' agreeableness and an individual's judgments of their behavioral effectiveness, and similarly for extraversion and conscientiousness.

To measure procedural knowledge, we calculated the correlation between each individual's ratings of the behavioral effectiveness of response alternatives and the mean of experts' ratings which we treat as estimates of the true effectiveness of the response options.

Correlations between individuals' traits and their associated ITPs were .18 ($p < .01$) for agreeableness, .07 (NS) for extraversion, and .14 ($p < .05$) for conscientiousness. These correlations largely support the central interaction hypothesis by showing that individuals' traits for agreeableness and conscientiousness are related to their associated ITPs. Correlations between procedural knowledge and ITPs were .81 ($p < .01$) for agreeableness, .63 ($p < .01$) for extraversion, and .89 ($p < .01$) for conscientiousness, supporting the hypothesis that ITPs for these personality traits are related to procedural knowledge. Correlations between individuals' trait and procedural knowledge scores were .18 ($p < .01$) for agreeableness, .02 (NS) for extraversion, and .11 ($p < .05$) for conscientiousness. Regressing procedural knowledge scores against all three personality traits yielded a multiple correlation of .21 ($p < .01$). We computed a regression analysis with procedural knowledge as the dependent variable entering the three ITP scores as one set of independent variables and then the three personality trait scores as a second set of independent variables. The multiple correlation was .934 for the three implicit policy scores and increased only trivially to .936 (although the increase was significant at $p < .05$) with the addition of the three personality trait scores, supporting the mediation hypothesis.

## SJT With a Most Likely/Least Likely Format

The sample for the second study consisted of 466 undergraduates who completed the SJT described by Motowidlo et al. (1990), which contained 30 situational stems, each with 5 response alternatives. They completed this SJT by picking one response alternative for each SJT stem that they would most likely carry out in that situation and one that they would least likely carry out. They also completed the NEO Five-Factor Inventory (Costa & McRae, 1989) for measures of extraversion, conscientiousness, and agreeableness.

We used the same scores for behavioral effectiveness and behavioral traits that that we used in the first study. However, we calculated ITP scores and procedural knowledge scores differently. For ITP scores, we summed the behavioral trait scores for all SJT response alternatives that a person would most likely carry out and subtracted behavioral trait scores for all response alternatives he or she would least likely carry out. This produced an ITP for each of the three traits under consideration. We followed a similar scoring procedure for procedural knowledge scores by summing behavioral effectiveness scores for all SJT response alternatives a person would most likely carry out and subtracting behavioral effectiveness scores for all response alternatives he or she would least likely carry out (see Knapp, Campbell, Borman, Pulakos, & Hanson, 2001, and Waugh, 2002, for other applications of this scoring method for SJTs).

Correlations between personal traits and their associated ITPs were .35 ($p < .01$) for agreeableness, .17 ($p < .01$) for extraversion, and .26 ($p < .01$) for conscientiousness, fully supporting the hypothesis that personal traits and behavioral traits interact to affect individuals' judgments of the effectiveness of SJT options. Correlations between procedural knowledge and ITPs were .73 ($p < .01$) for agreeableness, .66 ($p < .01$) for extraversion, and .88 ($p < .01$) for conscientiousness. Procedural knowledge was also correlated with the three personal traits: .25 ($p < .01$) for agreeableness, .20 ($p < .01$) for extraversion, and .27 ($p < .01$) for conscientiousness. The multiple correlation between all three traits together and procedural knowledge was .35 ($p < .01$). Finally, a hierarchical regression analysis in which we entered the set of three ITP scores followed by the set of three personal trait scores showed that the multiple correlation with procedural knowledge was .916 ($p < .01$) for the ITP scores alone and increased trivially to .918 (the increase was not statistically significant) with the addition of the three personality trait scores, thus supporting the hypothesis that ITPs mediate effects of personality traits on procedural knowledge measured by this SJT.

Taken together, these two studies with SJTs in two different formats provide strong support for hypotheses about relations between personality traits, ITPs, and procedural knowledge shown in Fig. 4.1. By showing that personality traits are correlated with their associated ITPs, these studies show that personal traits interact with behavioral traits in shaping individuals' judgments of the effectiveness of SJT options. They also show that ITPs are related to procedural knowledge and that after controlling for ITPs, personal traits have no discernible effect on procedural knowledge, a finding that supports the argument that effects of personal traits on procedural knowledge are mediated by ITPs.

The idea that personal traits interact with behavioral traits to affect individuals' judgments about the effectiveness of SJT response options is a cornerstone of the theoretical argument presented so far. That concept is what makes it possible to explain why and how personal traits are correlated with procedural knowledge measured by SJT scores. Framing that interaction effect in terms of a main effect of personal traits on ITPs (which are themselves main effects of traits expressed by response options on individuals' judgments of the effectiveness of the response options) highlights the fact that individuals' ITPs carry information about their basic traits. When people report their ITP for agreeableness, for instance, by reporting their beliefs about the effectiveness of SJT options that vary according to the level of agreeableness they express, they are also revealing something about their own standing on the trait of agreeableness. People who believe that agreeable SJT options are much more effective than disagreeable SJT options are likely to be more agreeable themselves than people who believe that agreeable SJT options are only slightly more effective than disagreeable SJT options. This means it might be possible to measure agreeableness indirectly, or at least, to develop a measure of ITP for agreeableness that is sufficiently saturated with the trait of agreeableness to serve as an indirect surrogate for the agreeableness trait.

## DEVELOPING SITUATIONAL JUDGMENT TESTS
## TO MEASURE IMPLICIT TRAIT POLICIES

The next set of studies summarized here reports results of efforts to develop SJTs specifically to measure ITPs saturated with information about selected personality traits. Earlier in this chapter, we argued that SJTs that are scored by comparing applicants' judgments of the effectiveness of SJT options to experts' judgments in effect measure procedural knowledge. Now we argue that when SJTs are scored in a different way by comparing applicants' judgments of the effectiveness of SJT options to others' judgments about the level of a trait the options express, they measure ITP for that trait. We are drawing an important distinction between the procedural knowledge construct and the ITP construct—in fact our theory predicts that the ITP construct is causally antecedent to the procedural knowledge construct.

### Implicit Versus Explicit Measures of Personality

If it turns out to be possible to capture enough personality trait information in an ITP measure to let it serve as a surrogate measure of that personality trait, such a measure might be considered an indirect or implicit measure of personality. It would differ from explicit measures such as the NEO-FFI (Costa & McRae, 1989) in that instead of asking participants to indicate directly whether statements that portray various trait characteristics are accurate self-descriptions, it would seek to assess their standing on the trait indirectly according to the assumption that their opinions about the effectiveness of SJT options contain information about their traits. This assumption makes it possible to measure traits inobtrusively.

One appealing characteristic of implicit measures in general is that their inobtrusiveness implies they are likely to be relatively free of social desirability concerns (Fazio & Olson, 2003) and less susceptible to faking and self-presentation biases (Bornstein, 2002). Bornstein, Rossner, Hill, and Stepanian (1994) compared the fakability of an implicit measure and an explicit measure of interpersonal dependency. The implicit measure was a projective test, the Rorschach Oral Dependency scale, and the explicit measure was an objective test, the Interpersonal Dependency Inventory. They induced faking by asking some participants to complete both tests as a very dependent person would and others to complete them as a very independent person would. Results showed that the instructional manipulation affected scores on the explicit measure but not the implicit measure.

An important paradox in this literature is that although implicit and explicit tests often both predict relevant behavioral criteria, they are often correlated only modestly with each other (Bornstein, 2002; Fazio & Olson, 2003). For example, Bornstein reported results of a meta-analysis showing that implicit measures of interpersonal dependency correlated .37 with various behavioral criteria and explicit measures correlated .31 with behavioral criteria (the difference is not statistically significant). Yet, in 12 studies that assessed correlations between the two types of tests, implicit and explicit measures of interpersonal dependency correlated only about .30 with each other. Results like these suggest that, although an implicit and an explicit measure might both be targeting the same general construct, they might be tapping different aspects of the construct that are both nevertheless related to the same behavioral criteria.

James' (1998) work on personality assessment through conditional reasoning is another example of implicit personality measurement. His implicit measures are objective, structured tests that aim to tap targeted personality constructs indirectly by asking about the kinds of justifications people use to rationalize actions expressing traits such as achievement motivation (James, 1998) and aggression (James, McIntyre, Glisson, Bowler, & Mitchell, 2004). James et al. summarized results of several studies of relations between the implicit conditional reasoning test for aggression, explicit tests of aggressive personality characteristics, and various behavioral criteria. Across 10 studies, correlations between the conditional reasoning test for aggression and behavioral criteria ranged from .32 to .64, with a mean of .44. Across four samples of undergraduates, correlations between the (implicit) conditional reasoning test for aggression and (explicit) self-report measures of personality characteristics related to aggression ranged from .00 to .26, with a mean of .14. These results are consistent with results from other research domains in showing that implicit measures often predict behavioral criteria reasonably well, but are not often strongly correlated with corresponding explicit measures (Bornstein, 2002; Fazio & Olson, 2003).

We conducted five studies to develop SJT measures of ITPs for agreeableness, extraversion, and conscientiousness (Motowidlo, Diesch [Hooper], & Jackson, 2003), examine their construct validity against explicit measures of personality and behavioral measures of selected traits (Hooper, Jackson, & Motowidlo, 2004b), and test their resistance to faking (Hooper, Jackson, & Motowidlo, 2004a).

## SJTs to Measure Implicit Policies for Agreeableness, Extraversion, and Conscientiousness (Motowidlo et al., 2003)

In the first study, we developed 5 SJT stems specifically to tap agreeableness, 5 to tap extraversion, and 6 to tap conscientiousness and wrote from 5 to 10 response options for each situational stem, including roughly half that we intended to express high trait levels and half that we intended to express low trait levels. We prepared a questionnaire that asked for ratings of the effectiveness of each situational response on a scale with anchors ranging from 1 (*very ineffective*) to 7 (*very effective*). Ninety-six undergraduates completed this SJT and the agreeableness, extraversion, and conscientiousness scales of the NEO Five-Factor Inventory (Costa & McRae, 1989). We computed ITP scores for each trait by summing effectiveness ratings for SJT options that we intended to express high levels of a targeted trait and subtracting effectiveness ratings for options intended to tap low levels of the trait. Correlations between these ITP scores and NEO scores for associated personality traits were .32 ($p < .01$) for agreeableness, .34 ($p < .01$) for extraversion, and .17 ($p < .05$) for conscientiousness.

In the second study, we developed another set of 19 SJT stems to tap agreeableness and a set of 19 SJT stems to tap conscientiousness and wrote three response options to express high levels of the targeted trait and three to express low levels of the trait. One hundred undergraduates completed this SJT by rating each response option for effectiveness on a scale ranging from 1 (*very ineffective*) to 7 (*very effective*). They also completed the agreeableness and conscientiousness scales of the NEO Five-Factor Inventory. As before, we computed ITP scores for agreeableness and conscientiousness by summing effectiveness ratings for SJT options intended to express high levels of one of these traits and subtracting effectiveness ratings for SJT options intended to express low levels of the trait. Correlations between these SJT implicit policy scores and NEO scores were .31 ($p < .01$) for agreeableness and $-.06$ (NS) for conscientiousness.

Results of these two studies offer further support for the theoretical prediction that individuals' traits interact with traits expressed by SJT response options to shape individuals' judgments of the effectiveness of the response options because they show again that personal traits are correlated with ITPs for those traits. In this way, they also provide preliminary evidence that ITP scores can carry information about personality traits, at least for agreeableness and extraversion. Correlations between these ITP scores for agreeableness and extraversion and explicit measures produced by the NEO are about as strong as correlations between implicit and explicit trait measures reported in other contexts. Thus, it might be reasonable to consider the ITP scores as implicit measures of agreeableness and extraversion, but we need evidence that the ITP scores can predict behavior that reflects these traits.

### Relations Between SJT Measures of Implicit Policy for Agreeableness and a Behavioral Measure of Agreeableness (Hooper et al., 2004b)

For the third study, we combined SJT items developed in the first two studies (Motowidlo et al., 2003) to develop two forms of SJTs intended to measure ITPs for agreeableness, each with 23 SJT stems and 2 response options per stem. Seventy-four undergraduates completed a questionnaire that included both forms of the agreeableness SJT. They also completed the NEO for an explicit measure of agreeableness. Students then took part in eight role-play exercises designed to elicit agreeableness. The role-plays were videotaped and later scored by four judges for the level of agreeableness shown. ITP for agreeableness measured by the two SJT forms correlated .83 ($p < .01$) with each other and .31 ($p < .01$) and .48 ($p < .01$) with the agreeableness score derived from the videotaped role-plays. They correlated .09 (NS) and .11 (NS) with NEO agreeableness, which correlated .09 (NS) with the role-play agreeableness score. These results show that ITPs for agreeableness can predict a behavioral measure of agreeableness reasonably well, even if they are not strongly correlated with the explicit measure of agreeableness produced by the NEO.

### Fakability of an SJT Measure of Implicit Trait Policy for Agreeableness (Hooper et al., 2004a)

If an ITP measure for agreeableness can usefully predict behavior, it becomes interesting to ask whether it might be more resistant to faking than an explicit measure of agreeableness like that produced by the NEO. Our fourth study tested this possibility with the two ITP measures for agreeableness that we developed in the first two studies described earlier. One hundred and fifty-two undergraduates participated in a laboratory experiment in which we manipulated faking in two ways. First, some students were instructed either to (a) simply complete the tests as part of the experiment (honest responding) or (b) imagine they were applying for a job and wanted to look their best (fake-good). Second, other students were instructed to imagine they were applying for a job that required either (a) highly agreeable people (fake-high agreeable) or (b) less agreeable people (fake-low agreeable). All students then completed the two SJT measures of ITP for agreeableness and the NEO agreeableness scale. For simplicity, we combined results of the honest condition with results of the fake-low agreeable condition and we combined results of the fake-good condition with results of the fake-high agreeable condition. The mean effect size ($d$) for the difference between (a) test score in the fake-good or fake-high agreeable condition and (b) test score in the honest or fake-low agreeable condition was .67 for the NEO agreeableness scale, .32 for the ITP score for agreeableness developed in the first study ($p = .07$ for the analysis of variance [ANOVA] effect representing this difference between NEO and SJT formats) and .37 for the ITP score for agreeableness developed in the second study ($p = .14$ for the ANOVA effect representing this difference between NEO and SJT formats. Although neither effect reached conventional levels of statistical significance, both were in the expected direction to support the argument that SJT scores will change less under pressures to fake than will NEO scores.

Our fifth study replicated the fourth study but with the ITP measures of agreeableness and conscientiousness that we developed in the first study described earlier. Two hundred and twenty-four undergraduates participated in another laboratory experiment in which we manipulated faking in two ways. First, some students were again instructed either to (a) simply complete the tests as part of the experiment (honest responding) or (b) imagine they were applying for a job and wanted to look their best (fake-good). Second, other students were instructed to imagine they were applying for a job that required either (a) highly agreeable and conscientious people (fake-high agreeable and conscientious) or (b) less agreeable and conscientiousness people (fake-low agreeable and conscientiousness). All students then completed the two SJT measures of ITP for agreeableness and the NEO agreeableness scale. For simplicity, we again combined results of the first and second ways in which we manipulated faking. The mean effect size ($d$) for the difference between the fake-high conditions and the honest or fake-low condition was .79 for the NEO agreeableness score and .27 for the ITP agreeableness score ($p < .01$). The mean effect size for this difference was .82 for the NEO conscientiousness score and .14 for the ITP conscientiousness score ($p < .01$). Thus, instructions to fake affected scores for both agreeableness and conscientiousness less when the traits were assessed by ITP scores than when they were assessed by the NEO format.

## SUMMARY

We began with the argument that when SJTs are scored by comparing applicants' indications of what they would or should do with experts' judgments about the effectiveness of those actions, the SJT scores can be regarded as measures of procedural knowledge. With that assumption, we described a theory about relations between the procedural knowledge construct measured by SJTs, its consequences for job performance, and its antecedents in dispositional and experiential variables. The theory predicts that procedural knowledge has causal effects on job performance, a prediction substantiated by many studies of the criterion-related validity of SJTs. It predicts that people learn through experience that behaviors that express some traits are more effective in certain situations than behaviors that express other traits and that some actions have consequences in work situations that are more organizationally desirable than the consequences of other actions in the same work situations, even if both kinds of actions express the same levels of the same traits. The theory also predicts that individuals' personality traits affect their procedural knowledge through their ITPs for those traits in specific work situations. If a particular trait is expressed by SJT response options, people with high levels of that trait implicitly hold that it is a relatively strong determinant of their effectiveness, whereas people with low levels of the same trait implicitly hold that it is not as strong a determinant of their effectiveness. If the trait truly does explain substantial variance in the effectiveness of SJT response options, then people with ITPs that weigh that trait more heavily in their effectiveness judgments (these are people who are themselves higher on that trait) will have more knowledge about the effectiveness of the SJT response options. In this way, ITPs mediate effects of personal traits on procedural knowledge.

We briefly reviewed two studies that tested and supported these theoretical predictions. Results suggest that ITPs about trait effectiveness measured through an SJT format carry information about individuals' standing on those traits. This suggests it might be useful to develop an SJT that would target ITPs as constructs, instead of procedural knowledge. We reviewed several studies that showed it is possible to develop SJTs to measure ITPs, that they correlate with explicit trait measures and behavioral criteria presumed to reflect the trait about as well as implicit trait measures do in other research contexts, and that they might therefore be considered implicit measures of the targeted traits. We also reviewed studies that showed these ITP measures are more resistant to faking than explicit measures of the same traits produced by the NEO.

The theoretical arguments and empirical results reviewed in this chapter have two important implications for practice. First, by explaining how and why some personality traits are correlated with SJT scores, they may provide a basis for arguing that correlations found between SJT scores and measures of these traits support the construct validity of the SJTs as measures of procedural knowledge. If, as we argued, the work situations described in the SJT used in our first two studies demand behavioral expressions of agreeableness, extraversion, and conscientiousness for effective performance, the correlations we found between scores on these traits and scores on this SJT might be taken as evidence for the construct validity of that SJT as a measure of procedural knowledge. More broadly, if work situations described in the SJTs included in the meta-analyses conducted by McDaniel and Nguyen (2001) demand behavioral expressions of agreeableness, conscientiousness, and emotional stability for effective performance, correlations reported between these traits and SJT scores in their meta-analyses might be taken as construct validity for the SJTs as measures of procedural knowledge.

The second implication for practice involves the possibility of developing SJTs to measure constructs different from the procedural knowledge construct that we presume is measured by SJTs that are scored by comparing applicants' responses to effectiveness judgments by experts. The theoretically expected interaction effect of individuals' traits and traits expressed by SJT options on individuals' judgments of the effectiveness of those SJT options implies that ITPs, which are the main effect of traits expressed by SJT options on individuals' judgments about their effectiveness, carry information about the individuals' traits. This means that an SJT built by preparing some response options that express some very high levels of a targeted trait and some response options that express very low levels of the same trait might measure ITP about that trait in a way that is especially saturated with information about individuals' own standing on the trait.

Although there is surely more than one way to develop tests specifically to measure ITPs for targeted personality traits, we summarize the procedures we followed in studies reported here in order to provide a quick reference guide:

1. We developed SJT stems that we hoped would describe situations likely to evoke responses that vary according to the targeted trait. For the trait

of agreeableness, for instance, our situations were designed to be ones in which some people are likely to behave agreeably and others are likely to behave less agreeably or even disagreeably.

2. For each SJT stem, we developed some response options that describe actions expressing high levels of the targeted trait and some that describe low levels of the targeted trait. For the trait of agreeableness, for example, we developed some response options to describe highly agreeable behavior and some to describe much less agreeable behavior. We tried to assure that there would be variance in response option endorsement by basing them on responses people actually said they would perform if they were in the situations described.

3. We developed a rating format that asked applicants to rate all response options for effectiveness on a 7-point scale.

4. We computed an ITP score for each targeted trait by summing effectiveness ratings given to response options that describe high levels of the trait and subtracting effectiveness ratings given to response options that describe low levels of the trait.

We have shown that SJT measures of implicit trait policies have some potential for predicting trait-relevant behavior, and this opens the door to the possibility that such measures might also be useful in predicting job performance. If they are usefully valid for predicting job performance, they might be able to take advantage of information about individuals' personality traits to predict job performance in a way that might be more resistant to faking than explicit trait measures like those produced by the NEO.

## REFERENCES

Bornstein, R. F. (2002). A process dissociation approach to objective-projective test score interrelationships. *Journal of Personality Assessment, 78*, 47–68.

Bornstein, R. F., Rossner, S. C., Hill, E. L., & Stepanian, M. L. (1994). Face validity and fakability of objective and projective measures of dependency. *Journal of Personality Assessment, 63*, 363–386.

Chan D., & Schmitt, N. (1997). Video-based versus paper-and-pencil method of assessment in situational judgment tests: Subgroup differences in test performance and face validity perceptions. *Journal of Applied Psychology, 82*, 143–159.

Chan, D., & Schmitt, N. (2002). Situational judgment and job performance. *Human Performance, 15*, 233–253.

Clevenger, J., Pereira, G. M., Wiechmann, D., Schmitt, N., & Harvey, V. S. (2001). Incremental validity of situational judgment tests. *Journal of Applied Psychology, 86*, 410–417.

Costa, P. T., & McRae, R. R. (1989). *The NEO-PI/NEO-FFI manual supplement*. Odessa, FL: Psychological Assessment Resources.

Fazio, R. H., & Olson, M. A. (2003). Implicit measures in social cognition research: Their meaning and use. *Annual Review of Psychology, 54,* 297–327.

Gosling, S. D., Rentfrow, P. J., & Swann, W. B. (2003). A very brief measure of the Big-Five personality domains. *Journal of Research in Personality, 37,* 504–528.

Hooper, A. C., Jackson, H. L., & Motowidlo, S. J. (2004a, April). *Faking on personality-based measures: SJT's compared to a traditional format.* Paper presented at the meeting of the Society for Industrial and Organizational Psychology, Chicago, IL.

Hooper, A. C., Jackson, H. L., & Motowidlo, S. J. (2004b, August). *Situational judgment measures of personality and work-relevant performance.* Paper presented at the 112th annual conference of the American Psychological Association, Honolulu, HI.

Hunter, J. E. (1983). A causal analysis of cognitive ability, job knowledge, job performance, and supervisory ratings. In F. Landy, & S. Zedeck, & J. Cleveland (Eds.), *Performance measurement and theory* (pp. ). Hillsdale, NJ: Lawrence Erlbaum Associates.

James, L. R. (1998). Measurement of personality via conditional reasoning. *Organizational Research Methods, 1,* 131–163.

James, L. R., McIntyre, M. D., Glisson, C. A., Bowler, J. L., & Mitchell, T. R. (2004). The conditional reasoning measurement system for aggression: An overview. *Human Performance, 17,* 271–295.

Knapp, D. J., Campbell, C. H., Borman, W. C., Pulakos, E. D., & Hanson, M. A. (2001). Performance assessment for a population of jobs. In J.P Campbell & D. J. Knapp (Eds.), *Exploring the limits in personnel selection and classification* (pp. 181–235). Mahwah, NJ: Lawrence Erlbaum Associates.

Latham, G. P., Saari, L. M., Pursell, E. D., & Campion, M. A. (1980). The situational interview. *Journal of Applied Psychology, 65,* 422–427.

McDaniel, M. A., Morgeson, F. P., Finnegan, E. B., Campion, M. A., & Braverman, E. P. (2001). Use of situational judgment tests to predict job performance: A clarification of the literature. *Journal of Applied Psychology, 86,* 730–740.

McDaniel, M. A., & Nguyen, N. T. (2001). Situational judgment tests: A review of practice and constructs assessed. *International Journal of Selection and Assessment, 9,* 103–113.

Motowidlo, S. J., Borman, W. C., & Schmit, M.J. (1997). A theory of individual differences in task and contextual performance. *Human Performance, 10,* 71–83.

Motowidlo, S. J., Diesch (Hooper), A. C., & Jackson, H. L. (2003, April). *Using the situational judgment format to measure personality characteristics.* Paper presented at the meeting of the Society for Industrial and Organizational Psychology, Orlando, FL.

Motowidlo, S. J., Dunnette, M. D., & Carter, G. W. (1990). An alternative selection procedure: The low-fidelity simulation. *Journal of Applied Psychology, 75,* 640–647.

Motowidlo, S. J., Hanson, M. A., & Crafts, J. L. (1997). Low fidelity simulations. In D. L. Whetzel & G.R Wheaton (Eds.), *Applied measurement methods in industrial psychology* (pp. 241–260). Palo Alto, CA: Consulting Psychologists Press.

Motowidlo, S. J., Jackson, H. L., & Hooper, A. C. (2005). *Why some personality traits are correlated with scores on situational judgment tests.* Unpublished manuscript.

Nguyan, N. T., McDaniel, M. A., & Biderman, M. D. (2002, April). *Response instructions in situational judgment tests: Effects on faking and construct validity.* Paper presented at the 17th annual conference of the Society for Industrial and Organizational Psychology, Toronto.

Ployhart, R. E., & Ehrhart, M. G. (2004). Be careful what you ask for: Effects of response instructions on the construct validity and reliability of situational judgment tests. *International Journal of Selection and Assessment, 11,* 1–16.

Waugh, G. W. (2002, April). *Developing a situational judgment test*. Paper presented at the 17th annual conference of the Society for Industrial and Organizational Psychology, Toronto, Ontario.

Weekley, J. A., & Jones, C. (1997). Video-based situational testing. *Personnel Psychology, 50,* 25–49.

Weekley, J. A., & Jones, C. (1999). Further studies of situational tests. *Personnel Psychology, 52,* 679–700.

# 5

# The Predictor Response Process Model

## Robert E. Ployhart
*University of South Carolina*

All current professional guidelines on assessment and validity give primary attention to predictor *scores* and less attention to predictors themselves. Consider these examples:

- The Standards (AERA, 1999, p. 9): "Validity refers to the degree to which evidence and theory support the interpretations of test scores entailed by proposed use of tests."
- The Principles (SIOP, 2003, p. 4): "Validity is the most important consideration in developing and evaluating selection procedures. Because validation involves the accumulation of evidence to provide a sound scientific basis for the proposed score interpretations, it is the interpretations of these scores required by the proposed uses that are evaluated, not the selection procedure itself."

As Messick (1995) so aptly noted, "Validity is not a property of the test or assessment as such, but rather of the meaning of the test scores" (p. 741). However, we frequently do not consider the full consequences of this thinking, and this is particularly true when the predictor methods assess multiple latent constructs, such as interviews, assessment centers, and situational judgment tests (that is why these assessments are typically referred to as *multidimensional* in nature). We tend to talk about the validity of such methods, and we tend to demonstrate *it* by correlating various predictors with other predictors to infer what the multidimensional methods must be measuring. We then might say a situational judgment test (SJT) measures cognitive ability, personality, experience, and so on, and hence it is a predictor method.

This is a reasonable validation strategy but it is by no means the only strategy or maybe even the most optimal. The reason is because we only consider an overall aggregate score, but neglect the multitude of factors that go into creating this score. We look at the end product of the score—its relationships with other scores—but not its determinants. We frequently treat these scores as a given but we neglect the processes that led to their creation. If we are to truly understand the meaning of predictor scores, we need to understand the psychological processes that led to the generation of those scores. For example, why should scores on a predictor change when we change the instructions or format in minor ways? Why are behavioral and situational interviews so weakly correlated? Why are there racial differences in cognitive ability tests? Our attempts to understand such questions by focusing on scale-level correlations provides only a rough approximation of what is occurring beneath the surface. If we remember that our interest is in predictor scores, there are multiple influences on such scores, and there are yet more ways we can manipulate these scores, then we realize that our understanding of validity must dig into the psychological and contextual processes that create such scores. We must think of the test scores as a consequence of a psychological response process.

This chapter presents a heuristic model for thinking about the processes that create predictor responses and ultimately the test scores used for selection. The underlying goal of the model is to unite contemporary conceptualizations of validity with research on psychological response processes and methodological models for testing such questions. Although each of these topics has been discussed in detail, the unique feature of the model is its attempt to merge practice, science, and methods into a single framework. The examples used in this chapter focus on SJTs, but the model applies to almost any form of psychological assessment and predictor method and may be particularly useful for understanding multidimensional predictors. It is a general model designed to help frame the relevant questions and identify the appropriate methods when trying to understand the processes involved in completing predictors. Hopefully, the model will contribute to a better understanding of SJTs and assessment methods used in selection contexts. It is called the Predictor Response PRocess model (PRPR; pronounced "proper").

In the following section, I first discuss a basic assumption of the PRPR model, that the psychological processes used to complete a predictor are a form of validity evidence. Next, I introduce the model, noting how it builds from similar models housed in several diverse literatures. This is followed by the model's implications for research and practice.

## PREDICTOR RESPONSE PROCESSES ARE A FORM OF VALIDITY

When applicants complete a test, they engage in a variety of psychological processes that ultimately produce a set of responses to individual test items (Snow & Lohman, 1989). These responses are then combined in some manner to produce an overall score (or subscores if the predictor has subdimensions), and it is the validity of these scores that is evaluated. Frequently, this evaluation will occur through examining whether the scores are related to various criteria (criterion-related validity) and similar constructs (convergent validity), and are unrelated to different constructs (discriminant validity). These forms of validity are well understood and routinely reported.

However, there is another form of validity evidence that is infrequently examined in selection circles. This form of validity is known as *substantive validity* in Messick (1995) or *response processes* in the Standards (AERA, 1999) and Principles (SIOP, 2003). According to the Standards "Theoretical and empirical analyses of the response processes of test takers can provide evidence concerning the fit between the construct and the detailed nature of performance or response actually engaged in by examinees" (p. 12). The Principles appear to give this form of validity less weight, indicating "in many employment contexts such evidence is irrelevant to the proposed use, as is the case where the only claim made is that the scores on the selection procedure are predictive of a particular work outcome" (p. 7). However, they still acknowledge that this form of validity may be useful for understanding the nature of the test scores. So, even though response-process validity may by itself be insufficient as a basis for justifying a selection procedure, it provides yet another form of validity evidence to help support such inferences. Perhaps more importantly, response-process validity offers an opportunity to explore the determinants of aggregate-level predictor scores. Such information may be most beneficial for understanding the nature of test scores for multidimensional predictors.

## UNDERSTANDING THE VALIDITY
## OF MULTIDIMENSIONAL PREDICTORS

When predictors are measurement methods, such as SJTs, interviews, and assessment centers, there are multiple forms of systematic variance that contribute to the overall score. This is reflected in less than homogenous predictor scores and relationships with numerous other knowledge, skills, ability, and other characteristic (KSAO) constructs. For example, research suggests SJTs are related to (but not entirely redundant with) cognitive ability, personality based on the Five Factor Model (FFM), experience, and job knowledge (McDaniel, Morgeson, Finnegan, Campion, & Braverman, 2001; McDaniel & Nguyen, 2001; Weekley & Ployhart, 2005).

When the predictors are multidimensional, we frequently observe moderately strong criterion-related validities, yet no clear understanding of construct validity. With assessment centers, this has been described as a paradox (Arthur, Woehr, & Maldegen, 2000), but the issue remains the same with other multidimensional predictor methods. From a practical perspective, one may suggest that it does not matter what these predictors measure because they relate to job performance in "vaguely" explainable ways. That is, we know these predictor methods assess a variety of KSAOs so we simply explain the predictive relationship through these numerous KSAOs. An SJT predicts performance because it captures variance in cognitive ability, personality, experience, and who knows what other constructs that relate to performance. However, this is a less than satisfying answer. First, from a scientific perspective we need to know what these predictors measure if we are to better understand, predict, and control responses to these tests in applicant settings. For example, knowing what a predictor measures could help understand why subgroup differences exist or why applicants score differently than incumbents. Second, from a practical perspective, we cannot make very informed choices about selection system design and implementation without having a clearer sense what these tests measure. We may inadvertently combine a SJT with a personality test and learn they are highly redundant with each other. Finally, it would seem prudent to be able to explain to the general public what we are measuring and why it relates to performance—which is one of the rights of test takers (Joint Committee on Testing Practices, 1998).

So when the predictor method is multidimensional and the predictor score relates to test scores from numerous other homogenous KSAOs, how shall one develop inferences of validity with the predictor? One potentially effective, but largely overlooked, method is to consider the psychological processes that are enacted when completing the predictor (Chan & Schmitt, in press; Snow & Lohman, 1989). As noted earlier, response processes are a form of validity and by taking a closer look at this response process we may provide clearer inferences of validity than simply looking at correlations with other constructs. It may be this form of validity evidence that is necessary to explain what a SJT and related predictor methods measure. Therefore, in the next several pages I describe a model and method for making such inferences.

## THE PREDICTOR RESPONSE PROCESS (PRPR) MODEL

### Background

The PRPR model described in this chapter draws from and integrates several closely related concepts. These include Messick's (1995) concepts of validity, process models of survey responses, typical/maximum performance, models of method bias, generalizability theory, and confirmatory factor analysis models.

***Messick's Validity Framework.*** Messick (1995) argued there are six major aspects of construct validity. These include *content, substantive* (response processes), *structural* (scoring), *generalizability* (including criterion-related), *external* (convergent and discriminant), and *consequential.* As noted earlier, selection experts frequently focus on external validity to infer what a predictor measures. But as also noted previously, when the predictor is multidimensional this information can at times become almost meaningless because the predictor seems to measure almost everything! This question cannot be answered solely with external validity; it requires an examination of what Messick called *substantive validity.*

Messick discussed another important aspect of validity, that of *invalidity.* This concept recognizes the fact that our assessment of a construct may be too narrow, a concept known as *construct underrepresentation,* or too broad, a concept known as *construct-irrelevant variance.* These may be known by their more familiar terms of deficiency and contamination, respectively. Of the two types, this chapter is most concerned with the concept of construct-irrelevant variance or contamination because it recognizes the fact there are multiple influences on a set of test scores, and some of these may not be relevant to the purpose of the assessment. For example, developing a written SJT with too high of a reading requirement will contribute to the SJT measuring reading ability along with whatever the SJT was designed to measure.

***Process Models of Survey Responses.*** The model draws heavily from research on psychological processes involved with survey responses (e.g., Krosnick, 1999; Tourangeau, Rips, & Rasinski, 2000). This research has identified the basic cognitive sequence in completing a survey item. The basic sequence is shown in Fig. 5.1 and although simplistic, captures the essence of the response process. First is the *comprehension* of the item. This involves a variety of cognitive processes involved with reading, interpreting, and understanding the purpose of the question. Second is

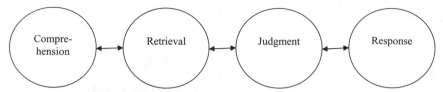

FIG. 5.1. Predictor response processes. (Adapted from Tourangeau et al., 2000.)

the *retrieval* of information from long-term memory that is relevant to the question. Note this may also involve the use of retrieval and memory strategies and shortcuts (e.g., Payne, Bettman, & Johnson, 1993). Third is the process of forming a *judgment*. This is itself a rather complicated process (see Brooks & Highhouse, chap. 3, this volume; Hastie & Dawes, 2001) that ultimately requires the test taker to integrate information from memory and develop an estimate of some likelihood of various events. Fourth is the *response*, where this judgment must be edited to fit the various response options provided. Note that this component may also involve editing the response to fit other considerations, such as impression management or a desire to appear consistent.

It is important to recognize that the process shown in Fig. 5.1 is a series of latent cognitive operations that contribute to a manifest response to an item. Therefore, it is an item-level process, meaning that this process may differ to varying degrees for different items based on the nature and structure of those items. This highlights the incredible cognitive sophistication required to complete a test question. Yet in reality, people process these questions very quickly and hence this is a very "fast" set of operations. It is also true that not every person will engage in the same set of operations for every question, nor will every operation be relevant for every question (largely because of differences in strategy selection and accessibility; see Payne et al., 1993). This is reflected in the two-headed arrows in Fig. 5.1, illustrating that different sequences or patterns of processing are possible. Yet to understand the response process we must start here. As noted in Tourangeau et al. (2000): "Both psychological and survey research provide ample evidence of the errors each component produces, and to understand how the response process can go awry, we need to take a closer look at them" (p. 8). I agree and believe this thinking may be very applicable and informative for understanding responses to predictors as well as surveys.

***Typical/Maximum Performance.*** Cronbach (1960) recognized that tests and assessments may be categorized into typical and maximum performance assessments. *Typical performance* measures tend to be assessments of motivation, willingness, and choice. These types of measures are typically treated as noncognitive in nature, such as personality tests and measures of motivation. It is for this reason they are frequently referred to as "will do" measures. *Maximum performance* measures tend to be assessments of ability, most frequently cognitive ability or some variation thereof. They are frequently referred to as "can do" measures because they assess the ability to perform rather than a willingness to perform.

With respect to criterion performance, there are three general ways of distinguishing between typical and maximum performance (Sackett, Zedeck, & Fogli, 1988). First, the setting for maximum performance measures contains an obvious sense that one is being evaluated. Second, maximum performance measures contain explicit (and accepted) instructions to expend maximum effort on the task. Third, maximum performance measures occur over reasonably short periods of time so that maximum energy can be expended. Obviously, when one completes a predictor for a job, it is likely that each of these elements is present. It might, therefore, be considered a maximum performance test because motivation is assumed to be a constant across test takers. However, this may not always be the case (think of the test-taking motivation of many students, even in "important" classes!), and if nothing else, the distinction between typical and maximum performance highlights the value of considering motivation in the testing process.

Frequently, one would assume test-taking motivation would be equal for all test takers, but this is not the case. First, research on applicant reactions suggests that test-taking motivation may relate to test performance and even account for a small amount of racial subgroup differences in test performance (Arvey, Strickland, Drauden, & Martin, 1990; Chan, Schmitt, DeShon, Clause, & Delbridge, 1997; Ployhart, Ziegert, & McFarland, 2003; Sanchez, Truxillo, & Bauer, 2000). Second, test-taking motivation may differ across applicant and incumbent contexts, and one hypothesized reason for higher test scores among applicants is their higher motivation to perform well on the test. Therefore, it appears that motivation is a relevant influence on test scores (see Bauer & Truxillo, chap. 11, this volume).

***Models of Method Bias.*** Another perspective incorporated into the model comes from models and theories of method bias. Podsakoff, MacKenzie, Lee, and Podsakoff (2003) recently provided an impressive overview of this research and its implications for evaluating method bias. A model of method bias is most frequently a confirmatory factor-analytic (CFA) model that includes both the latent "true score" factors and hypothesized "method" factors. The fundamental goal of method bias models is to isolate, estimate, and control the confounding sources of variance associated with the measurement method from those of the latent substantive construct or process. Method bias has usually been treated as a methodological concern, but Schmitt (1994) recognized the importance of treating method bias as yet another substantive source of variance. This has been the approach followed in several studies (e.g., Smith, Hanges, & Dickson, 2000; Williams & Anderson, 1994).

Consistent with the thinking of Podsakoff et al. (2003) and Schmitt (1994), it makes sense to consider these effects in more substantive ways. In fact, Podsakoff et al. (2003) provided a great service by linking the concept of method bias to the response process described by Tourangeau et al. (2000) previously described.

However, whereas Podsakoff et al. (2003) were most interested in accounting for method bias, the approach discussed here uses this thinking to model multiple sources of substantive variance in *predictor* responses. When predictors are multidimensional or have multiple sources of influence affecting the response process (e.g., context effects such as applicant or incumbent settings, or instruction effects such as "should do" and "would do"), this conceptualization can be used to model these effects and see how they influence the predictor response process. Although the proposed model is conceptually similar to the models described in Podsakoff et al. (2003), the major point of departure is that they were most interested in estimating method effects whereas here we are most interested in estimating method effects *and the effects of other KSAOs* on predictor responses.

***Generalizability Theory.*** Generalizability theory (Cronbach, Gleser, Nanda, & Rajaratnam (1972) is a general model that seeks to estimate several sources of variance in test scores. The model recognizes that different sources of variance are present in different situations, and that these sources of variance can be isolated and estimated. It is not necessary to belabor the basics of generalizability theory because they are well described elsewhere (Shavelson & Webb, 1991). Rather, for our purposes we need to recognize one critical implication of the theory: Test scores have multiple sources of variance that influence them, and subsequently, we must design research in the appropriate manner to model and estimate these sources.

***Confirmatory Factor Analysis.*** The basic CFA model has had a fundamental influence on how we model and evaluate measurement properties of assessments. Perhaps the beauty of this approach is that it allows us to separate measurement properties from latent properties. Like classical test theory, we can model and estimate "true score" variance (latent constructs) and error variance (uniquenesses). A basic example of this is shown in Fig. 5.2, where the  circle represents the latent construct, boxes

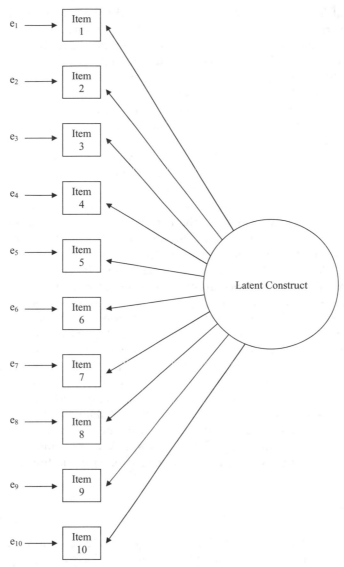

FIG. 5.2. Simple confirmatory factor analysis model.

represent measured (manifest) variables, and arrows indicate theoretical causal relationships. In this example, notice there is a single latent construct that is hypothesized to explain the covariance among 10 measured items. To the extent this model is correct, the arrows linking the latent construct and measured items (known as factor loadings) should be large and significant. This is never perfect, of course, so there is always some degree of error variance that is also related to a set of measured items. In reality, this may not be solely error variance because it is essentially all variance that is not associated with the latent construct. For example, this variance might include systematic variance caused by the wording of items, other constructs, mood, or other psychological and contextual factors.

One can model these other forms of systematic variance in CFA models. For example, in Fig. 5.2 we might find that half of the items were measured with "positively worded" items and half of the items were measured with "negatively worded" items. If the item wording produced a method effect, we might then have latent factors for (a) positively worded items, (b) negatively worded items, and (c) the true score (there would also be error variances associated with the items). Note that in such a model, the items have "cross-loadings" from more than one latent construct and hence there are multiple sources of systematic variance on the manifest items. When manifest items load on more than one factor, we can call it a "multiple cross-loading CFA model" to reflect the fact that the variance in each manifest item is explained by variance in more than one latent construct.

This type of CFA model is highly related to issues discussed in generalizability theory as well as recent publications on correctly modeling and controlling for "error variance" in psychological research. Schmidt and Hunter (1996) provided an excellent overview of these issues and the importance of specifying the correct form of error variance. DeShon (1998) published a critical article describing how to incorporate such thinking into CFA and structural equation modeling. Murphy and DeShon (2000a, 2000b) and Schmidt, Viswesvaran, and Ones (2000) provided alternative viewpoints on how we should deal with such issues operationally. All of these issues are interrelated and speak to the question, "What systematically influences the responses on a predictor and how do we deal with it?"

## The Model

The PRPR model is shown in Fig. 5.3 and integrates the aforementioned perspectives into a single framework. First, it is based on the graphical conventions used in structural equation modeling. Circles represent latent constructs, boxes represent manifest variables, one-headed arrows indicate theoretical causality, and two-headed arrows indicate covariance. This is more than just graphical convenience. It provides a means to test the model using CFA (particularly the method bias or multiple cross-loading models described earlier, except that the paths would go from the latent constructs to the response itself). Furthermore, it allows a means to test response

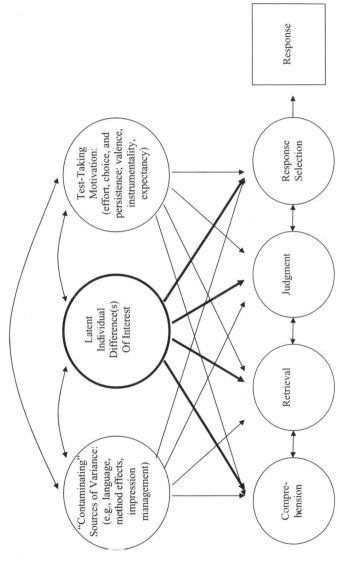

FIG. 5.3. A model of determinants of predictor response processes.

processes across groups (e.g., racial, context) using multiple group CFA, provided one has measured those processes.

Second, it is based on models of generalizability and method variance models by incorporating several sources of latent variance onto the manifest outcome. Notice that the true score variance or latent variable is denoted in bold. In a perfect world, there would only be this source of variance influencing the response, but in reality there are several sources of latent systematic variance that also may influence the manifest response—construct-irrelevant variance in Messick's (1995) terms and possibly method bias as well (Podsakoff et al., 2003). It also gives special attention to the role of test-taking motivation, helping to illustrate how motivation and ability may both be influential on responses and test scores (Cronbach, 1960).

Finally, the model incorporates the four-component model of survey response processes described in Tourangeau et al. (2000). These are latent cognitive processes that include comprehension, retrieval, judgment, and response. However, I have made a distinction between response selection (a latent process) and the actual response (a manifest outcome). This distinction is important because the manifest response is what is summed or manipulated in some manner to produce the overall score, whereas response selection is actually a cognitive process that may involve editing, revising, and strategizing the response (Tourangeau et al., 2000).

As Fig. 5.3 shows, each of these four components may be influenced by a variety of factors. This is perhaps the model's key contribution, to identify, isolate, and model the sources of systematic variance that influence response processes that ultimately determine predictor scores. For multidimensional predictors like SJTs, this may be the means through which we start to understand the meaning of SJT scores and ultimately construct validity, as illustrated in the next section.

## IMPLICATIONS OF THE PRPR MODEL

This section illustrates the implications of the model for understanding three difficult questions: the construct validity of SJTs, differences between applicant and incumbent contexts, and racial subgroup differences in test scores.

### Inferring the Construct Validity of Multidimensional Predictors: The SJT as an Example

SJTs are frequently considered to be a measurement method capable of assessing a variety of constructs like experience, knowledge, cognitive ability, and personality (as is typical of many measurement methods such as interviews and assessment centers). But as noted earlier, research has primarily focused on the relationship between the individual difference measures and the overall SJT score; it has not considered how the response processes may differ for different SJT items. The PRPR model provides another perspective on this issue and offers several ways of answering the question.

For example, manipulations of test instructions would tend to influence the comprehension, retrieval, and judgment components of the predictor response process. SJTs using "would do" instructions are only moderately correlated with SJTs using "should do" instructions (McDaniel & Nguyen, 2001; Ployhart & Ehrhart, 2003). We can better understand why this occurs using the PRPR model, as shown in Fig. 5.4. Notice in the figure there are two sources of variance, knowledge (the primary determinant of "should do" instructions) and personality (the primary determinant of "would do" instructions). (Note that in this example, test-taking motivation is assumed to be constant and is not present in the figure.) Thus, when a test taker completes an SJT item asking "would do" instructions, comprehension, retrieval, and judgment are driven primarily by personality (and possibly experience, as personality influences the types of experiences one will have). Alternatively, when a test taker completes an SJT item asking "should do" instructions, comprehension, retrieval, and judgment are driven primarily by knowledge. This is an idealized situation where respondents are entirely honest, and that is why there is no latent social desirability factor present. In applicant settings, latent social desirability may influence the response process and suppress the effects of experience irrespective of item type.

Legitimately, one could say we already acquire this information from aggregate correlations among knowledge, personality, and SJT scores. However, a common problem is that we find these relationships of varying magnitudes across different types of SJTs. Surely, some of this variance is sampling variability, but this is not likely to account for all of it. We can use the PRPR model to better understand why these differences exist by understanding how the latent KSAOs relate to different parts of the predictor response process. For example, what if the test taker has no direct experience with the situation? This is similar to what Hastie and Park (1986) referred to as making memory-based versus "on-line" judgments and the issue is whether there is actually a true memory that is assessed or whether such a memory is inferred or extrapolated from similar memories. The PRPR model provides a way to frame this question.

But suppose there are no measures or manipulations of the response process. Such a situation occurs frequently in practice where we might only have SJT and KSAO scores. One can still use the PRPR model to frame these issues in another way by adopting multiple cross-loading CFA models.

**96**

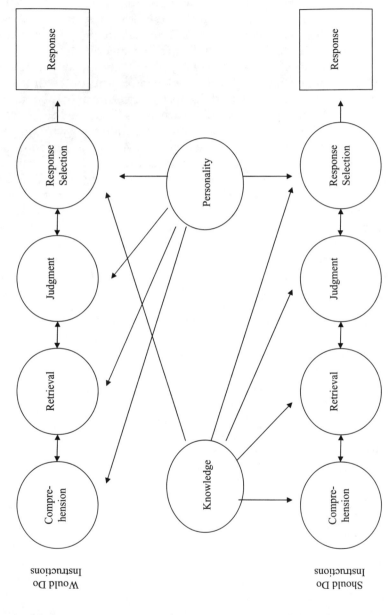

FIG. 5.4. Example of response processes involved with "would do" and "should do" instructions.

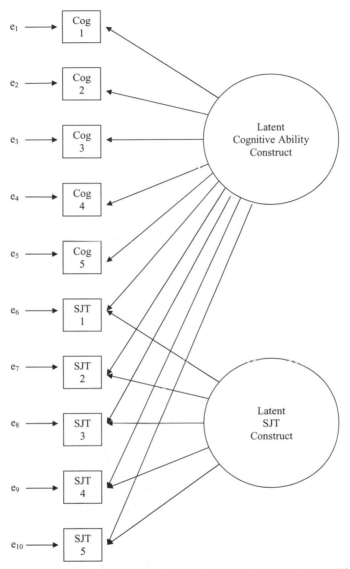

FIG. 5.5. Example of SJT cross-loading confirmatory factor analysis model.

Podsakoff et al. (2003) and Williams and Anderson (1994) provided several examples of such multiple cross-loading CFA models to model method bias. In terms of understanding what SJTs measure, one might have a model where cognitive ability cross-loads onto SJT manifest items along with the latent SJT true score. Such a model is shown in Fig. 5.5. Cognitive ability and the SJT are each measured with five items. To the extent the cognitive ability cross-loadings are large and statistically significant, it provides some evidence at the item level that cognitive ability contributes to manifest SJT scores. This is important because in the absence of a SJT measuring a homogeneous construct, such information could contribute to understanding the types of KSAOs that influence SJT responding. This provides information unique from scale-level correlations because one might find some SJT items are highly related to cognitive ability, whereas others are not. In doing so, one can then infer commonalities among the items that have the cognitive loading. Williams and Anderson (1994) provided details on how to use this approach operationally.

As these simple examples illustrate, there is potentially a lot of mental activity that corresponds to answering even a single item, much less an entire test, even though this processing happens relatively quickly. But by considering this information, we start to unlock the constructs assessed by the SJT through understanding how they influence comprehension, retrieval, judgment, and response selection. This means developers of SJTs should be cognizant of this processing sequence when generating items, trying to ensure consistency and homogeneity in such factors as instructions and options to ensure they do not influence the response process.

## Applicant–Incumbent Differences

Are noncognitive predictors influenced by context (applicant vs. incumbent), faking, and/or impression management? Research on personality suggests validity is not affected too substantially even though one finds higher mean scores among applicants (Hough, 1998). Research on SJTs is considerably smaller but tends to find similar results with validity (Weekley, Ployhart, & Harold, 2004; see Hooper, Cullen, & Sackett, chap. 10, this volume ). But how and why do such effects occur?

Smith et al. (2000) used the approach adopted by Williams and Anderson (1994) to model the cross-loadings of social desirability onto personality scores (similar to Fig. 5.5). More importantly, they did this across applicant and incumbent samples. They found the cross-loadings were similar across applicant and incumbent contexts, suggesting social desirability was not affecting one group more than another. The modeling of this question is consistent with the PRPR model, such that the hypothesized contaminant was measured and included within the CFA framework.

It is also interesting to understand why mean scores might differ across the two contexts. One of the hypothesized reasons is because of greater test-taking motivation among applicants. Yet, despite the large number of studies comparing these two contexts and the number of attributions made to motivational differences, I am not aware of a study that has actually measured and compared motivation between applicants and incumbents to explain such differences. Using multiple group CFA, one could include measures of test-taking motivation along with intended predictors when administering a predictor battery to applicants and incumbents. Although there might not be much variance within the applicant sample, it would be informative to compare the relative effects of motivation across the two contexts to see if motivation is truly the reason for higher (or sometimes lower) mean scores among applicants. This would be performed using a cross-loading CFA model similar to that shown in Fig. 5.5, except one would also include latent means in the analysis (see Ployhart & Oswald, 2004).

If one was able to measure the response process, one could make even more fine-grained predictions for SJTs. For example, impression management is likely to primarily influence the response-selection process. It may not have much of an influence on comprehension but could have a strong influence on retrieval, judgment, and response selection such that one draws from and selects those memories most favorable to a person.

## Racial Subgroup Differences

Subgroup differences are always important to minimize. With cognitive ability, racial subgroup differences are large and do not appear to be caused by measurement properties (e.g., Hough, Oswald, & Ployhart, 2001; Schmidt, 1988). However, one might question why the differences are present in multidimensional measurement methods like SJTs, interviews, and assessment centers. Do these differences occur because of the cognitive loading of the measures, or for some other reason? The answer to this question is to isolate and control for the variance associated with cognitive ability, to determine if subgroup differences still exist (note the interest so far has been primarily on racial subgroup differences and that is the situation considered here).

With assessment centers, some research suggests that controlling for cognitive ability will reduce the amount of subgroup difference found with overall scores without greatly reducing validity (Goldstein, Yusko, Braverman, Smith, & Chung, 1998; Goldstein, Yusko, & Nicolopoulos, 2001). Also important is the finding that some dimensions carry more of a cognitive load than others, indicating that subgroup differences are likely to be larger on those dimensions. With SJTs, Chan and Schmitt (1997) found that a SJT administered over video had a dramatically lower subgroup difference than the equivalent paper-and-pencil version. This difference appears to be largely due to subgroup differences in reading ability. Sacco and colleagues

(Sacco, Scheu, Ryan, & Schmitt, 2000; Sacco, Schmidt, & Rogg, 2000) found that the amount of racial subgroup difference in SJTs differed as a function of reading level, such that SJTs with higher reading levels showed larger subgroup differences. Finally, as noted earlier, research suggests test-taking motivation may differ between racial groups and show modest effects on test scores (e.g., Arvey et al., 1990; Chan et al., 1997).

In the PRPR model, one could consider these effects directly by using multiple group CFA and examine cross-loadings between cognitive ability and/or motivation with SJT scores. This would be similar to the model shown in Fig. 5.5, except that two (or more) racial groups would be examined simultaneously. One could invoke equivalence across the groups to test whether ability and/or motivation was equally influential on SJT scores for both samples (similar to Smith et al., 2000).

However, I believe the real value of incorporating the predictor response process for understanding subgroup differences will be to prompt a more fine-grained analysis of why the differences exist. Is it the case that racial groups differ in comprehension, and if so, why? It is probably true that cognitive ability, or at least reading ability, most impacts the comprehension part of the process. Do racial groups differ in their ability to retrieve information? In their judgment? Do they exhibit different response-selection strategies? Do different KSAOs influence these processes? There is almost no research on any of these questions but it is the kind of research that must be conducted if we are to reduce these differences.

Consider an example of using video-based versus written SJTs shown in Fig. 5.6. Here we see reading ability, a source of construct-irrelevant variance or contamination, influences the comprehension and response-selection components when using written SJTs because both the test question and responses are in written format. Alternatively, the video-based SJT shows effects for reading ability only on the retrieval component because it uses a written response format. Theoretically, if we were to further remove the written response component from the video SJT, the effects of reading ability should be eliminated.

The point is that if we know which components of the response process are associated with subgroup differences, we can try to change those aspects of the response process to reduce the subgroup differences.

## SUGGESTIONS FOR THE DESIGN OF FUTURE SJT RESEARCH

A serious consideration of the issues prompted by the PRPR model will require a change in the way we conduct SJT construct validity research.

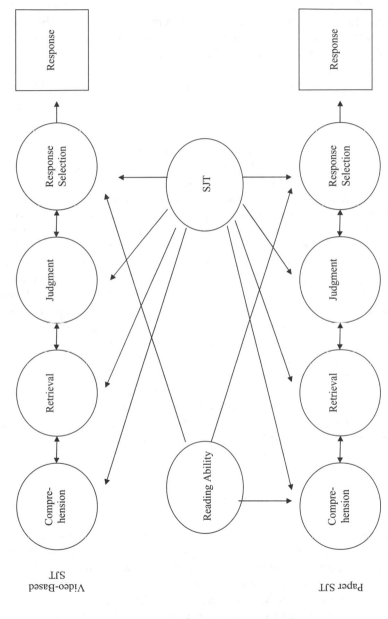

FIG. 5.6. Example of different response process determinants for paper and video-based SJTs.

101

The assessment of the response process is not something that can be easily conducted in the field and so there will need to be an increase in experimental research on SJTs. Currently, there is almost no such research and that must change if we are to more definitively conclude what SJTs measure. We already know that SJTs predict performance well, so it seems a reasonable next step to delve into the SJT response process.

In designing this research, we will need to borrow from methods used in cognitive psychology and cognitive science. For example, it would be quite informative to conduct a protocol tracing analysis as respondents complete SJTs. Test takers could describe orally what they are doing mentally as they complete the SJT. This would help infer whether or not participants follow the predictor response sequence in a linear manner, the kinds of strategies they might enact, and so on. One might conduct a cognitive task analysis of completing a SJT. Such analyses break down a task into the cognitive components necessary to perform the task and could provide an valuable sources of information about SJT response processes. One could also use reaction time measures to draw inferences about retrieval and judgment processes. For example, are judgments made in an "on-line" and relatively spontaneous manner or are they memory-based and require more time to complete (e.g., Hastie & Park, 1986)? If test takers do not have direct experience with a situation but must infer it from similar situations, longer reaction times are expected. We might develop actual manipulations of SJT items that target comprehension, retrieval, judgment, and response processes. For example, we could manipulate aspects of comprehension by altering response instructions (e.g., "would do" vs. "should do") and assess reaction times that differ between the two instructions. We could further assess a battery of relevant KSAOs and determine whether these differences in reaction time are explained by differences in KSAOs. And because, we are in this more micro-world anyway, we might also broaden our consideration of KSAOs to those more typically studied in cognitive psychology, such as working memory.

## CONCLUSION

This chapter has presented a broadly applicable model of the psychological process of completing predictors. Called the Predictor Response Process model, it is designed to help frame future research and practice on the cognitive processes involved with completing predictors. The model draws from several domains including modern conceptualizations of construct validity, response processes in survey research, models of method bias, typical/maximum performance, test-taking motivation, and generalizability theory and CFA. The model was presented and implications of the model were described. It is hoped the model will stimulate more considerations of validity from a response-process perspective. Although criterion-related validity must obviously remain central, response-process validity offers the potential to understand the many factors that influence test scores and hopefully enhance the science of selection.

## ACKNOWLEDGMENT

I thank Lynn McFarland and Jeff Weekley for their helpful comments on an earlier version of this chapter.

## REFERENCES

American Educational Research Association, American Psychological Association, & National Council on Measurement in Education. (1999). *Standards for educational and psychological testing*. Washington, DC: American Educational Research Association.

Arthur, W., Woehr, D., & Maldegen, R. (2000). Convergent and discriminant validity of assessment center dimensions: A conceptual and empirical reexamination of the assessment center construct-related validity paradox. *Journal of Management, 26*, 813–835.

Arvey, R. D., Strickland, W., Drauden, G., & Martin, C. (1990). Motivational components of test taking. *Personnel Psychology, 43*, 695–716.

Chan, D., & Schmitt, N. (1997). Video-based versus paper-and-pencil method of assessment in situational judgment tests: Subgroup differences in test performance and face validity perceptions. *Journal of Applied Psychology, 82*, 143–159

Chan, D., & Schmitt, N. (in press). Situational judgment tests. In N. Anderson, A. Evers, & O. Voskuijil (Eds.), *Blackwell handbook of selection*. Oxford, England: Blackwell Publishing.

Chan, D., Schmitt, N., DeShon, R. P., Clause, C. S., & Delbridge, K. (1997). Reactions to cognitive ability tests: The relationships between race, test performance, face validity perceptions, and test-taking motivation. *Journal of Applied Psychology, 82*, 300–310.

Cronbach, L. J. (1960). *Essentials of psychological testing* (2nd ed.). New York: Harper & Brothers.

Cronbach, L. J., Gleser, G. C., Nanda, H., & Rajaratnam, N. (1972). *The dependability of behavioral measurements: Theory of generalizability*. New York: John Wiley.

DeShon, R. P. (1998). A cautionary note on measurement error corrections in structural equation modeling. *Psychological Methods, 3*, 412–423.

Goldstein, H. W., Yusko, K. P., Braverman, E. P., Smith, D. B., & Chung, B. (1998). The role of cognitive ability in the subgroup differences and incremental validity of assessment center exercises. *Personnel Psychology, 51*, 357–374

Goldstein, H. W., Yusko, K. P., & Nicolopoulos, V. (2001). Exploring Black–White subgroup differences of managerial competencies. *Personnel Psychology, 54*, 783–807.

Hastie, R., & Dawes, R. M. (2001). *Rational choice in an uncertain world*. Thousand Oaks, CA: Sage.

Hastie, R., & Park, G. (1986). The relationship between memory and judgment depends on whether the judgment task is memory-based or on-line. *Psychological Review, 93*, 258–268.

Hough, L. M. (1998). Personality at work: Issues and evidence. In M. D. Hakel (Ed.), *Beyond multiple choice: Evaluating alternatives to traditional testing for selection* (pp. 131–166). Mahwah, NJ: Lawrence Erlbaum Associates.

Hough, L. M., Oswald, F. L., & Ployhart, R. E. (2001). Determinants, detection, and amelioration of adverse impact in personnel selection procedures: Issues, evidence, and lessons learned. *International Journal of Selection and Assessment, 9*, 152–194.

Joint Committee on Testing Practices. (1998). *The rights and responsibilities of test takers: Guidelines and expectations.* Washington, DC: American Psychological Association.

Krosnick, J. A. (1999). Survey research. *Annual Review of Psychology, 50*, 537–567.

McDaniel, M. A., Morgeson, F. P., Finnegan, E. B., Campion, M. A., & Braverman, E. P. (2001). Use of situational judgment tests to predict job performance: A clarification of the literature. *Journal of Applied Psychology, 86*, 730–740.

McDaniel, M. A., & Nguyen, H. T. (2001). Situational judgment tests: A review of practice and constructs assessed. *International Journal of Selection and Assessment, 9*, 103–113.

Messick, S. (1995). Validity of psychological assessment: Validation of inferences from persons' responses and performances as scientific inquiry into score meaning. *American Psychologist, 50*, 741–749.

Murphy, K. R., & DeShon, R. P. (2000a). Interrater correlations do not estimate the reliability of job performance ratings. *Personnel Psychology, 53*, 873–900.

Murphy, K. R., & DeShon, R. P. (2000b). Progress in psychometrics: Can industrial and organizational psychology catch up? *Personnel Psychology, 53*, 873–900.

Payne, J. W., Bettman, J. R., & Johnson, E. J. (1993). *The adaptive decision maker.* New York: Cambridge University Press.

Ployhart, R. E., & Ehrhart, M. G. (2003). Be careful what you ask for: Effects of response instructions on the construct validity and reliability of situational judgment tests. *International Journal of Selection and Assessment, 11*, 1–16.

Ployhart, R. E., & Oswald, F. L. (2004). Applications of mean and covariance structure analysis: Integrating correlational and experimental approaches. *Organizational Research Methods, 7*, 27–65.

Ployhart, R. E., Ziegert, J. C., & McFarland, L. A. (2003). Understanding racial differences on cognitive ability tests in selection contexts: An integration of stereotype threat and applicant reactions research. *Human Performance, 16*, 231–259.

Podsakoff, P. M., MacKenzie, S. B., Lee, J. Y., & Podsakoff, N. P. (2003). Common method biases in behavioral research: A critical review of the literature and recommended remedies. *Journal of Applied Psychology, 88*, 879–903.

Sacco, J. M., Scheu, C., Ryan, A. M., & Schmitt, N. W. (2000, April). *Understanding race differences on situational judgment tests using readability statistics.* Paper presented at the 15th annual convention of the Society for Industrial and Organizational Psychology, New Orleans, LA.

Sacco, J. M., Schmidt, D. B., & Rogg, K. L. (2000). *Using readability statistics and reading comprehension scores to predict situational judgment test performance, black-white differences, and validity.* Paper presented at the 15th annual convention of the Society for Industrial and Organizational Psychology, New Orleans, LA.

Sackett, P. R., Zedeck, S., & Fogli, L. (1988). Relations between measures of typical and maximum job performance. *Journal of Applied Psychology, 73*, 482–486.

Sanchez, R. J., Truxillo, D. M., & Bauer, T. N. (2000). Development and examination of an expectancy-based measure of test-taking motivation. *Journal of Applied Psychology, 85*, 739–750.

Schmidt, F. L., Viswesvaran, C., & Ones, D. S. (2000). Reliability is not validity and validity is not reliability. *Personnel Psychology, 53*, 901–912.

Schmidt, F. L. (1988). The problem of group differences in ability test scores in employment selection. *Journal of Vocational Behavior, 33*, 272–292.

Schmidt, F. L., & Hunter, J. E. (1996). Measurement error in psychological research: Lessons from 26 research scenarios. *Psychological Methods, 1*, 199–223.

Schmitt, N. (1994). Method bias: The importance of theory and measurement. *Journal of Organizational Behavior, 15*, 393–398

Shavelson, R. J., & Webb, N. M. (1991). *Generalizability theory: A primer.* Thousand Oaks, CA: Sage.

Smith, D. B., Hanges, P., & Dickson, M. (2000). Personnel selection and the five-factor model: Reexamining the effects of applicants frame of reference. *Journal of Applied Psychology, 86,* 2, 304–315.

Snow, R. E., & Lohman, D. F. (1989). Implication of cognitive psychology for education measurement. In R. L. Linn (Ed.), Educational measurement (3rd edition). New York: Macmillan.

Society for Industrial and Organizational Psychology. (2003). *Principles for the validation and use of personnel selection procedures.* Bowling Green, OH: Author.

Tourangeau, R., Rips, L. J., & Rasinski, K. (2000). *The psychology of survey response.* Cambridge, UK: Cambridge University Press.

Weekley, J. A., & Ployhart, R. E. (2005). Situational judgment: Antecedents and relationships with performance. *Human Performance, 18*, 81–104.

Weekley, J. A., & Ployhart, R. E., & Harold, C. (2004). Personality and situational judgment tests across applicant and incumbent contexts: An examination of validity, measurement, and subgroup differences. *Human Performance, 17*, 433–461.

Williams, L. J., & Anderson, S. E. (1994). An alternative approach to method effects by using latent-variable models: Applications in organizational behavior research. *Journal of Applied Psychology, 79*, 323–331.

# 6

# Using Situational Judgment Tests to Measure Practical Intelligence

Steven E. Stemler
Robert J. Sternberg
*Yale University*

Situational judgment tests (SJTs) have been shown to predict a variety of important professional outcomes, including technical proficiency, job dedication, and supervisors' ratings of participant performance (Chan & Schmitt, 2002; Motowidlo & Tippins, 1993). Yet, there remains some debate as to exactly why these tests are such powerful predictors. In this chapter, we argue that the theory of successful intelligence (Sternberg, 1997, 1999) provides a useful basis for understanding and explaining the predictive power of SJTs. Furthermore, we propose that SJTs developed in accordance with the theory of successful intelligence will ultimately provide a strong basis on which to build training programs for increasing participants' practical skills.

The chapter begins with a brief review of the evidence showing the practical utility of SJTs. We then discuss how the theory of successful intelligence can be used to provide a framework for understanding and explaining the predictive power of SJTs. Finally, we walk through an example of how the theory of successful intelligence has been used as a basis for constructing SJTs within the context of a project designed to assess teachers' levels of practical skills.

## THE PRACTICAL UTILITY OF SJTs

Researchers and practitioners alike have long searched for the holy grail of assessment that will allow them to predict with a high degree of accuracy which candidates are most likely to succeed in subsequent professional endeavors. Some believe that tests of general ability, or $g$, represent this holy grail (Gottfredson, 1997; Kuncel, Hezlett, & Ones, 2004). Although tests of $g$ do successfully predict at least some important variation in job performance, measures of $g$ alone still leave a substantial portion of the variability in work success and educational success unexplained (Gottfredson, 1997; Hunter, 1983). Thus, some researchers have continued to seek out alternative approaches to assessment that, in conjunction with other indicators, will help to explain more of the variability in professional and educational success. In constructing these expanded assessments, researchers have developed the methodology of situational judgment testing.

SJTs have a strong intuitive appeal because they ask participants to imagine themselves in the kind of situations they would be likely to face in their chosen occupation. Most SJTs are administered in paper-and-pencil format, where the stem is a written description of the scenario and all of the responses options are written out. Alternatively, some SJTs have taken the form of a video in which the main plot is acted out among the characters and the participant is asked to respond once the video has stopped playing (Sternberg & The Rainbow Project Collaborators, in press).

The strong intuitive appeal of SJTs is supplemented by their strong scientific appeal. Researchers using SJTs to predict job performance report validity coefficients, on average, of a magnitude of $r = 0.26$ (McDaniel, Morgenson, Finnegan, Campion, & Braveman, 2001). Furthermore, the predictive power of SJTs has been shown to be incremental to measures of general ability and personality. In other words, SJTs appear to capture some unique variance that is not captured by personality or by general ability.

## WHAT DO SJTs REALLY MEASURE?

The finding that SJTs have incremental predictive validity over and above tests of personality and general ability is a mixed blessing. On the one hand, SJTs appear to tap one or more different constructs that contribute to prediction. On the other hand, researchers have not been able to agree on exactly what the construct or constructs might be. Some authors have argued that SJTs represent a construct of situational judgment or job knowledge (Schmidt & Hunter, 1993), whereas others contend that variance explained by SJTs may simply be attributable to the method of measurement (Chan

& Schmitt, 2002; Schmitt & Chan, this volume; Weekley & Jones, 1999). Another potential explanation for the incremental predictive power of SJTs is that they measure part of a particular aspect of intelligence that Sternberg (1997, 1999) has called *practical intelligence*—the ability to adapt to, shape, and select real-world environments.

Indeed, the major limitation of SJTs is that there currently exists no over-arching theoretical framework holding the various SJTs together besides the fact that they share a common methodological heritage. As several re-searchers have noted (McDaniel & Nguyen, 2001; Weekley & Jones, 1999), the lack of a shared theoretical framework for the development of SJTs is an important problem for the field. Ployart and Ryan (2000, as cited in McDaniel & Nguyen, 2001) stated that without a firm knowledge of con-structs assessed by situational judgment measures, it is all the more dif-ficult to defend them both legally and professionally. Thus, theoretically grounded approaches to the development of SJTs are critical in order to more precisely target and assess the constructs of interest. We believe that using the theory of successful intelligence as a basis for the development of SJTs provides one potential solution.

## USING THE THEORY OF SUCCESSFUL INTELLIGENCE TO EXPLAIN THE PREDICTIVE POWER OF SJTs

Successfully intelligent people (Sternberg, 1997, 1999) are those who have developed the skills they need to realize their own goals within their sociocultural contexts. They recognize their strengths and weaknesses and capitalize on their strengths, while at the same time compensating for or correcting their weaknesses using a combination of creative, analytical, and practical skills. According to the theory, a common set of processes underlies all kinds of problem solving. These processes are hypothesized to be universal. For example, although what is considered an intelligent solution to a problem in one culture may be different from the solutions considered to be intelligent in another culture, the need to define prob-lems and translate strategies to solve these problems exists in any cul-ture. *Metacomponents*, or executive processes, plan what to do, monitor things as they are being done, and evaluate the things after they are done. *Performance components* execute the instructions of the metacomponents. *Knowledge-acquisition components* are used to learn how to solve problems or simply to acquire declarative knowledge in the first place. Although the same processes are used universally for all three aspects of intelligence (creative, analytical, and practical), these processes are applied to different kinds of tasks and situations as a function of the extent to which a given problem requires analytical, creative, or practical thinking, or a combination of these kinds of thinking. In particular, *creative* thinking is invoked when the components are applied to relatively novel tasks or situations. *Analytical* thinking is invoked when components are applied to somewhat familiar kinds of problems that are fairly abstracted from everyday life. *Practical* thinking is invoked when the components are applied to everyday life experiences in order to adapt to, shape, and select environments. Thus, the same components, applied in different contexts, yield different kinds of thinking—creative, analytical, and practical.

## THE CONSTRUCT OF PRACTICAL INTELLIGENCE

Practical intelligence represents one important branch of the triarchic theory of successful intelligence. Practical intelligence itself consists of two components: one cognitive, the other behavioral. The cognitive component requires knowledge, both tacit and explicit, about how to deal most effectively with situations that come up in the context of everyday experiences. Explicit knowledge is the kind of knowledge acquired through formal training. Tacit knowledge, on the other hand, is the kind of knowledge that people possess even if they are not able to articulate the principles guiding their behavior or to explain where this knowledge was acquired. Of course, knowledge is only part of the story. One may know the right course of action to take, but exhibit a breakdown in the implementation. Alternatively, a person may be able to react instinctively to a situation without being able to articulate how he or she knew what to do.

In assessing practical intelligence, it is best to assess both the cognitive and behavioral elements. Unfortunately, conducting behavioral assessments is extremely time- and resource-intensive. By contrast, cognitive assessments can be administered much more efficiently. For example, we have created assessments of tacit knowledge for several professions (e.g., teachers, school administrators, military leaders, business school applicants), most of which can be completed in less than 1 hour. Consequently, it would be reasonable to expect a job applicant to complete a SJT of tacit knowledge.

## THE CONSTRUCT OF TACIT KNOWLEDGE

Because our research program relies on SJTs to assess the construct of tacit knowledge, we now further discuss the relationship between tacit knowledge and practical intelligence. Most practical problem-solving scenarios involve at least three components: (a) the *situation*; (b) the response *strategy;* and (c) the *culture.* Tacit knowledge is related in an important way to each of these three components.

## The Situation

The first component of a practical problem is the situation, or the nature of the underlying problem being faced. Some potential situational descriptions include *uncertainty, insubordination, status exertion,* and *apathy. Uncertainty* occurs when a participant is asked to do something he or she does not know how to do. *Insubordination* results when a participant must act in such a way that could potentially undermine his or her supervisor's authority. *Status exertion* occurs when the participant's authority is challenged. *Apathy* occurs when a participant is faced with a task that he or she does not want to do or in which he or she has no motivation or investment. The specific details of any particular situation may vary, but overall, we believe that there is likely to be a finite number of general situations faced within the context of practical problem solving, and part of our current research efforts involves developing a taxonomy of these situations; however, as Gessner and Klimoski (this volume) point out, this task represents a major challenge.

## The Response Strategy

The second component of a problem-solving scenario is the response strategy for dealing with the situation. One of the main areas of research in the field of practical intelligence relates to problem-solving strategies. Among the central characteristics of strategies discussed in the research literature (Belmont & Butterfield, 1969; Berg, 1989; Brown, 1975; Flavell, 1970) are selectivity, goal-directedness, and intentionality. These are the same ingredients that make for success in the workplace, especially in for those in a leadership role (Antonakis, Cianciolo, & Sternberg, 2004; Sternberg, 2003).

Our own recent work has begun to focus on the strategic decisions that participants make about how best to respond to others, given potentially challenging social situations. Using Sternberg's (1997) theory as a guide, we conducted a study designed to examine teachers' levels of tacit knowledge. We conducted structured interviews with teachers ($N = 20$) and asked them to describe situations they had encountered during their teaching careers that they were never formally taught how to handle. We then asked them to recount specific situational examples and to describe how they handled them. The teachers with whom we spoke we employed at schools designated by the U.S. Department of Education as National Blue Ribbon Schools for the 2000–2001 school year. During the fall of 2001, we contacted the principals of all 243 Blue Ribbon schools via e-mail and invited them to participate in the project. Those principals who responded to our request were asked to nominate three teachers in their school whom they felt were particularly excellent. We then contacted those teachers for our interviews.

Because one of the main goals of this portion of the project was to develop a systematic and theoretical approach to the development of response strategies, we then asked the teachers to think about as many other

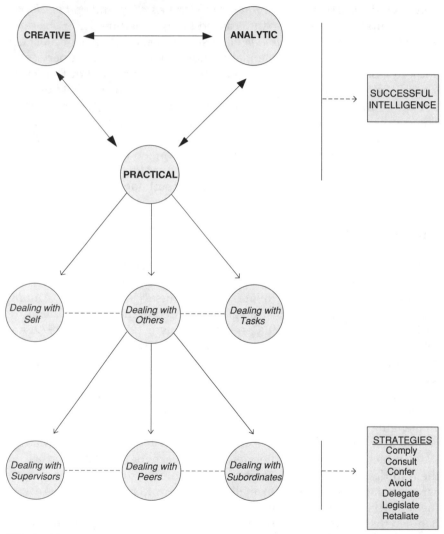

FIG. 6.1. Illustration of how the strategies fit within the broader framework of the theory of successful intelligence.

possible ways of handling the situation as they could. During the course of the project, we further refined the theory by dividing the category of dealing with others into three component parts: (a) *dealing with supervisors* (e.g., principals); (b) *dealing with peers* (e.g., teachers); and (c) *dealing with subordinates* (e.g., students). After compiling the information provided by teachers, as well as those potential responses generated by our research group, we conducted a content analysis of the responses (Fraenkel & Wallen, 2003; Stemler, 2001) to look for trends across the different situations. We arrived at seven practical strategies for dealing with others that seemed to apply across a wide variety of social situations: *avoid, comply, confer, consult, delegate, legislate,* or *retaliate.*

Figure 6.1 provides a graphical representation of how the seven strategies fit within the broader theoretical framework of successful intelligence.

Table 6.1 presents a summary of the key characteristics of the seven strategies, a description of circumstances where each may be appropriate or inappropriate, and some of their potential advantages and disadvantages. (For a more detailed review of the strategies, see Stemler, Elliott, Grigorenko, & Sternberg, 2005.) It is important to note that each of the seven strategies has advantages and disadvantages within any given social situation. Thus, no single strategy is uniformly best in all situations. Furthermore, the strategies themselves are not necessarily perfectly orthogonal. The strategies are defined in terms of the observable behaviors associated with each strategy. It is important to recognize that the exact same behavior may be driven by very different intentions. We chose to focus on the behavioral aspect of the strategy because, in life, it is people's actions that are most often interpreted, largely because they can be observed. People may later try to infer intentions, but misinterpretations may arise due to a variety of attributional errors (Aronson, Wilson, & Akert, 2001). From a theoretical standpoint, the practically intelligent person is keenly aware of what behavior interacts with which situational contexts to yield the desired outcomes.[1]

---

[1]It is reasonable to argue that practical skills involve at least two components. The first component involves understanding the kinds of actions teachers take in order to prevent problems from arising, and the second component involves understanding appropriate action to take once a challenging situation is presented. The seven strategies presented here are primarily concerned with the latter component, and therefore may be considered more reactive than preventive. This is not to underestimate the importance of prevention, however. Kounin's seminal work has led to recognition that a crucial element of behavior management resides in the teacher's ability to prevent difficulties by means of a variety of subtle verbal and nonverbal cues. By exercising these cues in a skillful fashion, problems are less likely to occur in the first place. Nevertheless, all teachers are likely to find themselves in situations where they are confronted by complex social challenges and the ways in which they deal with these will have an important bearing on their professional effectiveness.

**TABLE 6.1**

Key Characteristics of the Seven Strategies

| Strategy | Defining Characteristics and Behaviors | Appropriate Use/ Potential Advantages | Inappropriate Use/ Potential Disadvantages |
|---|---|---|---|
| Comply | • Actor does whatever is asked of him or her, regardless of who is asking<br><br>• Actor takes action that can be interpreted as actively condoning behaviors of others in the situation | • Actor agrees with what he or she is being asked to do<br><br>• Short-term compliance has long-term benefits (e.g., choose your battles) | • Actor fears emotional consequences of noncompliance<br><br>• Short-term compliance leads to negative long-term consequences |
| Consult | • Actor appeals to an external source for advice<br><br>• Actor asks people to work together to solve the problem | • Actor wishes to capitalize on other people's expertise | • Actor will be perceived as incapable of solving his or her own problems |
| Confer | • Actor engages in verbal discussion with source of interaction. Conversation takes place in a, private, one-on-one setting and is characterized by rational explanation of the actor's point of view | • Actor wishes to increase awareness and communication<br><br>• People are more apt to change when reasons for requests are revealed | • Revealing too much leaves actor vulnerable to being used as a pawn by others |
| Avoid | • Actor avoids, delays, or puts off dealing with a situation or problem<br><br>• No action is taken at all, or actions that are taken do not deal directly with the situation | • Actor believes that the situation or problem could resolve itself | • Rational discussion of each decision takes too much time to be practical<br><br>• Actor avoids action in order to put off emotionally difficult decisions |

| | | | |
|---|---|---|---|
| Delegate | • Actor either implicitly or explicitly delegates responsibility for taking action to someone else<br>• Actor absolves him or herself of responsibility for action | • Actor recognizes his or her own lack of expertise for dealing with situation. | • Actor is capable of dealing with situation him or herself |
| Legislate | • Actor explicates rules governing future actions of self and others | • Actor is interested in procedural justice<br>• A certain class of situations comes up frequently | • Actor creates too many policies<br>• Policies are too situation-specific<br>• Impossible to remember all policies |
| Retaliate | • Actor reacts physically or verbally in direct response to a situation. Direct response is often like for like in nature or involves punishment | • Other strategies have failed<br>• Antagonist does not respond to rational discussion | • Actor retaliates as an instinctive reaction<br>• Actor retaliates as an act of revenge without a strategy for changing antagonist's behavior |

As Mischel (1984) noted, endorsing a consistent strategy across different situational contexts may be maladaptive. Rather, some researchers have argued that successful everyday problem solving will involve carefully fitting strategies to the specific demands of a problem and modifying these strategies in response to changes in the problem (Berg & Sternberg, 1985; Rogoff, Gauvain, & Gardner, 1987; Scribner, 1984). Indeed, some research exists to support the notion that strategies that are supposedly effective across all contexts often fail in situations in which so-called ineffective strategies work (Berg, Calderone, & Gunderson, 1990 as cited in Berg & Calderone, 1994). Thus, tacit knowledge is the capacity to identify which strategy fits a given situation within a particular cultural context.

## The Cultural Context

Finally, the third component of a practical problem-solving scenario is the cultural context in which the situation unfolds. For example, a person may be confronted with the same scenario and potential response strategies within two different contexts (e.g., business and education). Even if the same mapping of strategy to situation is used in both contexts, the verdict of whether the behavior is practically intelligent may differ across contexts.

For example, imagine a person who moves to a new job. He knows that there are a finite number of both strategies and situations to be faced. Yet, the cultural context might require an adaptation of the fit between situations and strategies. Asking questions (i.e., the strategy of *consulting*) may have been perceived as a practically intelligent strategy in one context, but in the context of another culture, it may be deadly. Although the general strategies for dealing with practical problems remained constant (e.g., asking questions), as did the nature of the situation (e.g., the participant is uncertain about how to do something), the outcome of practically intelligent behavior, as determined by choosing the best strategy for the situation, may vary across cultures. Thus, tacit knowledge is the capacity to identify the optimal match between strategy and situation within a given culture. Understanding this match may be a universal process and a construct worth assessing.

Tacit knowledge is conceptualized by Sternberg and his colleagues (Sternberg, 1997; Sternberg et al., 2000; Sternberg & Horvath, 1999; Sternberg, Wagner, Williams, & Horvath, 1995) according to three main features, which correspond to the conditions under which it is acquired, its structural representation, and the conditions of its use.

First, tacit knowledge is viewed as knowledge that generally is acquired with little support from other people or resources. In other words, the individual is not directly instructed as to what he or she should learn, but rather must extract the important lesson from the experience even when learning is not the primary objective. Formal training environments facilitate certain knowledge-acquisition processes, including selective encoding (sorting relevant from irrelevant information in the environment), selective combination (integrating information into a meaningful interpretation of the situation), and selective comparison (relating new information to existing knowledge). When these processes are not well supported, as often is the case in learning from everyday experiences, the likelihood increases that some individuals will fail to acquire the knowledge. It also means that the knowledge will tend to remain unspoken, underemphasized, and poorly conveyed relative to its importance.

Second, tacit knowledge is viewed as procedural in nature. It is knowledge about how to perform various tasks in various situations. Tacit knowledge can be considered a subset of procedural knowledge that is drawn from personal experience. And as is often the case with procedural knowledge, it tends to guide action without being easily articulated (Anderson, 1983).

Part of the difficulty in articulating tacit knowledge is that it typically reflects a set of complex, multicondition rules (production systems) for how to pursue particular goals in particular situations (e.g., rules about how to judge people accurately for a variety of purposes and under a variety of circumstances). These complex rules can be represented in the form of condition–action pairings. For example, knowledge about confronting one's superior might be represented in a form with a compound condition:

IF <you are in a public forum>
AND
IF <the boss says something or does something that you perceive is wrong or inappropriate>
AND
IF <the boss does not ask for questions or comments>
THEN <speak directly to the point of contention and do not make evaluative statements about your boss>
BECAUSE <this saves the boss from embarrassment and preserves your relationship with him.>

In other words, tacit knowledge is more than a set of abstract procedural rules. It is context-specific knowledge about what to do in a given situation or class of situations. As discussed here, this representation serves as the basis of our approach to measuring tacit knowledge.

The third characteristic feature of tacit knowledge is that it has direct relevance to the individual's goals. Knowledge that is based on one's own practical experience will likely be more instrumental to achieving one's goals than will be knowledge based on someone else's experience or that is overly generic. For example, leaders may be instructed on what leadership approach (e.g., authoritative versus participative) is supposed to be most *appropriate* in a given situation, but they may learn from their own experiences that some other approach is more *effective* in that situation.

In describing tacit knowledge, it is also helpful to clarify that we do not equate tacit knowledge with job knowledge (see, e.g., Schmidt & Hunter, 1993). Rather we view the two as overlapping concepts. Job knowledge includes both declarative and procedural knowledge, and only some procedural knowledge can be characterized as tacit. Tacit knowledge represents a component of procedural knowledge that is used to solve practical, everyday problems, but that is not readily articulated or openly conveyed. Our research has shown that, although one can break down tacit knowledge into knowledge about self, others, and tasks, the three kinds of tacit knowledge are highly correlated (Sternberg et al., 2000).

Assessing tacit knowledge is not tantamount to assessing practical intelligence. Specifically, assessments of tacit knowledge may overlook how the strategy selected for the situation is actually implemented. For example, two participants could choose the same general strategy (e.g., consultation), but implement that strategy in entirely different ways. The first respondent might believe that the right way to ask a question is to be assertive, whereas the other participant might feel that the right way to ask the question is to be humble. Thus, even within the same strategy, the implementation itself may be the key factor preventing a course of action from being practically intelligent.

From the perspective of tacit knowledge, however, we are interested in assessing the extent to which a participant is able to adapt to the cultural context by detecting the optimal match between the situation and the response strategy within a given context.

## Disentangling Practical Intelligence, Social Intelligence, and Emotional Intelligence

The construct of practical intelligence shares some overlap with such constructs as social intelligence (Kihlstrom & Cantor, 2000; Marlowe, 1986; Neisser, 1976; Wong, Day, Maxwell, & Meara, 1995) and emotional intelligence (Mayer & Salovey, 1993; Mayer, Salovey, & Caruso, 2000; Mayer, Salovey, Caruso, & Sitarenios, 2003). Practical intelligence is different than either of the preceding constructs by virtue of the fact that the cognitive processes used need not always be directed at solving problems of a social nature (Hedlund & Sternberg, 2000). In fact, the construct of practical intelligence has been conceived of as encompassing three aspects: (a) dealing with self, (b) dealing with others, and (c) dealing with tasks (Stemler et al., 2005).

## Validity Evidence for Practical Intelligence

Most of the work validating the construct of practical intelligence has been conducted using SJTs designed to measure tacit knowledge (TKSJTs). The TKSJTs are typically scored against an expert response profile. In that sense, individuals' scores are compared to the distance of their scores from the average of a set of experts in the domain (e.g., expert managers, teachers). This approach to scoring follows from our theoretical assumption that tacit knowledge is a unidimensional construct.

TKSJTs have been found to have usually modest correlations with tests of academic intelligence. In our work, scores on TKSJTs for academic psychologists and managers correlated nonsignificantly (−.04 to .16) with verbal reasoning in undergraduate samples (Wagner, 1987; Wagner & Sternberg, 1985). Scores on the TKSJT for managers also exhibited nonsignificant correlations with measures of academic intelligence for a sample of business executives (Wagner & Sternberg, 1990) and a sample of air force recruits (Eddy, 1988). Similar findings were obtained with a TKSJT for sales in samples of undergraduates and salespeople (Wagner, Rashotte, & Sternberg, 1994). In one study, negative correlations were found between scores on tests of tacit knowledge and academic intelligence tests (Sternberg et al., 2001). In another, practical intelligence was a better predictor of practical behaviors, such as hunting skills, than was academic intelligence, among Yupi'ik Eskimos who need to hunt in order to survive (Grigorenko et al., 2004). Practical intelligence was also a better predictor of physical and mental health among Russian adults than was academic intelligence (Grigorenko & Sternberg, 2001). Scores on TKSJTs for military leaders exhibited nonsignificant as well as significant correlations (.02 to .25) with a measure of verbal reasoning ability (Hedlund et al., 1998). The more important finding of this research was that TKSJT scores explained variance in leadership effectiveness beyond verbal ability scores. In other words, TKSJT scores accounted for variance in performance not accounted for by a traditional test of academic intelligence.

In addition to exhibiting distinctions from academic intelligence, practical intelligence (at least as measured by tacit knowledge) appears to be distinct from personality variables. In a study with business executives, Wagner and Sternberg (1990) obtained data on several personality-type tests, including the California Psychological Inventory (Gough, 1986), the Myers–Briggs Type Indicator (Myers, 1962), and the Fundamental Interpersonal Relations Orientation–Behavior (FIRO-B; Schutz, 1989). TKSJT scores generally exhibited nonsignificant correlations with all of the personality measures, with the exception of the social presence factor of the California Psychological Inventory and the control expressed factor of the FIRO-B ($r = .29$ and $.25$, respectively).

Beyond the evidence for the empirical distinctiveness of the construct of tacit knowledge, there is also evidence to support the assertion that tacit knowledge predicts important outcomes. In studies with business managers, tacit knowledge scores correlated in the range of .2 to .4 with criteria such as salary, years of management experience, and whether the manager worked for a company in the Fortune 500 list (Wagner, 1987; Wagner & Sternberg, 1985). Wagner and Sternberg (1990) obtained a correlation of .61 between TKSJTs and performance on a managerial simulation and found that TKSJT scores explained additional variance beyond IQ and other personality and ability measures. In a study with bank branch managers, Wagner and Sternberg (1985) obtained significant correlations between TKSJT scores and average percentage of merit-based salary increase ($r = .48$, $p < .05$) and average performance rating for the category of generating new business for the bank ($r = .56$, $p < .05$). Williams and Sternberg (cited in Sternberg et al., 1995) further found that TKSJT scores were related to several indicators of managerial success, including compensation, age-controlled compensation, level of position, and job satisfaction, with correlations ranging from .23 to .39.

Finally, in addition to evidence for the discriminant and predictive validity of tacit knowledge, several studies by Sternberg and colleagues (Sternberg & The Rainbow Project Collaborators, in press; Sternberg, Torff, & Grigorenko, 1998) have shown that using expanded measures of intelligence tends to reduce the persistent ethnic differences in achievement that are frequently observed on more traditional assessments. Specifically, the ethnic group differences between White and minority students frequently observed on tests of analytical skills (Chubb & Loveless, 2002; Jencks & Phillips, 1998) tend to be drastically reduced on measures of tacit knowledge.

Our results are consistent with some results in the literature and appear, at face value, to be less consistent with other results, for example, of McDaniel et al. (2001). We believe that some of the inconsistencies are surface inconsistencies.

First, many investigators correct correlation coefficients for restriction of range. We do not. To begin with, we think the assumptions underlying corrections are somewhat dubious. In addition, we do not believe that the population mean and standard deviation are appropriate comparisons to most of our results. For example, when we measure tacit knowledge of business executives or Army battalion commanders, we are not dealing with a population that has a mean IQ of 100 and a standard deviation of 15. We do not even know what the mean and standard deviation for this population would be. But we believe that typical corrections inflate correlations by assuming an artificial population that does not apply. Business executives, for example, are not just drawn from the average population.

Second, many investigators correct correlation coefficients for attenuation. We do not. We have no great objection in principle to doing so, but we believe that such corrections once again entail dubious assumptions, at times even leading to correlations greater than 1. Moreover, the lower the reliability of the test and the greater the correction, the less likely it seems to represent reality.

Third, we have not used the full range of personality measures one might use. It is quite possible that other measures of personality would yield correlations higher than those few we have used.

In the end, we are not inclined to get into an argument over what the "true" correlations are, because there are no true correlations of tacit knowledge with $g$ or anything else. The correlations depend on many things—the tests used, the population sampled, the circumstances of testing, the context in which the tests are given, and so forth (see Sternberg, 2004). We have no dispute with those who believe that general ability is important to success in work as well as in school. We believe, however, that it is only part of the story.

As an aside, academics likely have, on average, very high IQs, in that they were selected for PhD programs on the basis of scores on related tests. But academics' success on IQ tests is not matched by their success in terms of societal norms. They are not at or near the top in prestige, and certainly not in terms of income. Indeed, in most parts of the world, academics, for all their high IQs, are among the poorest paid professionals for people with good educations. Most of them also have relatively little impact on the world, in comparison, say, with politicians or business executives, and their views are usually ignored or paid little attention when they try to influence policy. Finally, they write in journals that few people read and even fewer understand. If $g$ is highly correlated with societal measures of success, the very academics who trumpet the correlation at times seem to defy their own prediction, when success is measured in typical societal terms. Of course, there are many measures of success, but we refer here to the very ones that scholars tend to use as criteria, such as pay, prestige, and influence.

## USING THE THEORY OF SUCCESSFUL INTELLIGENCE TO CREATE SJTs

In the final section of this chapter, we focus on the development of SJTs that we designed to measure the extent to which teachers endorse each strategy across a variety of situations. We present three practical examples illustrating how the seven strategies can be used to measure various ways of handling social situations. Preliminary content-related validity evidence for the measures is reported using interrater reliability estimates.

### Examples of SJTs for Teachers

In this section, we present an account of how the seven strategies were used to develop potential response alternatives to SJTs for elementary, middle, and high school teachers, respectively. We developed three separate surveys because we found that the types of issues faced by each group of teachers were sufficiently different to warrant separate TKSJTs.

The social situations presented as the stem of each item were elicited from interviews conducted with teachers. We asked for examples of situations they had encountered throughout the course of their teaching careers that they had not been formally taught how to handle. Accompanying each stem was a list of the potential response options. In generating these options, we tried to retain as many as possible of the actual responses given by teachers during the interviews. We also drew up some further response options ourselves in order to ensure that we could provide options corresponding to all seven strategies described earlier.

Figure 6.2 presents an example item from the TKSJT for elementary school teachers. Figure 6.2 shows the item stem (i.e., the situation) followed by a list of potential response options (i.e., the response strategies). For illustrative purposes the corresponding strategy is listed in brackets. Note, however, that the strategy was not listed on the actual questionnaires for the respondents to see. Furthermore, the ordering of the response options was counterbalanced across items so that responses illustrating various strategies did not always occur in the same order (e.g., *avoid* was sometimes at the beginning of the response set, sometimes at the middle, and sometimes at the end). Finally, on the actual instruments, there may have been more than one response that illustrated a particular strategy (e.g., at times there were two or more responses that fit within the comply category).

Figure 6.3 presents an example item from the TKSJT for middle school teachers. Whereas Fig. 6.2 presented a situation fitting within the general category of dealing with subordinates, Fig. 6.3 represents a situation involving dealing with supervisors.

> Mrs. Smith had just finished teaching her first-grade class. All of her students were still in the classroom and had not yet left for their break when she received a note saying, "I love you, Mrs. Smith," from one of her students, Mike. Mike is a very shy boy and this was the first time he had shown his feelings for Mrs. Smith. Usually he would hide his eyes when she talked to him, and his cheeks would turn red.

Given the situation, please indicate in the box below what would be your primary concern in dealing with the situation.

Given the situation, please rate the quality of the following statements.

| 1 | 2 | 3 | 4 | 5 | 6 | 7 |
|---|---|---|---|---|---|---|
| Strongly Disagree | | | Neutral | | | Strongly Agree |

1. [COMPLY] By tomorrow morning, Mrs. Smith should write back to Mike saying how much she appreciated his note.
2. [CONSULT] Mrs. Smith should speak to another teacher who knows Mike and get his/her advice on how to respond.
3. [CONFER] Mrs. Smith should take Mike aside and thank him privately right after she reads the note.
4. [AVOID] Mrs. Smith should do nothing; just ignore the note.
5. [DELEGATE] Mrs. Smith should ask the school psychologist to talk to Mike.
6. [LEGISLATE] Mrs. Smith should announce to the class that any letters that she gets from students will be kept private.
7. [RETALIATE] In the presence of the whole class, Mrs. Smith should tell Mike that writing love letters to the teacher is not appropriate behavior.

FIG. 6.2.  Example elementary school scenario (dealing with subordinates).

Figure 6.4 presents an example item from the TKSJT inventory for high school teachers. Here, the particular situation presented in Fig. 6.4 represents the subcategory of dealing with peers.

*Content-Related Validity Evidence.*   After creating the various TKSJTs for teachers, we sought to gather evidence related to the content validity of the seven-strategy framework in order to demonstrate that the strategies were empirically distinguishable. Content-related validity evidence is a critical element of validity, especially within the context of situational judgment testing, as the courts have ruled against the legality of using SJTs in at least one case based on the lack content-related validity evidence (*Jerome Green*

The chairman of the department at Mr. Jackson's school has asked all of the teachers in his department to put together a portfolio illustrating their accomplishments as a teacher this year. The project has a very short time line and is in addition to his usual teaching tasks, but it is required by the department. Mr. Jackson really wants to do a great job, so he spends time working on it after school and during the weekend, and is proud of the final product he turns in. When he receives his evaluation, it says only that his portfolio was "average," as opposed to "excellent" or even "good." Mr. Jackson feels that it deserves a higher mark, especially given the amount of time he put into it.

Given the situation, please indicate in the box below what would be your primary concern in dealing with the situation.

Given the situation, please rate the quality of the following statements.

|  1  |  2  |  3  |  4  |  5  |  6  |  7  |
|-----|-----|-----|-----|-----|-----|-----|
| Strongly Disagree | | | Neutral | | | Strongly Agree |

1. [COMPLY] Mr. Jackson should try to put more effort into future projects.
2. [CONSULT] Mr. Jackson should talk to a few trusted colleagues about how angry he feels and ask them for their advice.
3. [CONFER] Mr. Jackson should talk to the department chair privately about his concerns.
4. [AVOID] Mr. Jackson should not make an issue out of it.
5. [DELEGATE] Mr. Jackson should ask a colleague to advocate for him.
6. [LEGISLATE] Mr. Jackson should decide that from now on, he will simply ignore any future remarks on his portfolio, good or bad, from the department chair.
7. [RETALIATE] Mr. Jackson should persuade his colleagues to oppose any other extra assignments from the chair in the future.

FIG. 6.3. Example middle school scenario (dealing with supervisors).

*vs. Washington State Patrol*, 1997, cited in McDaniel & Nguyen, 2001). Thus, the establishment of content validity of our strategic framework was an important part of the project.

Project team members worked together to refine the response options and independently rated each option according to the definitions above. They then reviewed the items, resolved areas of disagreement, and refined the response options and the scoring rubric. The next step was to ask two independent raters not previously involved in the project to evaluate each of the items according to the scoring rubric. The independent raters recruited were teachers who had practiced in the classroom within the previous 2

Mr. Thompson usually gets along well with his colleagues. One day, in a departmental meeting about the curriculum, a colleague personally attacks him because Mr. Thompson expresses a different opinion about a new program than most of his colleagues.

Given the situation, please indicate in the box below what would be your primary concern in dealing with the situation.

Given the situation, please rate the quality of the following statements.

| 1 | 2 | 3 | 4 | 5 | 6 | 7 |
|---|---|---|---|---|---|---|
| Strongly Disagree | | | Neutral | | | Strongly Agree |

1. [COMPLY] Mr. Thompson should reiterate his opinion about the curriculum but state that he is willing to go along with the group.
2. [CONSULT] After the meeting, Mr. Thompson should ask one of the other teachers how he or she thinks he should deal with his colleagueís comments.
3. [CONFER] Mr. Thompson should talk privately with his colleague and say that he felt the personal attack was inappropriate and out of line.
4. [AVOID] Mr. Thompson should ignore the attack and continue his discussion with another teacher.
5. [DELEGATE] Mr. Thompson should ask the principal speak to the colleague about his behavior.
6. [LEGISLATE] Mr. Thompson should propose the establishment of formal rules of order for faculty meetings.
7. [RETALIATE] Mr. Thompson should state that he is not interested in responding to petty personal attacks, but will be happy to answer questions about his opinion of the program.

FIG. 6.4. Example high school scenario (dealing with peers).

years. The results of the interrater reliability estimates between each of the two independent raters and the development team's ratings are presented in Table 6.2.

The results in the first column of Table 6.2 indicate the percentage agreement by rater and by strategy across all surveys. The results indicate fairly high levels of agreement between the classification of each response option between the raters and the development team. The percentage agreement overall and strategies for Rater 1 ranged from 67% to 97%, with a median percentage agreement of 79%. The percentage agreement for Rater 2 with the development team was slightly lower, ranging from 61% to 81%, with a median of 67% agreement.

TABLE 6.2

Interrater Reliability Estimates (Percent Agreement With Development Team)

| Strategy | Overall | Survey | | |
|---|---|---|---|---|
| | | Elementary | Middle | High |
| Comply | R1: 67% | R1: 67% | R1: 75% | R1: 58% |
| | R2: 61% | R2: 78% | R2: 67% | R2: 42% |
| Consult | R1: 97% | R1: 100% | R1: 92% | R1: 100% |
| | R2: 67% | R2: 56% | R2: 75% | R2: 67% |
| Confer | R1: 79% | R1: 56% | R1: 83% | R1: 92% |
| | R2: 67% | R2: 67% | R2: 58% | R2: 75% |
| Avoid | R1: 94% | R1: 89% | R1: 100% | R1: 92% |
| | R2: 81% | R2: 88% | R2: 82% | R2: 75% |
| Delegate | R1: 81% | R1: 63% | R1: 82% | R1: 92% |
| | R2: 71% | R2: 63% | R2: 55% | R2: 92% |
| Legislate | R1: 78% | R1: 88% | R1: 83% | R1: 67% |
| | R2: 78% | R2: 88% | R2: 83% | R2: 67% |
| Retaliate | R1: 73% | R1: 89% | R1: 83% | R1: 50% |
| | R2: 64% | R2: 56% | R2: 67% | R2: 67% |

The percentage agreement between each of the raters and the development team was also consistent across the three instruments, with a median percentage agreement of 73% for the elementary school instrument, 82% for the middle school instrument, and 71% for the high school instrument. Overall, the results provide some preliminary evidence supporting the idea that the seven categories are empirically distinguishable from one another. Although the strategies were not always perfectly orthogonal, our goal was to make them as orthogonal as possible. Our next step is to continue to examine and refine the item response options in light of our findings. In addition, we are currently analyzing data related to the criterion-related and construct-related validity of the TKSJTs.

## Implications for Data Analysis

The assumption that no single strategy is uniformly best in all situations has direct implications for how the data from this approach should be analyzed. As McDaniel and Nguyen (2001) pointed out, techniques such as exploratory factor analysis may not be particularly appropriate within such a paradigm, as the effectiveness of each response is a function of the scenario with which the response is associated. "Thus, the construct loading of two identical responses can be very different depending on

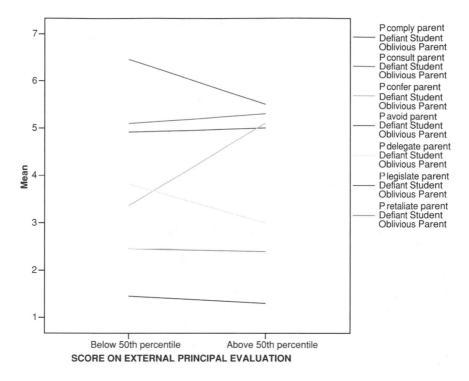

FIG. 6.5. Example results.

the scenario with which the responses are associated" (p. 106). The most appropriate technique for analyzing the data, then, may be through the use of Q-type factor analysis or cluster analysis techniques.

To date, we have used discriminant function analyses as an approach for analyzing the data. The goal of this approach has been to examine the extent to which certain sets of teachers (e.g., more effective vs. less effective; urban vs. suburban vs. rural; teachers of differing ethnic backgrounds) use systematically different strategies for dealing with others within the context of teaching. A graphical representation of this approach to analysis is presented in Fig. 6.5. In this example, the discriminant analysis results showed that more effective teachers tended to endorse the avoidance strategy as significantly more effective than did less effective teachers when the situation had to do with confronting disruptive students after the teacher had been absent for a day. Furthermore, a closer examination of the graph shows that expert teachers may have reduced the number of dimensions on which they classified the various strategies for dealing with this particular situation. Through the use of factor analyses, we can explore the number of dimensions seen in the data by experts and novices. The data analyses for this project are still ongoing, but the results to date show some promise for theory testing.

## CONCLUSIONS

In this chapter, we argued that the construct of practical intelligence, one aspect of the theory of successful intelligence, provides a useful basis for developing SJTs and for explaining their predictive power. We summarized evidence supporting the validity of the construct of practical intelligence and discussed how SJTs are useful for assessing the construct of practical intelligence via assessments of tacit knowledge. Finally, we provided a practical example of how the theory of successful intelligence can be used as a basis for the development of SJTs.

We believe that a theoretically based approach to assessing tacit knowledge through the use of SJTs holds tremendous promise both methodologically and substantively. From a methodological standpoint, the development and use of taxonomies of situations and response options like the ones proposed in this chapter (see also Motowidlo, Hooper & Jackson, this volume, for an alternative approach), may go a long way toward enhancing the comparability of SJTs across diverse cultural contexts. Furthermore, although there may be a finite number of situations and response strategies that exist across contexts, the capacity of a respondent to identify the optimal match between response strategy and situation within a given cultural context provides a measurable manifestation of his or her tacit knowledge.

From a substantive standpoint, school leaders can utilize the results of SJTs for teachers to add to the quality of mentor programs for younger or newer teachers. School administrators may potentially use the results for professional development purposes to stimulate dialogue about the different strategies outlined in this chapter and to create a well-targeted and empirically based professional development and/or training programs for teachers and administrators. In addition, the use of theoretically based SJTs may ultimately provide a more objective and defensible basis for hiring and evaluation of teachers in the United States.

## ACKNOWLEDGMENTS

This chapter was prepared under subcontract to the Temple University Laboratory for Student Success (LSS) as part of a grant from the U.S. Department of Education (award no. 31-1992-701), Institute for Educational

Sciences. Their financial support does not imply their acceptance of the ideas in this chapter.

## REFERENCES

Anderson, J. R. (1983). *The architecture of cognition.* Cambridge, MA: Harvard University Press.

Antonakis, J., Cianciolo, A., & Sternberg, R. J. (Eds.). (2004). *The nature of leadership.* Thousand Oaks, CA: Sage.

Aronson, E., Wilson, T., & Akert, R. M. (2001). *Social psychology* (4th ed.). New York: Pearson Education.

Belmont, J. N., & Butterfield, E. C. (1969). The relations of short-term memory to development and intelligence. In L. Lipsitt & H. Reese (Eds.), *Advances in child development and behavior* (Vol. 4, pp. 30–83). New York: Academic Press.

Berg, C. A. (1989). Knowledge of strategies for dealing with everyday problems from childhood through adolsecence. *Developmental Psychology, 25,* 607–618.

Berg, C. A., & Calderone, K. (1994). The role of problem interpretations in understanding the development of everyday problem solving. In R. J. Sternberg & R. K. Wagner (Eds.), *Mind in context* (pp. 105–132). New York: Cambridge University Press.

Berg, C. A., & Sternberg, R. J. (1985). A triarchic theory of intellectual development during adulthood. *Developmental Review, 5,* 334–370.

Brown, A. L. (1975). The development of memory: Knowing, knowing about knowing, and knowing how to know. In H. Reese (Ed.), *Advances in child development and behavior* (Vol. 10, pp. 103–152). New York: Academic Press.

Chan, D., & Schmitt, N. (2002). Situational judgment and job performance. *Human Performance, 15*(3), 233–254.

Chubb, J. E., & Loveless, T. (Eds.). (2002). *Bridging the achievement gap.* Washington, DC: Brookings Institute.

Eddy, A. S. (1988). *The relationship between the Tacit Knowledge Inventory for Managers and the Amred Services Vocational Aptitude Battery.* Unpublished master's thesis, St. Mary's University, San Antonio, TX.

Flavell, J. H. (1970). Developmental studies of mediated memory. In H. Reese (Ed.), *Advances in child development and child behavior* (Vol. 5, pp. 181–211). New York: Academic Press.

Fraenkel, J. R., & Wallen, N. E. (2003). *How to design and evaluate research in education* (5th ed.). Boston: McGraw-Hill.

Gottfredson, L. S. (1997). Why g matters: The complexity of everyday life. *Intelligence, 2,* 79–132.

Gough, H. G. (1986). *California Psychological Inventory.* Palo Alto, CA: Consulting Psychologists Press.

Grigorenko, E. L., Meier, E., Lipka, J., Mohatt, G., Yanez, E., & Sternberg, R. J. (2004). Academic and practical intelligence: A case study of the Yup'ik in Alaska. *Learning & Individual Differences, 14,* 183–207.

Grigorenko, E. L., & Sternberg, R. J. (2001). Analytical, creative, and practical intelligence as predictors of self-reported adaptive functioning: A case study in Russia. *Intelligence, 29,* 57–73.

Hedlund, J., Horvath, J. A., Forsythe, G. B., Snook, S. A., Williams, W. M., Bullis, R. C., Dennis, M., & Sternberg, R. J. (1998). *Tacit knowledge for military leadership: Evidence for construct validity* (Tech. Rep. No. 1080). Alexandria, VA: U.S. Army Research Institute for the Behavioral and Social Sciences.

Hedlund, J., & Sternberg, R. J. (2000). Too many intelligences? In R. Bar-On & J. D. A. Parker (Eds.), *The handbook of emotional intelligence* (pp. 136–167). San Francisco: Jossey-Bass.

Hunter, J. E. (1983). *Test validation for 12,000 jobs: An application of job classification and validity generalization analysis to the General Aptitude Battery (GATB)* (No. 45). Washington, DC: U.S. Employment Service, U.S. Department of Labor.

Jencks, C., & Phillips, M. (Eds.). (1998). *The Black–White test score gap.* Washington, DC: Brookings Institution Press.

Kihlstrom, J. F., & Cantor, N. (2000). Social intelligence. In R. J. Sternberg (Ed.), *Handbook of intelligence* (pp. 359–379). New York: Cambridge University Press.

Kuncel, N. R., Hezlett, S. A., & Ones, D. S. (2004). Academic performance, career potential, and job performance: Can one construct predict them all? *Journal of Personality & Social Psychology, 86*(1), 148–161.

Marlowe, H. A. (1986). Social intelligence: Evidence for multidimensionality and construct independence. *Journal of Educational Psychology, 78,* 52–58.

Mayer, J. D., & Salovey, P. (1993). The intelligence of emotional intelligence. *Intelligence, 17*(4), 433–442.

Mayer, J. D., Salovey, P., & Caruso, D. (2000). Models of emotional intelligence. In R. J. Sternberg (Ed.), *Handbook of intelligence.* New York: Cambridge University Press.

Mayer, J. D., Salovey, P., Caruso, D. R., & Sitarenios, G. (2003). Measuring emotional intelligence with the MSCEIT V2.0. *Emotion March, 3*(1), 97–105.

McDaniel, M. A., Morgenson, F. P., Finnegan, E. B., Campion, M. A., & Braveman, E. P. (2001). Use of situational judgment tests to predict job performance: A clarification of the literature. *Journal of Applied Psychology, 86*(4), 730–740.

McDaniel, M. A., & Nguyen, N. T. (2001). Situational judgment tests: A review of practice and constructs assessed. *International Journal of Selection & Assessment, 9*(1–2), 103–113.

Mischel, W. (1984). Convergences and challenges in the search for consistency. *American Psychologist, 39,* 351–364.

Motowidlo, S. J., & Tippins, N. (1993). Further studies of the low-fidelity simulations in the form of a situational inventory. *Journal of Occupational and Organizational Psychology, 66,* 337–344.

Myers, I. B. (1962). *The Myers–Briggs type indicator.* Palo Alto, CA: Consulting Psychologists Press.

Neisser, U. (1976). General, academic, and artificial intelligence. In L. Resnick (Ed.), *Human intelligence: Perspectives on its theory and measurement* (pp. 179–189). Norwood, NJ: Ablex.

Rogoff, B., Gauvain, M., & Gardner, W. (1987). Children's adjustment of plans to circumstances. In S. L. Friedman, E. K. Scholnick, & R. R. Cocking (Eds.), *Blueprints for thinking* (pp. 303–320). Cambridge, MA: Harvard University Press.

Schmidt, F. L., & Hunter, J. E. (1993). Tacit knowledge, practical intelligence, general mental ability and job knowledge. *Current Directions in Psychological Science, 2,* 8–9.

Schutz, W. (1989). *FIRO-B.* Palo Alto, CA: Consulting Psychologists Press.

Scribner, S. (1984). Studying working intelligence. In B. Rogoff & J. Lave (Eds.), *Everyday cognition: Its development in social context* (pp. 9–40). Cambridge, MA: Harvard University Press.

Stemler, S. E. (2001). An overview of content analysis. *Practical Assessment, Research and Evaluation, 7*(17) [Online], Available http://ericae.net/pare/getvn.asp?v=7&n=17.

Stemler, S. E., Elliott, J., Grigorenko, E. L., & Sternberg, R. J. (2005). *There's more to teaching than instruction: Seven strategies for dealing with the social side of teaching.* Manuscript submitted for publication.

Sternberg, R. J. (1997). *Successful intelligence: How practical and creative intelligence determine success in life.* New York: Plume.

Sternberg, R. J. (1999). The theory of successful intelligence. *Review of General Psychology, 3,* 292–316.

Sternberg, R. J. (2003). WICS: A model for leadership in organizations. *Academy of Management Learning & Education, 2,* 386–401.

Sternberg, R. J. (2004). Culture and intelligence. *American Psychologist, 59*(5), 325–338.

Sternberg, R. J. (2004). Intelligence in humans. In C. Spielberger (Edition-in-chief), *Encyclopedia of applied psychology* (Vol. 2, pp. 321–328). Oxford: Academic Press.

Sternberg, R. J. (Ed.). (2004). *International handbook of intelligence.* New York: Cambridge University Press.

Sternberg, R. J. (2004). North American approaches to intelligence. In R. J. Sternberg (Ed.), *International handbook of intelligence* (pp. 411–444). New York: Cambridge University Press.

Sternberg, R. J. (2004). Reply to Sjöberg's Commentary. *European Psychologist, 9*(3), 152–153.

Sternberg, R. J. (2004). The role of biological and environmental contexts in the integration of psychology: A reply to Posner and Rothbart. *Canadian Psychology, 45*(4), 279–283.

Sternberg, R. J. (2004). What do we know about the nature of reasoning? In J. P. Leighton & R. J. Sternberg (Eds.), *The nature of reasoning* (pp. 443–455). New York: Cambridge University Press.

Sternberg, R. J. (2004). What skills should be measured in the second century of ability testing? *Measurement: Interdisciplinary research and perspectives, Vol. 2*(1), 51–54.

Sternberg, R. J., Forsythe, G. B., Hedlund, J., Horvath, J. A., Wagner, R. K., Williams, W. M., et al. (2000). *Practical intelligence in everyday life.* New York: Cambridge University Press.

Sternberg, R. J., & Horvath, J. (Eds.). (1999). *Tacit knowledge in professional practice.* Mahwah, NJ: Lawrence Erlbaum Associates.

Sternberg, R. J., Nokes, K., Geissler, P. W., Prince, R., Okatcha, F., Bundy, D. A., & Grigorenko, E. L. (2001). The relationship between academic and practical intelligence: A case study in Kenya. *Intelligence, 29,* 401–418.

Sternberg, R. J., & The Rainbow Project Collaborators. (in press). The Rainbow Project: Enhancing the SAT through assessments of analytical, practical, and creative skills. *Intelligence.*

Sternberg, R. J., Torff, B., & Grigorenko, E. L. (1998). Teaching triarchically improves school achievement. *Journal of Educational Psychology, 90,* 374–384.

Sternberg, R. J., Wagner, R. K., Williams, W. M., & Horvath, J. (1995). Testing common sense. *American Psychologist, 50,* 912–927.

Wagner, R. K. (1987). Tacit knowledge in everyday intelligent behavior. *Journal of Personality & Social Psychology, 52,* 1236–1247.

Wagner, R. K., Rashotte, C. A., & Sternberg, R. J. (1994, April). *Tacit knowledge in sales: Rules of thumb for selling anything to anyone.* Paper presented at the annual meeting of the American Educational Research Association, Washington, DC.

Wagner, R. K., & Sternberg, R. J. (1985). Practical intelligence in real-world pursuits: The role of tacit knowledge. *Journal of Personality & Social Psychology, 49,* 436–458.

Wagner, R. K., & Sternberg, R. J. (1990). Street smarts. In K. E. Clark & M. B. Clark (Eds.), *Measures of leadership* (pp. 1990). West Orange, NJ: Leadership Library of America.

Weekley, J. A., & Jones, C. (1999). Further studies of situational tests. *Personnel Psychology, 52,* 679–700.

Wong, C. M. T., Day, J. T., Maxwell, S. E., & Meara, N. M. (1995). A multitrait-multimethod study of academic and social intelligence in college students. *Journal of Educational Psychology, 87,* 117–133.

# II

# Measurement

# 7

# Situational Judgment Tests: Method or Construct?

Neal Schmitt
*Michigan State University*

David Chan
*National University of Singapore*

Personnel selection research has always been characterized appropriately by concerns about methods. The impact of measurement error and range restriction are commonly recognized as having a great impact on the magnitude of effect sizes observed in applied research (Schmidt, Hunter, & Urry, 1976). Emphases on producing reliable measurement (across time, raters, as well as items) and research designs that alleviate the impact or allow the assessment of range restriction are well placed in a discipline that is concerned with the prediction of performance.

Unfortunately, the concern with methods and prediction of employee performance also has led to lessened concern with the underlying constructs measured by selection instruments. For example, high internal consistency is usually assumed by researchers as indicative that a single construct is being measured and is often not examined as closely as predictive criterion-related validity. In fact, a measure that is multidimensional is often more predictively valid because it is likely that it better represents criterion dimensionality. However, the emphasis on predictive criterion-related validity, and the correspondingly lower interest in unidimensional measures that produce clearly interpretable constructs does decrease the possibility that we understand fully the predictor or criterion constructs we measure.

This emphasis on methods and criterion-related validity is evident in many areas of selection research. We often speak of the validity of interviews, assessment centers, work samples and other measurement instruments when the more appropriate question should be: What is the validity of this method for the measurement of which knowledge, skill, ability, or other characteristics (KSAOs)? In other words, there should be a concern with the validity of the measurement of individual difference or KSAO constructs; the validity of a method of measurement is not meaningful outside of the context of some construct (Guion, 1998; Nunnally & Bernstein, 1994; Schmitt & Chan, 1998). Our profession as a whole, however, is more apt to discuss the validity of methods rather than the validity of measurement of constructs as was evidenced by a meta-analytic effort by Schmitt, Clause, and Pulakos (1996) who could not address method by construct demographic differences for lack of data. As further evidence of a concentration on methods as opposed to constructs, we also have meta-analyses of assessment centers (Gaugler, Rosenthal, Thornton, & Bentson, 1987), interviews (McDaniel, Whetzel, Schmidt, & Maurer, 1994), work samples (Schmidt & Hunter, 1998), and other methods, such as situational judgment tests (SJTs, McDaniel, Morgerson, Finnegan, Campion, & Braverman, 2001).

This chapter examines whether the SJT is a method of measurement or a construct. To address this question, we thought it would be useful to consider the nature of construct validity as outlined in Cronbach and Meehl's (1955) article on the nomological net as well as the most recent version of the *Standards for Educational and Psychological Testing* (American Educational Research Association, American Psychological Association, & National Council on Measurement in Education [AERA, APA, & NCME], 1999), and then apply these criteria in evaluating the nature of SJTs. In doing so, we discuss the difficulty in ascertaining the nature of the constructs underlying SJT performance and the associated evidence available in the literature. This leads us to arrive at a tentative answer to the question of whether SJT is a construct or a method. We end the chapter with suggestions for future research to derive a more conclusive answer to the question.

## NATURE OF CONSTRUCT VALIDITY

Cronbach and Meehl defined a *construct* as "some postulated attribute of people assumed to be reflected in test performance," a definition consistent with our understanding of KSAOs in selection research. So, in the case of

SJTs, we are asking if scores are indicative of some attribute that resides in individuals or if it is a method that we use to assess a variety of such attributes.

Cronbach and Meehl (1955) specified several criteria to be used in the investigation of construct validity. First are *group differences*. If the understanding of a construct leads to the expectation that two groups should differ on a measure, this can be tested directly. In the case of an SJT, for example, we might hypothesize that groups with differing levels of experience in the situational context specified in an item will have differing probabilities of answering the item, or a group of items, in the scored direction.

A second criterion mentioned by Cronbach and Meehl is the *homogeneity* of the items that have been written to assess a single construct. If a number of items are written to assess the hypothesized construct, then these items should be correlated. If there are groups of items in the measure such that the within-group item correlations are higher than the between-group item correlations, it suggests an additional construct(s) (method or substantive) may explain some of the variance in the measure. High item intercorrelations, however, are not a sufficient criterion to conclude that a set of items measures an intended construct; they could, for example, be a function of the method of measurement or some other construct. In other words, high internal consistency does not necessarily imply high construct validity.

Along with internal consistency, a construct valid measure should reflect a *predictable and interpretable pattern of correlations* with other established measures. The target measure should correlate highly with measures of similar constructs and be less correlated or uncorrelated with dissimilar constructs. Confirmatory and exploratory factor analyses are often employed to assess both homogeneity of items on the measure (in which case, evidence of a single factor is desired) and an appropriate pattern of correlations between the measure and external variables. Related to this concern with intercorrelations between measures of similar and dissimilar constructs is the concern with convergent and discriminant validity and the use of the multitrait–multimethod matrix (Campbell & Fiske, 1959).

*Stability of scores* on the measure may or may not be indicative of the construct validity of a measure depending on the theory that defines the construct. Mean change in situational judgment measures might, for example, be expected as individuals confront similar situations over time assuming that experience affects performance. If, however, situational judgment is a stable individual construct, mean scores may not change while correlations with performance measures that require situational judgment may be substantial.

Finally, Cronbach and Meehl (1955) suggested the consideration of *process issues* in determining the nature of the construct underlying a measure.

Such studies require a theory of how a person comes to achieve a high or low score on some measure and then generate empirical data that test the associated hypotheses. For example, one hypothesis is that SJT performance represents general cognitive ability (Schmidt & Hunter, 1993), whereas an alternative hypothesis is that it represents practical intelligence (Chan & Schmitt, 2002; Sternberg et al., 2000).

A modern interpretation of validity does not differentiate content, criterion-related, and construct validity as did psychologists at the time Cronbach and Meehl (1955) wrote their article on construct validity and the nomological net. Rather, the *Standards for Educational and Psychological Testing* (AERA, APA, & NCME, 1999) considers validity as a single notion and refers to various sources of validity evidence. The content of the test should tell us much about the construct the measure is supposed to represent. Content includes the themes, test tasks, and wording of the items but also the scoring and administration of the test. *Standards* also mentions evidence based on response processes as do Cronbach and Meehl. However, *Standards* mentions ways in which individual responses can be examined (e.g., verbal protocol analyses of respondents of judges who score test data) to provide information or generate hypotheses about how individuals respond to a measure. Discussion of evidence based on internal structure, relationships to other variables, convergent and discriminant validation, and test-criterion relationships are all remarkably similar to discussions by Cronbach and Meehl. Evidence based on validity generalization or meta-analyses provides a novel way in which to aggregate data from multiple studies to allow much stronger statements about the nature of constructs. Finally, evidence based on the consequences of testing can be similar to Cronbach and Meehl's idea that group differences tell us about constructs. In this context, however, it is important to distinguish between what group differences tell us about the nature of the construct measured and the social policy implications of those differences. That is, we need to distinguish between psychometric issues of validity and societal issues that affect test use or are affected by test use. We may not desire a large difference between males and females on a measure being used to make employment decisions (a societal issue of test use) but such differences on a measure purporting to measure upper body strength would be supportive of its validity (a psychometric issue of validity).

The nature of the constructs underlying SJT has been especially difficult to ascertain for several reasons. First, the development of SJT begins with the generation of critical incidents. Resolution of such incidents which serve as the stem of SJT items almost always requires multiple knowledges, skills, abilities, or traits. Second, the focus in most early studies of SJT was on the prediction of multidimensional criteria. Predictors whose utility is judged by their relationship to a multidimensional outcome will themselves tend to be multidimensional. Third, the importance of the response instructions in determining the nature of the construct being measured has only recently been recognized. In the remainder of this chapter, we use the considerations posed by Cronbach and Meehl (1955) and in the *Standards* (AERA, APA, & NCME, 1999) in judging a measure's construct validity and to organize our discussion of whether the SJT represents a construct or a method.

## SUBGROUP DIFFERENCES

Conceptually, one would expect an SJT to be related to experience; that is, groups with more experience with a situation should understand better how to handle it. Several studies provide data on the relationship between job experience measured on a continuum and situational judgment measures. McDaniel and Nguyen (2001) reported a mean correlation across 17 studies of .07. If one examines those studies (e.g., Weekley & Jones, 1997, 1999; Smith & McDaniel, 1998) that use a SJT developed based on critical incidents related to job performance, the correlations are typically in the high teens and low 20s. Weekley and Jones (1997, 1999) were also more careful in their measurement of job experience than most other researchers who considered the experience–SJT relationship. Job experience is usually considered a proxy for job knowledge, but there are also some studies in which job knowledge is measured more directly. This research is summarized here.

Race and gender subgroup differences on SJTs have also been examined. Although there is no conceptual reason to expect such differences, social and legal concerns dictate such examinations. Most studies (e.g., Clevenger, Pereira, Wiechmann, Schmitt, & Schmidt Harvey, 2001; Motowidlo, Dunnette, & Carter, 1990; Pulakos & Schmitt, 1996; Weekley & Jones, 1997, 1999) have reported that African-American examinees score lower than Whites by about 0.5 standard deviations (effect sizes ranged from $ds = .37$ to .85 in the studies cited previously). Fewer studies have reported gender differences but most report that females score as well or better than males; Weekley and Jones (1999) reported a d = .30. Women also did slightly better than men (d = .18) on an SJT developed for medical school admissions decisions (Lievens & Coetsier, 2002).

## HOMOGENEITY OF SJT ITEMS

Cronbach's alpha is an imperfect measure of the homogeneity of items, but it is usually the only index presented. Cronbach's alpha coefficients are usually relatively low unless the SJT is comprised of a very large number of items. Clevenger et al. (2001) reported alphas of .63, .90, and .82 for SJTs consisting of 33, 43, and 39 items, respectively. Lievens and Coetsier (2002) reported alphas between .41 and .56 for video-based SJTs. Weekley and Jones (1997) reported alphas of .29 and .32 for 20-item SJTs. In a subsequent study, Weekley and Jones reported alphas of .73 for a 34-item SJT and .87 for a 46-item SJT. The artifact distribution provided by McDaniel et al.'s (2001) meta-analysis included alpha values ranging from .43 to .94 with a mean value of .60. All the above alpha values reported for SJTs need to be interpreted along with the factor-analytic results and other data related to homogeneity (Hattie, 1985).

## FACTOR ANALYSES OF SJT MEASURES

Gillespie, Oswald, Schmitt, Manheim, and Kim (2002) reported a study in which SJT items were written to represent 12 *a priori* content areas. These content areas were represented by three to six items each and had predictably low alphas (.22 to .56). Confirmatory factor analysis of this 12-factor model yielded disappointing results. Exploratory factor analysis yielded results similar to other efforts (e.g., Chan & Schmitt, 2002; Pulakos, Schmitt, & Keenan, 1994). That is, the first dimension accounted for 12% of the variance, whereas the second dimension account for 5% of the variance in responses. Subsequent dimensions each accounted for slightly less variance so that use of the scree criterion to determine the number of dimensions represented by the measure would lead one to the conclusion that a single dimension represents the data well. However, the percent of variance accounted for would generally be considered weak evidence for unidimensionality. The first factor accounts for almost three times as much variance as the second, but a relatively small portion of the total variance. Examination of the factor loadings yielded no convincing substantive interpretation. Because of the relatively large number of items and the low positive item intercorrelations, the alpha of the 57 item composite was .87.

Given the relatively low alphas that are typically reported, along with the factor-analytic results, it seems safe to conclude that a general "judgment" factor accounts for response variance in most SJT items, but a relatively large portion of variance is accounted for by other factors that are represented in fewer items that do not seem to share similar content or constructs. What is left unanswered is the precise conceptual nature of the general "judgment" factor and the more specific factors, although we have speculated that the concept of practical intelligence may be represented by the general factor (Chan & Schmitt, 2002, 2005).

## STABILITY OF TEST SCORES

There are some data on the stability or test–retest reliability of SJTs. Ployhart, Porr and Ryan (2004) found a test–retest reliability estimate for a 41-item SJT of .84 over a 1-month interval. Becker (2004) reported a test–retest reliability of .71 for a 20-item SJT over a 2-month interval. Ployhart and Ehrhart (2003) reported test–retest reliabilities for different rating instructions ranging from .20 to .92. Theoretically, it is not clear what level of test–retest reliability one would expect to find. If SJT scores are a function of one's experiences, then there should be mean differences in SJT scores across time. However, persons who receive higher SJT scores that reflect higher levels of ability to make good judgments may benefit more from experiences that reflect the situations in the SJT measure than persons with lower SJT scores. If so, the increase in SJT score over time will be larger for those with higher SJT scores to begin with compared with those with lower SJT scores. This will translate into an increase in test variance, in addition to an increase in test mean. If the amount of benefit from experience is highly and positively correlated with initial SJT scores, then test–retest reliability would still be high. However, if the amount of benefit from experience is not a simple linear function of SJT scores, then it is possible that test–retest reliability would be low as scores on the SJT would be a complex function of both an individual difference characteristic and the situations to which persons are exposed. Both additional theoretical development as well as empirical studies of change in SJT scores across time is needed.

## CORRELATIONS BETWEEN SJTS AND MEASURES OF OTHER CONSTRUCTS: PROCESS ISSUES

Probably the most frequent effort to understand the construct validity of the SJT and to determine whether SJTs measure a unique construct(s) as opposed to simply measuring similar established constructs assessed by traditional methods using a different method has been to correlate SJT with other well-known measures. These correlations also provide some information about the process underlying responses on SJT items; that is, what might be the social, experiential, and cognitive determinants of SJT responses. Reflecting the notion that SJTs, or measures of tacit knowledge, are simply measures of job knowledge and dependent on cognitive ability (Schmidt & Hunter, 1993), many studies have examined the correlation between measures of cognitive ability, job knowledge, and SJTs. McDaniel et al. (2001) reported a mean observed correlation between SJT and cognitive ability of .36 (corrected to .46) across 79 coefficients. However, only 12% of the variance was due to artifacts and the credibility interval (10th and 90th percentile) was .17 to .75. This indicates that in some instances the observed relationship was quite high, whereas in other cases it was low or nearly zero. One conclusion, with respect to this variability, is that the SJT is a method that can be used to assess cognitive ability, but that it does not necessarily do so and may be used to assess a variety of other constructs that may or may not be correlated with cognitive ability (Chan & Schmitt, 2002, 2005). Note that it is also the case that SJTs add incrementally above cognitive ability measures when predicting job performance (e.g., Chan & Schmitt, 2002; Clevenger et al., 2001; Lievens & Coetsier, 2002; Motowidlo et al., 1990; Weekley & Jones, 1997, 1999).

Correlations with measures of job knowledge are less frequently reported. Pulakos et al. (1994) reported a correlation of .11 between a 33-item SJT and a 117-item measure of job knowledge for a group of federal investigative agents. Across 17 studies, McDaniel and Nguyen (2001) found an average correlation of .07, excluding a single large study (Clevenger & Haaland, 2000) in which the correlation was negative. The 90% credibility interval was −.14 to .29. Neither correlations with cognitive ability nor job knowledge should lead us to the conclusion that SJTs are simply alternative measures of these constructs. Given the range of correlations with cognitive ability measures, it appears that one can develop a SJT that is highly cognitive, but that an SJT can also be developed to assess other constructs.

A summary of the relationships between SJTs and constructs other than cognitive ability is provided by McDaniel and Nguyen (2001). Average observed correlations between SJTs and Agreeableness, Conscientiousness, Emotional Stability, Extroversion, and Openness were .25, .26, .31, .06, and .09, respectively. SJT correlations with Openness were reported for only three studies, whereas the other averages were based on 8 to 13 correlations. In all cases but Openness, almost all the variation in correlations was unexplained on the basis of sampling error and the 90% credibility intervals were quite large. Several studies subsequent to McDaniel and Nguyen (2001) also reported correlations between SJTs and personality measures. Chan and Schmitt (2002) reported SJT correlations of .23, .24, and .29 with Conscientiousness, Extraversion, and Agreeableness and −.20 with Neuroticism. In the Lievens and Coetsier (2002) study, none of the reported correlations between measures of the Big Five and the SJT exceeded .15. Clevenger et al. (2001) reported correlations of .00, .16, and .21 between SJTs and Conscientiousness in three different samples. In short, the empirical findings that SJT scores may be correlated with a variety of different variables including cognitive ability and personality measures are consistent with our suggestion that SJTs can be developed to correlate with cognitive ability or personality measures and it is in this sense that the SJT is a method that can be developed to assess different constructs (Chan & Schmitt, 2005). Note, however, that the correlations between SJT scores and personality (or cognitive ability) test scores often vary quite widely depending on the specific content of the SJT and the typical correlations are only modest in magnitude. This pattern of results has led us to draw two conclusions (Chan & Schmitt, 2005). First, we believe that the specific content of a particular SJT is the critical determinant of the nature of constructs being in fact assessed and therefore the magnitude of the correlations between SJT scores and personality/cognitive ability measures. Second, we believe that the modest magnitude of typical SJT correlations with personality/cognitive ability measures is indicative that the dominant constructs assessed by typical SJTs are not identical to, although they may be correlated with, cognitive ability or personality traits (as elaborated later in this chapter).

In addition to the studies cited here, data collected as part of a study conducted by Oswald, Schmitt, Kim, Ramsay, and Gillespie (2004) affords an opportunity to examine correlations between SJT and a broad array of other psychological measures. In that study of 644 college freshmen, academic performance was predicted using SJT measures of 12 content domains, Big Five measures (Goldberg, 1999), a measure of Holland's (1985) six interest dimensions, and ACT/SAT scores (considered cognitive ability). The SJT did provide incremental validity above cognitive ability measures in the prediction of college grade point average (GPA), absenteeism, and self- and peer reports of performance in 12 performance domains. For purposes of considering the construct validity of SJTs, we provide here an alternative analysis of these data and other available data on these examinees. Table 7.1 summarizes the results of a series of regression analyses in which we examined the degree to which variance in SJT responses was related to four different psychological domains that are relatively independent of one another. SJT measures of 12 different performance domains considered important in the development of college students were regressed in hierarchical fashion on ACT/SAT scores, freshman-year GPAs, which in this context was considered analogous to job knowledge, personality, and interest, in that order. The hierarchical order was arbitrary, but with some exceptions (e.g., GPA and ACT/SAT, Artistic interests and Openness) these four sets of variables were uncorrelated.

In parentheses in the first column of Table 7.1, we present the Cronbach's alphas associated with each SJT. The first number in remaining columns of the table is the percent of SJT variance explained by the set of variables involved. In Columns 4 and 5, we also present the predictors that contributed

**TABLE 7.1**

Estimates of True Relationships Between SJT Measures, Cognitive Ability, Academic Performance, Personality, and Interest

| SJT Content | ACT/SAT | GPA | Personality | Interest | Other |
|---|---|---|---|---|---|
| Knowledge (.38)[a] | .022 (.058, .064)[b] | .048 (.126, .141) | .078 (.205, .242) Agreeableness, conscientious | .023 (.061, .071) Realistic, investigative, enterprising | .829 (.550, .482) |
| Continuous Learning (.22) | .023 (.105, .116) | .001 (.004, .005) | .045 (.204, .241) Agreeableness | .017 (.077, .091) Investigative, artistic | .914 (.610, .547) |
| Artistic (.47) | .000 | .006 (.013, .014) | .084 (.178, .210) Agreeableness, openness | .042 (.089, .105) Artistic, investigative, realistic | .868 (.720, .671) |
| Multicultural Appreciation (.40) | .004 (.010, .011) | .000 | .126 (.315, .371) Agreeableness, emotional stability | .066 (.165, .194) Artistic, social, conventional | .821 (.510, .424) |
| Leadership (.38) | .000 | .009 (.023, .026) | .125 (.329, .388) Extraversion, conscientiousness | .013 (.034, .040) Investigative | .852 (.614, .546) |
| Interpersonal skills (.44) | .009 (.020, .023) | .000 | .115 (.261, .308) Agreeableness, emotional stability | .010 (.029, .034) | .865 (.696, .642) |
| Social responsibility (.28) | .000 | .003 (.011, .012) | .076 (.272, .319) Agreeableness, emotional stability | .026 (.073, .087) Investigative, social | .896 (.644, .582) |

| | | | | |
|---|---|---|---|---|
| Health (.28) | .016 (.057, .063) | .003 (.011, .012) | .059 (.211, .248) Agreeableness, conscientious-ness | .008 (.029, .034) | .914 (.692, .643) |
| Career orientation (.39) | .012 (.031 .034) | .001 (.003, .003) | .055 (.141, .166) Agreeableness, conscientious-ness, emotional stability | .017 (.044, .051) Realistic, investigative | .915 (.781, .746) |
| Adaptability (.28) | .006(.021, .024) | .006(.021, .024) | .044(.157, .185) Conscientious-ness, emotional stability | .026(.093, .109) | .918(.708, .658) |
| Perseverance (.37) | .006 (.016 .018) | .032 (.087, .096) | .065 (.176, .207) Conscientious-ness, emotional stability | .015 (.041, .048) Realistic | .892 (.680, .631) |
| Ethics/integrity (.56) | .051 (.091, .101) | .029 (.052, .058) | .058 (.104, .122) Agreeableness, conscientious-ness | .028 (.050, .059) Investigative, social | .853 (.703, .660) |

[a] Numbers in parentheses next to the situational judgment content areas are reliability estimates.

[b] The first number in parentheses is corrected for attenuation due to unreliability in the situational judgment measure; the second effect size in parentheses has been corrected for both situational judgment unreliability and unreliability in the other measure. All numbers are percent variance that SJT shares with a set of other constructs. The "Other" column represents the variance remaining after the sum of the variances associated with the other four sets of constructs is summed.

significantly at that step in the regressions. The first number in parentheses is corrected for unreliability in the SJT. The second number in parentheses is corrected for unreliability in both the SJT and the predictor variable. We had no direct measure of reliability for these predictors or predictor sets, so we estimated conservatively high reliabilities of .90 for ACT/SAT and GPA and .85 for the personality and interest measures. The last column, labeled "Other," represents the SJT variance unaccounted for in each of the regressions. Our intent in presenting these data is to examine the degree to which SJTs share variance with a variety of psychological constructs and performance (or academic knowledge) and to assess the degree to which SJTs represent unique information or a novel construct. Second, to the degree to which they are redundant with these existing measures, we can better understand what SJTs measure or can be adapted to measure.

The first thing that is apparent in this table is that a great deal of the variance in each of the SJT measures is unrelated to performance, cognitive ability, personality, and interests even after making what seem to be reasonable corrections for unreliability. This might be taken to mean that there is a situational judgment construct that is independent of most other individual difference variables that we usually use in personnel selection.

It is also the case that this set of SJTs is most highly related to measures of the Big Five. Percents of shared variance (corrected for unreliability in SJT and the correlates of SJT) range from 12% for Ethics/Integrity to 39% for Leadership. Agreeableness was a significant contributor to nine of the regressions, and Emotional Stability and Conscientiousness to seven of the regressions. These data are consistent with the meta-analysis by McDaniel and Nguyen (2001) that indicated these three Big Five dimensions were most highly correlated with SJT measures. There are interpretable deviations from this pattern; for example, the Artistic SJT measure is related to Openness and the Leadership SJT measure is related significantly to Extraversion.

Interest measures are also related in interpretable ways to several SJT measures. Investigative interests are significant correlates of many of the dimensions including Knowledge (academic interest and aptitude) and Continuous Learning (efforts to learn outside the required curriculum) as well as several other SJT measures. Social interests are related significantly to Leadership, Multicultural Appreciation, and Social Responsibility. GPA is related most highly to Knowledge, Perseverance, and Ethics/Integrity. The latter may not appear substantively reasonable, but many of the Ethics/Integrity items were related to classroom or academic honesty. Cognitive ability, as represented by students' ACT/SAT scores is most highly correlated with Knowledge, Continuous Learning, and Ethics/Integrity. The latter, again, may be a function of the inclusion of academic honesty situations in this measure or the fact that academically capable students are more likely to be more honest in dealing with cheating situations than their less able peers. The Ethics/Integrity and Knowledge dimensions seem to be most multidimensional in that each of the four sets of correlates are significantly correlated with these measures.

This analysis certainly has limitations. It represents one set of SJT measures developed in an academic setting (most SJT applications have been in the employment setting). Our corrections for reliability were based on assumptions rather than empirical estimates of the reliability of the correlates of the SJT measures. Finally, because these various sets of correlates are themselves correlated in some instances, the division of variance into these four portions is ambiguous. Nevertheless, we believe this analysis does tell us something valuable about the major question to which this chapter is oriented. It is obvious that SJT, as a method of measurement, can be oriented to the measurement of a variety of constructs such as cognitive ability and personality variables. But it also appears that the SJTs are unique in some way, perhaps most obviously, as measures of the practical use of a variety of information in sometimes ambiguous situations to make good decisions (see the discussion on adaptability and contextual knowledge).

## CONTENT CONSIDERATIONS

The *Standards* suggest that a consideration of the content of a measure can also tell us about its construct validity. In the case of SJTs, their development has usually begun with generation of critical incidents that reflect the important job or academic performance areas. Although this likely makes them valid representations of job-relevant knowledge, skills and abilities, it does not follow that they are measures of the traits usually measured by individual difference psychologists. What they all have in common is that they require that the respondent consider a briefly described situation and indicate what course or action they think best or what they would be most likely (and sometimes least likely) to pursue. So the conclusion that SJTs are measures of some decision-making or judgment dimension that is independent of the nature of the situation seems supported by the manner in which these measures are usually developed and the seemingly diverse content that comprises these items.

A search of the literature on SJTs shows that there is virtually no direct investigation of the relationships linking SJT scores and test content, despite our belief that explicating these relationships is one of the fundamental steps toward obtaining an answer to the question of whether SJT is a method or a construct. In Chan and Schmitt (2005), we provided a detailed review and discussion of SJTs including how our understanding of SJT performance may be enhanced by linking SJT content and the construct–method distinction to the examination of SJT scores. In the following sections, we summarize these issues and relate them to the construct validity issues discussed earlier in this chapter.

The central question in this chapter is whether the SJT is a method of measurement that can be used to assess different constructs or an indicator of an identifiable and meaningful new construct(s) (i.e., situational judgment constructs that are distinct from established constructs such as cognitive ability and personality traits). We think that the answer is "both," in the sense that although SJTs can be construed as a method that can be used to assess different constructs, the core characteristics of the test content of typical SJTs impose constraints on the range of constructs being assessed and the dominant constructs are probably conceptually distinct from established constructs such as cognitive ability and personality traits. Before we elaborate on the arguments to support our position, we need to discuss the efforts to conceptually and empirically disentangle construct and method.

## EFFORTS TO DISENTANGLE CONSTRUCT AND METHOD

For empirical studies to yield findings that would adequately address the general question of whether SJT is a method or construct, we need to deal with a more specific question concerning the method–construct distinction. This more specific question concerns distinguishing between the format of testing used by a given SJT (i.e., the specific test method) and the situation/item content of the SJT (i.e., the intended test construct[s]). This level of distinction between construct and method is important because it allows the researcher to isolate unintended constructs measured by a given SJT and thereby avoid several problems associated with construct contamination.

In Chan and Schmitt (1997), we addressed the specific level distinction between construct and method by comparing a video-based SJT with a written paper-and-pencil version (i.e., two different methods of testing) of the same test. We found that substantially smaller Black–White subgroup difference on the video-based version of this SJT than on the written version (d = −.21 vs. d = −.95 favoring the White group). We also found that part of the Black–White differences in performance across the two different methods of test presentation were attributable to Black–White differences in reading comprehension and reactions to the tests. If the intent is to use this SJT to measure constructs other than reading comprehension, for example, the correlations with reading comprehension would be evidence that the SJT is contaminated. This argument is consistent with the application of Cronbach and Meehl's (1955) criterion on correlations with established variables and Campbell and Fiske's (1959) consideration on low or no correlation with different constructs as evidence of discriminant validity.

We highlighted the importance of making a clear distinction between test construct and test method and showed one way in which sources of variance due to construct versus method can be isolated. However, we recognize that empirical studies in which the impact of construct and method are separately estimable are very difficult to devise especially in field situations, primarily because test methods differ in the ease with which they can be adapted to assess similar test content (Chan & Schmitt, 2005).

## CONCEPT OF DOMINANT CONSTRUCTS AND THE DOMINANT CONSTRUCTS MEASURED BY SJTs

Based on the extant findings on the significant correlations between SJT scores and measures of established constructs including cognitive ability and personality traits, as well as the significant incremental validities of SJTs over the measures of these established constructs, we think we have a tentative answer to the question of whether SJT is a method or a construct. We propose that SJTs, like the interview, be construed as a method of testing that can be used to measure different constructs but that the method places constraints on the range of constructs measured and the dominant constructs are different from those assessed in the interview or with established measures of cognitive ability and personality traits. Like the interview, SJTs have dominant constructs that are readily or almost inherently assessed. We propose that the primary dominant constructs assessed by SJTs are *adaptability constructs* that are likely a function of both individual difference traits and the result of acquisition through previous experiences and a *contextual knowledge construct* that may be gained through experience in various real-world contexts. Collectively, these SJT-dominant constructs can be represented by the global construct called *practical intelligence* (Chan & Schmitt, 2002; Motowidlo et al., 1990; Pulakos, Arad, Donovan, & Plamondon, 2000; Sternberg et al., 2000) or a general judgment factor as we suggested was true earlier in this chapter. We are speculating at this point about the nature of the SJT construct(s), but we believe that the bulk of the theorizing and empirical research supports this speculation. This speculation also seems consistent with the data reported in Table 7.1 in that SJTs seem to be related to a variety of better known constructs, but that they also represent something novel—what we and others variously call adaptability, practical intelligence, contextual knowledge, or simply judgment.

Dominant constructs assessed in the interview are associated with the structural format of the interview which almost dictates that dimensions such as oral communication and person composure dominate. Unlike the interview, SJT-dominant constructs are not associated with the structural format of the SJT but instead are associated with the core characteristics of the test content of typical SJTs. We have proposed three distinct but interrelated core characteristics of SJT content: practical situational demands, multidimensionality of situational response, and criterion-correspondent sampling of situations and response options in test content development (Chan & Schmitt, 2002). For the purpose of this chapter, we discuss only the first two core characteristics, which we believe are related to practical situational demands and multidimensionality, respectively.

## PRACTICAL SITUATIONAL DEMANDS: PRACTICAL INTELLIGENCE, ADAPTABILITY, AND CONTEXTUAL KNOWLEDGE

The content of a typical SJT describes realistic demands found in practical or everyday situations. These practical problems are best understood by contrasting them with academic problems. Academic problems tend to be well-defined, provide complete information, have one correct answer, and are often solvable by only one correct method. Practical problems are ill-defined, incomplete in information provided, do not have one clearly correct answer, and often have multiple "solutions" each with varying degrees of effectiveness as well as different liabilities and assets (Chan, 2000b; Hedlund & Sternberg, 2000). In addition, practical or real-world situational demands on the job often go beyond technical task knowledge to include requirements of contextual knowledge (knowledge of the interpersonal, organizational, and resource environment that affects how work gets accomplished) and adaptability requirements (Chan, 2000a, 2000b; Chan & Schmitt, 2002; Pulakos et al., 2000; Sternberg et al., 2000). Successful SJT performance is defined as overall effectiveness in responses to a variety of these practical situational demands (as indexed by the composite test score) which reflects high levels of contextual knowledge of what to do and how to do it such that one adapts and functions well in the practical situations and contexts (Chan & Schmitt, 2005).

We, and others before us, have argued that SJT performance is a manifestation of these knowledge and ability dimensions, which collectively constitute what Sternberg and his colleagues have called *practical intelligence* (Chan & Schmitt, 2002, 2005; Motowidlo et al., 1990; Sternberg et al., 2000). Practical intelligence refers to the ability or expertise to effectively respond and successfully adapt to a variety of practical problems or situational demands. It also refers to the contextual knowledge acquired from every-day experience and the ability to apply this knowledge effectively in prac-tical situations to achieve personally valued goals (Sternberg et al., 2000). Practical intelligence and contextual knowledge in particular, is typically procedural in nature with an implicit learning/processing quality. The pro-cedural nature refers to the characteristic structure of the knowledge rep-resentation in the form of production rules and the implicit quality refers to the acquisition of these rules from everyday experiences without con-scious or deliberate intention to learn (for details, see Chan & Schmitt, 2005).

Applying Cronbach and Meehl's (1955) criteria on construct validation, we could build on the conceptual definitions of academic intelligence and practical intelligence (and associated constructs such as adaptability and contextual knowledge) to develop a nomological net to be empir-ically tested for predictable and interpretable patterns of correlations linking SJT scores and other established measures. If our analysis of the practical nature of situational demands is correct, we would also expect predictable subgroup differences in SJT scores. For example, criterion groups of individuals who have been independently (of SJT performance) assessed, say by supervisors and peers, as having higher levels of practical intelligence or adaptability should yield higher SJT scores than those assessed as having lower levels. Of course, a com-prehensive theory will also specify how individuals come to achieve a high (or low) level of practical intelligence or adaptability that involves consideration of what Cronbach and Meehl (1955) referred to as process issues.

## MULTIDIMENSIONALITY OF SITUATIONAL RESPONSE

We believe that the response to situations on a typical SJT is multidimen-sional in nature, often even at the level of a single response option to a situation (Chan & Schmitt, 2005). This is consistent with the multidi-mensional nature of the practical intelligence (or adaptability) construct. Because most practical situations are complex, good judgment in these sit-uations is likely to be a function of multiple, more narrowly defined traits and abilities. This may explain the typical findings from SJT studies show-ing relatively low internal consistency estimates of reliability (despite a large number of items) and low test variance accounted for by the single general factor in factor analyses. As we reported earlier in the chapter, identifying multiple interpretable situational judgment dimensions from factor-analytic studies of SJT has been difficult (Chan & Schmitt, 1997, 2002; Motowidlo et al., 1990; Pulakos & Schmitt, 1996). This may be due to the multidimensionality of the response option (i.e., SJT item) itself. In factor analyses of SJT items, researchers explicitly or implicitly assumed a simple structure in the solution (i.e., that each item loads on one and only one factor) when they search for interpretable factors to represent meaningful SJT dimensions. Solutions that allow cross-loadings (i.e., an item is allowed to load on more than one factor) are probably more adequate factorial representations of the SJT content. In other words, factor-analytic solutions need to explicitly model the multidimensionality of the adaptive response (i.e., SJT item) and not just the multidimensionality of the entire test. Unfortunately, unambiguous interpretation of the substantive nature of factors is difficult in the presence of items with cross-loadings. However, this difficulty should not detract us from the importance of considering internal structure as a criterion for construct validity as noted by Cronbach and Meehl (1955) and in the *Standards* (AERA, APA, & NCME, 1999).

## CONCLUSION AND SUGGESTED RESEARCH ISSUES

Throughout this chapter, we have made suggestions for future research that involve a careful analysis of the situation content to understand SJTs, which is one of several major strategies for designing future research to understand and explain what it is that SJTs are measuring (for more details on other strategies and substantive areas for future research on SJTs, see Chan & Schmitt, 2005), We end this chapter by suggesting some other avenues of research that might be pursued based on our analysis of the Cronbach and Meehl (1955) construct validity criteria as well as the discussion in the *Standards*, along with the data discussed in this chapter. We focus on future research directions that might help us arrive at a more conclusive answer to the question of whether SJT is a method, construct, or both.

First, we have little theory or empirical data that relate to the stability of SJTs. What should we expect (i.e., from a theoretical viewpoint) if we request SJT measures of the same persons across time and what would we find (i.e., from empirical studies)? Second, following the logic of convergent and discriminant validities explicated by Campbell and Fiske (1959), it might be helpful to include SJT measures in a multitrait–multimethod matrix to assess the degree to which there is trait (construct) convergence across various methods of measurement or if SJT measures are relatively independent of measures of the same construct assessed in other ways. Third, it might be useful to analyze the response process in SJT performance using verbal protocol analyses or techniques other than self-reports that ascertain what a person considers, thinks, and feels when responding to these situations. Fourth, it is relatively common to find that SJT item stems (and sometimes the options) are complex verbal statements. Some analysis of the reading level of these statements or an evaluation of efforts to simplify these item stems without losing important content may tell us something about potential "contaminants" of SJT measures. Finally, given the complexity and multifaceted nature of SJTs, future meta-analyses involving SJTs will need to be more theory-driven and exercise greater care in coding and aggregating SJT data from multiple studies to allow stronger statements to be made about SJT as method or construct.

Given the extant research, our tentative position that SJT is both method and construct in the sense that although it can be construed as a method that can be used to assess different constructs, the core characteristics of the test content of typical SJTs impose constraints on the range of constructs being assessed and the dominant constructs are probably conceptually distinct from established constructs such as cognitive ability and personality traits. But we stand corrected by future research.

## REFERENCES

American Educational Research Association, American Psychological Association, & National Council on Measurement in Education. (1999). *Standards for educational and psychological testing*. Washington, DC: American Educational Research Association.

Becker, T. E. (2004, April). *Development and validation of a scenario-based measure of employee integrity*. Paper presented at the 19th annual convention of the Society for Industrial and Organizational Psychology, Chicago, IL.

Campbell, D. T., & Fiske, D. W. (1959). Convergent and discriminant validation by the multitrait–multimethod matrix. *Psychological Bulletin, 56*, 81–105.

Chan, D. (2000a). Conceptual and empirical gaps in research on individual adaptation at work. *International Review of Industrial and Organizational Psychology, 15*, 143–164.

Chan, D. (2000b). Understanding adaptation to changes in the work environment: Integrating individual difference and learning perspectives. *Research in Personnel and Human Resources Management, 18*, 1–42.

Chan, D., & Schmitt, N. (1997). Video-based versus paper-and-pencil method of assessment in situational judgment tests. *Journal of Applied Psychology, 82*, 143–159.

Chan, D., & Schmitt, N. (2002). Situational judgment and job performance. *Human Performance, 15*, 233–254.

Chan, D., & Schmitt, N. (2005). Situational judgment tests. In N. Anderson, A. Evers, & O. Voskuijil (Eds.), *Blackwell handbook of selection* (pp. 219–242). Oxford, England: Blackwell.

Clevenger, J., & Haaland, D. E. (2000, April). *Examining the relationship between job knowledge and situational judgment performance*. Paper presented at the 15th annual convention of the Society for Industrial and Organizational Psychology, New Orleans, LA.

Clevenger, J., Pereira, G. M., Wiechmann, D., Schmitt, N., & Schmidt Harvey, V. (2001). Incremental validity of situational judgment tests. *Journal of Applied Psychology, 86*, 410–417.

Cronbach, L. J., & Meehl, P. E. (1955). Construct validity in psychological tests. *Psychological Bulletin, 52*, 281–302.

Gaugler, B. B., Rosenthal, D. B., Thornton, G. C. III, & Bentson, C. (1987). Meta-analyses of assessment center validity. *Journal of Applied Psychology, 72*, 493–511.

Gillespie, M. A., Oswald, F. L., Schmitt, N., Manheim, L., Kim, B. (2002, April). *Construct validation of a situational judgment test of college student success.* Paper presented at the 17th annual convention of the Society for Industrial and Organizational Psychology, Toronto, Canada. April.

Goldberg, L. R. (1999). A broad-bandwidth, public-domain, personality inventory measuring the lower-level facets of several five-factor models. In I. Mervielde, I. Deary, F. DeFruyt, & F. Ostendorf (Eds.), *Personality psychology in Europe* (Vol. 7, pp. 7–28). Tilburg, Netherlands: Tilburg University Press

Guion, R. M. (1998). *Assessment, measurement, and prediction for personnel decisions.* Mahwah, NJ: Lawrence Erlbaum Associates.

Hattie, J. (1985). Methodology review: Assessing unidimensionality of tests and items. *Applied Psychological Measurement, 9*, 139–164.

Hedlund, J., & Sternberg, R. (2000). Practical intelligence: Implications for human resources research. *Research in Personnel and Human Resources Management, 19*, 1–52.

Holland, J. L. (1985). *Making vocational choices: A theory of careers* (2nd Ed.) Englewood Cliffs, NJ: Prentice Hall.

Lievens, F., & Coetsier, P. (2002). Situational tests in student selection: An examination of predictive validity, adverse impact, and construct validity. *International Journal of Selection and Assessment, 10*, 245–257.

McDaniel, M. A., Morgerson, F. P., Finnegan, E. B., Campion, M. A., & Braverman, E. (2001). Use of situational judgment tests to predict job performance: A clarification of the literature. *Journal of Applied Psychology, 86*, 730–740.

McDaniel, M. A., & Nyugen, N. T. (2001). Situational judgment tests: A review of practice and constructs assessed. *International Journal of Selection and Assessment, 9*, 103–113.

McDaniel, M. A., Whetzel, D. L., Schmidt, F. L., & Maurer, S. D. (1994). The validity of the employment interview: A comprehensive review and meta-analysis. *Journal of Applied Psychology, 79*, 599–616.

Motowidlo, S. J., Dunnette, M. D., & Carter, G. W. (1990). An alternative selection procedure: The low-fidelity simulation. *Journal of Applied Psychology, 75*, 640–647.

Nunnally, J. C., & Bernstein, I. H. (1994). *Psychometric theory.* New York: McGraw-Hill.

Oswald, F. L., Schmitt, N., Kim, B. H., Ramsay, L. J., & Gillespie, M. A. (2004). Developing a biodata measure and situational judgment inventory as predictors of college student performance. *Journal of Applied Psychology, 89*, 187–207.

Ployhart, R. E., & Ehrhart, M. G. (2003). Be careful what you ask for: Effects of response instructions on the construct validity and reliability of SJT. *International Journal of Selection and Assessment, 11*, 1–16.

Ployhart, R. E., Porr, W., & Ryan, A. M. (2004, April). *New development in SJTs: Scoring, coaching, and incremental validity.* Paper presented at the 19th annual convention of the Society for Industrial and Organizational Psychology, Chicago, IL.

Pulakos, E. D., Arad, S., Donovan, M. A., & Plamondon, K. E. (2000). Adaptability in the workplace: Development of a taxonomy of adaptive performance. *Journal of Applied Psychology, 85*, 612–624.

Pulakos, E. D., & Schmitt, N. (1996). An evaluation of two strategies for reducing adverse impact and their effects on criterion-related validity. *Human Performance, 9*, 241–258.

Pulakos, E. D., Schmitt, N., & Keenan, P. A. (1994). *Validation and implementation of the FBI special agent entry-level selection system.* Alexandria, VA: Human Resources Research Organization (FR-PRD-94-20).

Schmidt, F. L., & Hunter, J. E. (1993). Tacit knowledge, practical intelligence, general ability, and job knowledge. *Current directions in psychological science, 2,* 7–8.

Schmidt, F. L., & Hunter, J. E. (1998). The validity and utility of selection methods n personnel psychology: Practical and theoretical implications of 85 years of research findings. *Psychological Bulletin, 124,* 262–274.

Schmidt, F. L., Hunter, J. E., & Urry, V. (1976). Statistical power in criterion-related validation studies. *Journal of Applied Psychology, 61,* 473–485.

Schmitt, N., & Chan, D. (1998). *Personnel selection: A theoretical approach.* Thousand Oaks, CA: Sage.

Schmitt, N., Clause, C. S., & Pulakos, E. D. (1996). Subgroup differences associated with different measures of some common job-relevant constructs. In C. R. Cooper & I. T. Robertson (Eds.), *International review of industrial and organizational psychology* (Vol. 11, pp. 115–140). New York: Wiley.

Smith, K. C., & McDaniel, M. A. (1998, April). *Criterion and construct validity evidence for a situational judgment measure.* Paper presented at the 13th annual convention of the Society for Industrial and Organizational Psychology, Dallas, TX.

Sternberg, R. J., Forsythe, G. B., Hedlund, J., Horvath, J. A., Wagner, R. K., Williams, W. M., Snook, A. A., & Grigorenko, E. L. (2000). *Practical intelligence in everyday life.* Cambridge, UK: Cambridge University Press.

Weekley, J. A., & Jones, C. (1997). Video-based situational testing. *Personnel Psychology, 50,* 25–50.

Weekley, J. A., & Jones, C. (1999). Further studies of situational tests. *Personnel Psychology, 52,* 679–700.

# 8

# On the Development of Situational Judgment Tests: Issues in Item Development, Scaling, and Scoring

Jeff A. Weekley
*Kenexa*

Robert E. Ployhart
*University of South Carolina*

Brian C. Holtz
*University of Calgary*

Although situational judgment tests (SJTs) have been around for more than 80 years (McDaniel, Morgeson, Finnegan, Campion, & Braverman, 2001), they have only recently begun to garner serious research attention. Given such sporadic research focus, it is not surprising that there is no consensus on how such measures should be developed, scaled, or scored. Indeed, as increasingly more research examines SJTs, an increasing number of varied means of developing, scaling, and scoring such measures are being used. In this chapter, we examine various issues regarding the development of SJTs. Specifically, these issues include determination of both the (a) item stem and (b) response option, (c) the effect of response instructions, (d) methods for determining the effectiveness of responses, (e) and methods for scoring SJTs. Table 8.1 provides an overview of the various issues

**TABLE 8.1**

An Overview of SJT Development, Scaling, and Scoring Alternatives and Issues

|  | \multicolumn{4}{c}{*SJT Development Issues*} | |
| --- | --- | --- | --- | --- |
|  | *Item-Stem Content* | *Response-Option Content* | *Response Instructions* | *Response Effectiveness* | *Scoring Methods* |
| Alternatives | Origin (source) | Origin (source) Construct-based | Would do vs. Should do | Subject matter experts Empirical Keying | Forced choice Continuous (Likert) |
|  | Complexity Fidelity Content | Complexity Fidelity Fakability |  | Theory Hybrids |  |

considered in this chapter. As becomes apparent, there is currently little systematic research on any of these topics and, as a result, there are many gaps in the SJT literature. Consensus regarding optimal SJT development methods, of course, is a prerequisite to establishing SJTs as a means to measure a specific construct.

## DETERMINING ITEM-STEM CONTENT

The bases for any SJT are the situations, or item stems, presented to the examinee. There are four key issues to consider when developing item stems (or situations). These include (a) the origin or source used to determine the item stems (including whether the item stems are designed to target particular constructs) (b) the complexity of the item stems, (c) the fidelity of the item stems, and (d) the content of the item stems.

### Origin of Stem Development

The first issue concerns the source from which the item-stem content is derived. From our literature review, there are at two general methods that have been used to develop item stems: critical incidents and theory-based methods. These correspond roughly to inductive and deductive test development methods.

The critical incident method (Flanagan, 1954) is by far the most common approach used to identify the content of SJT item stems (see also Motowidlo, Hanson, & Crafts, 1997). In the typical critical incident method, subject matter experts (SMEs; e.g., incumbents and supervisors of incumbents) are asked to recall exceptionally good and exceptionally poor examples of performance. In most cases, the three-part or antecedent–behavior–consequence (A–B–C) format is used, where an antecedent is what led up to the incident, behavior refers to what the person actually did that was effective or ineffective, and consequence describes what happened as a result of the person's behavior. The antecedent provides the impetus for the item stem and the actual behavior can become one of the response options (discussed in next section).

Critical incidents have typically been collected from incumbents and/or supervisors. However, it is not always clear why incumbents or supervisors are chosen, and often the choice is made without consideration of differences in their perspectives. This leads one to wonder if the two groups might generate different situations. For example, retail incumbents might focus more on customer-oriented situations, whereas supervisors might focus more on policy compliance situations. Other sources might provide even more unique incidents that cover work behaviors from a different perspective. Developers of SJTs for managerial positions, for example, might benefit by collecting critical incidents from direct reports. Employees who report to managers undoubtedly have many recollections of good and poor managerial performance of which managers may not be aware. Direct reports may provide unique insights not identified as critical incidences by the managers themselves. Similarly, an SJT for a sales or customer service job may be enhanced by collecting incidents from customers. Behaviors that incumbents and/or supervisors perceive as effective might be perceived negatively by some customers. Future research should determine whether the source of critical incidents used in SJT development matters and, if so, which of the key stakeholders should be used under what conditions.

Critical incidents have also been harvested from archival sources. In his study of aviation judgment, Hunter (2003) used accident reports to identify challenging situations encountered by pilots. Particularly where events are recorded for other purposes (e.g., accident reports, insurance investigative reports, after action reports), archival records should be a rich source of incidents on which an SJT might be based.

The second approach to stem development is to write the SJT items to reflect some underlying model, be it a set of competencies, attributes identified from a job analysis, review of the literature, or theory as to important determinants of effective performance. Already in the literature are several attempts to develop items stems to measure a particular set of homogeneous constructs, dimensions, or competencies. For example, Stevens and Campion (1994, 1999) used such an approach in developing the Teamwork KSA test; essentially an SJT designed to assess teamwork knowledge, skills, and abilities (KSAs). The items for this test were based on an extensive review of the literature regarding the types of KSAs necessary for effective teamwork.

Motowidlo, Dunnette, and Carter (1990) attempted to develop an SJT around two dimensions—interpersonal skills and problem-solving skills. The authors did so by soliciting critical incidents from incumbents related to these two areas. Reynolds, Winter, and Scott (1999) used a similar approach in developing an SJT for professional jobs. From job-analysis interviews and surveys, these authors identified dimensions important for this job family and directed incumbents and managers to provide critical incidents relevant to the dimensions. Many other examples of model-driven SJT development exist (e.g., Arad, Borman, & Pulakos, 1999; Gillespie, Oswald, Schmitt, Manheim, & Kim, 2002; Kim, Schmitt, Oswald, Gillespie, & Ramsay, 2003).

One variation of this theme has been for the test developer to write the situations, without the help of critical incidents, to fit a conceptual model. Stevens and Campion (1999), as mentioned, identified five dimensions of teamwork and wrote items to fit these dimensions. Arad et al. (1999) had experienced psychologists write situations that required adaptive performance in the eight dimensions underlying their model. Similarly, Becker (2004) developed an SJT to measure integrity by writing items to reflect the seven values that his theoretical model indicated underlie integrity (benevolence, honesty, independence, justice, productivity, pride, and rationality). It is important to note that although numerous attempts have been made to develop SJTs around constructs or competencies, few of these developers have sought to create subscores reflecting these dimensions. Probably due to the multidimensionality and poor psychometric characteristics of the subscales, most have instead collapsed across items to create an overall SJT score.

Which of these sources of stem content may be considered "best" or most efficient is open to study. Critical incident methods provide a rich source of information, but they are also expensive and time-consuming to collect. Model-based methods seem promising, but a major limitation is the lack of theory about work situations (and situationally based theories in general; Frederickson, 1972). Research comparing these and related approaches would be helpful. Despite this, there are several advantages to construct-driven approaches. Where a thorough job analysis exists, indicating several behavioral dimensions as being important to job performance, SJT developers would be well advised to consider this information when creating the content for their SJTs. Devising items to reflect specific dimensions that are identified through an analysis of job requirements helps ensure the representativeness and job-relatedness of the resulting measure. Furthermore, as SJT development methods become more refined, it may be possible to develop SJTs that capture unique dimensional constructs.

At present, developing a model, from theory or job analyses, and then collecting critical incidents from a variety of sources to fit the model, would appear to be the most comprehensive means of developing SJT stems. The issue of whether or not SJTs benefit psychometrically from being based on a model is an important area for future research.

## Stem Complexity

The second issue concerns the degree of complexity, detail, and specificity in the item stem (McDaniel & Nguyen, 2001). Although some SJTs have relatively simple item stems, others are lengthy and have quite detailed descriptions of situations—indeed, some have used branching techniques, with multiple "subsituations" being based on a common "primary situation" (see Table 8.2 for an example). Some SJT researchers have theorized that more specific items would be more valid (McDaniel et al., 2001; Reynolds, Sydell, Scott, & Winter, 2000). Unlike many predictors, which are "signs" of performance (Wernimont & Campbell, 1968), highly specific SJTs are thought to be more a "sample" of performance because the items are sampled directly from the performance domain they are designed to predict. As Chan and Schmitt (2002) and Lievens, Buyse, and Sackett (2005) noted, the high degree of correspondence between the test content and criterion domain may explain much of the validity of SJTs. Research on the comparative validity of specific versus general SJTs has been mixed. Contrary to their expectations, McDaniel et al.'s (2001) meta-analysis indicated that more detailed SJTs showed lower criterion-related validity than did relatively general SJTs. On the other hand, Reynolds et al. (1999) examined specificity within their instrument at the item level and found that specific items were more valid and generalizable across cultures than were less specific items. In a follow-up study, Reynolds et al. (2000) replicated their results and again found that more specific items had greater validity than did relatively general items. Highly detailed and specific stems may also have the advantage of greater face validity and more positive test-taker reactions, although this issue remains to be researched.

One of the implications of complexity was illustrated by Sacco and colleagues (Sacco, Scheu, Ryan, & Schmitt, 2000; Sacco, Schmidt, & Rogg, 2000), who showed reading level to be related to subgroup differences in SJT performance. In two separate studies, these researchers found various reading-level indices were significantly related to Black–White, Asian–White, and Hispanic–White differences in SJT performance. In one of the studies, they also found some support for the notion that reading-ability differences accounted for some of the race differences in SJT performance and item validity. The SJTs used in these studies were relatively complex, presenting the respondent with a situation, several subsituations

**TABLE 8.2**

Examples of SJT Items and Instructions

|  | *Example SJT* |
|---|---|
| Low-complexity SJT item | A customer asks for a specific brand of merchandise the store doesn't carry. How would you respond to the customer? |

a. Tell the customer which stores carry that brand, but point out that your brand is similar.

b. Ask the customer more questions so you can suggest something else.

c. Tell the customer that the store carries the highest quality merchandise available.

d. Ask another associate to help

e. Tell the customer which stores carry that brand.

High-complexity SJT item[a]

[Situation]:
Your organization purchased an applicant-tracking software package a couple of months back and it is finally up and running. You have just been assigned to coordinate the team responsible for training recruiters to use the program. The recruiting season starts in 3 weeks and your supervisor has informed you that all recruiters must be trained and proficient in the new software before the season starts.

[Subsituation]:
One of the trainers assigned to your team informs you that he is scheduled for 7 days of medical leave starting the next week. The trainer scheduled the medical leave months ago to allow recovery time for a minor surgical procedure. Rate the effectiveness of the following responses.

[Items]:

1. Ask your supervisor for another trainer to replace the individual going on leave.
2. Inform the trainer that he is responsible for finding a co-worker to fill in in his absence.

(continued)

**TABLE 8.2**

|  |  |
|---|---|
|  | 3. Inform your supervisor that you will not be able to train all recruiters before the season starts because you are short one trainer for an entire week. |
| Should do/knowledge instructions | Which of the options above do you believe is the *best* under the circumstances? Which of the options above do you believe is the *worst* under the circumstances? |
| Would do/behavioral tendency instructions[b] | You are in a large lecture class where attendance is not mandatory. The class meets once a week. The class is not interesting, and all of the notes are provided on the Web. |

1. Which one of the following *would you most likely* do?———
2. Which one of the following *would you least likely* do?———

    (A) Skip class all semester and just show up for the exams.
    (B) Attend class every other week.
    (C) Attend class every week.
    (D) Find a friend and take turns going to class.

Behaviorally uniform response options[c]

You are talking to some customers and promise to call them the next day. However, after they leave you realize you have the next 3 days off. What do you do?

A. Call the customers immediately and tell them you won't be able to contact them for 3 days.
B. Call the customers later and tell them you won't be able to contact them for 3 days.
C. Call the customers after you return from your 3 days off.
D. Wait until the customers call you back.

[a] From Sacco et al. (2000), with permission.
[b] From Ployhart and Ehrhart (2003), with permission.
[c] From Ployhart et al. (2004), with permission.

(extending the previous situation), and multiple response-options. That reading-level effects were observed at the item-stem level, and not the response-option level, suggest that only the greater detail and complexity in the former were reflected in reading-level ability effects. Importantly, they projected that reducing the reading grade level of the situations would have reduced race differences on one SJT by more than 30%. In a third study, using simpler and shorter situations, subgroup differences were quite small (e.g., $d = .07$) and unrelated to reading-level indices.

Because one of the attractions to SJT testing has been the typically smaller subgroup differences observed (at least relative to cognitive ability), this represents an important line of research and one worthy of continued exploration. Although it appears reading level accounts for some of the cognitive load of SJTs, and therefore some of the subgroup difference observed, the impact of reading level on criterion-related validity is less clear. Future research should continue to examine the interrelationships between item specificity/complexity, reading level, subgroup differences, cognitive ability, and validity. Specific guidance on the best way to write situations (e.g., at what reading level, the maximum length of sentences/situations, etc.) to maximize validity while minimizing subgroup differences should find a wide audience among SJT developers. Unfortunately, we are a long way from being able to provide such guidance, although the theories and models described in chap. 2–6 may help in this regard.

## Stem Fidelity

Another related issue pertains to the degree of fidelity in the item stem. Fidelity typically refers to the degree of realism in the item or the degree to which it realistically recreates the task requirements of the job itself (e.g., Hanson, Borman, Mogilka, & Manning,1999; Motowidlo et al., 1997). There is a distinction between physical fidelity (e.g., does the test require the same types of behavioral operations as tasks performed on the job?) and psychological fidelity (e.g., does the test require the same types of cognitive operations as tasks performed on the job?). Goldstein, Zedeck, and Schneider (1993) noted psychological fidelity is the critical type of fidelity. Fortunately, SJTs tend to be at least moderate on both types of fidelity.

We do not provide a comprehensive review of this literature because this topic is covered in depth by Olson-Buchanan and Drasgow (chap. 12, this volume). The important point to recognize for now is that differences in response formats, such as paper-and-pencil, computerized, Internet, and so on, may produce differences in responses. Changing the fidelity of the stem from written to video format may not only affect physical fidelity but also psychological fidelity. As one implication of this, Chan and Schmitt (1997) showed how converting an SJT from paper to video reduced Black–White subgroup differences in test performance.

## Stem Content

The last issue concerns the content of SJT item stems. Many SJTs appear to focus on interpersonal situations, but there is no reason they could not be used to assess procedural knowledge. For example, where incumbents are expected to follow an established procedure (e.g., troubleshooting a failed car engine given certain "symptoms" or diagnosing the cause of a computer crash), SJTs could be used to assess mastery of the procedural knowledge. By expanding beyond interpersonal situations into more factual contexts, SJTs could be used as training certification assessments and, in the case of well-established crafts, as job knowledge-based selection tools (see Fritzsche, Stagl, Salas, & Burke, chap. 14, this volume).

In essence, what we are talking about is the construct validity of the SJT (and how this is affected by the nature of the item stem). Many of the chapters in this book address this issue in some detail. Therefore, we do not belabor the point here other than to recognize that what the SJT measures may influence how we measure it—and vice versa.

## DETERMINING RESPONSE OPTIONS

A second set of issues related to the development of SJTs concerns the creation of response options. In most SJTs, the item stem is followed by anywhere from 3 to 12 (or even more) possible means of handling the situation. Issues in response-option development include (a) the origin (source) of the response options, (b) construct-based response options, (c) the complexity in response options, (d) the fidelity of response options, and (e) "fakability" or the degree of transparency in the effectiveness of the options presented.

## Origin of Response Options

In terms of the origin of response options, in most cases, SMEs are used to generate alternative courses of action to a given situation (e.g., Motowidlo et al., 1997). In other cases (e.g., Stevens & Campion, 1999; Weekley & Jones, 1999; Weekley & Ployhart, 2005) the SJT developers wrote most of the options. At present, no empirical research has examined the issue of whether SME-generated SJTs are any different from those developed by the test developer—we simply do not know which might be better, or if it makes any difference at all. However, there are at least two advantages to using SMEs in all stages of SJT development. First, the realism of the SJT stems and response options is likely to be higher. Having experience in the situations presented, SMEs are less likely to identify options that are unrealistic. Second, a large group of SMEs can generate a large pool of different possible responses to a given situation. As some SJTs have included as many as 20 possible responses to a given situation (e.g., Wagner & Sternberg, 1985), having a large group of people with varying perspectives is likely to make the generation of such a large number of different options easier. If SMEs are not used to write the response options, they should be used to review them for realism, reasonableness, and the like.

## Construct-Based Response Options

Construct-based response options have been used when the test developer seeks to create an SJT where the options represent indicators of particular constructs. Keep in mind that most SJTs only provide an overall score; even those designed to target particular constructs tend not to report homogenous subscale scores. So beyond trying to write the item stem to target a particular construct, one may also try to write the response options to target particular constructs (see Motowidlo et al., chap. 4 and Stremmler & Sternberg, chap. 6, this volume).

Trippe and Foti (2003) and Motowidlo, Diesch, and Jackson (2003) attempted to develop SJTs to measure traits of the Big Five framework. Trippe and Foti, for example, developed an SJT to measure conscientiousness, agreeableness, and openness. They wrote the response options so that each represented a different level of the trait of interest and arrayed them on a continuous 4-point scale. Despite the careful development, their results showed that method factors accounted for a larger proportion of the variance in the SJT items than in traditional personality-type items. Similarly, Motowidlo et al. (2003) wrote response options to represent both high and low levels of agreeableness, extraversion, and conscientiousness. Their results demonstrated that individuals' level of these traits were positively and negatively related to endorsing response options designed to express high and low levels of the traits, respectively.

Ployhart and colleagues (Ployhart & Ryan, 2000; Porr & Ployhart, 2004) took a slightly different approach to the issue by examining the issue of behavioral uniformity in a couple of studies. Because most SJT development efforts rely on SMEs to generate response options, a wide variety of different behaviors are typically identified as possible means of handling a given situation. The wide variation in behaviors embedded in the response options ensures the multidimensional nature of the final measure. As an alternative, Ployhart and Ryan (2000) developed an SJT in which the response options lay on a behavioral continuum, with different options reflecting slightly different forms of the same behavior (see Table 8.2 for an example). By aligning the behaviors along a continuum, Ployhart and Ryan sought to increase the construct orientation of the final measure. Their results showed this SJT to be moderately related to neuroticism, agreeableness, and conscientiousness, but not to cognitive ability. In a subsequent study, Porr and Ployhart (2004) employed the same SJT, along with a traditionally developed SJT (i.e., one with multiple behaviors reflected in the response options), in a customer service context. Their results found the construct-oriented SJT provided incremental prediction over the traditional SJT, and vice versa, suggesting there may be some important validity benefits for adopting a construct-oriented approach.

Finally, Beauregard (2000) sought to develop an SJT capable of measuring specific constructs. In addition to ensuring that each of the response options, rated on a Likert-type scale, represented a single behavior, he had SMEs sort the response options into categories representing an a priori set of constructs. Scores for each response option were determined by computing the absolute difference between the examinee's ratings and those of a different group of SMEs. Construct scores were then created by summing the response options judged as being related to that construct. Note that what is unique about Beauregard's (2000) approach is that response options are aggregated across situational stems. His data showed good internal consistency reliabilities for some constructs, but not for others. Further research using this approach is needed to determine if summing response options from different stems is a reasonable approach to construct measurement.

As noted earlier, response options are usually derived from SMEs without much reference to specific constructs. Although there have been attempts to write SJTs that target constructs (e.g., Ployhart & Ryan, 2000; Trippe & Foti, 2003; Wagner & Sternberg, 1985), more studies need to compare construct-based response options to those derived from the critical incidents methodology. Therefore, at this point we simply do not know the extent to which construct-based response options are desirable. Continued research that focuses directly on manipulating response content with the goal of having different responses measure different constructs and comparing such an approach to the traditional method is warranted.

## Complexity

Issues of complexity and specificity in response options have received a little recent attention in the literature. In the Sacco et al. (2000) research, the stem-level reading effects were not observed at the level of the response option. This means the driver of subgroup differences was coming from the item stem, not the response options. We are aware of no other research that has systematically examined the impact of highly detailed and specific responses versus less detailed and more general responses. In keeping with previous thinking, it would seem reasonable to expect that more detailed and specific response options might have greater local validity and less generalizability. For example, responses that use a lot of jargon or organization-specific procedures are unlikely to be transportable to other organizations. For that matter, there may be important cultural differences in response options in terms of what is a plausible alternative (see Lievens, chap. 13, this volume). Again, there is a need for research that systematically manipulates the complexity characteristics of response options.

## Fidelity of Response Options

Similar to issues noted on the fidelity of item stems, one may also consider the fidelity of response options. For example, one could present a video-based SJT that shows the situations in video, but has the response options presented on paper. In this case, the item stem is video but the response options are written. Alternatively, one might have both the situation and response options presented on video (although the applicant would most likely have to remember the options to make a response on an answer sheet). As we noted in the section on fidelity of item stems, Olson-Buchannon and Drasgow (chap. 12, this volume) discuss these issues in detail and we refer readers to their chapter for more information on various response formats.

## Fakability

One potential downside to the use of behaviorally uniform response options concerns the degree of transparency in those options. The issue of transparency is not limited, however, to SJTs developed using behaviorally uniform response options. The issue of the "fakability" of SJTs has only recently begun to receive research attention and the mixed results suggest that different SJTs used thus far have varying degrees of transparency in their response option sets (see Hooper, Cullen, and Sackett, chap. 10, this volume for a review of this literature). Importantly, we believe the degree of fakability has very much to do with the manner in which the SJT's response options are developed and selected for inclusion. In other words, the test developer may control the degree of fakability in SJTs and could conceivably create an SJT resistant to faking by including only response options of comparable social desirability. For example, in a study by Olson-Buchanan, et al. (1998), the response options ultimately used were selected from a larger pool if they were "reasonably socially desirable." Conversely, if the social desirability or appropriateness of the options is dramatically different, the fakability of the measure should increase. One as yet untried approach might to be to borrow from the performance appraisal literature the logic of mixed standard scales (Blanz & Ghiselli, 1972). That is, one might present two "positive" items, matched in social desirability but only one predictive of performance, and two negative items, again matched in desirability but only one predictive. Research on the fakability of SJTs must begin to consider the content of the SJT itself before substantial progress can be made.

## RESPONSE INSTRUCTIONS

One issue that has garnered a fair amount of research attention has been the effects of response instructions on SJTs (McDaniel, Hartman & Grubb, 2003; McDaniel & Nguyen, 2001; Nguyen, Biderman, & McDaniel, 2003; Ployhart & Ehrhart, 2003). Essentially, response instructions for SJTs have been of two types: behavioral tendency or "would do" instructions and knowledge or "should do" instructions. With *behavioral tendency* instructions, the test taker is asked to express his or her behavioral intentions or what he or she would do (or would not do) given the situation. *Knowledge* or "should do" instructions, on the other hand, ask the test taker to identify the correct or best course of action given the situation. The latter have also been referred to as "knowledge" instructions because the ability to identify the correct/incorrect responses is reliant on job knowledge and cognitive ability (Nguyen et al., 2003).

Ployhart and Ehrhart (2003) examined the effects of six different types of SJT instructions in terms of reliability and validity. Their results indicated asking what one would do showed more favorable characteristics than asking what one should do. Not only were criterion-related validities substantially more favorable in the "would do" conditions, but correlations between these two types were relatively low despite the fact that the same items were used in both conditions. McDaniel and Nguyen

(2001) hypothesized that the knowledge-based response format (pick the best/worst) would be more resistant to faking than the behavioral tendency (would/would not do) format because the former assess *knowledge* of procedure, fact, or concept, knowledge which is more difficult to fake. Nguyen et al. (2003) examined this hypothesis and determined that knowledge instructions were more resistant to faking and had a stronger relationship with cognitive ability than did behavioral tendency instructions. Finally, McDaniel et al. (2003) conducted a meta-analysis of 62 validity coefficients (41 knowledge instructions and 21 behavioral tendency instructions) and concluded that response instructions impacted the constructs measured by SJTs. Specifically, they found that knowledge-based instructions had higher criterion-related validities than did behavioral tendency instructions. Furthermore, SJTs employing knowledge instructions were more highly correlated with cognitive ability than behavioral tendency-based SJTs, whereas the latter were more strongly related to personality constructs (conscientiousness, agreeableness, and emotional stability) than knowledge-based SJTs.

Almost all research with SJTs has been based on concurrent validation designs (McDaniel et al., 2001), and this is true of the McDaniel et al. (2003) meta-analysis on the effects of response instructions. As Weekley and Jones (1999) noted, there is reason to suspect that these findings will not generalize to an applicant setting. It seems unlikely that an applicant motivated to secure employment would select, under behavioral tendency instructions, as his or her course of action an option other than the one he or she believed to be the best. For the same results reported earlier to be observed, applicants would have to admit that what they would do is different from what they believe they should do (see also McDaniel, Hartman, Nguyen, & Grubb, chap. 9; Motowidlo et al., chap. 4, this volume). Research in applicant settings is needed to determine if response instructions have a significant impact on SJT measurement properties.

## DETERMINING RESPONSE EFFECTIVENESS

At least three different methods for determining the effectiveness of various response options have been explored in the literature: SMEs, empirical keying, and theory. A number of studies have compared these various methods (e.g., Krokos, Meade, Cantwell, Pond, & Wilson, 2004; MacLane, Barton, Holloway-Lundy, & Nickles, 2001; Paullin & Hanson, 2001; Weekley & Jones, 1997, 1999). Drawing heavily on the biodata literature, these researchers have compared SJT empirical scoring keys, using various weighting methods, with one another and with rationally derived keys. MacLane et al. (2001), for example, compared an empirical key (developed using a correlational method) with a rational key developed using a large group of SMEs within a governmental agency. Their results showed the two keys to have very similar levels of validity (indeed, the two keys correlated at $r = .84$) and they echoed Weekley and Jones' (1999) conclusion that empirical keying offered no real advantages over rationally developed keys, at least in terms of validity. Similarly, Paullin and Hanson (2001) compared a rationally scored SJT with a series of empirical keys developed using the following empirical keying methods: vertical percent method, horizontal percent method, correlational method, and mean criterion method. On cross-validation, they found no difference between the various empirical keying methods (median validities across different criteria/empirical keying methods varied by .03) or between empirically keyed and rationally derived key validities.

Bergman, Drasgow, Donovan, and Juraska (2003) compared scoring keys developed rationally, empirically, and theoretically for a leadership SJT (they also included a fourth group of hybrid keys or keys developed by combining the methods mentioned previously). Their results showed the SME and empirical keys to both be related to performance and incrementally so over cognitive ability and personality. Although none of the theory-based keys had significant criterion-related validity, one hybrid theory key (crediting as correct both the theory-based and the empirically derived answers) was significantly related to performance. Interestingly, although the empirical key was moderately related to one SME based key ($r = .54$) it was unrelated to another based on the modal responses of novices versus experts. Krokos et al. (2004) also compared five empirical keying methods with a rationally derived key. Their results showed only one of the empirical keys (based on the correlational method) to hold up on cross-validation. The rationally derived key was not related to the criterion. Finally, Such and Schmidt (2004) examined the effectiveness of empirically keying versus rationally scoring an SJT across four different cultures. Using the vertical percent method, their results showed a slight advantage for the empirical key (e.g., $r = .35$) over the rational key (e.g., $r = .29$). Importantly, they found an average correlation of .70 between the empirical and rational keys across four cross-validation samples.

For the most part, these studies have shown that empirically derived and SME-based keys are roughly equivalent in terms of validity, even though the correlations between the two keys are not always large. The fact that two similar measures show similar validity but low intercorrelations may suggest they measure different constructs, or capture different parts of the criterion space. Alternatively, it may simply be the case that more than one item stem is "correct" and the different scoring methods identify the

different but equally correct answers. These results are somewhat inconsistent and surprising and need to be explored in future research. Given
that the large samples required to empirically key an SJT might often be
unavailable, that SMEs represent a reasonable alternative is good news.
Rather than merely transporting from the biodata literature the issue of
which empirical weighing method works best in SJT scoring, we suggest
future research also consider whether different groups of SMEs might yield
rational keys of varying validity.

The SMEs used to develop rational scoring keys have variously been
incumbents (Pulakos & Schmitt, 1996), supervisors of incumbents in the
target job (e.g., Reynolds et al., 1999; Weekley & Ployhart, 2005), trainers
(Hunter, 2003), customers (e.g., Weekley & Jones, 1997), unidentified "experts" (Sinar, Paquet, & Scott, 2002), and even "nonexperts" (Legree, 1995).
For example, in a study of a video-based SJT to be used to select employees to work in nursing homes, family members of residents were used to
develop a rational scoring key by identifying the courses of action they
would prefer the employees take (Weekley & Jones, 1997). This key was
significantly related to performance and moderately related to an empirically derived key for the same items ($r = .48$ and $.53$, respectively). Hunter
(2003) had certified flight instructors identify the best response options
in his SJT of aviation judgment. Legree (1995), based on the assumption
that the common variance in observed scores is expert variance while the
unique variance in the same scores is nonexpert variance, argued that an
SJT can be effectively scored by simply surveying large numbers of nonexperts.

Interestingly, although SMEs are the foundation of most SJT scoring
protocols, there has been little systematic research regarding SMEs. This is
unfortunate because it would appear likely that different groups of SMEs
would develop different keys (e.g., would identify different response options as most and least effective). To the extent different types of SMEs
derive different rational keys, the selection of the SME group may go a
long way toward determining who gets hired by the organization. Utilizing senior-level executives, for example, could help ensure that the organization's dominant cultural values are reflected in the scoring key. On the
other hand, using customers as SMEs could help ensure that those hired
subsequently behave in ways the customers' prefer. Finally, incumbents
as SMEs could well identify a key that reflects the prevailing performance
management and reward systems. That these keys could all be different
seems likely. Continuing the above example, an SJT for sales people that
is scored against customer preferences might have various high-pressure
sales tactics as the poor courses of action, even though the incumbents
know that such tactics work and result in higher sales. Again, research that

compares various groups of SMEs and the effects their perspective has on the scoring of SJTs would be insightful. The issue of who constitutes a "subject matter expert" is an important one worthy of additional research.

The third and least frequently used means of developing scoring keys is to rely on theory. In the previously described Bergman et al. (2003) study, the researchers scored an SJT on the basis of two leadership theories; initiation of structure versus empowerment and Vroom's decision model (Vroom, 2000, Vroom & Yetton; 1973; ). Unfortunately, neither key was related to performance. In contrast, Olson-Buchanan et al. (1998) found a key based on theory was predictive of conflict-management performance, albeit less so than an empirically derived key. Finally, Stevens and Campion's (1999) SJT of teamwork was dichotomously scored, with the correct answer "determined from findings in the research literature." This SJT was found to be significantly related to performance in a couple of studies. Research is needed to better understand when theory-based approaches will result in higher/lower validity and such research will undoubtedly lead to refinement in theory.

## SCORING METHODS

Once the effectiveness of the response options has been determined, it is still necessary to compare test takers' choices to these judgments in some fashion in order to determine how well the test takers did on the SJT. That is, one may know the effectiveness of different options, but how to combine those options and items to create an overall score poses a new issue. Two broad categories of methods have been used: forced-choice methods and continuous or Likert-type-scale methods. In the simplest of forced-choice methods, one response is designated "correct" and all others as incorrect. This enables the SJT to be scored as an ability test would be scored, with each item receiving 1 point if the "correct" response option was chosen and no points if one of the distracters was chosen. This simple approach has been used successfully in several studies (e.g., Hunter, 2003; O'Connell, Doverspike, Norris-Watts, & Hattrup, 2001; Sinar et al., 2002; Stevens & Campion, 1999). For example, Hunter developed an SJT for general aviation pilots using the "pick best" scoring format and found it to be related to the number of hazardous aviation events experienced and with the certification level of the pilot groups (e.g., commercial pilots scored higher than did student pilots). Also using a "pick best" format, Hanson et al. (1999) recognized that not all "wrong" answers are equally poor. They scored their SJT by assigning each response option its mean effectiveness rating (from SMEs). In effect, this gives examinees "partial credit" for choosing answers, other than the best, that were still better than the worst answer (see also Legree, 1995). Additional research on this innovative approach is warranted.

Motowidlo et al. (1990) extended this approach and had test takers identify the best and worst (or the most/least likely) courses of action to each situation. Under this method, scores on each item can range from +2 to −2 and are calculated as follows:

1. To receive a +2, a person would have to choose as the *best* response the designated "best" answer and as the *worst* response the designated "worst" answer (i.e., get both right).
2. To receive a −2, a person would have to chose as the *best* response the designated "worst" answer and as the *worst* response the designated "best" answer (i.e., get both wrong).
3. A +1 was received if the respondent successfully identified either the designated "best" or "worst" answers, but not both.
4. A −1 was indicated if the respondent chose as the *best* response the designated "worst" answer or chose as the *worst* response the designated "best" answer, but not both.
5. A 0 was received by those choosing distracters for both questions.

The score for each item is the sum of the points received from responses to the best and worst questions and a total test score is created by summing across the situational items.

There are a number of advantages to this approach over the simple "pick the best/most likely" approach. First, assessing responses using the best/most likely and worst/least likely approach tends to increase the variance in any one item score (e.g., Weekley, Harding, Creglow, & Ployhart, 2004). Increased variance could increase the potential validity of the SJT. Second, there is some evidence the correlates of the "pick best/most likely" responses are different than the correlates of the "pick worst/least likely" responses. For example, Cucina, Vasilopoulos, and Leaman (2003) separately summed most likely and least likely responses and found the former to be more strongly related to the Big Five personality factors than the least likely responses. Furthermore, using separate measures of most and least likely responses enabled these researchers to account for more variance in the criterion than a single SJT score based on the combination of the two (i.e., scored in the manner first prescribed by Motowidlo et al., 1990). In a related study, McElreath and Vasilopoulos (2002) found least likely responses to be more highly related to cognitive ability than were most likely responses. Although these results bear replication, they may help explain the multidimensionality inherent in most SJTs. If these findings are robust, they may also expand the potential criterion space SJTs could tap into, again increasing the potential validity of SJTs. Furthermore, to the extent that this format taps into different job-relevant attributes, some of the answer in our search for construct measurement with SJTs may lie in how these data are combined. Accumulating separately within "pick best/most likely" and "pick worst/least likely" responses may result in potentially more homogeneous measures of different constructs than the multidimensional measure typically resulting from accumulations across these questions. Additional research is needed on this issue: whether knowing what to do is fundamentally different than knowing what not to do; whether what one is most likely to do indicates meaningfully different information than what one is least likely to do.

Others have extended this forced-choice format to its logical conclusion by measuring across the full range of response options. Weekley et al. (2004), for example, had respondents rank-order five response options from "best to worst." To score the SJTs (in this study there were four different SJTs), responses were compared to SMEs' rank ordering by means of Spearman's rank-order correlations. Higher values, of course, indicated greater overall consistency with the SMEs, whereas negative values indicated a tendency to reverse the SMEs' ordering of the options. In two of the four SJTs, the rank-ordering method produced slightly, but significantly, better validity than did the "pick best" method or the "pick best/pick worst" format. These results bear further replication with other SJTs using various response instructions. Because additional increments in validity from rank-order scoring are likely to be small, future research should also consider the trade-offs involved (e.g., the greater time required to rank order all options vs. simply selecting the best and worst from that set).

The other common means of scoring SJTs has been to have respondents use Likert-type scales and rate the effectiveness of each of the response options. For example, Chan and Schmitt (2002) had respondents rate the effectiveness of each response option on a 6-point scale. These ratings were compared to SME ratings and assigned a value of 1, 2, or 3, depending on the percentage of agreement. This SJT predicted performance incrementally over cognitive ability, experience, and the Big Five personality traits (Chan & Schmitt, 2002). In the Sacco et al. (2000) research, SJT scores were derived by taking the inverse of the absolute value of the difference between respondents' effectiveness ratings and those of a SME group. This distance-measure approach gives lower scores to those whose ratings are most dissimilar to the SMEs (be they above or below the SMEs) and higher scores to those whose profile of ratings most closely matches the SME group. Unfortunately, they reported no validity information. Wagner

(1987) used a similar approach in his study of tacit knowledge and academic success. In his SJT, each of 12 situations were paired with anywhere from 9 to 11 responses rated on a 7-point scale. Scores for each of the 12 items were derived by summing the squared deviations of the subjects' scores from the mean of a SME groups' scores. Wagner (1987) found that there were individual differences between subjects in terms of their use of the entire range of ratings such that he standardized the resulting scores (see also Legree, 1995). His SJT was significantly related to a number of measures of research productivity.

Wagner and Sternberg (1985) developed an SJT to predict academic success in the discipline of psychology. Each of their 12 situations was followed by 6 to 20 response options rated on a 7-point scale (ranging from *not important* to *extremely important*). Interestingly, they scored their SJT by retaining those items that were significantly correlated with group membership (psychology professors, psychology graduate students, and undergraduates). Within the faculty sample, this key was significantly related to a number of criteria such as the number of publications, number of conferences attended, and the percentage of time spent in research. In a second study, Wagner and Sternberg (1985) developed an SJT to predict success in business management. As before, each of the 12 work-related situations were followed by anywhere from 9 to 20 response options, each of which was rated on an importance scale. A key was developed by summing across the 39 items that significantly differentiated business managers, business graduate students, and undergraduates students. Within the business manager group, this SJT was significantly related to organizational level, years of schooling beyond high school, and salary. What is particularly interesting about these studies is that the differentiating items were identified not through traditional empirical keying methods or SME review, but by determining which items differentiated between experts and novices. That it still predicted performance measures within the expert groups suggests this novel approach to scoring deserves further attention (although see Bergman et al., 2003, for an unsuccessful attempt at using such an approach).

It is suspected that the use of Likert-type scales with SJTs will find a wider audience in the future, probably at the expense of the forced choice format. As McDaniel and Nguyen (2001) noted, this approach offers several potential advantages. First, because responses to each option/item are independent (which is not entirely the case with pick best/worst formats), there is no ipsativity in the resulting scores. Second, because each response option is rated, the SJT developer has as many scorable items as there are responses. More data points offer potential benefits in terms of reliability and validity. In that some SJTs present up to 20 different potential responses to a single situation (e.g., Wagner & Sternberg, 1985), this represents a potentially dramatic increase in the predictive potential of each situational item. Third, because such an approach allows the accumulation of response option ratings *across* situations, it might enable the SJT developer to measure more homogeneous constructs within a single SJT. For example, to the extent that different response options reflect the personal characteristics of those endorsing them, it may be possible to measure traits such as agreeableness and conscientiousness more homogeneously by independently summing the ratings of response options loaded with such traits. Such measures are likely to be substantially less transparent than the typical personality measure. Finally, we also speculate that the Likert-type rating approach might reduce the cognitive load of SJTs, at least as compared to the forced-choice format. In the forced choice format, one must correctly identify the best (or the best and worst) answers to the situation or receive no points (or even negative points). In contrast to this all-or-nothing scoring, the Likert approach, by allowing for partial credit across all response options, may be less related to general mental ability than the forced-choice method. We are aware of no research examining this proposition.

The Likert-type scale approach does have a few issues associated with it. For one, the items cannot be as independent as items associated with separate scenarios because they are all tied to the same scenario. Some of the responses will be redundant with respect to the variance they capture. There are also individual differences in the extent to which people use the entire scale or only parts of it. In turn, this effects scoring when, for example, it is done by computing absolute distance scores from the mean rating of experts. Wagner (1987) observed this in his data and responded by first standardizing all SJT item ratings to a standard deviation of 1.5 (see also Legree, 1995). Additional research is needed to determine the most appropriate way to handle this issue.

One final issue related to scoring SJTs concerns the potential for branching in SJTs. In Olson-Buchanan et al. (1998), examinees responded to nine "first-stage" situations, each having four possible responses. Each response then resulted in the presentation of a new situation, related to the examinee's choice and the original first-stage situation, followed by four new response options. The use of branching has seen very little application, despite its potential benefits. Having follow-up situations vary as a function of first-stage responses would appear to be an ideal means of illustrating the possible consequences of choices. The implications of such an application for training (see Fritzsche et al., chap. 14, this volume) are obvious. Such an approach may also enhance psychological fidelity because in real life, choices and judgments are usually not made in isolation but within an ongoing stream of consciousness and changing context.

At the same time, branching does come with its own set of unique complications. Beyond the complexities involved in developing a multistage SJT, their use for selection might be compromised in that different applicants would literally take different tests, depending on the branches their choices led them down. This creates several difficulties with scoring and interpretation (e.g., not all applicants would complete the same items, item responses are not independent, etc.). Again, research into the advantages and disadvantages of multistage SJTs is warranted.

## THE CONSEQUENCES OF SJT DEVELOPMENT ALTERNATIVES

Throughout this chapter, we have discussed various consequences of using different SJT development, scaling, and scoring alternatives. It is clear there is little systematic research examining these issues. Rather, the extant literature may best be described as a hodge-podge of findings, where one feature of SJT development may be manipulated (e.g., instructions) but others left untouched (e.g., item stems). Even less systematic has been the nature of the dependent variables examined in such manipulations. Some studies look at the psychometric equivalence of SJT versions, others examine validity (nearly always on incumbent samples), and a few examine subgroup differences.

What is desperately needed is research examining these alternatives in a systematic manner. Table 8.1 shows a general overview of the various issues for each part of SJT development. This table can be used as a guide for future research. For example, one could manipulate various features across the cells (e.g., item-stem development, response-option development) and the effects on SJT psychometric equivalence, validity, subgroup differences, user reactions, and utility could be examined. It is quite possible that many of the variations in development, scaling, and scoring will not produce large differences. However, determining which of these characteristics really matter and which do not would go a long way to advancing the science and practice of SJTs.

## ACKNOWLEDGMENT

We thank Mike McDaniel for his helpful suggestions on an earlier draft of this chapter.

# REFERENCES

Arad, S., Borman, W. C., & Pulakos, E. D. (1999, April). *Construct validation of a situational judgment test of adaptive behavior.* Paper presented at the 14th annual convention of the Society for Industrial and Organizational Psychology, Atlanta, GA.

Beauregard, R. S. (2000). *Construct explication of a situational judgment test: Addressing multidimensionality through item development, content analysis, and scoring procedures.* Unpublished doctoral dissertation, Wright State University, Dayton OH.

Becker, T. E. (2004, April). *Development and validation of a scenarios-based measure of employee integrity.* Paper presented at the 19th annual conference of the Society for Industrial and Organizational Psychology, Chicago, IL.

Bergman, M. E., Drasgow, F., Donovan, M. A., & Juraska, S. E. (2003, April). *Scoring situational judgment tests.* Paper presented at the 18th annual conference of the Society for Industrial and Organizational Psychology, Orlando, FL.

Birkeland, S., Manson, T., Kisamore, J., Brannick, M., & Liu, Y. (2003, April). *A metaanalytic investigation of job applicant faking on personality measures.* Paper presented at the 18th annual conference of the Society for Industrial and Organizational Psychology, Orlando, FL.

Blanz, F., & Ghiselli (1972).The mixed standard scale: A new rating system. *Personnel Psychology, 25,* 185–199.

Chan, D., & Schmitt, N. (1997). Video-based versus paper-and-pencil method of assessment in situational judgment tests: Subgroup differences in test performance and face validity perceptions. *Journal of Applied Psychology, 82,* 143–159.

Chan, D., & Schmitt, N. (2002). Situational judgment and job performance. *Human Performance, 15,* 233–254.

Cucina, J. M., Vasilopoulos, N. L., & Leaman, J. A. (2003, April). *The bandwidth-fidelity dilemma and situational judgment test validity.* Paper presented at the 18th annual conference of the Society for Industrial and Organizational Psychology, Orlando, FL.

Flanagan, J. C. (1954). The critical incident technique. *Psychological Bulletin, 41,* 237–358.

Frederickson, N. (1972). Toward a taxonomy of situations. *American Psychologist, 27,* 114–123.

Gillespie, M. A., Oswald, F. L., Schmitt, N., Manheim, L., & Kim, B, H. (2002, April). *Construct validation of a situational judgment test of college student success.* Paper presented at the 17th annual conference of the Society for Industrial and Organizational Psychology. Toronto, CA.

Goldstein, I. L., Zedeck, S., & Schneider, B. (1993). An exploration of the job analysis-content validation process. In N. Schmitt & W. C. Borman (Eds.), *Personnel selection in organizations* (pp. ). San Francisco, CA: Jossey-Bass.

Haas, A. C., Smith, K. C., & McDaniel, M. A. (1999, April). Faking strategies: *Effects on a situational judgment test.* Paper presented at the 14th annual convention of the Society for Industrial and Organizational Psychology, Atlanta, GA.

Hanson, M. A., Borman, W. C., Mogilka, H. J., & Manning, C. (1999). Computerized assessment of skill for a highly technical job. In F. Drasgow & J. B. Olson-Buchanan (Eds.), *Innovations in computerized assessment* (pp. ). Mahwah, NJ: Lawrence Earlbaum Associates.

Hooper, A. C., Jackson, H. L., & Motowidlo, S. J. (2004, April). *Faking on personality-based measures: SJTs compared to a traditional format.* Paper presented at the 19th annual conference of the Society for Industrial and Organizational Psychology, Chicago, IL.

Hunter, D. R. (2003). Measuring general aviation pilot judgment using a situational judgment technique. *International Journal of Aviation Psychology, 13,* 373–386.

Juraska, S., & Drasgow, F. (2001, April). *Faking situational judgment: A test of the conflict resolution skills assessment.* Paper presented at the 16th annual conference of the Society for Industrial and Organizational Psychology, San Diego, CA.

Kim, B. H., Schmitt, N., Oswald, F. L., Gillespie, M., & Ramsay, L. J. (2003, April). *Job knowledge tests on the path to successful performance.* Paper presented at the 18th annual conference of the Society for Industrial and Organizational Psychology, Orlando, FL.

Krokos, K.J., Meade, A. W., Cantwell, A. R., Pond, S. B., & Wilson, M. A. (2004, April). *Empirical keying of situational judgment tests: Rationale and some examples.* Paper presented at the 19th annual conference of the Society for Industrial and Organizational Psychology, Chicago, IL.

Legree, P. (1995). Evidence for an oblique social intelligence factor established with a likert-based testing procedure. *Intelligence, 21,* 247–266.

Lievens, F., Buyse, T., & Sackett, P. R. (in press). The operational validity of a video-based situational judgment test for medical college admissions: Illustrating the importance of matching predictor and criterion construct domains. *Journal of Applied Psychology.*

MacLane, C. N., Barton, M. G., Holloway-Lundy, A. E., Nickles, B. J. (2001, April). *Keeping score: Expert weights on situational judgment responses.* Paper presented at the 16th annual conference of the Society for Industrial and Organizational Psychology, San Diego, CA.

McDaniel, M. A., Hartman, N. S., & Grubb, W. L. (2003, April). *Response instructions as moderators of the validity of situational judgment tests.* Paper presented at the 18th annual conference of the Society for Industrial and Organizational Psychology, Orlando, FL.

McDaniel, M. A., Morgeson, F. P., Finnegan, E. B., Campion, M. A., & Braverman, E. P. (2001). Use of situational judgment tests to predict job performance: A clarification of the literature. *Journal of Applied Psychology, 80,* 730–740.

McDaniel, M. A., & Nguyen, N. T. (2001). Situational judgment tests: A review of practice and constructs assessed. *International Journal of Selection and Assessment, 9,* 103–113.

McElreath, J., & Vasilopoulos, N. L. (2002, April). *Situational judgment: Are most and least likely responses the same?* Paper presented at the 17th annual conference of the Society for Industrial and Organizational Psychology, Toronto, Canada.

Motowidlo, S. J., Diesch, A. C., & Jackson, H. L. (2003, April). *Using the situational judgment format to measure personality characteristics.* Paper presented at the 18th annual conference of the Society for Industrial and Organizational Psychology, Orlando, FL.

Motowidlo, S. J., Dunnette, M. D., & Carter, G. W. (1990). An alternative selection procedure: The low-fidelity simulation. *Journal of Applied Psychology, 75,* 640–647.

Motowidlo, S. J., Hanson, & Crafts, J. L. (1997). Low-fidelity simulations. In D. L. Whetzel & G. R. Wheaton (Eds.), *Applied measurement methods in industrial psychology* (pp. 241–260). Palo Alto, CA: Davies-Black.

Nguyen, N. T., Biderman, M., & McDaniel, M. A. (2005). Effects of response instructions on faking in a situational judgment test. Manuscript submitted for publication.

O'Connell, M. S., Doverspike, D., Norris-Watts, C., & Hattrup, K. (2001). Predictors of organizational citizenship behavior among Mexican retail salespeople. *International Journal of Organizational Analysis, 9,* 272–280.

Olson-Buchanan, J. B., Drasgow, F., Moberg, P. J., Mead, A. D., Keenan, P. A., & Donovan, M. A. (1998). Interactive video assessment of conflict resolution skills. *Personnel Psychology, 51,* 1–24.

Paullin, C., & Hanson, M. A. (2001, April). *Comparing the validity of rationally-derived and empirically-derived scoring keys for a situational judgment inventory.* Paper presented at the 16th annual conference of the Society for Industrial and Organizational Psychology, San Diego, CA.

Peeters, H., & Lievens, F. (2005). Situational judgment tests and their predictiveness of college students' success: The influence of faking. *Educational and Psychological Measurement, 65*, 70–89.

Ployhart, R. E., & Ehrhart, M. G. (2003). Be careful what you ask for: Effects of response instructions on the construct validity and reliability of situational judgment tests. *International Journal of Selection and Assessment, 11*, 1–16.

Ployhart, R. E., & Ryan, A. M. (2000, April). *Integrating personality tests with situational judgment tests for the prediction of customer service performance.* Paper presented at the 15th annual conference of the Society for Industrial and Organizational Psychology, New Orleans, LA.

Ployhart, R. E., Weekley, J. A., Holtz, B. C., & Kemp, C. F. (2003). Web-based and paper-and-pencil testing of applicants in a proctored setting: Are personality, biodata, and situational judgment tests comparable? *Personnel Psychology, 56*, 733–752.

Porr, W. B., & Ployhart, R. E. (2004, April). *The validity of empirically and construct-oriented situational judgment tests.* Paper presented at the 19th annual conference of the Society for Industrial and Organizational Psychology, Chicago, IL.

Pulakos, E. D., & Schmitt, N. (1996). An evaluation of two strategies for reducing adverse impact and their effects on criterion-related validity. *Human Performance, 9*, 241–258.

Reynolds, D. H., Sydell, E. J., Scott D. R., & Winter J. L. (2000, April). *Factors Affecting Situational Judgment Test Characteristics.* Paper presented at the 15th annual conference of the Society for Industrial and Organizational Psychology, New Orleans, LA.

Reynolds, D. H., Winter, J. L., & Scott, D. R. (1999, April). *Development, validation, and translation of a professional-level situational judgment inventory.* Paper presented at the 14th annual conference of the Society for Industrial and Organizational Psychology, Atlanta, GA.

Sacco, J. M., Scheu, C., Ryan, A. M., & Schmitt, N. W. (2000, April). *Understanding race differences on situational judgment tests using readability statistics.* Paper presented at the 15th Annual Convention of the Society for Industrial and Organizational Psychology, New Orleans, LA.

Sacco, J. M., Schmidt, D. B., & Rogg, K. L. (2000, April). *Using readability statistics and reading comprehension scores to predict situational judgment test performance, black-white differences, and validity.* Paper presented at the 15th annual convention of the Society for Industrial and Organizational Psychology, New Orleans, LA.

Schmidt, D. B., & Wolf, P. P. (2003). *Susceptibility of SJTs to applicant faking: An examination of applicant and incumbent samples.* Paper presented at the 18th annual conference of the Society for Industrial and Organizational Psychology, Orlando, FL.

Sinar, E. F., Paquet, S. L., & Scott D. R. (2002, April). *Internet versus paper selection tests: Exploring comparability issues.* Paper presented at the 17th annual conference of the Society for Industrial and Organizational Psychology, Toronto, Canada.

Stevens, M. A., & Campion, M. J. (1994). The knowledge, skill, and ability requirements for teamwork: Implications for human resource management. *Journal of Management, 20*, 503–530.

Stevens, M. A., & Campion, M. J. (1999). Staffing work teams: Development and validation of a selection test for teamwork settings. *Journal of Management, 25*, 207–208.

Such, M. J., & Schmidt, D. B. (2004, April). *Examining the effectiveness of empirical keying: A cross-cultural perspective.* Paper presented at the 19th annual conference of the Society for Industrial and Organizational Psychology, Chicago, IL.

Trippe, M. D., & Foti, R. J. (2003, April). *An evaluation of the construct validity of situational judgment tests.* Paper presented at the 18th annual conference of the Society for Industrial and Organizational Psychology, Orlando, FL.

Viswesvaran, C., & Ones, D.S. (1999). Meta-analysis of fakability estimates: Implications for personality measurement. *Educational and Psychological Measurement, 59*, 197–210.

Vroom, V. H. (2000). Leadership and the decision-making process. *Organizational Dynamics, 28*, 82–94.

Vroom, V. H., & Yetton, P. W. (1973). *Leadership and decision making.* Pittsburgh, PA: University of Pittsburgh Press.

Wagner, R. K. (1987). Tacit knowledge in everyday intelligent behavior. *Journal of Personality and Social Psychology, 52*, 1236–1247.

Wagner, R. K., & Sternberg, R. J. (1985). Practical intelligence in real-world pursuits: The role of tacit knowledge. *Journal of Personality and Social Psychology, 48*, 436–458.

Weekley, J. A., Harding, R., Creglow, A., & Ployhart, R. E. (2004, April). *Scoring situational judgment tests: Does the middle matter?* Paper presented at the 19th annual conference of the Society for Industrial and Organizational Psychology, Chicago, IL.

Weekley, J. A., & Jones, C. (1997). Video-based situational testing. *Personnel Psychology, 50*, 25–49.

Weekley, J. A., & Jones, C. (1999). Further studies of situational tests. *Personnel Psychology, 52*, 679–700.

Weekley, J. A., & Ployhart, R. E. (2005). Situational judgment: Antecedents and relationships with performance. *Human Performance, 18*, 81–104.

Weekley, J. A., & Ployhart, R. E., & Harold, C. (2004). Personality and situational judgment tests across applicant and incumbent contexts: An examination of validity, measurement, and subgroup differences. *Human Performance, 17*, 433–461.

Wernimont, P., & Campbell, J. P. (1968). Signs, samples, and criteria. *Journal of Applied Psychology, 52*, 372–376.

# 9

# Situational Judgment Tests: Validity and an Integrative Model

Michael A. McDaniel
*Virginia Commonwealth University*

Deborah L. Whetzel
*Work Skills First, Inc.*

Nathan S. Hartman
*John Carroll University*

Nhung T. Nguyen
*Towson University*

W. Lee Grubb, III
*East Carolina University*

This chapter offers insights and data concerning factors that can affect the construct and criterion-related validity of situational judgment tests (SJTs). First, we review the history of the debates concerning the validity of SJTs. Next, we review four characteristics of SJT items that are logically related to issues of construct and criterion-related validity. Then, we summarize evidence on construct validity, criterion-related validity, and incremental validity of SJTs. Next, we present a model that integrates the findings.

Finally, we offer topics for future research concerning the construct and criterion-related validity of SJTs.

## VALIDITY DEBATES CONCERNING SJTs ARE AS OLD AS SJTs

The development and use of SJTs have a long history in personnel selection. In fact, the use of SJTs dates back to the 1920s. For a detailed history of SJTs, the reader is referred to the first chapter of this book and McDaniel, Morgeson, Finnegan, Campion, and Braverman (2001). Despite the long history of these tests, substantial attention to the construct and criterion-related validity has been a recent phenomenon. Still, some early work foreshadows recent debates about the validity of SJTs, particularly their construct validity. The first test known to use situational judgment items was the George Washington Social Intelligence Test. One of the subtests, called Judgment in Social Situations, included many items in work situations. This subtest required "keen judgment, and a deep appreciation of human motives, to answer correctly" (Moss, 1926, p. 26). Thorndike and Stein (1937) began the construct validity debate in SJTs by arguing that the George Washington Social Intelligence Test did not correlate with other tests designed to measure social intelligence and was highly correlated with measures of general intelligence. Cardall (1942) offered the Practical Intelligence Test, but some researchers criticized it for its high correlations with measures of general intelligence (Carrington, 1949; Taylor, 1949). Northrop (1989) reviewed World War II-era SJTs and made observations on their complex construct domain. More recently, Sternberg et al. (2000) made bold claims about the construct validity of practical intelligence measures that are composed of situational judgment items. These claims have received substantial critique (Gottfredson, 2003; McDaniel & Whetzel, 2005).

## CHARACTERISTICS OF SJTs THAT MIGHT AFFECT VALIDITY

There are several characteristics of SJTs that may affect their validity. This section draws on and expands the McDaniel and Nguyen (2001) discussion of the characteristics of SJTs. These characteristics include the degree of fidelity of the SJT, the cognitive complexity of the items, the content of the scenario, and the response instructions. A discussion of some of these characteristics is also relevant to issues of development and scoring of SJTs and is addressed in chapter 8 of this volume. In our chapter, these characteristics are presented as they relate to the construct and criterion-related validity of SJTs.

## Degree of Fidelity

SJTs vary in the degree of fidelity of presentation. Fidelity can be defined as the extent to which the test resembles the work required on the job. For example, work samples would have high fidelity and cognitive ability tests would have low fidelity. Typically, video-based SJTs are considered to have higher fidelity than written SJTs. However, within a given format, one might expect fidelity to vary across SJTs.

Video-based SJTs consist of a series of situations or scenarios in a video media as well as some number of plausible response options, also on video media. Several such measures have been developed to predict customer service performance. For example, Alignmark's AccuVision Customer Service System (Alignmark, 2001) is a video-based selection test that has been developed to measure customer service skills and abilities. Job-analysis information provided the basis for the design and content of the system and varying degrees of customer contact are represented by the different scenarios (e.g., employee-to-customer, employee-to-employee, and telephone interactions).

We believe video-based SJTs are popular for three reasons. First, video simulations have stronger visual and affective appeal than written SJTs. Typically, video-based SJTs are more interesting to view than written tests are to read. Thus, employers who use video-based SJTs can speak of how innovative and technologically sophisticated their selection systems are. Likewise, applicants can be impressed by the sophistication of the selection system and be attracted to the organization. Second, high-fidelity simulations are valued because of their philosophy of measurement. They reflect the sample approach to measurement as opposed to sign measurement (Wernimont & Campbell, 1968). In their review of inferential and evidential bases of validity, Binning and Barrett (1989) discussed this measurement approach as one seeking to demonstrate that the predictor is isomorphic with the performance domain. Based on this measurement philosophy, many academics and practitioners shun low-fidelity instruments such as cognitive ability tests and embrace higher fidelity methods (e.g, video SJTs, work sample tests, and assessment centers) because they are considered samples of job content and are viewed as intrinsically better selection tools. Sometimes this belief is based on evidence and sometimes it is not. Third, video-based based SJTs are popular because they are perceived to have lower Black–White racial differences. (Nguyen, McDaniel, & Whetzel, 2005) The rationale is that video-based testing formats reduce the cognitive variance in the test by reducing the reading demands. Given the large mean differences between Blacks and Whites in cognitive ability (Roth, BeVier, Bobko, Switzer, & Tyler, 2001), reducing the cognitive variance in a test likely will reduce Black–White score differences on the test. Reducing the cognitive demands is a common approach to manipulating racial outcomes in test performance (Gottfredson, 1996). Reducing Black–White differences in test scores is a common motivation for developing video-based SJTs. We have often seen them used by employers facing race-based employment litigation. Developers of video-based SJTs promote them as tests designed to minimize adverse impact.

Typically, however, SJTs are presented in a written format, whether as paper-and-pencil or computer-administered tests. In written-format SJTs, the scenario is described rather than shown via video. Written SJTs are developed more frequently due to the cost differences in development between written and video formats and the need for expanded skills sets for video production. Although both formats share the cost of developing the scenarios and response options, video-based tests require costs associated with scripting, actors, and video production. These factors make video-based SJTs substantially more expensive to develop than paper-and-pencil measures. Personnel psychologists typically have the skills needed to develop SJTs in written format. Video-based SJTs typically would require the personnel psychologist to obtain assistance from those with video competencies. Separate from the cost considerations, video-based SJTs require the test-development project to involve more people and a longer time to completion. Thus, simplicity of production likely makes written format SJTs more common than video-based SJTs.

In summary, the fidelity of the SJT might affect both construct and criterion-related validity. A video-based SJT has a reasonable chance of reducing the cognitive variance of the SJT primarily by reducing the reading demands. Thus, in contrast to written SJTs, video-based SJTs can be expected to have a lower correlation with cognitive ability and yield lower Black–White test score differences. If the construct validity of the SJT changes with fidelity, one might observe criterion-related validity differences among SJTs of varying fidelity. Cognitive ability is the best predictor of job performance (Schmidt & Hunter, 1998). If one removes the cognitive variance from a test, one runs the risk of reducing its prediction of job performance. However, the remaining noncognitive variance may also have useful levels of validity. We suggest that if one removes cognitive variance from a SJT, the SJT will be correlated with personality traits such as conscientiousness, agreeableness, and emotional stability as well as job knowledge. All of these constructs can contribute to the prediction of job performance. Also, the high fidelity of the video might contextualize the measurement properties in a manner to enhance the validity of the test. We recognize that this assertion is speculative, but there is some evidence to suggest that adding contextualization to personality tests can improve validity (Robie, Born, & Schmit, 2001; Robie, Schmit, Ryan, & Zickar, 2000; Schmit, Ryan, Stierwalt, & Powell, 1995). Thus, it is reasonable to suggest that if high-fidelity SJTs offer more work-related contextualization than low-fidelity SJTs, the greater contextualization of high-fidelity SJTs may add to their validity. However, we know of no evidence that examines the relationship between the fidelity of an SJT and its validity and find the topic worthy of investigation.

## Cognitive Complexity

SJTs vary in the level of cognitive complexity of the scenarios. We offer this example as a low-complexity situational judgment item:

> Everyone in your workgroup but you has received a new computer. Nobody has said anything to you about the situation.
>
> a.  Assume it was a mistake and talk to your supervisor
> b.  Take a computer from a coworker's desk
> c.  Confront your boss about why you are being treated unfairly
> d.  Quit

The Tacit Knowledge Inventory for Managers (TKIM; Wagner & Sternberg, 1991), on the other hand, presents scenarios that are considerably longer and more detailed than the typical SJT. The TKIM presents situations that are typically several paragraphs long and involve fairly complex interactions. Given the increased reading and reasoning requirements imposed by complex scenarios, they are likely to be more highly correlated with cognitive ability than other SJTs composed of lower complexity scenarios. McDaniel and Nguyen (2001) suggested that the complexity of the situation is related to the length of the scenario and that more words are typically required to describe complex situations than less complex situations. A related issue concerns the comprehensibility of the stems. It is harder to understand the meaning and import of some situations than other situations. Sacco et al. (2000) examined the comprehensibility of item stems using readability formulas and found variability in the reading demands. It is a reasonable assertion that the length, complexity, and comprehensibility of the situation are interrelated and may drive the cognitive loading of the situational stems.

The cognitive complexity of the items in a SJT can be expected to affect both construct and criterion-related validity. Cognitively demanding SJTs relative to less cognitively demanding SJTs can be expected to have relatively more of their variance driven by cognitive ability and less of their variance associated with noncognitive traits. This difference in the relative degree of cognitive and noncognitive constructs assessed might impact the criterion-related validity. Whereas cognitive tests have higher validity than personality tests, on average, for most job performance criteria, increasing the cognitive loading of the SJT might increase its criterion-related validity. The Sacco et al. (2000) data supported this assertion. However, a SJT may not be the sole screening tool. If one increases the cognitive load of a SJT, the SJT may contribute little additional variance to a battery containing a cognitive ability test. In contrast, a SJT with lower cognitive load, may have a lower correlation with cognitive ability and provide better incremental validity to a battery containing a cognitive ability test.

## Content of the Scenario

There is variability in the content of scenarios of SJTs. Some scenarios use interpersonal situations that do not require any kind of job knowledge. Others involve job knowledge that is fairly generic (e.g., decision making or problem solving) and others may involve technical job knowledge (e.g., knowledge of electronics or mechanics).

We suggest that the content of the scenario affects both construct and criterion-related validity and offer the following observations. It is difficult to assess the correlates of situational judgment items by inspecting their content. One's response to an item concerning an interpersonal conflict would certainly reflect one's interpersonal competencies but it may also reflect other traits. In interpersonal conflicts some possible responses reflect stupid behavior and others reflect behavior driven by complex reasoning. Some responses might reflect low or high levels of conscientiousness or emotional stability. In our sample item concerning not receiving a new computer, endorsement of the response of taking a new computer from a co-worker's desk might simultaneously reflect low cognitive ability, low conscientiousness, and low emotional stability. However, it is reasonable that content must drive constructs assessed. SJT items that present interpersonal scenarios should tap interpersonal constructs to a greater degree than scenarios focused on resolving problems with automobile engines. It is also reasonable that the content assessed must drive the criterion-related validity. Some content is more job-related than others and some content will better predict job performance than other content.

## Response Instructions

Two different kinds of response instructions are typically used for SJTs: behavioral tendency and knowledge. Tests with behavioral tendency in-structions ask respondents to identify how they would likely behave in a given situation. These instructions, asking people about their typical behavior, look like personality measures that ask people to describe their behavioral inclinations. A variant of this approach is to ask the respondent to identify the response they would most likely perform and those they would least likely perform (Dalessio, 1994; Smith & McDaniel, 1998).

SJTs with knowledge instructions ask respondents to evaluate the effectiveness of possible responses to a particular situation. These judgments take the form of effectiveness ratings or rankings of best response and/or worst response. Alternatively, an applicant might be asked to identify the best response or the best and worst response.

McDaniel and Nguyen (2001) suggested that knowledge instructions make the SJT more faking resistant than behavioral tendency instructions. Consider, as a metaphor, the distinction between a personality item and a mathematical knowledge item. As with a SJT with behavioral tendency instructions, personality test instructions encourage respondents to describe their typical behavior. In the assessment of conscientiousness, an item might ask if the respondent maintains an orderly work area. A disorderly person could answer truthfully or could falsely indicate that he or she maintains a neat work area. As with a SJT using knowledge instructions, a respondent on a mathematics knowledge item is asked to provide the best answer. In the assessment of cube-root knowledge, a mathematics test might ask the respondent for the cube-root of 4,913. A mathematically deficient person cannot pick the correct answer with certainty. The individual might correctly guess the answer (17) but he or she cannot knowingly provide the correct answer as can the disorderly person who claims that he or she is orderly. Thus, in a SJT with behavioral intention instructions it is possible for an ill-suited applicant to answer in a manner that mimics an applicant with highly desirable behavioral tendencies. In a knowledge instruction SJT, it is more difficult for an applicant who lacks knowledge of the best responses to mimic a knowledgeable applicant. Nguyen, Biderman, and McDaniel (in press) provided preliminary evidence that faking can raise scores on a SJT with behavioral tendency instructions to a much greater extent than on a SJT with knowledge instructions.

Response instructions are likely to affect construct validity. Responses to behavior tendency items describe typical behavior when applicants are responding without the intent of distorting. These responses are similar to personality items and are likely to assess or be correlated with personality dispositions. On the other hand, knowledge items assess one's knowledge of the best way to behave. Assessments of knowledge generally have cognitive correlates. Job knowledge is gained as a result of opportunities and ability to learn. The opportunity to learn and the ability to learn may be influenced by personality dispositions. For example, anxiety may impede learning or cause one to avoid situations that offer the opportunity to learn and introversion may impede one's knowledge acquisition through an avoidance of active learning situations (e.g., introverts may have less knowledge gained through public speaking). However, knowledge acquisition places large demands on cognitive skills. Thus, SJTs using behavioral tendency instructions may correlate higher with personality traits and personality-loaded criteria (contextual performance) than SJTs using knowledge instructions that may correlate more highly with cognitive ability tests and cognitively loaded criteria (task performance).

Response instructions likely influence criterion-related validity in two ways. The first way relates to differential faking between response formats. We made arguments and cited preliminary evidence that SJTs using behavioral tendency instructions may be more readily faked than SJTs using knowledge instructions. If this is true, and to the extent that some respondents fake and faking diminishes validity, one would expect SJTs with behavioral tendency instructions to have lower criterion-related validity than SJTs with knowledge instructions. This validity difference should be more pronounced in applicant samples than in incumbent samples because incumbents typically have less motivation to fake.

The second way in which response formats might affect criterion-related validity is through their effects on constructs assessed. Whereas cognitive ability tests have substantially larger correlations with job performance than personality tests (Schmidt & Hunter, 1998), SJTs with knowledge instructions, with their associated larger cognitive load, may yield higher validities than SJTs with behavioral tendency instructions. On the other hand, a SJT with behavioral tendency instructions might provide a reliable measure of cognitive ability and supplement cognitive variance with job-related personality variance. Thus, an SJT with behavioral tendency instructions may have similar levels of validity as a test battery containing both a cognitive ability test and a set of personality measures. Optimally weighted composites of cognitive and personality measures can yield higher validities than cognitive tests alone (Schmidt & Hunter, 1998).

## THE EVIDENCE FOR CONSTRUCT AND CRITERION-RELATED VALIDITY

So far, we have offered speculation on factors that may be associated with the construct and criterion-related validity of SJTs. There has been substantial research on the construct and criterion-related validity of SJTs that addresses some but not all of the factors on which we have speculated.

Here, we present a summary of empirical evidence addressing the construct and criterion-related validity of SJTs.

## Construct Validity Evidence

Several classic primary studies have been conducted documenting the validity of SJTs (e.g., Chan & Schmitt, 1997; Motowidlo, Dunnette, & Carter, 1990; Olson-Buchanan et al., 1998; Smith & McDaniel, 1998). Given the attention of SJTs in the recent psychological literature, meta-analyses have been conducted on the construct validity of SJTs (McDaniel, Hartman, & Grubb, 2003; McDaniel, Morgeson, Finnegan, Campion, & Braverman, 2001; McDaniel & Nguyen, 2001). McDaniel et al. (2001) examined the cognitive correlates of SJTs. McDaniel and Nguyen (2001) summarized personality and job-experience correlates of SJTs. McDaniel et al. (2003) extended the construct-validity analyses of McDaniel and Nguyen (2001) and McDaniel et al. (2001) with more data and the inclusion of a response-instruction moderator. The construct validity highlights of the McDaniel et al. (2003) effort are shown in Table 9.1.

SJTs are shown to measure cognitive ability and the Big Five personality traits to varying degrees. The extent to which SJTs measure these constructs

TABLE 9.1

Meta-Analytic Results of Correlations Between Situational Judgment Tests and Cognitive Ability, Agreeableness, Conscientiousness, and Emotional Stability

| Distribution of correlations with SJTs | N | No. of rs | ρ |
|---|---|---|---|
| Cognitive ability | 22,553 | 62 | .39 |
| Behavioral tendency instructions | 5,263 | 21 | .23 |
| Knowledge instructions | 17,290 | 41 | .43 |
| | | | |
| Agreeableness | 14,131 | 16 | .33 |
| Behavioral tendency instructions | 5,828 | 11 | .53 |
| Knowledge instructions | 8,303 | 5 | .20 |
| | | | |
| Conscientiousness | 19,656 | 19 | .37 |
| Behavioral tendency instructions | 5,902 | 11 | .51 |
| Knowledge instructions | 13,754 | 8 | .33 |
| | | | |
| Emotional Stability | 7,718 | 14 | .41 |
| Behavioral tendency instructions | 5,728 | 10 | .51 |
| Knowledge instructions | 1,990 | 4 | .11 |

is moderated by the SJT response instructions. McDaniel et al. (2003) found that for the three most researched personality constructs, SJTs with behavioral tendency instructions are more correlated with personality than SJTs with knowledge instructions (Agreeableness .53 vs. .20; Conscientiousness .51 vs. .33; Emotional Stability .51 vs. .11). SJTs with knowledge instructions are more correlated with cognitive ability than SJTs with behavioral tendency instructions (.43 vs. .23). They noted that some of the distributions had relatively small numbers of coefficients and that results should be replicated as more data cumulate.

As shown in Table 9.1, the primary correlates with SJTs are cognitive ability, agreeableness, conscientiousness, and emotional stability. Given the wide range of constructs correlated with SJTs, their multifaceted nature does not make it easy to target them to specific constructs to the exclusion of other constructs. Efforts at such targeting have not been fully successful (Ployhart & Ryan, 2000). Our reading of this literature is that SJTs can be targeted to assess specific constructs but that the targeted SJTs will continue to measure multiple constructs.

In summary, SJTs are typically correlated with cognitive ability, agreeableness, conscientiousness, and emotional stability. SJTs with behavioral tendency instructions are more correlated with personality than SJTs with knowledge instructions. SJTs with knowledge instructions are more correlated with cognitive ability than SJTs with behavioral tendency instructions. These findings suggest that one can change the construct validity of a situational judgment test by altering the response instructions. Furthermore, the finding that SJTs have moderate correlates with personality and cognitive ability suggests that the tests are best viewed as methods and not assessment of a judgment construct.

We note that the construct-validity data are drawn almost entirely from concurrent studies. Thus, for studies using incumbents, it is clear that SJTs with behavioral tendency instructions appear to assess more personality and less cognitive ability, whereas the opposite is found for SJTs with knowledge instructions. Applicant data, when they become available, may show a less clear distinction between behavioral tendency instructions and knowledge instructions. We believe the cause of any potential difference will be due to applicant faking. It is reasonable that some applicants will respond in a manner to make themselves look better than they are and other applicants will not. It is also reasonable that among those applicants who choose to fake, some will be better at faking than others. We argue that applicants will have more difficulty faking the SJTs using knowledge instructions than the SJTs using behavioral tendency instructions. Deceitful applicants may not provide a response indicative of their behavioral tendency but rather a response consistent with their perception of what is the best response. As such, deceitful applicants will respond to a behavioral tendency SJT as if it had the instructions of a knowledge SJT. To the extent that this happens with some frequency among applicants, we anticipate that the construct validity differences between behavioral tendency and knowledge instruction SJTs will be smaller because the results for the behavioral tendency SJTs will become more similar to the results for knowledge instruction SJTs. Thus, an SJT that is more personality loaded in an incumbent sample, may become more cognitively loaded in an applicant sample.

## Criterion-Related Validity Evidence

As a result of the large number of SJT instruments and studies conducted to assess their validity, McDaniel et al. (2001) conducted a meta-analysis to determine the criterion-related validity of these kinds of instruments. McDaniel et al. (2003) re-analyzed and updated the 2001 data and found that knowledge-response instructions yielded higher validity (.33) than behavioral tendency instructions (.27). We note that this is not a large magnitude moderator and is based primarily on concurrent studies with incumbent data. Earlier, we speculated that the construct validity evidence based on applicant samples may be somewhat different from the construct validity data using incumbent samples. We hold the same caveat for the criterion-related validity data. To the extent that some applicants fake when completing SJTs, faking respondents on SJTs with behavioral tendency instructions may respond not with behavioral dispositions but with their perception of the best answer. To the extent that this happens, the criterion-related validity of behavioral tendency SJTs may approximate those of SJTs with knowledge instructions. We recognize that this argument may lead to the conclusion that faking can enhance validity. This is not a position with which we are comfortable or which we endorse and we encourage research to evaluate this possibility.

## Incremental Validity Evidence

The incremental validity of SJTs over measures of cognitive ability has been a topic of several primary studies (Clevenger, Pereira, Wiechmann, Schmitt, & Schmidt Harvey, 2001; Chan & Schmitt, 2002; O'Connell, McDaniel, Grubb, Hartman, & Lawrence, 2002; Weekly & Jones, 1997, 1999) and two meta-analyses (McDaniel et al., 2001; McDaniel et al., 2003). All studies showed that SJTs provide incremental validity over cognitive ability. The incremental prediction is reasonable in that SJTs typically measure job-related personality traits including conscientiousness, agreeableness, and emotional stability. Whereas SJTs are measurement methods and can measure a variety of constructs in varying magnitudes, the incremental validity of SJTs over cognitive ability can expect to vary with the cognitive saturation of the SJT. SJTs that are highly correlated with cognitive ability can not be expected to have much incremental validity over cognitive ability. SJTs that measure noncognitive job-related constructs can be expected to have useful levels of incremental validity over cognitive ability.

Data on incremental validity of SJTs over both cognitive ability and personality are rare. O'Connell et al. (2002) found incremental validity of the SJT over cognitive ability but very little incremental validity over both cognitive ability and personality. They did not report incremental validity of the SJT over personality alone. Whereas SJTs typically measure both personality and cognitive ability, one might expect an SJT to have incremental validity over cognitive ability or over personality. However, it is likely to be more difficult for SJTs to have incremental validity over both cognitive ability and personality. Still, Weekley and Ployhart demonstrated that a SJT provided incremental validity beyond cognitive ability, personality, and experience. Future research should examine whether this is a rare or a common event.

## A MODEL TO INTEGRATE CONSTRUCT AND CRITERION-RELATED VALIDITY EVIDENCE FOR SJTS

Figure 9.1 presents a model that integrates validity evidence for SJTs. The four personal traits that affect performance on SJTs are cognitive ability, agreeableness, conscientiousness, and emotional stability. This assertion is consistent with the correlations between measures of these constructs and SJTs. The four personal traits also affect the extent to which job knowledge is gained through education and training. For example, the smart and dependable gain more job knowledge through education and training than do the stupid and the slothful. The four personal traits also affect the extent to which one gains job knowledge through job experience. We have divided job knowledge into general job knowledge and technical job knowledge. We envision general job knowledge to be composed of basic knowledges common to most jobs and might be viewed as work socialization knowledge. These knowledges would include the value of showing up to work, being nice to co-workers, dressing appropriately, following the directions of one's supervisor, and refraining from employee theft and inappropriate language. These are knowledges that one might gain in one's initial job and might show more variance among applicants for entry-level positions than more senior positions. However, general job knowledge might

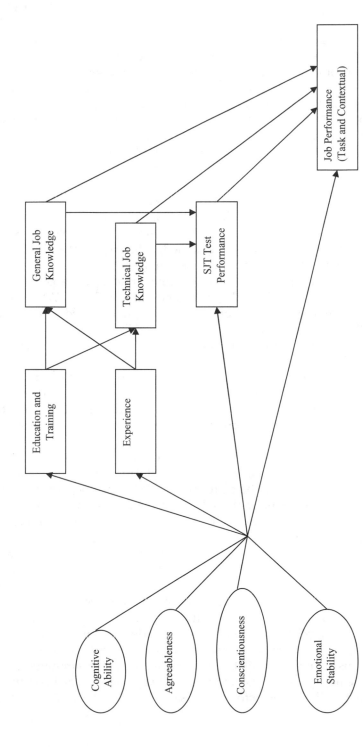

FIG. 9.1. A conceptual model of the factors affecting the construct and criterion-related validity of situational judgment tests.

also include some knowledges needed at supervisory levels. For example, some supervisors have more knowledge related to dealing with subordinates than others. Many SJTs are designed to tap general supervisory knowledge. Technical job knowledge is knowledge specific to a job or an industry and is gained through education, training, and experience. Some SJTs might tap technical knowledge such as techniques useful in closing a sale or knowledge related to managing a large project. There is little research addressing knowledge correlates of SJTs but SJTs are often assumed to measure knowledge, tacit or explicit (Schmidt & Hunter, 1993; Sternberg et al., 2000).

Our model assumes that test performance on SJTs is a function of cognitive ability, agreeableness, conscientiousness, and emotional stability, both directly and through their effects on job knowledge as mediated by education, training, and experience. Job knowledge, both general and technical, is assumed to directly affect performance on SJTs.

Job performance is predicted by cognitive ability, agreeableness, conscientiousness, emotional stability, SJTs, and job knowledge. Whereas different SJTs assess the four personal traits and job knowledge to varying degrees, the incremental validity of a specific SJT will vary based on its correlates. SJTs with substantial cognitive correlates may have little incremental validity over cognitive ability but substantial incremental validity over personality. SJTs with substantial noncognitive correlates may have little incremental validity over personality but substantial incremental validity over cognitive tests. SJTs with both high cognitive and noncognitive saturation, may offer little incremental validity over a battery of cognitive and noncognitive tests.

The model also recognizes that job performance can be measured with varying emphases on task and contextual performance. We anticipate that knowledge-based SJTs will be better predictors of task performance than behavioral tendency SJTs. If the job performance construct space were weighted to be more contextually oriented, one would expect an increase in the validity of behavioral tendency SJTs.

Our model is not rocket science, but it is meant as a heuristic for understanding the construct, criterion-related, and incremental validity of SJTs. The model's separation of job knowledge into general and technical is speculative. The model's description of SJT variance as a function of only cognitive ability, three personality traits and knowledge may be too restrictive. The model also needs to be expanded to consider differential loading of job performance on task and contextual factors. However, the model is consistent with available data, can aid in understanding the roles of cognitive and personality constructs in SJTs, and can facilitate understanding of the differences across studies in incremental validity. Certainly, more theory and better models of the nomonological net of SJTs can be developed.

## FUTURE RESEARCH

Although we know much about the construct and criterion-related validity of SJTs, we believe that research on SJTs is in its infancy and that there are a large number of issues that need further attention. We offer eight areas in need of additional research.

### Response Instructions and Item Content

Our discussion of the effects of response instructions on criterion-related and construct validity assumes that there is nothing different in the content of the items in knowledge-instruction versus behavioral tendency instruction SJTs. It could be that all or part of the response instruction effect is actually due to differences in item content. Nguyen et al. (in press), using a single set of SJT items, found the expected effects with respect to faking and correlations with cognitive ability. Specifically, a SJT with knowledge instructions was less fakable and more correlated with cognitive ability than was the same SJT with behavioral tendency instructions. However, that study did not examine correlations with personality or job performance. The chapter authors have done a small sample study in which raters were asked to guess whether SJT items were from a knowledge instruction or a behavioral tendency instruction SJT and found that raters were not able to make accurate decisions. Thus, these results argue against an item-content confound. Despite this preliminary evidence against an item-content confound, more study of item-content and other possible confounds is warranted. We recognize that some will not find it credible that one can change the construct and criterion-related validity of a test simply by changing the response instructions. More research is needed to evaluate our assertions about the impact of response instruction effects on SJTs.

### Job Knowledge

Most SJT researchers assume that SJTs measure knowledge and some explicitly assert this (Schmidt & Hunter, 1993; Sternberg et al., 2000). Yet no research has adequately assessed job-knowledge correlates of SJTs. McDaniel and colleagues (McDaniel & Nguyen, 2001; McDaniel et al., 2003) have summarized the small literature that has related SJTs to length of job experience as a remote surrogate measure of job knowledge. More research is clearly needed.

## Constructs of a Moving Target

Most researchers acknowledge that SJTs are measurement methods that can and do measure multiple constructs. Different SJTs can and do measure constructs differentially. The Stevens and Campion (1999) teamwork SJT has substantial correlates with cognitive ability, whereas other SJTs have much lower correlations with cognitive ability. Likewise, some SJTs have large correlations with some personality traits and others have lower correlations. Thus, any attempt to draw conclusions about the constructs assessed by SJTs must recognize that these are "constructs assessed on the average" and that any given SJT can deviate from these typical correlations. Much more work needs to be done to better target the constructs measured by SJTs. Ployhart and Ryan (2000) offered a very reasonable method for constructing SJTs to measure specific constructs. Although the SJT scales did measure the intended constructs, the correlations with other measures of the constructs were not large and the discriminant validity of the measures was low. Given that a reasonable approach to building SJTs to target specific constructs yielded less than satisfying results, we are not hopeful that SJTs can be readily targeted to specific constructs to the exclusion of others. However, research to refute our pessimism is encouraged.

## Search for More Constructs

We have offered evidence that SJTs in part assess cognitive ability, conscientiousness, agreeableness, and emotional stability. We have also speculated that SJTs tap job knowledge and encouraged more research of SJTs and job knowledge. Sternberg and colleagues (2000) argued that one can measure a general factor of practical intelligence with situational judgment items. Although we agree with Gottfredson (2003) and McDaniel & Whetzel (2005) that the available evidence finds no support for the existence of a practical intelligence construct let alone a general factor of practical intelligence, we do encourage more theory and research concerning other constructs that are or can be assessed by SJTs.

We note that our findings that SJTs typically are correlated with cognitive ability, conscientiousness, agreeableness, and emotional stability may be a function of the jobs examined to date and might differ for other jobs. For example, SJTs designed for sales jobs could reasonably have large magnitude correlations with extroversion. It is worthwhile to examine the extent to which job content moderates the correlates of SJTs.

## Fidelity and Validity

All validity evidence cumulated by McDaniel and colleagues (McDaniel et al., 2001; McDaniel & Nguyen, 2001; McDaniel et al., 2003) has been restricted to written SJTs. As more validity data on video-based SJTs become available, cumulative evidence on their construct and criterion-related validity should be summarized. In this chapter, we have also restricted fidelity to describe the difference between video and written formats. This is a constrained definition of fidelity. We have also considered fidelity for its effect on the cognitive load of SJTs. We suspect fidelity has more import than its effect on cognitive load. We also speculated on the contextualization of items as an aspect of fidelity that might affect validity. The notion of fidelity and its relation to validity needs further examination.

## Applicant Data

Almost the entire knowledge base concerning the construct and criterion-related validity of SJTs is based on concurrent data. Concurrent studies use incumbents as respondents and the task of completing the SJT is typically explained as a research effort that does not affect the career of the respondents. Applicants complete SJTs under much different situations that serve to manipulate the motivation of the respondents. Compared to incumbents, applicants are much more likely to be concerned about the evaluations of their responses. Motivational and other differences between applicants and incumbents may affect the construct and criterion-related validity of SJTs. In this chapter, we speculated that the differences between behavioral tendency and knowledge instruction SJTs may be less pronounced in applicant data than the results we described.

## Cognitive Loading

We have speculated about cognitive loading of SJT items and its effect on Black–White score differences, construct validity, and criterion-related validity. There is very little research (Sacco et al., 2000; Nguyen et al. 2005) that has directly assessed cognitive loading of items on their racial differences and validity. Clearly, more research is needed.

## Publication Bias

Developments in meta-analytic methods in industrial/organizational (I/O) psychology has largely stalled. However, meta-analysis in medical research is a hot-bed of methodological developments. Foremost among these developments are statistical techniques to evaluate publication bias in literatures (Dickerson, in press; Halpern & Berlin, in press). Fail-safe Ns, the most common approach to publication bias assessment in I/O psychology has been shown to be a very poor procedure to assess publication bias (Becker, in press) and a number of more accurate and powerful approaches have been offered (Duval, in press; Hedges & Vevea, in press; Sterne & Egger, in press; Sutton & Pigott, in press). Personnel psychologists may ignore this research to their eventual detriment. Authors who have results counter to the typical results may be discouraged from submitting them for publication because the results do not fit the "known facts." Likewise, editors who receive small sample, low-validity studies are likely to reject them as flawed due to sample size and other factors because they are counter to "known facts." This is not a situation that is conducive to the advancement of cumuletetive live knowledge. Consistent with many publication bias investigations, one might expect small sample, low-validity studies to be suppressed. If this were the case, there would be an upward bias in the reported validity of SJTs and possibly some effect on the correlations with other measures relevant to construct validity. Current validity data on SJTs should be evaluated for potential publication bias and efforts to evaluate and prevent publication bias (Berlin & Ghersi, in press) in this and other I/O literatures is warranted.

## SUMMARY

This examination of SJT construct validity has focused primarily on cognitive ability, conscientiousness, emotional stability, and agreeableness. We suggest that job knowledge is also an important correlate of SJT performance. The criterion-related validity of SJTs is well established, which is reasonable given that the constructs associated with SJTs also tend to be useful predictors of job performance. We offer evidence that the instructions used with SJTs can moderate the construct and criterion-related validity of the measures. We also provide a heuristic model that helps to integrate the relations between other constructs, SJTs, and job performance. Finally, we note several areas of research that will help advance our knowledges of SJTs.

# REFERENCES

Alignmark. (2001). *AccuVision customer service system validation Report*. Maitland, FL: Author.

Becker, B. J. (in press). The failsafe N or file-drawer number. In H. Rothstein, A. J. Sutton, & M. Borenstein (Eds.), *Publication bias in meta-analysis: Prevention, assessment and adjustments*. New York: Wiley.

Berlin, J. A., & Ghersi, D. (in press). Preventing publication bias: Registries and prospective meta-analysis. In H. Rothsetin, A.J. Sutton, & M. Borenstein (Eds.), *Publication bias in meta-analysis: Prevention, assessment and adjustments*. New York: Wiley.

Binning, J. F., & Barrett, G.V. (1989). Validity of personnel decisions: A conceptual analysis of the inferential and evidential bases. *Journal of Applied Psychology, 74*, 478–494.

Cardall, A. J. (1942). *Preliminary manual for the Test of Practical Judgment*. Chicago: Science Research Associates.

Carrington, D. H. (1949). Note on the Cardall Practical Judgment Test. *Journal of Applied Psychology, 33*, 29–30.

Chan, D., & Schmitt, N. (1997). Video-based versus paper-and-pencil method of assessment in situational judgment tests: Subgroup differences in test performance and face validity perceptions. *Journal of Applied Psychology, 82*, 143–159.

Chan, D., & Schmitt, N. (2002). Situational judgment and job performance. *Human Performance, 15*, 233–254.

Clevenger, J., Pereira, G. M., Wiechmann, D., Schmitt, N., & Schmidt Harvey, V. (2001). Incremental validity of situational judgment tests. *Journal of Applied Psychology, 86*, 410–417.

Dalessio, A. T. (1994). Predicting insurance agent turnover using a video-based situational judgment test. *Journal of Business and Psychology, 9*, 23–32.

Dickerson, K. (in press). Publication bias: Recognizing the problem, understanding its origins and scope, and preventing harm. In H. Rothsetin, A. J. Sutton, & M. Borenstein (Eds.), *Publication bias in meta analysis: Prevention, assessment and adjustments*. New York: Wiley.

Duval, S. (in press). The "Trim and Fill" method. In H. Rothsetin, A. J. Sutton, & M. Borenstein (Eds.), *Publication bias in meta analysis: Prevention, assessment and adjustments*. New York: Wiley.

Gottfredson, L. S. (1996). Racially gerrymandering the content of police tests to satisfy the U.S. Justice Department: A case study. *Psychology, Public Policy, and Law, 2*, 418–446.

Gottfredson, L. S. (2003). Dissecting practical intelligence theory: Its claims and evidence. *Intelligence, 31*, 343–397.

Halpern, S. D., & Berlin, J. A. (in press). Beyond Conventional Publication Bias: Other Determinants of Data Suppression. In H. Rothsetin, A. J. Sutton, & M. Borenstein (Eds). *Publication Bias in Meta Analysis: Prevention, Assessment and Adjustments*. Wiley.

Hedges, L., & Vevea, J. (in press). The selection model approach to publication bias. In H. Rothsetin, A.J. Sutton, & M. Borenstein (Eds.), *Publication bias in meta analysis: Prevention, assessment and adjustments*. New York: Wiley.

McDaniel, M. A., Hartman, N. S., & Grubb W. L. III. (2003, April). *Situational judgment tests, knowledge, behavioral tendency, and validity: A meta-analysis*. Paper presented at the 18th annual conference of the Society for Industrial and Organizational Psychology, Orlando, FL.

McDaniel, M. A., Morgeson, F. P., Finnegan, E. B., Campion, M. A., & Braverman, E. P. (2001). Use of situational judgment tests to predict job performance: A clarification of the literature. *Journal of Applied Psychology, 86*, 730–740.

McDaniel, M. A., & Nguyen, N. T. (2001). Situational judgment tests: A review of practice and constructs assessed. *International Journal of Selection and Assessment, 9*, 103–113.

McDaniel, M. A., & Whetzel, D. L. (in press). Situational judgment research: Informing the debate on practical intelligence theory. *Intelligence, 33*, 515–525.

Moss, F. A. (1926). Do you know how to get along with people? Why some people get ahead in the world while others do not. *Scientific American, 135*, 26–27.

Motowidlo, S. J., Dunnette, M. D., & Carter, G. W. (1990). An alternative selection procedure: The low-fidelity simulation. *Journal of Applied Psychology, 75*, 640–647.

Nguyen, N. T., Biderman, M. D., & McDaniel, M. A. (in press). Effects of response instructions on faking a situational judgment test. *International Journal of Selection and Assessment*.

Nguyen, N. T., McDaniel, M. A., & Whetzel, D. L. (2005, April). *Subgroup differences in situational judgment test performance: A meta-analysis.* Paper presented at the 20th annual conference of the society, for Industrial and Organizational Psychology, Los Angeles.

Northrop, L. C. (1989). *The psychometric history of selected ability constructs.* Washington, DC: U. S. Office of Personnel Management.

O'Connell, M. S., McDaniel, M. A., Grubb, W. L., III, Hartman, N. S., & Lawrence, A. (2002, April). *Incremental validity of situational judgment tests for task and contextual performance.* Paper presented at the 17th annual conference of the Society of Industrial Organizational Psychology, Toronto, Canada.

Olson-Buchanan, J. B., Drasgow, F., Moberg, P. J., Mead, A. D., Keenan, P. A., & Donovan, M. A. (1998). Interactive video assessment of conflict resolution skills. *Personnel Psychology, 51*, 1–24.

Ployhart, R. E., & Ryan, A. M. (2000, April). *Integrating personality tests with situational judgment tests for the prediction of customer service performance.* Paper presented at the 15th annual conference of the Society for Industrial and Organizational Psychology, New Orleans, LA.

Porr, W. B., & Ployhart, R. E. (2004, April). *The validity of empirically and construct-oriented situational judgment tests.* Paper presented at the 19th annual conference of the Society for Industrial and Organizational Psychology, Chicago, IL.

Robie, C., Born, M. P., & Schmit, M. J. (2001). Personal and situational determinants of personality responses: A partial reanalysis and reinterpretation of the Schmit et al. (1995) data. *Journal of Business & Psychology, 16*, 101–117.

Robie, C., Schmit, M. J., Ryan, A. M., & Zickar, M. J. (2000). Effects of item context specificity on the measurement equivalence of a personality inventory. *Organizational Research Methods, 34*, 348–365.

Roth, P. L., BeVier, C. A., Bobko, P., Switzer, F. S. III, & Tyler, P. (2001). Ethnic group differences in cognitive ability in employment and educational settings: A meta-analysis. *Personnel Psychology, 54*, 297–330.

Sacco, J. M., Scheu, C. R., Ryan, A. M., Schmitt, N., Schmidt, D. B., & Rogg, K. L. (2000, April). *Reading level and verbal test scores as predictors of subgroup differences and validities of situational judgment tests.* Paper presented at the 15th Annual Conference of the Society of Industrial and Organizational Psychology, New Orleans, LA.

Schmidt, F. L., & Hunter, J. E. (1993). Tacit knowledge, practical intelligence, general mental ability, and job knowledge. *Current Directions in Psychological Science, 2*, 8–9.

Schmidt, F. L., & Hunter, J. E. (1998). The validity and utility of selection methods in personnel psychology: Practical and theoretical implications of 85 years of research findings. *Psychological Bulletin, 124*, 262–274.

Schmit, M. J., Ryan, A. M., Stierwalt, S. L., & Powell, A. B. (1995). Frame-of-reference effects on personality scale scores and criterion-related validity. *Journal of Applied Psychology, 80*, 607–620.

Smith, K. C., & McDaniel, M. A. (1998, April). *Criterion and construct validity evidence for a situational judgment measure.* Paper presented at the 13th annual convention of the Society for Industrial and Organizational Psychology, Dallas, TX.

Sternberg, R. J., Forsythe, G. B., Hedlund, J., Horvath, J. A., Wagner, R. K., Williams, W. M., Snook, S. A., & Grigorenko, E. L. (2000). *Practical intelligence in everyday life.* New York: Cambridge University Press.

Sterne, J. A. C. & Egger, M. (in press). Regression methods to detect publication and other bias in meta-analysis. In H. Rothsetin, A. J. Sutton, & M. Borenstein (Eds.), *Publication bias in meta analysis: Prevention, assessment and adjustments.* New York: Wiley.

Stevens, M. J., & Campion, M. A. (1999). Staffing work teams: Development and validation of a selection test for teamwork settings. *Journal of Management, 25,* 207–208.

Sutton, A. J., & Pigott, T. D. (in press). Bias in meta-analysis induced by incompletely reported studies. In H. Rothsetin, A. J. Sutton, & M. Borenstein (Eds.), *Publication bias in meta analysis: Prevention, assessment and adjustments.* New York: Wiley.

Taylor, H. R. (1949). Test of practical judgment. In O. K. Buros (Ed.), *The third mental measurements yearbook* (pp. 694–695). New Brunswick, NJ: Rutgers University Press.

Thorndike, R. L., & Stein, S. (1937). An evaluation of the attempts to measure social intelligence. *Psychological Bulletin, 34,* 275–285.

Wagner, R. K., & Sternberg, R. J. (1991). *Tacit Knowledge Inventory for Managers: User manual.* San Antonio, TX: The Psychological Corporation.

Weekley, J. A., & Jones, C. (1997). Video-based situational testing. *Personnel Psychology, 50,* 25–49.

Weekley, J. A., & Jones, C. (1999). Further studies of situational tests. *Personnel Psychology, 52,* 679–700.

Weekley, J. A. & Ployhart, R. E. (2005). Situational judgment: Antecedents and relationships with performance, *Human performance, 18,* 81–104.

Wernimont, P. F., & Campbell, J. P. (1968). Signs, samples, and criteria. *Journal of Applied Psychology, 52,* 372–376.

# 10

# Operational Threats to the Use of SJTs: Faking, Coaching, and Retesting Issues

Amy C. Hooper
*University of Minnesota*

Michael J. Cullen
*Personnel Decisions Research Institutes*

Paul R. Sackett
*University of Minnesota*

This chapter focuses on issues that arise when one considers the use of situational judgment tests (SJTs) in operational settings. We note that a relatively small proportion of SJT research has been done in operational settings. For example, only six validity studies summarized in the McDaniel, Morgeson, Finnegan, Campion, and Braverman (2001) meta-analysis of SJT validity use a predictive design, whereas 96 were concurrent studies where the SJT was not used operationally. The first issue addressed here is faking. Although faking can be an issue in nonoperational settings (i.e., concern about positive self-presentation may be present in any setting), the high-stakes nature of testing in an operational setting may create heightened motivation to respond in a manner seen as likely to be well received. The second issue addressed is coaching. In operational settings there is concern about the possibility of some type of external intervention aimed at enhancing test scores. This may range from commercial test preparation efforts, such as those common for highly publicized tests (i.e., the SAT); to local organized efforts, such as those conducted by a labor union or an incumbent group; to individual efforts, as in the case of an individual receiving information from a friend who has successfully passed a test. The third issue is retesting. In operational settings, a policy of permitting an individual to retest is widespread. An individual receiving a failing score must first decide whether to retest, and then decide on a strategy for the retest. A wide variety of strategies are available, including seeking coaching, deciding to change one's approach to the test (e.g., choosing to fake after adopting a "respond honestly" approach on the initial effort, undertaking a program of study to improve one's standing on the construct of interest, and simply trying again).

We note in advance that research on these issues in the domain of SJTs is quite limited. In total, fewer than a dozen papers have explored the fakability of SJTs, only two papers have explored their coachability, and only one has examined retest effects. The purpose of this chapter is to critically review the state of knowledge about fakability, coachability, and retesting effects when using SJTs.

## FAKING AND SJTs

There are a number of reasons to be concerned about the effects of faking on SJTs. One important concern is the impact of faking on the criterion-related validities of SJTs (e.g., Douglas, McDaniel, & Snell, 1996; Ones, Viswesvaran, & Reiss, 1996). Another concern is that faking can seriously affect the kinds of decisions that are made about who gets hired and who does not. Faking may lead to the hiring of individuals whose true score on the characteristic being measured is less than what it appears to be; there is considerable debate in the literature about whether faking has these effects on the hiring process (Ellingson, Smith, & Sackett, 2001; Griffith, Chmielowski, Snell, Frei, & McDaniel, 2000; Hough, Eaton, Dunnette, Kamp, & McCloy, 1990; Mueller-Hanson, Heggestad, & Thornton, 2003; Ones et al., 1996 ).

Results from studies investigating the fakability of SJTs have varied widely, making integration of the literature difficult. Because studies have not produced consistent results, a meta-analysis would be an ideal method of summarization under most conditions. However, the current state of SJT faking research has not yet provided an adequate sample of studies with which to conduct a meta-analysis with reasonable confidence. There are several variables that could be posited as moderators for strong theoretical or empirical reasons, but splitting such variables into groups frequently creates samples of approximately two. Nevertheless, given the prevalence of these tests, we believe that integration of the literature is useful and important at this point.

Investigations of the fakability of the SJT have largely paralleled that of other noncognitive predictors such as personality, with several distinct streams of research (Visveswaran & Ones, 1999). In particular, we first review the lab studies that have examined whether it is possible for respondents to achieve higher scores on SJTs when instructed to do so. Next, we discuss whether the results from the lab have been supported in practice as well. Finally, we identify characteristics of SJTs that might make them more or less susceptible to faking relative to other SJTs, as well as why SJTs might differ in fakability relative to other noncognitive predictors such as personality. Table 10.1 provides a basic summary of the findings regarding SJTs and faking. It also provides a reference for relevant SJT characteristics that are discussed in subsequent sections.

## SJT Lab Studies

Although several lab studies have examined whether respondents can fake on SJTs when instructed to do so, a single, consistent trend has not emerged as it has in the personality literature, where researchers agree that respondents can significantly alter their scores (e.g., Visveswaran & Ones, 1999). In this section, we summarize the findings of available studies and later examine characteristics that might account for inconsistencies in the current state of the literature. Although the primary inquiry in these studies was whether a particular SJT could be faked, most were also concerned with fakability relative to traditional measures of personality.

Two studies by Peeters and Lievens (2005) and Juraska and Drasgow (2001) are illustrative of the variance in research findings. First, Peeters and Lievens found a large faking effect ($d = .89$) for their SJT when students were asked to respond to the SJT with honest responses or as if they were taking the SJT for admission into college and were trying to maximize their score. To the contrary, Juraska and Drasgow (2001) found that an SJT could not be faked ($d = .08$), whereas a set of personality measures could (mean $d = 1.05$), when undergraduate participants were asked to either respond honestly or respond in a manner that would maximize their chances of being hired by a company.

Studies by McDaniel and colleagues found results somewhere between those just described. Nguyen, McDaniel, and Biderman (2002) found that one version of their SJT (asking for the individual's most likely and least

**TABLE 10.1**

Summary of SJT Study Characteristics and Fakability

| Study[a] | Response Instructions | Faking Condition[b] | Sample Size[c] | Constructs: Cognitive ability and Personality[d] (range for r; mean r) | | | | | | | Faking Effects for SJT (in **bold**) and Personality Measures (range for d; mean d)[e] | Confidence Intervals for SJT (in **bold**) and Personality Effect Sizes[f] |
|---|---|---|---|---|---|---|---|---|---|---|---|---|
| | | | | gma | E | A | C | O | ES | Other | | |
| [B]Hooper et al. (2004a), Agr scale 1 | Rate effectiveness of each response | [B]Honest vs. applicant | 37 (38) | n/a | n/a | .18 | .01 | n/a | n/a | n/a | **.23** .34 | **(−.22 to .68)** (−.12 to .80) |
| [B]Hooper et al. (2004a), Agr scale 2 | Rate effectiveness of each response | [B]Honest vs. applicant | 37 (38) | n/a | n/a | .29* | .04 | n/a | n/a | n/a | **.21** .31 | **(−.24 to .66)** (−.15 to .77) |
| [B]Hooper et al. (2004a), Agr scale 1 | Rate effectiveness of each response | [B] Applicant with low trait demands vs. applicant with high trait demands | 41 (36) | n/a | n/a | .39* | −.05 | n/a | n/a | n/a | **.40** 1.01 | **(−.05 to .85)** (.53 to 1.49) |
| [B]Hooper et al. (2004a), Agr scale 2 | Rate effectiveness of each response | [B] Applicant with low trait demands vs. applicant with high trait demands | 41 (36) | n/a | n/a | .52* | .03 | n/a | n/a | n/a | **.52** 1.01 | **(.06 to .98)** (.53 to 1.49) |
| [B]Hooper et al. (2004b), Agr scale | Rate effectiveness of each response | [B]Honest vs. applicant | 54 (58) | n/a | n/a | .25* | .16 | n/a | n/a | n/a | **.25** .40 | **(−.12 to .62)** (.03 to .77) |
| [B]Hooper et al. (2004b), Con scale | Rate effectiveness of each response | [B]Honest vs. applicant | 54 (58) | n/a | n/a | .13 | .17 | n/a | n/a | n/a | **.04** 1.03 | **(−.33 to .41)** (.64 to 1.42) |
| [B]Hooper et al. (2004b), Agr scale | Rate effectiveness of each response | [B] Applicant with low trait demands vs. applicant with high trait demands | 56 (56) | n/a | n/a | .30* | .03 | n/a | n/a | n/a | **.28** 1.17 | **(−.09 to .65)** (.77 to 1.57) |
| [B]Hooper et al. (2004b), Con scale | Rate effectiveness of each response | [B] Applicant with low trait demands vs. applicant with high trait demands | 56 (56) | n/a | n/a | .14 | .20* | n/a | n/a | n/a | **.24** .61 | **(−.13 to .61)** (.23 to .99) |

**TABLE 10.1**

(Continued)

| Study | Instruction | Comparison | N | | r/a | | | | | | | |
|---|---|---|---|---|---|---|---|---|---|---|---|---|
| [superscript *]Juraska & Drasgow (2001) | Would do | [B]Honest vs. applicant | 58 (67) | n/a | n/a | n/a | n/a | n/a | n/a | n/a | .08 (.74–1.38; 1.05) | (−.27 to .43) (.63 to 1.47) |
| [superscript *]Nguyen et al. (2002)–SJT 1 | Most likely / least likely | [W]Honest vs. customer service representative applicant | 203 (203) | .32* (.33*) .33 | .11 (.29*) .20 | .13 (.29*) .21 | .27* (.34*) .31 | .30* (.32*) .31 | .19* (.32*) .26 | n/a | .25 (.35–.75; .51) | (.05 to .45) (.31 to .71) |
| [superscript *]Nguyen et al. (2002)–SJT 2 | Best action / worst action | [W]Honest vs. customer service representative applicant | 203 (203) | .47* (.34*) .41 | .15* (.30*) .23 | .26* (.39*) .33 | .29* (.32*) .31 | .26* (.29*) .28 | .06 (.25*) .16 | n/a | .06 (.35–.75; .51) | (−.13 to .25) (.31 to .71) |
| [superscript *]Peeters & Lievens (2005) | Most effective / least effective | [B]Honest vs. "get the highest score on an admission exam" | 138 (153) | .06 (−.05) .00 | .20* (−.02) .08 | .26* (.04) .14 | .48* (.18*) .32 | .28* (−.03) .12 | .10 (−.01) .04 | n/a | .89 n/a | (.65 to 1.31) n/a |
| Ployhart et al. (2003) | Most likely / least likely | [B]Incumbent vs. applicant | 425 (2,544) | n/a | n/a | .24* (.25*) .25 | .43* (.28*) .30 | n/a | .30* (.26*) .27 | n/a | .88 (.62–1.42; 1.05) | (.77 to .99) (.94 to 1.16) |
| Reynolds et al. (1999) | Best response / worst response | [B]Incumbent vs. applicant | 172 (661) | n/a | .10 | .15 | .24* (.14*) .16 | .10 | n/a | .05–.07 (.05*–.19*) .12 | −.30 n/a | (−.47 to −.13) n/a |
| Schmidt & Wolf (2003), SJT 1, achievement/initiation | n/a | [B]Incumbent vs. applicant | 436 (2,352) | n/a | n/a | n/a | n/a | n/a | n/a | −.02–.06; (−.04–.02) −.03 | −.39 .70–.81; .75 | (−.49 to −.29) (.64 to .86) |
| Schmidt & Wolf (2003), SJT 1, interpersonal sensitivity | n/a | [B]Incumbent vs. applicant | 436 (2,352) | n/a | n/a | n/a | n/a | n/a | n/a | .02–.23* (.34*) .31 | −.26 .70–.81; .75 | (−.36 to −.16) (.64 to .86) |
| Schmidt & Wolf (2003), SJT 2, achievement/initiation | n/a | [B]Incumbent vs. applicant | 439 (2,352) | n/a | n/a | n/a | n/a | n/a | n/a | −.11–.09 (.04–.05*) .02 | −.54 .70–.81; .75 | (−.64 to −.44) (.65 to .85) |
| Schmidt & Wolf (2003), SJT 2, interpersonal sensitivity | n/a | [B]Incumbent vs. applicant | 439 (2,352) | n/a | n/a | n/a | n/a | n/a | n/a | .25*–.39* (.33*–.34*) .33 | −.24 .70–.81; .75 | (−.34 to −.14) (.65 to .85) |

(Continued)

**TABLE 10.1**

(Continued)

| Study[a] | Response Instructions | Faking Condition[b] | Sample Size[c] | Constructs: Cognitive ability and Personality[d] (range for r; mean r) | | | | | | | Faking Effects for SJT (in **bold**) and Personality Measures (range for d; mean d)[e] | Confidence (Intervals for SJT in **bold** and Personality Effect Sizes)[f] |
|---|---|---|---|---|---|---|---|---|---|---|---|---|
| | | | | gma | E | A | C | O | ES | Other | | |
| Smith et al. (1999) | Most likely / least likely | [B]Honest vs. applicant | 217 (240) | n/a | n/a | n/a | n/a | n/a | n/a | n/a | **.53** n/a | **(.34 to .72)** n/a |
| Vasilopoulos et al. (2000) | Most likely | [B]Low social desirability score vs. high social desirability score | 97 (101) | n/a | n/a | n/a | -.08 (-.07) -.07 | n/a | n/a | -.12--.07 (-.13--.17) .00 | **.27** .58-1.03; .83 | **(-.01 to .55)** (.54 to 1.12) |
| Weekley et al. (2003) | Best option / worst option | [B]Incumbent vs. applicant | 2989 (7,259) | n/a | .09* (.27*) .25 | .20* (.12*) .13 | .13* (.11*) .11 | n/a | n/a | n/a | **-.60** .47-.83; .64 | **(-.64 to -.56)** (.60 to .68) |

[a] ^ indicates that the study was conducted in a lab. All other studies are field studies.

[b] B indicates a between-subject design for faking condition.
W indicates a within-subject design for faking condition.

[c] The first sample size represents the honest (or incumbent) sample and the second sample size in parentheses is the fake good (or applicant) sample. The sample sizes differed slightly for the personality measures in the Juraska and Drasgow (2001) and Schmidt and Wolf (2003) papers; in both cases these adjusted figures were used in all relevant calculations for personality effects.

[d] E = extraversion; A = agreeableness; C = conscientiousness; O = openness; ES = emotional stability; Other = any personality relation from a non–Big Five measure.
Where three coefficients are provided, the first represents the relation within the honest (or incumbent) condition, the second coefficient in parentheses represents the relation within the fake good (or applicant) condition, and the third coefficient represents the sample size-weighted mean correlation for the two groups.

[e] Positive effect sizes indicate higher test scores for fake good or applicant groups; negative effect sizes indicate higher test scores for honest or incumbent groups. SJT effect sizes are presented first in **bold**, followed by personality effects.

[f] Where a range of effect sizes are provided for personality measures, the sample size-weighted mean effect size was used to compute a confidence interval.

n/a = statistic or information not available; * p < .05

likely responses) could be faked, whereas the other version (asking the respondent to identify the best and worst action) was fakable only under some conditions (i.e., when the faking condition preceded the honest condition). However, the degree to which the SJT was faked (mean $d = .16$) still tended to be less than that for the personality measures (mean $d = .51$). Similarly, students were able to increase their SJT scores ($d = .53$) when they were encouraged, under a faking condition, to lie on the SJT if they believed a given response would maximize their chances of getting a job that they desperately needed (Smith, Sydell, Snell, Haas, & McDaniel, 1999).

Another line of research questioned whether an SJT and traditional personality measure that were designed to measure the same constructs would be equally fakable (Hooper, Jackson, & Motowidlo, 2004). In two studies, participants completed personality and SJT measures, all of which were designed to assess the personality traits agreeableness and/or conscientiousness, and the participants were asked to respond in one of three ways: honestly, as a job applicant, or in a way that would maximize chances of obtaining a job with a specific company. These studies demonstrated that, when an SJT tapped into specific Big Five personality traits, it was less fakable than a traditional measure of these same traits (mean $d = .75$ for personality and mean $d = .26$ for SJT measures).

This handful of lab studies demonstrates that at least some SJTs can be faked, although the degree of faking varies from $d = .08$ to $d = .89$. Reasons why some SJTs might be less fakable than others, as well as why an SJT might be less fakable than a traditional personality measure will be addressed in subsequent sections.

## SJT Field Studies

A small number of studies have also addressed the degree to which faking might occur in practice, and some of the results differ from those found in the lab, such that the honest group (i.e., incumbents) score better than the fake good sample (i.e., applicants). A study by Reynolds, Winter, and Scott (1999) demonstrated that incumbents in nonsupervisory positions performed better on an SJT than applicants for those positions ($d = -.30$). Similarly, another study (Weekley, Ployhart, & Harold, 2003) investigating an SJT and a personality measure across incumbent and applicant samples for retail customer service positions found that incumbent SJT scores were higher than those of applicants ($d = -.60$), whereas the opposite pattern occurred for the personality measure (mean $d = .64$). Schmidt and Wolf (2003) also reported that applicants performed significantly better than incumbents on two biodata-formatted measures of a number of noncognitive traits (mean $d = .75$), whereas the reverse occurred across two SJTs each with two scales measuring interpersonal sensitivity and achievement/ initiative (mean $d = -.36$). Thus, applicants appeared to be able to increase their scores on the personality measure but not on the SJT.

Two additional studies, however, reported results more in the range of those found in the lab. In a sample of call center incumbents and applicants, applicants had significantly higher SJT scores ($d = .88$), although the effect was smaller than every personality trait measured (mean $d = 1.05$; Ployhart, Weekley, Holtz, & Kemp, 2003). Another study (Vasilopoulos, Reilly, & Leaman, 2000) tested applicants for U.S. border patrol positions. Applicants scoring above the median on an impression management scale achieved significantly higher scores on the personality measures (mean $d = .83$) relative to the SJT ($d = .27$). These latter two studies tend to concur with the lab studies in that, if SJTs are indeed fakable, they appear to be less fakable than self-report personality measures. Nevertheless, it is interesting that three of the five field studies show substantially different patterns of effect sizes relative to those in other field and lab settings.

A number of factors may operate in the field to contribute to the unique set of results where incumbents perform better than applicants on SJTs but not on personality measures. Because SJTs can measure a variety of characteristics that are commonly used in selection batteries (e.g., personality variables, cognitive ability; McDaniel et al., 2001; McDaniel & Ngyen, 2001), scores on the SJT may be restricted in range indirectly via the SJT's relations to measures that were used to select the incumbents. To the extent that the SJT and selection battery measure similar constructs, the incumbent and applicant groups should not be equivalent and the incumbent group should be higher on the constructs tapped by the SJT. Weekley et al. (2003) found evidence of nonequivalent samples in their study, where there were significantly more minority members in the applicant sample than in the incumbent sample.

A second type of range restriction that would also produce nonequivalent samples is through the relations between the SJT and criterion. Even if incumbents were not selected on those constructs measured by the SJT, the SJT should have been developed to predict job performance. Given that the SJT does indeed relate to job performance, those incumbents who have performed at a level such that they have been retained by an organization should score higher than a group of applicants. Although both types of range restriction would apply to personality measures as well as to SJTs, these effects could be larger with SJTs given that (a) they tend to be multidimensional and related to a larger number of constructs used in selection batteries than are personality measures and (b) their validities are substantially higher than those of personality (McDaniel et al., 2001).

Finally, incumbents may score higher than applicants on SJTs because SJTs tend to measure job knowledge (Motowidlo, Hanson, & Crafts, 1997; Motowidlo, Hooper, & Jackson, chap. 4, this volume), a domain in which incumbents should have a distinct advantage. Reasons for an SJT effect size that favors incumbents, contrary to what the lab studies would suggest should occur, may be influenced by a number of factors, including range restriction and reliance on job knowledge. A better understanding of factors operating in SJT studies in the field is needed before disparities between lab and field studies can be understood. Future studies should explore these as well as other avenues.

## Potential Moderators of SJT Fakability

Because both conclusions and effect sizes vary across the lab and field studies, the degree to which an SJT can be faked probably depends on one or more factors that have not yet been explicitly accounted for. We propose that there are at least four important factors that may moderate the fakability of a given SJT: constructs measured, transparency of response options, SJT instructions, and study design.

*Constructs.*    SJTs are a method that can be used to measure any number of traits (e.g., McDaniel & Nguyen, 2001), and some traits are less fakable than others. SJTs, then, that tap into less fakable domains such as cognitive ability should be less susceptible to faking than those that tap into domains such as personality. McDaniel et al.'s (2001) meta-analysis reported strong correlations with general cognitive ability as well as personality, although there was large variation across tests. Thus, if the SJTs examined in the current faking studies are representative of the SJTs summarized in the meta-analysis, some should be more cognitively loaded than others, and these differences may account for differences in magnitude of faking across studies. As can be seen in Table 10.1, the two studies that reported relationships between an SJT and cognitive ability tend to support this hypothesis. Unfortunately, because other studies did not report measures of cognitive ability, it is difficult to determine what degree the role of different constructs play in the present findings.

*Transparency.*    Transparency of response options relates to the degree that the correct, or keyed, answer(s) can be determined by respondents

(Holden & Jackson, 1979). To the extent that respondents are easily able to identify the correct response(s), an SJT should be more susceptible to faking. Reducing transparency of items to decrease fakability has received some support with biodata (Lautenschlager, 1994). Weekley, Ployhart, and Holtz (chap. 8, this volume) discuss the impact of transparency on SJTs, and present potential solutions.

***Would Versus Should Instructions.***   Nguyen et al. (2002) proposed that the instructional set that accompanies an SJT can affect fakability. Specifically, students were asked to respond both honestly and as an ideal job applicant on an SJT, and the order of the conditions were counterbalanced. Additionally, participants responded to this single SJT in two distinct manners. They indicated (a) what the worst and best action was and (b) what their least likely and most likely course of action would be. The authors found that respondents were consistently able to fake when they responded with what they would most and least likely do, but fakability of the best action/worst action response format depended on the order of the faking condition, such that faking only occurred when the faking instructions preceded the honest instructions. However, in the best/worst action scenario, where faking instructions preceded honest instructions, the faking effect was comparable to, or larger than, those effects found in the most likely/least likely format. The researchers concluded that when respondents are asked to give their best answers (as opposed to what they believe they would do), less faking may occur, although future research is needed to untangle the order effects and account for the equivalent faking effects across response formats when the condition eliciting honest responses first is removed from consideration.

***Study Design.***   Although the previous characteristics have related to SJT designs, differential fakability might also be attributed to study design. Between-subject designs tend to obtain smaller faking effect sizes than within-subject designs (Viswevaran & Ones, 1999). Several researchers have also argued that the type of faking condition can affect the magnitude of faking, such that applicants probably fake with less abandon than do participants asked to "fake good" in a lab (Ellingson et al., 2001). A similar effect may occur within lab studies where participants asked to respond as applicants might be less extreme in their attempts than those asked to respond in the most desirable manner possible or to do their best to maximize their score. As Table 10.1 shows, there is considerable variability in faking instructions across studies. At this point, it is difficult to tell whether some of the variability in results may be affected by between- or within-subject designs as well as faking instructional set.

## Faking on SJTs Versus Personality Measures

The previous section discussed characteristics of SJTs that might account for differential findings regarding the fakability of SJTs, but characteristics common to SJTs might generally make faking less likely as well. Indeed, as can be seen in Table 10.1, the pattern of standardized effect sizes tend to support that traditional personality measures are more fakable than SJTs. To facilitate this comparison, we calculated a mean sample-size weighted $d$ and standard deviation (SD) for personality variables and SJTs separately. Given the disparity discussed earlier in effect sizes found across lab and field studies, effect sizes are calculated separately for these settings. For lab studies, the mean $d$ was .70 (SD = .04) for personality variables and .33 (SD = .03) for SJTs. For field settings, the mean $d$ was congruent with the lab findings for personality (.68; SD = .15) and dissimilar for SJTs (−.38; SD. = .12). Thus, even if SJTs can be faked to some degree in some situations, they might still be less fakable than personality measures. Level of transparency, as discussed earlier, relative to personality measures, may be one source of differences in fakability. Other such factors may include complexity inherent in faking on a given measure and the degree to which measures are explicitly or implicitly measuring relevant constructs.

*Complexity of Faking an SJT.* On a typical self-report personality measure, the respondent interested in increasing his or her score need only identify the desirable end of a continuous scale and then select the extreme option on this scale. In other words, one must decide "is higher or lower better in this domain?" The scoring procedure for SJTs, however, naturally makes for a more complex faking procedure. At the simplest level of scoring procedures, respondents might have four noncontinuous options for each SJT item, and of the four options they need to determine which answer is the best, where two options are negative and two are positive (e.g., Juraska & Drasgow, 2001). Thus, unlike the personality test that requires one step to fake (i.e., identify whether the positive or negative end of the scale is more desirable), the SJT requires at least two steps (i.e., identify the positive response options, and then identify which of these positive options is the best before selecting a response). In the more common case, however, respondents might be required to select both the best and worst options on an SJT with four response options (e.g., Weekley et al., 2003). In this scenario, an additional step of selecting the worst option would be added to the SJT procedure just described. Additionally, SJTs vary in the number of response options offered for each item, and the complexity of this procedure would increase as the number of response options increased.

The difficulty to dissimulate on SJTs would increase from the complexity of the procedure alone, where respondents simply cannot effectively process enough information to do as well as they can on a traditional personality inventory. At an even more basic level, however, the increased number of steps required to fake an SJT introduces more possibility for error. Probability requires that respondents will make more errors in this process than in a process with fewer steps and more errors would result in lower scores.

***Explicit Versus Implicit Tests.*** A theoretical framework that explains why SJTs, even if they measure personality, might be less fakable than standard personality measures can be found in the distinction between explicit and implicit personality measures in the social psychological literature (Hooper et al., 2004; Motowidlo, Hooper, & Jackson, chap. 4, this volume). Explicit personality tests measure self-attributed characteristics, and common personality measures such as the NEO Five-Factor Inventory fall into this category. Implicit personality tests measure characteristics that operate automatically, and responses to such tests are not filtered through an individual's deliberate thought processes (McClelland, Koestner, & Weinberger, 1989). Hooper et al. explained that a typical SJT that asks respondents what they would do or asks respondents to rate the effectiveness of personality-laden behaviors can measure personality in an automatic, or implicit, manner. Because implicit personality measures have demonstrated resistance to faking (e.g., Bornstein, Rossner, Hill, & Stephanian, 1994), an SJT that measures personality constructs should be less fakable than its explicit counterpart.

## Conclusions Regarding Fakability and SJTs

The current literature has not pointed to a clear relation between SJTs and faking. Considerable variability across studies on important moderator variables might contribute to such inconsistencies. Furthermore, characteristics unique to SJTs generally might explain the trend that, even if SJTs can be faked somewhat, they appear to be less vulnerable than traditional personality measures. The current review contributes to the resolution of both issues by proposing moderators and characteristics of SJTs that could account for the present state of the literature.

Future research is needed in the SJT faking literature and should account for SJT moderators that can impact fakability. First, it would be useful if researchers provided relations for cognitive ability as well as personality, as this is the only way to determine whether resistance to faking is a function of a given SJT's cognitive loading. Second, researchers should be aware of differences between would and should instructions, as well as transparency of response options. Third, researchers have tended to use idiosyncratic faking instructions when more standard and uniform instructions might be more warranted and informative at this early stage of exploration.

In summary, although research on the fakability of SJTs has been mixed, SJTs appear to be less fakable than personality. Various SJT characteristics and research designs might contribute to fakability of a given SJT, and more research is needed to verify and clarify the relations between SJTs and faking.

## COACHING AND SJTs

In this section, we explore issues and research associated with coaching SJTs. To date, very little research has addressed the general question of whether noncognitive predictors can be coached. To our knowledge, only two studies have specifically addressed the question of whether SJTs can be coached.

As Sackett, Burris, and Ryan (1989) pointed out, there are at least three reasons to study the effects of coaching in selection contexts. One concern is that coaching can affect the construct validity of a test. The effect may be either positive or negative. Coaching may increase the construct validity of a test by eliminating the error variance associated with test unfamiliarity. However, when coaching improves an observed score without affecting the true score, it decreases construct validity because it leads to incorrect inferences about a person's true standing on the characteristic being measured by the test. A second concern is that coaching may affect criterion-related validity. If the effect of coaching is to add a constant to the test score of all test takers, validity will remain unaffected. However, if a coaching intervention increases test scores for low-ability test takers more than for high-ability test takers, or vice versa, validity will be affected. Third, even if criterion-related validity is relatively unaffected by coaching interventions, coaching may contribute to perceptions of unfairness in the hiring process. Coaching, like faking, may lead to the hiring of individuals whose true score on the characteristic being measured is less than what it appears to be (e.g., Rosse, Stecher, Miller, & Levin, 1998), and thus coached individuals have an advantage over uncoached individuals. This last concern is intimately connected to the problem of differential access to coaching programs.

The question of the coachability of SJTs is a pressing one in light of recent attempts to develop SJTs for use in the college admissions process (Oswald, Schmitt, Kim, Ramsey, & Gillespie, 2004; Sternberg and Rainbow Project Collaborators, 2002). SJTs that measure noncognitive constructs are potentially attractive selection tools in the college admissions process in part because they have smaller subgroup differences than traditional, $g$-loaded selection instruments such as the SAT (Clevenger, Pereira, Weichmann, Schmitt, & Schmidt Harvey, 2001). As such, when combined with the SAT, they offer the possibility of decreased adverse impact and increased validity. However, there is concern that interested parties will eventually capture the scoring key for any SJT developed, and that test preparation firms will use these keys to devise coaching programs. Given this possibility, the resiliency of SJTs to coaching interventions arises as a key issue for their use in admissions settings. The resiliency of SJTs to coaching interventions in employment contexts is also a concern. Although we are not aware of any test preparation firms in an employment context that prepare job candidates for an SJT-based test specifically, commercial testing programs for civil service jobs and certification tests required for employment (e.g., Microsoft certification, CPA certification, automotive certification, etc.) are widespread. Thus, as the popularity of the SJT format increases in employment contexts, concerns about the resiliency of SJTs to coaching interventions in this context will also increase.

## Conceptualizing Coaching

In keeping with past discussions on this topic (Anastasi, 1981; Maurer, Solaman, & Troxtel, 1998; Messick & Jungeblut, 1981), we draw a distinction between coaching and practice. Practice involves an examinee taking an alternate form of a test in order to become familiar with the test format and procedure. In contrast, we conceptualize coaching as a broader set of interventions aimed at enhancing test scores. Coaching itself, often referred to as "test preparation," does not have a universally agreed on definition (Sackett et al., 1989). However, it usually has one of three goals: increasing test familiarization, increasing test-wiseness, and increasing knowledge of the content of the domain being tested.

It is instructive to consider the goals of coaching in terms of the sources of test variance it is intended to target. Bond (1989) suggested that standardized tests can be considered to have three sources of variance: true score variance, test-specific variance, and random error. The first two strategies, increasing familiarization and test-wiseness, target test-specific variance, whereas the third strategy of increasing knowledge targets true score variance.

To increase test familiarization, coaching programs acquaint the test taker with procedural elements of a test, such as test instructions, item type, time limits, and the answer sheet format. To increase test-wiseness, a coaching program teaches a set of strategies for taking the test. The strategies may be general strategies applicable across many tests, or they may be tailored to a specific test. They may include showing test takers how the test is scored; encouraging them to do their best; teaching them how to manage their time, select questions, and set priorities; and showing them how to reduce anxiety and manage stress (Messick & Jungeblut, 1981). Finally, coaching aimed at increasing knowledge of the content domain may teach basic skills, such as mathematical skills, that the test is constructed to test. Messick and Jungeblut (1981) conceptualized coaching on a continuum, with coaching strategies on one end of the continuum and coaching test content on the other end.

By limiting our conceptualization of coaching to the three goals set out previously, we clearly distinguish coaching from other test preparation activities that focus on learning strategies, such as elaboration, goal-setting, self-monitoring, and metacognitive processing, which have themselves been the focus of much research (Alderman, Klein, Seeley, & Sanders, 1993; Clause, Delbridge, Schmitt, Chan, & Jennings, 2001; Pintrich, Smith, Garcia, & McKeachie, 1993). We also distinguish coaching from faking. Because faking is a deliberate attempt to increase test scores through use of a very specific strategy—knowing how the test is scored and adapting responses in order to exploit that knowledge—it may qualify as a very specific type of coaching in test-wiseness. Armed with knowledge of how a test is scored, test takers can be coached in the "strategy" of deliberately lying in order to maximize scores. Although coaching and faking are conceptually distinct, however, it is important to note that faking and coaching raise many of the same concerns about their effect on validity and fairness in the selection process.

## Coaching on Noncognitive Measures

Very little research has focused on coaching noncognitive tests. In 1989, Sackett et al. thoroughly reviewed the coaching literature and were not able to find any coaching studies on personality tests in an employment setting. The situation has not changed dramatically, although there has been some progress. Some research has examined the effects of coaching on interview performance (Campion & Campion, 1987; Maurer, Soloman, Andrews, &

Troxtel, 2001; Maurer et al., 1998) but results have been inconsistent, with two studies finding a positive effect for coaching and one study finding no effect. Studies on the effect of coaching on overt and personality-based integrity tests have shown small but significant effects for both types of tests, with stronger effects for overt than personality-based integrity tests (Alliger & Dwight, 2000; Alliger, Lilienfield, & Mitchell, 1996; Hurtz & Alliger, 2002). In their meta-analytic review, Alliger and Dwight reported a mean coaching effect size of 1.54 for overt tests ($N = 7$) and a more modest effect size of .36 for personality-based tests ($N = 6$). At least three studies found that the unlikely virtues scales of many integrity tests may be highly susceptible to coaching (Alliger et al., 1996; Dwight & Alliger, 1997; Hurtz & Alliger, 2000). One recent study examined the effect of coaching on a biodata inventory (Ramsey et al., 2003). As the coaching intervention, researchers provided test takers with information on the dimensions being tapped by the sample questions, and a brief explanation of how items were scored. Results indicated an effect size of 0.48. Finally, an earlier line of research indicates that scores on assessment centers can be modesty improved through coaching (see Sackett et al., 1989, for a review).

## Existing Research on Coaching SJTs

Two recent studies by Cullen, Sackett, and Lievens (2004) and Ramsey et al. (2003) addressed whether SJTs are amenable to coaching. Because both studies investigated the coachability of the same SJT—the Situational Judgment Inventory (SJI)—some discussion of that instrument is warranted.

The SJI is a 57-item instrument developed for possible use in the admissions process (Oswald et al., 2004). It was developed to tap 12 dimensions of college performance: knowledge acquisition, learning, artistic appreciation, multicultural tolerance, leadership, interpersonal skill, citizenship behavior, physical and psychological health, career orientation, adaptability, perseverance, and integrity. Each item presents respondents with a situation related to one of these educational objectives, as well as a set of alternative courses of action. Respondents are asked to indicate which alternative, in their judgment, is the "best" and "worst" course of action and scoring is determined by the degree to which responses accord with expert judgment about the "best" and "worst" alternatives.

Cullen et al. (2004) also tested the coachability of the Common Sense Questionnaire (CSQ; Sternberg & Rainbow Project Collaborators, 2002). The CSQ is a 30-item instrument that was also developed for potential use in the admissions process. It is a tacit knowledge measure, or test of "practical know-how" applied to the life of college students. Students are once again presented with situations likely to occur at college, as well as a set of alternative courses of action. However, the response format is different from the SJI, as respondents are asked to rate the quality of each possible course of action, rather than choosing the best and worst options. This test is also scored very differently than the SJI. In contrast to the SJI, scores on the CSQ are determined by computing a "distance" score for each item alternative from the mean for the specific sample that is taking the test. Scores for individual item alternatives are summed for items, and item scores are summed to compute an overall score for the test. The practical result of this procedure is that lower scores on the CSQ are better than higher scores. Another consequence of this procedure is that a given set of responses produces different test scores from one sample to another, because individual responses are compared with sample mean responses.

Ramsey et al. (2003) were interested in the effect of coaching, motivation and warnings on SJI performance. The researchers used a $2 \times 2 \times 2$ orthogonal design to randomly assign students to the different conditions. This design meant there were eight different cells with approximately 45 students assigned to each cell. Those students assigned to the coaching condition were provided with a 10-minute coaching component, which included information on the dimensions being tapped by the SJI, and a brief explanation of how items were scored. To encourage students in the motivated condition to do their best, a financial incentive of $10 was offered to those who scored above the 50th percentile. Students in the warning condition were told that responses may be verified, and that if dishonest responding was detected, it would invalidate their chance to receive $10 for high performance.

Results indicated that this very brief coaching intervention had a moderately positive effect on SJI performance, with an effect size of .34. One interaction, that of motivation and coaching, was statistically significant but the results were not consistent with expectations in that the presence of warning produced larger SJI scores than no warning, the difference being larger in the two conditions that did not receive the motivational manipulation.

To investigate the coachability of the SJI and CSQ, Cullen et al. (2004) utilized a $3 \times 2$ factorial design with experimental condition as the between-subjects condition and test form as the within-subjects condition. Four hundred and fifty participants were randomly assigned to one of three experimental conditions. In the "control" condition, participants completed both the SJI and CSQ pretests and posttests (which were both random halves of the full-length test) without any strategy training. The order in which students received the pretests and posttests was counterbalanced. In the "CSQ" condition, participants completed the CSQ pretest, received strategy training for the CSQ, and then completed the CSQ posttest. In the "SJI" condition, participants completed the SJI pretest, received strategy training for the SJI, and then completed the SJI posttest.

For both the CSQ and SJI, the strategy training involved watching a 20-minute videotape conducted by a human resource professional on techniques for raising scores on the tests. The strategies reviewed in the videotape had previously been generated by a group of graduate students who had examined the tests and scoring keys for each test. Remarkably, many of the strategies generated by the graduate students were similar for the two tests. The strategies for both SJTs involved acting responsibly, being organized, never taking the easy way out, and avoiding aggressive displays in interpersonal disputes. The commonality of the strategies was surprising in light of the fact that the two test themselves were only modestly positively correlated ($r = .25$) and that the tests seemed to be tapping somewhat different constructs. In this study, the CSQ was more cognitively loaded than the SJI (uncorrected $r$'s with a college entrance exam: ACT = .32 and .18, respectively) and although the SJI was positively correlated with agreeableness and conscientiousness ($r = .25$ and .28, respectively), the CSQ was negatively correlated with these personality traits ($r = -.15$ and $-.17$, respectively).

Results indicated that that the coaching program developed for the CSQ was effective in raising scores on the CSQ ($d = .24$), but that the coaching program for the SJI was ineffective in raising scores on the SJI. In keeping with the majority of past studies, the validity of the CSQ and SJI in predicting undergraduate grade point averages (GPAs) remained unaffected by the coaching intervention (Allalouf & Ben-Shakhar, 1998).

Results also indicated that the manner in which the CSQ was scored (i.e., by comparing individual responses with sample means for each item) left it vulnerable to a very specific coaching strategy. In the initial stages of the project, a graduate student suggested that a reasonable strategy for enhancing scores on the CSQ would be to avoid endorsing extreme responses on the 7-point Likert scale. The student reasoned that it was unlikely that sample means for any given item alternative would be extreme. Rather, mean scores would be closer to the center of the distribution, perhaps between 3 and 5 on the Likert scale. According to this reasoning, participants should be able to increase their scores on the CSQ simply by avoiding endorsing 1s, 2s, 6s, and 7s. Cullen et al. (2004) viewed this logic as sound, and decided prior to the study to test whether such a "scale" effect existed for the CSQ. Rather than train participants on this strategy for the CSQ, they decided to wait until the end of the study and run a simulation of what would have happened had they trained students on this scale strategy. This manner of proceeding had the advantage of allowing Cullen et al.

to separate the training effects due to strategy training from any potential scale effects.

They conducted the simulation in two steps. First, for the posttest in the CSQ condition, they changed all "1s" in their database to "2s" and all "7s" to "6s." Total scores and a new group mean for the CSQ posttest were then recomputed in the CSQ condition and effect sizes were recomputed for CSQ posttest scores in the CSQ condition versus the control condition. The new effect size included the effect size due to strategy training as well as the effect size due to the scale effect. They subtracted out the effect due to training and were left with a scale strategy effect size of $d = 1.28$. Thus, had Cullen et al. (2004) instructed participants to answer "2" whenever they would normally answer "1" and "6" whenever they would normally answer "7," participants would have increased their scores by 1.28 SD on the CSQ. Results were even more impressive when they changed all 1s and 2s to "3s" and all 7s and 6s to "5s" in the database. In this case, the scale effect increased from 1.28 SD to 1.57 SD.

## Conclusions Regarding Coaching and SJTs

The two studies to date used very different coaching interventions. Ramsey et al. focused on a very simple intervention, namely, making clear to participants the dimensions on which the SJT would be scored. In contrast, Cullen et al. focused on teaching the respondents the characteristics of responses that were likely to receive a favorable evaluation.

The fact that the CSQ was coachable as the result of a very short coaching intervention sounds an important note of caution for the use of SJTs in the college admission process. There is little doubt that test preparation firms would expend considerably more resources than Ramsey et al. (2003) and Cullen et al. (2004) did in developing a coaching program for these tests, and that students would receive intensive, distributed coaching in an effort to enhance SJT scores. In addition, the large-scale effect found for the CSQ renders it impractical for use without revision to the current scoring procedure.

Note that both coaching studies to date reported on SJTs focus on instruments designed for use in a higher education context. In that setting, any testing program will undergo intense public scrutiny, and the high test volumes make for a viable market for commercial test preparation firms. A few organizational settings might approach this level of public scrutiny, but many clearly will not. Although it is important to gain understanding of the potential coachability of SJTs, the degree to which a finding that SJTs are coachable is a threat to operational use will vary from setting to setting.

## RETEST EFFECTS ON SJTs

It is a widespread practice to give individuals the opportunity to retake tests. In employment settings, the Uniform Guidelines on Employee Selection Procedures (1978) state that test users should provide a reasonable opportunity to test takers for retesting. In educational settings, the *Standards for Educational and Psychological Testing* (AERA, APA, & NCME, 1999) state that retest opportunities should be provided for tests used for promotion or graduation decisions. Rationales behind endorsing retesting include the possibility that the initial assessment was an error, either due to a transient characteristic of the applicant (e.g., illness) or the testing situation (e.g., noise, distractions), or to random measurement error, as well as the possibility that candidates have improved their standing on the construct of interest during the interval between two administrations.

We use the term *retest effects* to describe changes in test performance after prior exposure to an alternate form (identical or parallel) of a test under standardized conditions. Using this definition, retest effects encompass both practice effects and coaching effects. In particular, practice effects relate to individuals' learning from their own experience by taking an alternate form of a test under standard conditions (i.e., there is no external intervention). This may involve familiarization effects due to exposure to the type of test, as well as attempts to change one's test taking strategy, as in a decision to attempt to fake on a retest following a decision to respond honestly on the initial test. Conversely, for retest effects to be coaching effects, there has to be learning through instruction (in the form of an external intervention such as feedback from others, information sharing, tutoring, and test preparation). These definitions are in line with conceptualizations outlined by various authors (Kulik, Bangert-Drowns, & Kulik, 1984; Messick & Jungeblut, 1981; Sackett et al., 1989).

Thus, retest effects do not reflect a single process, and may include the two other major topics of this chapter (i.e., faking and coaching), as well as additional processes, such as familiarization with item format, and reduction in test anxiety, among others.

There is a lack of studies on retest effects in operational testing contexts (i.e., situations where tests are used for making actual selection decisions). Most prior studies have examined retest effects in a laboratory setting (Kulik, Kulik, & Bangert, 1984). However, it is doubtful that the motivation of research participants to improve on their initial test scores is representative of the motivation of actual applicants in a high-stakes selection context (Kelley, Jacobs, & Farr, 1994; Sackett et al., 1989). Actual applicants have greater incentive to try to learn as much as possible from their first exposure to the test, and to engage in various test preparation activities after failing the first examination. Note that retest effects refer to systematic changes in scores on the measure of interest. Thus, studies of test–retest reliability that produce only a correlation between two test administrations (thus indexing the stability of the rank ordering of candidates) do not provide evidence regarding the presence or magnitude of mean score change upon retesting.

## Existing Research on Retesting Effects and SJTs

It is in this context that we turn to the only study of SJT retest effects that we have been able to locate. Lievens, Buyse, and Sackett (2004) examined a video-based SJT used as part of the medical school admissions process in Belgium. The intent of the SJT was to assess interpersonal skills, and candidates were presented with scenes involving physician–patient interaction and asked to evaluate various possible courses of action. The test is given twice a year, and a different form of the SJT was used for each administration. The study used 4 years of data, and thus involved eight forms of the test.

SJT scores are combined with science, cognitive, and medical reading work sample scores. Candidates who passed the exam received a certificate that guaranteed entry in the university in which they wanted to start their medical studies. So, contrary to the United States, there was no further selection on the part of universities. The overall passing rate is about 30%. The SJT carries a relatively small weight in the overall composite; the part–whole correlation is .29.

Over the 4 years, 1,985 individuals took the test twice, permitting an examination of retesting effects. Lievens et al. found that SJT scores improved by .32 SD upon retesting (.40 after correcting for measurement error), whereas science and cognitive scores improved .27 and .42 SDs, respectively (.30 and 46 after correcting for measurement error). Note that it is unclear what mechanism is responsible for the score improvement on the SJT, or on the other tests. One piece of contextual information may be useful: The authors noted that because the cognitive and science knowledge components are more heavily weighted, test preparation activities in Belgium focus on these domains. There is no evidence of any systematic coaching activities involving the SJT.

Lievens et al. attempted to gain insight into the mechanism underlying the score improvement by examining the criterion-related validity for initial tests versus retests. This analysis was based on a much smaller sample. Of the 1,985 who retested, 556 passed on the second attempt and entered one of several Belgian medical schools; their GPA over the first 3 years of study was obtained for use as a criterion. Neither the first nor the second administration SJT score was significantly related to this criterion. This was not unexpected; the SJT focused on interpersonal skills and overall GPA is primarily driven by performance in basic science and medical procedure courses. Of more interest, Lievens et al. created a second criterion measure, namely GPA in courses with an interpersonal skills component (e.g., training in physician–patient interaction). Such courses were present in some medical schools and not in others, resulting in a smaller sample ($N = 143$) for whom this criterion was available. The correlation between the SJT and this interpersonal skills criterion was ($r = .13$) for the first and .23 for the second SJT administration. Thus, the second administration turned out to provide a more valid assessment of the candidate's standing on the construct measured by SJTs. Note that the same result was found for the knowledge test as a predictor of the overall GPA criterion. The validity of the cognitive ability test did not change upon retesting. There are competing possible explanations. One is that these students gained additional knowledge (either in sciences or in how to deal with interpersonal situations) between the two administrations; another is that there was reduced construct-irrelevant variance in the second administration, due to increased familiarity with the testing format or to reduced test anxiety.

Lievens et al. then moved from within-person analysis (i.e., comparing first and second administration scores for the same people) to between-person analysis. That analysis compared individuals whose qualifying score (e.g., the score resulting in them gaining admission for medical school) was their first and only attempt with individuals passing on their second try. The question is whether a given test score results in the same expected level of criterion performance regardless of whether it is an initial score or a retest score.

They posited that a moderated multiple regression model can be used to examine this question. Consider a regression model relating test scores to a criterion. The scores represent the entry-gaining score for each tester. For some, the entry-gaining score is the initial attempt at taking the test; for others the entry-gaining score is a retest. The inclusion of a dummy variable reflecting whether a test score is an initial attempt or a retest provides a test of intercept differences (i.e., whether a given test score produces a systematically different level of criterion performance if it is an initial test than if it is a retest). Adding an interaction term (test score multiplied by the dummy variable reflecting initial test versus retest) provides a test of slope differences between initial testers and retesters.

Lievens et al. applied this model to the use of the overall selection composite to predict the overall GPA criterion, and found significant slope and intercept differences. In short, the same test score produced a lower level of criterion performance if it was obtained on a second attempt than on a first attempt. This approach could not be applied separately to the SJT due to an omitted variables problem (i.e., the dummy variable for first versus second attempt is correlated with the test components other than the SJT, which are correlated with the criterion).

Thus, although the repeat test score may prove more valid than the initial test score among the group of repeat test takers, a given overall test score translated to lower predicted performance if it is obtained by repeat test takers than if obtained by novel (one-time) test takers. This suggests that score improvements upon retesting are not artifactual; if they were, one would expect lower validity for retests than for initial tests within the sample of repeat test takers. Nonetheless, a retest score predicts lower performance than the same score obtained by a novel (one-time) test taker, suggesting that the fact it requires two attempts to obtain a given score signals something about the test taker (e.g., lack of diligence in preparing for the test) that is not specific to the testing situation, but also affects subsequent performance. Investigating the characteristics (e.g., personality) of individuals requiring a retest to obtain a given passing scores is a fruitful area for subsequent study.

## Conclusions Regarding Retesting Effects and SJTs

In summary, there is extremely limited information available about retest effects on SJTs, with only one study reported to date. That study does indicate higher scores upon retesting in an operational environment, with effect sizes comparable to those reported for other measures, such as cognitive ability. Preliminary evidence from this single study also finds differences in criterion-related validity for first versus second adminstrations among individuals testing twice, with higher validity for second administration scores. Although second administration scores may be more informative than first administration scores in within-person comparisons, the study suggests that a given score may signal a lower level of subsequent performance if obtained on a second attempt than if obtained on a first.

## CONCLUSION

Conclusions about each individual issue addressed in this chapter have been presented at the end of the sections on faking, coaching, and retesting, respectively. We do not reiterate those conclusions here. We do offer a few overall comments. First, although we have treated each of these topics separately, we caution against interpreting these as independent effects. Resting effects may reflect coaching, faking, or both. Some coaching programs may simply reinforce the faking strategies that candidates would devise on their own should they choose to distort their responses.

Second, and most pressing, is the small amount of research to date on each of the key issues addressed in this chapter. As such, any broad conclusions are premature. We believe that several features of SJTs themselves, as well as features of the testing environment, are likely to emerge as very important. The fact that SJTs are a measurement method, potentially tapping a variety of different constructs, makes it unlikely that the end result will be unqualified main effects for the effects of faking, coaching, or retesting. The most obvious factor is the varying cognitive load of SJTs; as noted earlier, we believe this is likely to moderate the effectiveness of faking attempts and coaching interventions. From a practical standpoint, the fact that SJTs are primarily a measurement method makes it unlikely that a single coaching program can be developed to increase scores on SJTs generally. Rather, we expect that coaching programs will need to be tailored to individual SJTs based on an examination of the constructs being measured.

Another factor is the use of "would do" versus "should do" instruction, which mirror the often drawn distinction between typical and maximum performance measures. In terms of features of the testing environment, the most pressing is likely to be the scale of the application, which we see as closely related to public scrutiny. In some settings, it is likely that the prototypic candidate encounters an SJT with no prior information about the selection method or process; in others it is likely that candidates have access to a wide array of sources of information (perhaps differing in credibility) about selection system content and process.

The limited research to date on these topics means that additional research is certainly in order. We highlight a few areas that we view as being of particular importance. First, the contrasting findings from laboratory and field settings on the fakability of SJTs merit careful investigation. We view the laboratory findings as an estimate of the upper bound of fakability: They estimate the degree to which candidates can fake an SJT. The question of the degree to which applicants actually do fake SJTs in operational settings would benefit from approaches other than applicant–incumbent comparisons. Such comparisons require the suspect assumption that motivation to fake is the only feature differentiating these two groups. One possible approach is to seek opportunities for within-subject studies in applied settings (e.g., test applicants, and retest those selected shortly after the hiring decision). We note a study by Ellingson and Sackett (2003) in which the same individuals completed a personality inventory in an operational selection setting and in a development setting, with the two settings posited as differing in motivation to fake. Second, in the coaching area, studies to date have taken contrasting approaches: informing candidates about the dimensions that the SJT is intended to measure versus the use of rule-based coaching strategies. As each has been the focus of only a single study, further work on these approaches, including an examination of the joint effects of using both approaches, would be useful. Third, retest effects have been examined to date in only a single study. Opportunities may be available to examine data in ongoing operational settings where SJTs are used to document score changes among individuals who reapply after an initial unsuccessful attempt. We note that little is known in general about how candidates approach a retest after an initial unsuccessful attempt, and research examining changes in test-taking strategies after an initial failure would be quite useful.

In conclusion, the presence of this volume signals the high degree of interest in SJTs, and the operational issues addressed in this chapter are an important piece of the puzzle. We trust that a clearer picture will emerge as research on these issues continues.

## REFERENCES

Alderman, M. K., Klein, R. Seeley, S. K. & Sanders, M. (1993). Metacognitive portraits: Preservice teachers as learner. *Reading Research and Instruction, 32*, 38–54.

Allalouf, A., & Ben-Shakhar, G. (1998). The effect of coaching on the predictive validity of scholastic aptitude tests. *Journal of Educational Measurement, 35*, 31–47.

Alliger, G., & Dwight, S. (2000). A meta-analytic investigation of the susceptibility of integrity tests to faking and coaching. *Educational and Psychological Measurement, 60*, 59–72.

Alliger, G., Lilienfeld, S., & Mitchell, K. (1996). The susceptibility of overt and covert integrity tests to coaching and faking. *Psychological Science, 7*, 32–39.

American Educational Research Association, American Psychological Association, & National Council on Measurement in Education (AERA, APA, & NCME). (1999). *Standards for educational and psychological testing*. Washington, DC: American Psychological Association.

Anastasi, A. (1981). Coaching, test sophistication and developed abilities. *American Psychologist, 36*, 1086–1093.

Bond, L. (1989). The effects of special preparation on measures of scholastic ability. In R. L. Linn (Ed.), *Educational measurement* (3rd ed., pp. 429–444). New York: American Council on Education and Macmillan.

Bornstein, R. F., Rossner, S. C., Hill, E. L., & Stepanian, M. L. (1994). Face validity and fakability of objective and projective measures of dependency. *Journal of Personality Assessment, 63*, 363–386.

Campion, M., & Campion, J. (1987). Evaluation of an interview skills training program in a natural field experiment. *Personnel Psychology, 40*, 675–691.

Clause, C. S., Delbridge, K., Schmitt, N., Chan, D., & Jennings, D. (2001). Test preparation activities and employment test performance. *Human Performance, 14*, 45–75.

Clevenger, J., Pereira, G. M., Wiechmann, D., Schmitt, N., & Schmidt Harvey, V. S. (2001). Incremental validity of situational judgment tests. *Journal of Applied Psychology, 86*, 410–417.

Cullen, M. J., & Sackett, P. R. (2004, April). Threats to the operational use of situational judgment tests in a student admission context. In P. R. Sackett (Chair), *New developments in SJTs: Scoring, coaching and incremental validity*. Symposium conducted at the 19th annual conference of the Society for Industrial and Organizational Psychology, Chicago, IL.

Cullen, M. J., Sackett, P. R., & Lievens, F. (2005). Threats to the operational use of situational judgment tests in the college admission process. *Submitted to the International Journal of Selection and Assessment*.

Douglas, E. F., McDaniel, M. A., & Snell, A. F. (1996, August). *The validity of non-cognitive measures decays when applicants fake*. Paper presented at the Academy of Management Proceedings, Cincinatti, OH.

Dwight, S. A., & Alliger, G. M. (1997, April). *Using response latencies to identify overt integrity test dissimulation*. Paper presented at the 12th annual conference of the Society for Industrial and Organizational Psychology, St. Louis, MO.

Ellingson, J. E., & Sackett, P. R. (2003, April). *Consistency of personality scale scores across selection and development contexts*. Paper presented at the 18th annual conference of the Society for Industrial and Organizational Psychology, Orlando, FL.

Ellingson, J. E., Smith, D. B., & Sackett, P. R. (2001). Investigating the influence of social desirability on personality factor structure. *Journal of Applied Psychology, 86*, 122–133.

Griffith, R. L., Chmielowski, T. S., Snell, A. F., Frei, R. L., & McDaniel, M. A. (2000, April). *Does faking matter? An examination of rank-order changes in applicant data*. Paper presented at the 15th annual conference of the Society for Industrial and Organizational Psychology, New Orleans, LA.

Holden, R. R., & Jackson, D. N. (1979). Item subtletly, and face validity in personality assessment. *Journal of Consulting and Clinical Psychology, 47*, 459–468.

Hooper, A. C., Jackson, H. L., & Motowidlo, S. J. (2004, April). *Faking on personality-based measures: SJTs compared to a traditional format*. Paper presented at the 19th annual conference of the Society for Industrial and Organizational Psychology, Chicago, IL.

Hough, L. M., Eaton, N. K., Dunnette, M. D., Kamp, J. D., & McCloy, R. A. (1990). Criterion-related validities of personality constructs and the effect of response distortion on those validities. [Monograph]. *Journal of Applied Psychology, 75*, 581–595.

Hurtz, G. M., & Alliger, G. M. (2002). Influence of coaching on integrity test performance and unlikely virtues scale scores. *Human Performance, 15*, 255–273.

Juraska, S.E., & Drasgow, F. (2001, April). Faking situational judgment: A test of the Conflict Resolution Skills Assessment. In F. Drasgow (Chair), *Situational judgment tests: Assessing the assessments*. Symposium conducted at the 16th annual conference of the Society for Industrial and Organizational Psychology, San Diego, CA.

Kelley, P. L., Jacobs, R. R., & Farr, J. L. (1994). Effects of multiple administrations of the MMPI for employee screening. *Personnel Psychology, 47*, 575–591.

Kulik, J. A., Bangert-Drowns, R. L., & Kulik, C. C. (1984). Effectiveness of coaching for aptitude tests. *Psychological Bulletin, 95*, 179–188.

Kulik, J. A., Kulik, C. C., & Bangert, R. L. (1984). Effects of practice on aptitude and achievement test scores. *American Educational Research Journal, 21*, 435–447.

Lautenschlager, G. J. (1994). Accuracy and faking of background data. In G. A. Stokes, M. D. Mumford, & W. A. Owens (Eds.), *Biodata handbook* (pp. 391–419). Palo Alto, CA: Consulting Psychologists Press.

Lievens, F., Buyse, T., & Sackett, P. R. (2004, August). *The effects of retaking tests on test performance and predictive validity: An examination of cognitive ability, knowledge, and situational judgment tests*. Paper presented at the American Psychological Association conference, Honolulu, HI.

Maurer, T., Solamon, J., Andrews, K., & Troxtel, D. (2001). Interviewee coaching, preparation strategies, and response strategies in relation to performance in situational employment interviews: An extension of Maurer, Solamon, and Troxtel (1998). *Journal of Applied Psychology, 86,* 709–717.

Maurer, T., Solamon, J., & Troxtel, D. (1998). Relationship of coaching with performance in situational employment interviews. *Journal of Applied Psychology, 83,* 128–136.

McClellan, D. C., Koestner, R., & Weinberger, J. (1989). How do self-attributed and implicit motives differ? *Psychological Review, 96,* 690–702.

McDaniel, M. A., Morgeson, F. P., Finnegan, E. B., Campion, M. A., & Braverman, E. P. (2001). Use of situational judgment tests to predict job performance: A clarification of the literature. *Journal of Applied Psychology, 86,* 730–740.

McDaniel, M. A., & Nguyen, N. T. (2001). Situational judgment tests: A review of practice and constructs assessed. *International Journal of Selection and Assessment, 9,* 103–113.

Messick, S., & Jungeblut, A. (1981). Time and method in coaching for the SAT. *Psychological Bulletin, 89,* 191–216.

Motowidlo, S. J., Hanson, M. A., Crafts, J. L. (1997), Low-fidelity simulations. In D. L. Whetzel and G. R. Wheaton (Eds.), *Applied Measurement Methods in Industrial Psychology* (pp. 241–260), Palo Alto, CA: Davies-Black Publishing Inc.

Mueller-Hanson, R., Heggestad, E. D., & Thornton, G. C., III. (2003). Faking and selection: Considering the use of personality from select-in and select-out perspectives. *Journal of Applied Psychology, 88,* 348–355.

Nguyen, N. T., McDaniel, M. A., & Biderman, M. D. (2002, April). *Response instructions in situational judgment tests: Effects of faking and construct validity.* Symposium presented at the 17th Annual Conference of the Society for Industrial and Organizational Psychology, Toronto, Canada.

Ones, D. S., Viswesvaran, C., & Reiss, A. D. (1996). Role of social desirability in personality testing for personnel selection: The red herring. *Journal of Applied Psychology, 81,* 660–679.

Oswald, F. L., Schmitt, N., Kim, B. H., Ramsay, L. J., & Gillespie, M. A. (2004). Developing a biodata measure and situational judgment inventory as predictors of college student performance. *Journal of Applied Psychology, 89,* 187–208.

Peeters, H., & Lievens, F. (2005). Situational judgment tests and their predictiveness of college student success: The influence of faking. *Educational and Psychological Measurement, 65,* 70–89.

Pintrich, P. R., Smith, D. A . F., Garcia, T., & McKeachie, W. J. (1993). Reliability and predictive validity of the Motivated Strategies for Learning Questionnaire (MSLQ). *Educational and Psychological Measurement, 53,* 801–813.

Ployhart, R. E., Weekley, J. A., Holtz, B. C., & Kemp, C. (2003). Web-based and paper-and-pencil testing of applicants in a proctored setting: Are personality, biodata, and situational judgment tests comparable? *Personnel Psychology, 56,* 733–752.

Ramsey, L. J., Gillespie, M. A., Kim, B. H., Schmitt, N., Oswald, F. L., Drzakowski, S. M., & Friede, A. J. (2003, November). *Identifying and preventing score inflation on biodata and situational judgment inventory items.* Invited presentation to the College Board, New York.

Reynolds, D. H., Winter, J. L., & Scott, D. R. (1999, May). *Development, validation, and translation of a professional-level situational judgment inventory.* Paper presented at the 14th annual conference of the Society for Industrial and Organizational Psychology, Atlanta, GA.

Rosse, J. G., Stecher, M D, Miller, J. L. & Levin, R. A. (1998). The impact of response distortion on preemployment personality testing and hiring decisions. *Journal of Applied Psychology 83(4),* 634–644.

Sackett, P. R., Burris, L. R., & Ryan, A. M. (1989). Coaching and practice effects in personnel selection. In C. L. Cooper & I. T. Robertson (Eds.), *International Review of Industrial and Organizational Psychology 1989*. Chicester: Wiley.

Schmidt, D. B., & Wolf, P. P. (2003, April). *Susceptibility of SJTs to applicant faking: An examination of applicant and incumbent samples*. Paper presented at the 18th annual conference of the Society for Industrial and Organizational Psychology, Orlando, FL.

Smith, K. C., & McDaniel, M. A. (1998). *Criterion and construct validity evidence for a situational judgment measure*. Paper presented at the 13th annual conference of the Society for Industrial and Organizational Psychology, Dallas, TX.

Smith, K. C., Sydell, E., Snell, A. F., Haas, A. C., & McDaniel, M. A. (1999, May). *Flanagan's critical incident technique meets the faking controversy*. Paper presented at the 14th annual conference of the Society for Industrial and Organizational Psychology, Atlanta, GA.

Sternberg, R. J., and the Rainbow Project Collaborators. (2002). *Enhancing the SAT through assessments of analytical, practical, and creative skills*. Unpublished manuscript.

Vasilopoulos, N. L., Reilly, R. R., & Leaman, J. A. (2000). The influence of job familiarity and impression management on self-report measure scale scores and response latencies. *Journal of Applied Psychology, 85*, 50–64.

Visweswaran, C., & Ones, D. S. (1999). Meta-analysis of fakability estimates: Implications for personality measurement. *Educational and Psychological Measurement, 59*, 197–210.

Weekley, J. A., Ployhart, R. E., & Harold, C. (2003, April). *Personality and situational judgment tests across applicant and incumbent settings: An examination of validity, measurement, and subgroup differences*. Paper presented at the 18th Annual Conference of the Society for Industrial and Organizational Psychology, Orlando, FL.

# 11

# Applicant Reactions to Situational Judgment Tests: Research and Related Practical Issues

Talya N. Bauer
*Portland State University*

Donald M. Truxillo
*Portland State University*

The use of situational judgment tests (SJTs) has grown since the 1980s. This growth is partly a result of interest in selection methods that appear more job-related and are less likely to draw litigation than more abstract methods such as cognitive-ability tests. It is not surprising that during this same time, there has been increased interest in how applicants perceive the selection process because such perceptions are theorized to relate to important outcomes such as attraction to the organization and reduced litigation (e.g., Gilliland, 1993). In other words, interest in SJTs and applicant perceptions have largely stemmed from the same interest in improving the selection process from the applicant's perspective.

In this chapter, we review SJTs in terms of applicant perceptions. We begin by describing a framework for classifying SJTs that explains how applicants perceive the selection process. We then use organizational justice theory to explain how applicants should react to different types of SJTs in practice, and from this develop research propositions regarding

SJTs. Finally, we describe key directions for future research on applicant perceptions of different types of SJTs.

## CATEGORIZATION OF SJTs RELEVANT TO APPLICANT PERCEPTIONS

When it comes to SJTs there is no "one" type. They vary from high-fidelity, hands-on work samples (e.g., Arvey, Strickland, Drauden, & Martin, 1990; Cascio & Phillips, 1979; Mount, Muchinsky, & Hanser, 1977), multimedia simulations (Olson-Buchanan et al., 1998; Schmitt & Mills, 2001), video simulations (Chan & Schmitt, 1997; Funk & Schuler, 1998; Weekley & Jones, 1997), and paper-and-pencil simulations (Hattrup & Schmitt, 1990; Stevens & Campion, 1999).

Research linking applicant reactions to SJTs has been scarce and primarily limited to reactions to batteries of tests rather than any focus on SJTs in particular. This is surprising given that situational judgment tests may have more of the characteristics that applicants want: face validity, samples of job behavior, and even information about the job (e.g., Truxillo, Donahue, & Kuang, 2003). Moreover, some of these tests provide quick feedback. However, there are differences among different types of SJTs that will affect applicant reactions. We think that the two key dimensions of the SJT format that are likely to affect applicant reactions are the format of the stimulus, and the format of the response.

With regard to the stimulus format, SJTs may give written descriptions of situations, or may provide very realistic video presentations of stimulus information. Similarly, response formats for SJTs can be low fidelity, providing multiple-choice response options that are either written or video-based, or open-ended response options that are presented in either written or oral format. This 2 (stimulus format) × 2 (response format) × 2 (test format) classification for SJTs is presented in Table 11.1, creating eight cells or types of SJTs. These eight cells are helpful for explaining how applicants perceive and react to the hiring process through their effects on fairness perceptions, motivation, and self-efficacy, as well as to more distal outcomes such as organizational attractiveness and litigation.

## EXPLAINING APPLICANT REACTIONS TO SJTs: ORGANIZATIONAL JUSTICE THEORY

Applicant reactions to selection is a relatively new area of research. For decades, researchers have devoted considerable attention to what could be done by recruiters, test developers, organizational members, and

TABLE 11.1

Classification for SJTs in Terms of Stimulus and Response
Format

| | | | Stimulus Format | |
|---|---|---|---|---|
| | | | Written | Video |
| Response format | Written | Multiple-choice | | |
| | | Open-ended | | |
| | Video | Multiple-choice | | |
| | | Open-ended | | |

This classification should help understand applicant reactions and
perceptions.

organizations to improve the reliability, validity, and utility of their selection systems. What was missing was the role of the applicant in the
selection process. Applicant reactions tap into the perceptions of applicants in understanding how fair and just they perceive a selection system
to be, and the effects of these reactions on important outcomes such as
job-acceptance decisions, litigation, and applicant self-perceptions. The realization that applicants' perceptions of selection procedures could have
important consequences for the organization has caused organizations and
researchers alike to examine these reactions. In addition, it has initiated efforts by practitioners to make selection procedures as positive as possible
while still maintaining their validity, practicality, and legal defensibility.

The theoretical basis for much of the applicant reactions research is organizational justice theory (e.g., Lind & Tyler, 1988). Research in this area has
been largely driven by Gilliland's (1993) model of applicant reactions to
selection systems. According to Gilliland's model, justice (or fairness) has
two key components, procedural and distributive justice. Whereas procedural justice elements focus on characteristics of the selection process
itself (e.g., its job-relatedness), distributive justice elements focus on the
favorability of outcomes received by job applicants. Gilliland proposed
that these fairness perceptions should affect a range of outcomes such as
job-acceptance decisions, litigation, and self-efficacy. Although the model
hypothesizes a key role for distributive justice, and distributive justice (or
outcome favorability) has been shown to be a key predictor of applicant reactions (e.g., Ryan & Ployhart, 2000), in this chapter we focus primarily on

procedural justice issues as these seem to be more within the organization's control.

Gilliland's (1993) model includes 10 procedural justice rules that are hypothesized to affect the perceived fairness of an organization's selection process. These justice rules fall under three broad categories of variables that are proposed to influence overall reactions, that in turn lead to important organizational and individual outcomes. The first is the *formal characteristics* category, which is comprised of job-relatedness, chance to perform, reconsideration opportunity, and consistency. Under the *explanation* heading is feedback, information known, and openness. Within the *interpersonal treatment* umbrella is treatment at the test site, two-way communication, and propriety of questions.

Potential outcomes noted by Gilliland include *reactions during hiring* such as organizational attractiveness, job acceptance, and test-taking motivation (a reaction that has generated its own literature, e.g., Arvey et al., 1990; Sanchez, Truxillo, & Bauer, 2000), *reactions after hiring* such as legal actions, on-the-job performance or attitudes, and reapplication intentions, and *self-perceptions* such as self-esteem and test-taking self-efficacy. Researchers have generally supported this model (e.g., Bauer, Maertz, Dolen, & Campion, 1998; Hausknecht, Day, & Thomas 2004; Ryan & Ployhart, 2000).

In the following sections, we review potential effects of different types of SJTs on three key applicant perceptions: fairness perceptions, motivation, and self-efficacy. Note that although there is now a fairly well-developed applicant reactions literature, there is still relatively little research that examines applicant reactions to SJTs per se. Therefore, as we review the possible effects of different types of SJTs on each of these applicant perceptions, we develop propositions as a guide to future research.

## RELATING APPLICANT REACTIONS TO SJTs: PROCEDURAL JUSTICE

As seen in Table 11.2, we believe that 5 of Gilliland's (1993) 10 procedural justice rules are most directly relevant to SJTs. They are job-relatedness, opportunity to perform, consistency of administration, feedback, and two-way communication. We did not focus on the other rules for three reasons. First, Gilliland proposed that the type of selection test was not relevant to these other justice rules. Second, we did not find research to support the importance of the other five rules to test-type. Third, logically, we did not perceive that these other five factors are affected by test-type; rather they are more likely affected by the company's selection policy, individual

TABLE 11.2

Propositions for SJTs in Terms of Ratings of Applicants Reactions

| Justice Rule | How SJT Fares Regarding This Justice Rule |
|---|---|
| Job-relatedness | High |
| Opportunity to perform | Low to high (interaction) |
| Reconsideration opportunity | Not necessarily affected |
| Consistency of administration | High |
| Feedback | Low to high (interaction) |
| Selection information | Not necessarily affected |
| Honesty | Not necessarily affected |
| Interpersonal effectiveness of administrator | Not necessarily affected |
| Two-way communication | Low |
| Propriety of questions | Not necessarily affected |

differences, or the human resources staff. For example, regardless of test-type, a rude or ineffective administrator is sure to offend applicants.

In this section, we present some research propositions based on these procedural justice rules as a guide to future research on how applicants perceive SJTs. Such work will be critical to understand not only how to improve these applicant reactions, but which factors will cause the greatest improvement in applicant perceptions at the least cost.

## Job-Relatedness

Gilliland (1993) defined job-relatedness as the extent to which a test either appears to measure content relevant to the job situations or appears to be valid. A sample item from the job-relatedness subscale of the Selection Procedural Justice Scale (SJPS), a scale designed to tap the 10 dimensions in Gilliland's model (Bauer et al., 2001), is "Doing well on this test means a person can do the job well." Job-relatedness is the most studied and one of the most salient procedural justice dimensions. It is clear that applicants (as well as the legal community) see job-relatedness as a key dimension relating to fairness. High perceptions of job-relatedness have been shown to relate to perceived fairness (e.g., Bauer et al., 1998; Kluger & Rothstein, 1993; Smither, Reilly, Millsap, Pearlman, & Stoffey, 1993). In their early study of applicant reactions, Smither et al. (1993) found that applicant assessments of job-relatedness were higher for interviews and assessment centers were rated higher than were personality tests and biodata. In a creative study of applicants for a student job, Gilliland manipulated job-relatedness and found that it related to ratings of procedural and distributive fairness. Research has also shown that simply communicating or explaining the research and rationale behind the selection method can enhance positive applicant reactions (e.g., Lounsbury, Bobrow, & Jensen, 1989; Ostberg, Truxillo, & Bauer, 2001; Truxillo, Bauer, Campion, & Paronto, 2002).

> **Proposition 1a:** SJTs of all types will be rated high on job-relatedness compared with more abstract types of selection procedures.
>
> **Proposition 1b:** Explaining the validity and job-relatedness of SJTs to applicants will increase perceptions of job-relatedness.

However, we also believe that both the stimulus and response format of the SJT itself should affect perceptions of job-relatedness. For example, SJTs that present situations to applicants in terms of written, scenario-based SJTs should appear less job-related to applicants than SJTs with video-based formats. Similarly, SJTs that present applicants with multiple-choice response options rather than open-ended options should appear less life-like to applicants and therefore less job-related.

> **Proposition 1c:** SJTs with more clearly job-related stimulus formats (e.g., video) should appear more fair to applicants than those with less clearly job-related formats (e.g., written scenario).
>
> **Proposition 1d:** SJTs with more clearly job-related response formats (e.g., open-ended) should appear more fair to applicants in terms of job-relatedness than those with less clearly job-related formats (e.g., multiple choice).

## Consistency of Administration

A major concern that applicants have is the degree to which selection is carried out in a consistent manner. To the extent that applicants perceived that all applicants are treated in the same way, undergo the same screening, and are administered the same questions, the higher they should perceive procedural justice. Therefore, selection systems that are higher on this dimension are desirable. A sample item from the SPJS (Bauer et al., 2001) is "There were no differences in the way the test was administered to different applicants." Bauer et al. (1998) found that consistency was related to general perceptions of testing fairness. Overall, we propose that SJTs will fare well on this dimension relative to more abstract selection methods as they tend to be highly structured and routinized. For example, stimulus formats that are written or videotaped do not vary by applicant, and this should lead to higher ratings on this dimension.

> **Proposition 2:** SJTs of all types will be rated high in terms consistency of administration compared to selection procedures that allow for differences in test administration across interviewees (e.g., unstructured interviews).

## Feedback

Feedback refers to applicants receiving timely and informative information about their performance in the test or selection process. Feedback given to applicants about how well they do is another key dimension to understanding applicant reactions. Applicants who do not hear anything about their performance tend to assume the worst (e.g., Rynes, Bretz, & Gerhart, 1991). Lounsbury et al. (1989) found that people who received feedback following a test had more favorable reactions than those who did not. The response format of an SJT is predicted to affect this dimension to the extent that it affects the time needed to score test responses and provide feedback to applicants. For example, a response format that is open-ended should take much longer to score than a multiple-choice format. Therefore, we propose the following:

> **Proposition 3:** The amount of time needed to score the SJT will affect fairness perceptions. SJTs with multiple-choice response formats may be rated more highly in terms of feedback timeliness than SJTs with open-ended formats due to the time required to score open-ended responses.

## Opportunity to Perform

The opportunity to perform relates to how much an applicant is able to offer input into the selection process in terms of showing his or her knowledge, skills, and abilities during a selection situation. A sample item from the SJPS (Bauer et al., 2001) is "This test gives applicants the opportunity to show what they can really do." In an interesting study of interviews, Bies and Shapiro (1988) provided both scenarios that allowed and did not allow interviewees to have input and ask questions. The interview that allowed greater interviewee input was rated higher in terms of procedural fairness.

To the extent that SJTs are highly structured and routinized, they will be rated low on this opportunity to perform. However, we believe that the response format of the SJT may affect applicants' perceived opportunity to perform. For example, the opportunity to give open-ended responses versus multiple-choice formats would allow applicants the chance to share insights into their answers above and beyond one single answer. Therefore we propose the following:

> **Proposition 4:** The response format of an SJT will affect perceptions of opportunity to perform. Specifically, SJTs with a multiple-choice format will be rated lower than open-ended SJTs in terms of opportunity to perform.

## Two-Way Communication

Two-way communication relates to an applicant's ability to ask questions and have them answered as well as to interpersonally offer input into the process (as opposed to opportunity to perform, which relates specifically to performance; Gilliland, 1993). A sample item from the communication subscale of the SPJS (Bauer et al., 2001) is "There was enough communication during the testing process." This is similar to the concept of voice. Perceptions of fair treatment may come from the opportunity to voice opinions about decisions (Thibaut & Walker, 1975). For example, when people feel they can give voice to their opinions it can enhance fairness perceptions. Due to the structured nature of most SJTs, we expect that applicants would rate SJTs low on this dimension. However, SJTs that involve more interaction between applicants and testing staff may lead to increased perceptions of communication and thus to fairness perceptions.

> **Proposition 5:** SJTs that involve more interaction with testing staff (e.g., those with certain types of open-ended response formats) will be rated more positively in terms of two-way communication.

## EFFECTS ON SELF-PERCEPTIONS

Outcome favorability refers to the result of the selection process. For example, did the applicant pass the selection hurdle? Did he or she receive a job offer? Research has shown that outcome favorability (also thought of as distributive justice) is a consistent predictor of applicant perceptions (e.g., Ryan & Ployhart, 2000). It has also shown that failure in selection can lower self-perceptions when performance is related to ability (McFarland & Ross, 1982).

As noted earlier, self-efficacy toward testing ability has been identified as a key self-perception outcome in theoretical models such as Gilliland's (1993), as well as research findings (e.g., Bauer et al., 1998; Gilliland, 1994). In studies with student samples, self-efficacy researchers have found that both trait-like factors (e.g., intelligence, need for achievement) and situational factors (e.g., goal orientation, state anxiety) influence performance (e.g., Chen, Gully, Whiteman, & Kilcullen, 2000; Phillips & Gully, 1997). A general finding is an interaction between being hired and ratings of procedural justice: Specifically, although rejection leads to lower self-efficacy for all applicants, this effect is especially strong among those rejected by means of a fair test (e.g., Gilliland, 1994). This is similar to the interaction proposed to exist between fairness and outcomes across a range of outcomes (e.g., Brockner, 2002; Brockner & Wiesenfeld, 1996).

In general, because most SJTs should be perceived as highly job-related by applicants, those who pass SJTs should experience high self-efficacy, whereas those who fail should experience very low self-efficacy. This will not be the case for more abstract selection methods such as cognitive-ability tests. In other words, because of their particularly high job-relatedness, SJTs may cause very low self-perceptions among those applicants who do not pass.

> **Proposition 6a:** Test type (SJT vs. abstract test) will interact with applicant outcome to affect self-perceptions such as self-efficacy. Specifically, those who pass SJTs should experience very high self-perceptions, whereas those who fail should experience very low self-efficacy. This effect will not be as pronounced for more abstract selection methods.

The realism (job-relatedness) of the SJT format should cause similar effects.

> **Proposition 6b:** Applicants who do not pass SJTs that are high in realism (e.g., video format) will experience lower self-perceptions than those who do not pass SJTs that are lower in realism (e.g., written format).

In summary, the possibility of more fair selection procedures such as SJTs leading to negative self-perceptions among unsuccessful applicants creates a dilemma for organizations. In other words, although increasing applicant fairness perceptions is believed to accrue a number of positive outcomes such as increased job acceptance and decreased litigation, it may also result in negative self-perceptions among those who do not pass the test. Clearly, we are not suggesting that organizations should reduce face validity or, worse yet, the psychological fidelity of their selection procedures to enhance the self-perceptions of those who fail. However, human resources practitioners may wish to consider techniques that buffer the negative effects on self-perceptions among applicants who fail. Such methods include explaining particularly low selection ratios to rejected applicants and providing positive interpersonal treatment when providing applicants with feedback (both in person and in writing).

## TEST-TAKING MOTIVATION

In addition to fairness perceptions, test-taking predispositions have begun to be explored, and one predisposition that has received considerable attention is test-taking motivation (e.g., Arvey et al., 1990; Sanchez et al., 2000; Schmit & Ryan, 1992). The study of test-taking motivation is important for several reasons. Test-taking motivation has been shown to relate to test validity (e.g., Schmit & Ryan, 1992), test performance (e.g., Arvey et al., 1990; Chan, Schmitt, DeShon, Clause, & Delbridge, 1997; Ryan, Ployhart, Greguras, & Schmit, 1998; Sanchez et al., 2000), ethnic differences in test performance (e.g., Arvey et al., 1990), and the likelihood of applicants remaining in a selection process (e.g., Schmit & Ryan, 1997). Researchers have found that applicant perceptions of fairness and job relevance are influenced by their perceived performance on tests they have taken (Chan, Schmitt, Jennings, Clause, & Delbridge, 1998). It seems that perceived performance matters a great deal for test-taking motivation. Furthermore, the more familiarity applicants have with a testing format such as video or written tests, the higher their test-taking motivation (e.g., Gilliland, 1993).

In terms of test-taking motivation, we expect the realism of the SJT format to be most motivating to applicants because it enhances job-relatedness. SJTs with more realistic stimulus and response formats should lead to increased motivation in terms of expectancy and instrumentality (see Sanchez et al., 2000). Because video SJTs actually *show* scenarios rather than describe them, we propose that video stimuli will be rated more favorably than paper-and-pencil SJTs in terms of job-relatedness.

**Proposition 7a:** SJTs with video stimulus will be rated higher than SJTs with written stimuli or scenarios.

In addition to job-relatedness, consistency of the treatment of applicants should also increase motivation in terms of expectancy and instrumentality. Therefore, SJTs should result in higher applicant motivation than selection methods that may allow for inconsistency in the way they are administered to applicants.

**Proposition 7b:** SJTs of all types will result in higher test-taker motivation compared with selection procedures that allow for differences in test administration across interviewees (e.g., unstructured interviews) due to increased fairness perceptions in terms of consistency of administration.

Similarly, opportunity to perform should also increase motivation in terms of expectancy and instrumentality.

**Proposition 7c:** SJTs will be rated as high or low in terms of opportunity to perform depending on response format, such that SJTs with a multiple-choice response format will be rated lower than open-ended SJTs.

## RECENT DEVELOPMENTS IN ORGANIZATIONAL JUSTICE: IMPLICATIONS FOR SJTs

Although some researchers have questioned the usefulness of fairness-based models of applicant reactions (e.g., Ryan & Ployhart, 2000), and some have proposed the integration of attribution theory (e.g., Ployhart & Harold, 2004) and social identity theory (e.g., Herriot, 2004), support for the organizational justice approach to explaining applicant reactions has generally been promising. Support has been found for selection fairness on "soft" outcomes such as attitudes and intentions, although research on behavioral outcomes (e.g., actual litigation) has been lacking (Truxillo, Steiner, & Gilliland, 2004). However, there have been developments in organizational justice theory that could further explain applicant reactions, and some of which are particularly relevant to SJTs.

*Justice–Injustice Asymmetry.* Gilliland and Chan (2001) discussed a threshold for unfairness. Relatively fair procedures would have little effect on reactions, whereas unfair procedures would cross a threshold that should lead to very negative reactions. In the context of SJTs, most applicants should consider SJTs relatively fair because of their obvious face validity, suggesting that SJTs should result in relatively few highly negative outcomes. However, this is an issue that needs further research.

*Fairness Early in the Person–Organization Relationship.* Lind's (2001) fairness heuristic theory holds that fairness perceptions develop from a general fairness judgment early in the relationship, after which the general perception of the organization becomes less likely to change. And once the fairness heuristic is established, it forms a lens through which subsequent information about the organization is interpreted. Similarly, Cropanzano and Ambrose (2001) presented a monistic view of justice, such that procedural and distributive fairness perceptions are highly related because both are influenced by early perceptions. For this reason, we argue that it is important to positively influence perceptions early in the organizational relationship, such as during the selection process, and that the generally positive views applicants should have of SJTs are an excellent ways to do this.

## TECHNOLOGY AND SJT AND APPLICANT REACTIONS

One of the most revolutionary changes in applicant selection is the development of high-tech selection methods (see Olson-Buchanan & Drasgow, chap. 12, this volume for more detail on technology and SJT). Such methods provide employers with several advantages, such as increased validity and reduced adverse impact, whereas applicants may gain quicker feedback (Lievens & Harris, 2003). Regarding SJTs, high-tech approaches will allow for the cheaper, more efficient delivery of tests with greater fidelity. Given the importance of job-relatedness and quick feedback to applicant reactions, we believe that this will enhance the perceived fairness of SJTs. On the other hand, there may be some drawbacks to more high-tech SJTs. For example, people who are less familiar with computers or who have less access to the Internet (e.g., older workers, some minority group members, people of lower socioeconomic status) may see high-tech SJTs in a less positive light (Truxillo et al., 2004). Clearly, what is thought today to be high-tech by applicants will be considered less so over time. But as new technologies are introduced, researchers and practitioners should focus on how to make newer technologies available and acceptable to all members of their applicant pools.

## RECOMMENDATIONS FOR PRACTICE

As noted earlier, there is little research on reactions to SJTs, so practice recommendations must be made based on some general conclusions from the applicant reactions literature. Overall, SJTs of all sorts should be perceived positively by applicants. They all provide greater face validity and obvious job-relatedness than abstract types of tests such as cognitive ability and personality tests. Therefore, SJTs provide a valuable option for organizations seeking to improve applicant reactions. This could be particularly useful when an employer seeks to increase job acceptance or to reduce the possibility of litigation. Of course, these considerations must be balanced with the increased cost sometimes associated with an SJT (e.g., if the test is developed in-house) and with the assumption that an SJT is available that provides adequate validity.

This last point raises an interesting issue, both when choosing between an SJT and a more abstract test format, or among different types of SJTs (i.e., those differing in terms of their stimulus or response formats.) For example, although video-based SJTs may lead to more positive applicant reactions, the costs associated with the development and administration of a video-based SJT may be prohibitive. But development costs may be well worth it when there is a large enough applicant pool, and the costs associated with administration may be worth it if facilities are readily available. Moreover, such costs may be worth it in litigious environments or it is important for applicants to become familiar with the job during the selection process. Similarly, although a multiple-choice response format may cause some reduction in job-relatedness, this may be worth the trade-off to gain speedier feedback to applicants. In making any decisions regarding the components of a selection system, a consideration of applicant reactions should be balanced with validity, practicality, utility, and legal issues.

Finally, we conclude our chapter with some key factors that organizations can use to enhance applicants' perceptions of SJTs. We present these factors in Table 11.3, along with some specific suggestions for each factor. First, although SJTs are considered high in face validity, methods that can increase face validity (e.g., more realistic scenarios) should be considered when possible. Second, when using any test, it is important to enhance interpersonal fairness. For example, human resources staff should show consideration for applications. Third, and relatedly, we suggest that information be shared with applicants. This is important to provide reasonable expectations for what the testing process will involve, or how long it will take to score the test. Information may be particularly important to reduce applicants' concerns when a novel (e.g., high-tech) test format is used. Fourth, we also suggest that explanations be provided after the testing process is complete, so applicants can understand their scores, how they were derived, and how they fit into the hiring decision. There has been relatively little research on organizational interventions to improve applicant reactions (Truxillo et al., 2004), the work on reactions to SJTs is particularly

TABLE 11.3

Factors Underlying Applicant Perceptions of SJTs and Methods
for Enhancing These Factors

| Factor | Potential Methods for Enhancement |
|---|---|
| Face validity | 1. Use realistic, job-related scenarios.<br>2. Use less artificial media (e.g., video).<br>3. Use realistic response formats (e.g., open-ended rather than multiple-choice.<br>4. Enhance psychological fidelity (i.e., be sure the test elicits key knowledge, skills, and abilities). |
| Interpersonal fairness | 1. Ensure that human resource staff treat applicants with respect. |
| Information (pretest) | 1. Provide information about what to expect in the test.<br>2. Inform applicants about any new technology involved in the test.<br>3. Explain how long it will take to score the SJT and why.<br>4. Although it may be obvious, explain the job-relatedness of the SJT, that it was validated, and so on. |
| Explanation (posttest) | 1. Provide explanations for how the scoring was done.<br>2. Explain how the test score will affect the hiring procedure. |

sparse. However, we believe this chapter provides a guide for future research into how applicants perceive SJTs and what organizations can do to enhance these perceptions. Such work will be critical to understanding not only how to improve these applicant reactions, but which factors will cause the greatest improvement in applicant perceptions at the least cost. Future work should continue to investigate the impact that technology has on applicant reactions to SJTs. Integrating this chapter with chapter 12 by Olson-Buchanan and Drasgow should help researchers and practitioners identify key areas for pursue in the future.

# REFERENCES

Arvey, R. D., Strickland, W., Drauden, G., & Martin, C. (1990). Motivational components of test-taking. *Personnel Psychology, 43,* 695–716.

Bauer, T. N., Maertz, C., Dolen, M., & Campion, M. A. (1998). A longitudinal assessment of applicant reactions to an employment test. *Journal of Applied Psychology, 83,* 892–903.

Bauer, T. N., Truxillo, D. M., Sanchez, R., Craig, J., Ferrara, P., & Campion, M. A. (2001). Development of the Selection Procedural Justice Scale (SPJS). *Personnel Psychology, 54,* 387–419.

Bies, R. J., & Shapiro, D. L. (1988). Voice and justification: Their influence on procedural fairness judgments. *Academy of Management Journal, 31,* 676–685.

Brockner, J. (2002). Making sense of procedural justice: How high procedural fairness can reduce or heighten the influence of outcome favorability. *Academy of Management Review, 27,* 58–76.

Brockner, J., & Wiesenfeld, B. M. (1996). An integrative framework for explaining reactions to decisions: Interactive effects of outcomes and procedures. *Psychological Bulletin, 120,* 189–208.

Cascio, W. F., & Phillips, N. (1979). Performance testing: A rose among thorns? *Personnel Psychology, 32,* 751–766.

Chan, D. & Schmitt, N. (1997). Video-based versus paper-and-pencil method of assessment in situational judgment tests: Subgroup differences in test performance and face validity perceptions. *Journal of Applied Psychology, 82,* 143–159.

Chan, D., Scmitt, N., DeShon, R. P., Clause, C. S., & Delbridge, K. (1997). Reactions to cognitive ability tests: The relationship between race, test performance, face validity perceptions, and test-taking motivation. *Journal of Applied Psychology, 82,* 300–310.

Chan, D., Schmitt, N., Jennings, D., Clause, C. S., & Delbridge, K. (1998). Applicant perceptions of test fairness: Integrating justice and self-serving bias perceptions. *International Journal of Selection and Assessment, 6,* 232–239.

Chen, G., Gully, S. M., Whiteman, J. A., & Kilcullen, R. N. (2000). Examination of relationships among trait-like individual differences, state-like individual differences, and learning performance. *Journal of Applied Psychology, 85,* 835–847.

Cropanzano, R., & Ambrose, M. L. (2001). Procedural and distributive justice are more similar than you think: A monistic perspective and a research agenda. In J. Greenberg & R. Cropanzano (Eds.), *Advances in organizational justice* (pp. 119–151). Stanford, CA: Stanford University Press.

Funk, U., & Schuler, H. (1998). Validity of stimulus and response components in a video test of social comparisons International. *Journal of Selection and Assesment, 6,* 115–123.

Gilliland, S. W. (1993). The perceived fairness of selection systems: An organizational justice perspective. *Academy of Management Review, 18,* 694–734.

Gilliland, S. W. (1994). Effects of procedural justice and distributive justice on reactions to a selection system. *Journal of Applied Psychology, 79,* 691–701.

Gilliland, S. W., & Chan, D. (2001). Justice in organizations: Theory, methods, and applications. In N. Anderson, D. S. Ones, H. K. Sinangil, & C. Viswesvaran (Eds.), *International handbook of work and organizational psychology* (pp. 143–165). Newbury Park, CA: Sage.

Hattrup, K., & Schmitt, N. (1990). Prediction of trades apprentices' performance on job sample criteria. *Personnel Psychology, 43,* 453–466.

Hausknecht, J. P., Day, D. V., & Thomas, S. C. (2004). Applicant reactions to selection procedures: An updated model and meta-analysis. *Personnel Psychology 57,* 639–683.

Herriot, P. (2004). Social identities and applicant reactions. *International Journal of Selection & Assessment, 12(1–2),* 75–83.

Kluger, A. N., & Rothstein, H. R. (1993). The influence of selection test type on applicant reactions to employment testing. *Journal of Business & Psychology, 8,* 3–25.

Lievens, F., & Harris, M. M. (2003). Research on internet recruitment and testing: Current status and future directions. *International Review of Industrial and Organizational Psychology.* Chichester, England: Wiley.

Lind, E. A. (2001). Fairness heuristic theory: Justice judgments as pivotal cognitions in organizational settings. In J. Greenberg & R. Cropanzano (Eds.), *Advances in organizational justice* (pp. 56–88). Stanford, CA: Stanford University Press.

Lind, E. A., & Tyler, T. (1988). *The social psychology of procedural justice.* New York: Plenum.

Lounsbury, J. W., Bobrow, W., & Jensen, J. B. (1989). Attitudes toward employment testing: Scale development, correlates, and "known-group" validation. *Professional Psychology: Research and Practice, 20,* 340–349.

McFarland, C., & Ross, M. (1982). Impact of causal attributions on affective reactions to success and failure. *Journal of Personality and Social Psychology, 43,* 937–946.

Mount, M. K., Muchinsky, P. M., & Hanser, L. M. (1977). The predictive validity of a work sample: A laboratory study. *Personnel Psychology, 30,* 637–645.

Olson-Buchanan, J. B., Drasgow, F., Moberg, P. J., Mead, A. D., Keenan, P. A., & Donovan, M. A. (1998). Interactive video assessment of conflict resolution skills. *Personnel Psychology, 51,* 1–24.

Ostberg, D. E., Truxillo, D. M., & Bauer, T. N. (2001, April). Effects of pre-test information on applicants' perceptions of selection fairness. In R. E. Ployhart & D. M. Truxillo (Co-Chairs), *Presenting selection information to applicants: Theoretical and practical implications.* Symposium presented at the 16th annual meeting of the Society for Industrial and Organizational Psychology, San Diego, CA.

Philips, J. M., & Gully, S. M. (1997). Role of goal orientation, ability, need for achievement, and locus of control in the self-efficacy and goal-setting process. *Journal of Applied Psychology, 82,* 792–802.

Ployhart, R. E., & Harold, C. M. (2004). The applicant attribution-reaction theory (AART): An integrative theory of applicant attributional processing. *International Journal of Selection & Assessment, 12(1–2),* 84–98.

Ryan, A. M., & Ployhart, R. E. (2000). Applicants' perceptions of selection procedures and decisions: A critical review and agenda for the future. *Journal of Management, 26,* 565–606.

Ryan, A. M., Ployhart, R. E., Greguras, G. J., & Schmit, M. J. (1998). Test preparation programs in selection contexts: Self-selection and program effectiveness. *Personnel Psychology, 51,* 599–621.

Rynes, S. L., & Boudreau, J. W. (1986). College recruiting in large organizations: Practice, evaluation, and research implications. *Personnel Psychology, 39,* 729–757.

Rynes, S. L., Bretz, R. D., & Gerhart, B. (1991). The importance of recruitment in job choice: A different way of looking. *Personnel Psychology, 44,* 487–521.

Sanchez, R. J., Truxillo, D. M., & Bauer, T. N. (2000). Development and examination of an expectancy-based measure of test-taking motivation. *Journal of Applied Psychology, 85,* 739–750.

Schmit, M. J., & Ryan, A. M. (1992). Test-taking dispositions: A missing link? *Journal of Applied Psychology, 77,* 629–637.

Schmit, M. J., & Ryan, A. M. (1997). Applicant withdrawal: The role of test-taking attitudes and racial differences. *Personnel Psychology, 50,* 855–876.

Schmitt, N., & Mills, A. E. (2001). Traditional tests and job simulations: Minority and majority performance and test validities. *Journal of Applied Psychology, 86,* 451–458.

Smither, J. W., Reilly, R. R., Millsap, R.E., Pearlman, K., & Stoffey, R. W. (1993). Applicant reactions to selection procedures. *Personnel Psychology, 46,* 49–76.

Stevens, M. J., & Campion, M. A. (1999). Staffing work teams: Development and validation of a selection test for teamwork settings. *Journal of Management, 25,* 207–228.

Thibaut, J., & Walker, T. J. (1975). *Procedural justice: A psychological analysis.* Hillsdale, NJ: Lawrence Erlbaum Associates.

Truxillo, D. M., Bauer, T. N., Campion, M. A., & Paronto, M. E. (2002). Selection fairness information and applicant reactions: A longitudinal field study. *Journal of Applied Psychology, 87,* 1020–1031.

Truxillo, D. M., Donahue, L. M., & Kuang, D. (2003). Job sample tests, performance testing, and competency testing. In J. Thomas (Ed.), *Comprehensive handbook of psychological assessment, Vol. 4: Industrial/organizational psychology* (pp. 345–370). New York: Wiley.

Truxillo, D. M., Steiner, D. D., & Gilliland, S. W. (2004). The importance of organizational justice in personnel selection: Defining when selection fairness really matters. *International Journal of Selection & Assessment, 12(1–2),* 39–53.

Weekley, J. A., & Jones, C. (1997). Video-based situational testing. *Personnel Psychology, 50,* 25–49.

# III

# Application

# 12

# Multimedia Situational Judgment Tests: The Medium Creates the Message

Julie B. Olson-Buchanan
*California State University, Fresno*

Fritz Drasgow
*University of Illinois, Urbana–Champaign*

A considerable amount of research has documented the effectiveness and efficiency of low-fidelity situational judgment tests (SJTs) that present stimuli in written form and provide multiple-choice options for responses. However, recent advances in multimedia computer technology have opened the door to the development and implementation of alternative SJT formats. For example, situational test items could be presented through the use of video clips, allowing assessees to see and hear people interacting, perceive or, importantly, fail to perceive their emotions and stress, and confront dilemmas about one's choice of action or inaction. Multimedia situational judgment tests (MMSJTs) frequently retain a multiple-choice answer format, but provide a much richer assessment environment that allows the situational context to be richly portrayed. With this format, we may be able to better understand how the assessee will interpret verbal and nonverbal behaviors of others in the workplace and choose to respond.

In this chapter, we describe and analyze MMSJTs. MMSJTs became technologically feasible around 1990, which sparked the interest of several researchers. As a result, we begin with a description of the benefits and challenges of MMSJTs that were anticipated when research in this area was initiated. Next, we discuss what is now known about developing MMSJTs and summarize research findings. We then evaluate the benefits and challenges of MMSJTs and conclude with a discussion of the major issues that need to be addressed to advance our understanding of MMSJTs.

## THE ANTICIPATED BENEFITS AND CHALLENGES OF MMSJTs

The use of multimedia technology gained early acceptance and application in the education (e.g., Broadus, 1991) and training fields (e.g., "Interactive video training," 1991). Although such technology was not as quickly adopted for assessment purposes, its potential benefits and challenges generated substantial discussion and debate since it became available around 1990 (e.g., Dyer, Desmarais, Midkiff, Colihan, & Olson, 1992). The ability to present stimuli in the form of full-motion video and audio via personal computers (PCs) seemed especially applicable to SJTs.

There were several advantages hypothesized for multimedia assessment. First, it was anticipated that full-motion video/audio would heighten assessee interest (Drasgow, Olson, Keenan, Moberg, & Mead, 1993) and enhance perceptions of face validity (Weekley & Jones, 1997) as it had in educational settings (e.g., Petty & Rosen, 1987). Although multimedia technology was available to personal and business consumers in the late 1980s, it was still novel in the context of assessment. Given the proliferation of electronic entertainment, there was some concern that paper-and-pencil assessments, particularly in the domain of situational judgment, would soon seem old fashioned to digital-savvy consumers. Presenting assessment stimuli via an electronic medium seemed like a logical solution.

A number of researchers argued that the fidelity of SJTs would be enhanced with the use of multimedia technology relative to the traditional paper-and-pencil format (e.g., Drasgow et al., 1993; Weekley & Jones, 1997). Thorndike (1949) touted enhanced realism as a benefit of video (film)–based tests long before they were widely available. In particular, multimedia may be able to present a more veridically representative workplace stimulus in that voice inflections, facial expressions, and other nonverbal behaviors would be more similar to what one would experience face-to-face on the job (Desmarais et al., 1992; Drasgow et al., 1993). That is, a video presentation of an employee complaining about the difficulty of a work assignment might require the assessee to notice and interpret how the employee presents her complaint (e.g., is the employee exasperated or calm?) and this interpretation may be an important factor in selecting the "right" answer. Indeed, personality research (e.g., Chiu, Hong, Mischel, & Shoda 1995; Shoda, Mischel, & Wright, 1993) suggests that "this type of discriminative facility seems to be a component of social intelligence, a sensitivity to the subtle cues in the situation that influences behavior" (Mischel & Shoda, 1998, p. 244). In contrast, a paper-and-pencil SJT may have to directly state some aspects of the nonverbal or verbal cues. To the extent that it is important for an individual to perceive accurately verbal and nonverbal situational cues in the workplace, an MMSJT may provide a superior assessment of job-related skills.

In addition, it was anticipated that the increased realism of MMSJTs would not be at the expense of standardization or reliability. That is, much like paper-and-pencil SJTs, the stimuli would be presented in exactly the same way to all assessees, with no variations due to, say, changes in role-playing actor's performance (Drasgow et al., 1993).

The technological possibility of developing interactive SJTs was considered an especially intriguing potential benefit of MMSJTs (McHenry & Schmitt, 1994). In contrast to linear MMSJTs where the content of the test does not vary, an interactive MMSJT would present different video/audio to the test taker based on the test taker's response to earlier video/audio (Drasgow et al., 1993). This would allow the SJT to simulate the dynamics of interaction, while maintaining some level of standardization. Researchers argued that this interactivity would increase the fidelity of the MMSJT even further because the test taker would be interacting with the SJT (McHenry & Schmitt, 1994).

Some researchers argued that MMSJTs may serve to mitigate subgroup differences because they minimize the use of written stimuli material (Drasgow et al., 1993). McDaniel, Morgeson, Finnegan, Campion, and Braverman's (2001) meta-analysis revealed a substantial relation between SJTs (typically paper-and-pencil) and cognitive-ability measures on average (mean correlation of .46), albeit with considerable variation. Given the ability to present stimuli (and even responses) in video or audio, several researchers argued that MMSJTs would be less related to general cognitive ability than paper-and-pencil SJTs and subsequently would have smaller differences between groups.

In addition, it was anticipated that MMSJTs would enjoy the benefits typically associated with computer-based assessment (Olson-Buchanan, 2001). These benefits include increased ease of administration (automated delivery and recording of answers), ability to provide immediate feedback (Schmitt, Gillliland, Landis, & Devine, 1993), and enhanced flexibility in accommodating disabled individuals (e.g., Johnson, 1983).

The potential challenges of creating and maintaining MMSJTs generated a similar amount of discussion. Perhaps the largest barrier to entry was the anticipated development costs (Olson-Buchanan, 2001). In addition to the resources typically needed to develop the content for paper-and-pencil SJTs, early MMSJTs also required specialized hardware (e.g., a PC equipped with a laserdisc player and adaptor), programming, and video/audio production costs (Mead, 1991). In the early 1990s, a typical station with the requisite specialized hardware cost approximately $5,000. Programming costs were harder to estimate. Although there were some primitive authoring systems available at the time, they did not have the requisite flexibility for MMSJTs. Video/audio production costs varied depending on whether a professional production company or the researcher's own production talents were used (Midkiff, Dyer, Desmarais, Rogg, & McCusker, 1992; Olson & Keenan, 1994). Note that an interactive MMSJT would incur additional costs to produce the branching scenes.

A related concern surrounded the maintenance costs associated with changes in technology (Midkiff et al., 1992). Multimedia programming was generally platform-specific. Suppose a MMSJT was custom-programmed in 1991 to use the IBM M-motion adaptor card for the DOS or OS/2 operating systems. When IBM stopped supporting this hardware and software, what resources would be required to upgrade or change to a new system?

Just as technology becomes obsolete, the content of a video may also become dated (Desmarais et al., 1992). The clothing, hairstyles, and office décor depicted in a workplace in 1988 could appear out of style just a few years later. Imagine, for example, how a cell phone from 1995 might appear today. Although every effort could be made to minimize or neutralize the date-related appearance of video content, clearly updating MMSJT content would require more resources than a paper-and-pencil SJT.

Another anticipated challenge inherent in developing MMSJTs involved maintaining or verifying the integrity of the item content in video/audio production (Drasgow, Olson-Buchanan, & Moberg, 1999; Olson & Keenan, 1994). The content for a paper-and-pencil SJT might be initially developed through the critical-incidents technique and modified or further developed through extensive paper-and-pencil pilot testing. The content for an MMSJT would be similarly developed and then the video/audio would be prepared. However, an additional task would be to determine whether the video/audio stimuli accurately represent the content as originally intended. Here the test developer should examine the video to determine whether the nuances of vocal tone, inflection, and facial expression conveyed what had originally been intended. This could be done with additional pilot testing of the video/audio, but changes at that point would be expensive.

Finally, some of the challenges associated with traditional SJTs would also be issues for MMSJTs as well. In particular, response scaling and scoring (see chap. 3, this volume) was a significant issue to address in MMSJTs (e.g., Desmarais, Masi, Olson, Barbera, & Dyer, 1994; McHenry & Schmitt, 1994). Scoring for interactive video assessments would introduce additional challenges because branched or nested items are not independent and all test takers would not respond to the same items, making it difficult to assess reliability (McHenry & Schmitt, 1994).

## REVIEW OF MMSJTs

Despite concerns about cost and commensurate gains (e.g., incremental validity), test developers have created MMSJTs. As a result, today we can begin to evaluate whether the anticipated benefits and drawbacks of MM-SJTs have been realized. Although it has been about 15 years since multimedia technology became available, it has taken some time for a significant literature to develop in this area (Drasgow & Olson-Buchanan, 1999; Olson-Buchanan, 2001).

### Videotape-Based SJTs

Although the term *multimedia* often refers to computer-driven media, research using video-based assessments is also relevant to this discussion. That is, many of the hypothesized benefits and challenges of MMSJTs are equally applicable to non-computer-based media assessments that incorporate video and audio (e.g., Weekley & Jones, 1997).

For example, Dalessio (1994) developed a video-based SJT to predict turnover among insurance agents. To minimize development costs (he estimated it would cost $2,000 to $3,000 per minute of filming), he created a video SJT by editing existing sales training tapes from several insurance companies. He developed the multiple-choice response options with several subject matter experts (SMEs) who provided original responses for the most effective and least effective options to the scenarios. Using a predictive validity design, he asked assessees (newly hired agents) to select the options describing what they would most likely and least likely do when confronted with the situation depicted in the video. Delassio used an empirical method (the horizontal percent method) to develop a scoring key and found the assessees' most likely score was significantly related to turnover one year after the assessment.

Pine (1994) developed a video-based SJT for correctional officers. He created 47 officer–inmate scenarios from critical incidents and filmed the scenarios with one camera using current officers to play the roles. The multiple-choice responses were developed with input from current incumbents, job applicants, and an expert panel. In addition to presenting the responses in written form, a narrator read the responses and test takers were asked to indicate their most and least likely responses to each situation. The scoring system was based on expert ratings, where one option was identified as most effective (+1), one response was identified as least effective (−1) and the remaining responses were neither (0 points). A concurrent validity study ($N = 100$) demonstrated significant correlations between the total scores and four of six performance criteria. Interestingly, the test takers' least likely response scores were significantly related to five of the six criteria, whereas the most likely scores were only significantly related to one of the six criteria.

Weekley and Jones (1997) developed and validated two video-based SJTs, one for hourly retail workers and another for nursing home caregivers. The scripts for both SJTs were developed through the critical incidents technique with SME input throughout the revision process. The SJTs were professionally filmed on site, with SMEs available to ensure realism. The video was later edited onto videotape along with the accompanying response options. Task performance, cognitive ability, and amount of experience measures were also collected for both studies. The scoring for the retail workers' SJT was empirically based, whereas both an empirical and rational (customer/family member preference) was developed for the caregiver SJT. Both the empirical keys and the customer-preference key (rational) were significantly related to the appropriate criterion measure. Moreover, Weekley and Jones demonstrated that the SJT scores provided predictive power above and beyond cognitive ability and experience. Similarly, significant validity results were found for other SJTs developed for the customer service/relations industry (Jones & DeCotiis, 1986; McHenry & Schmitt, 1994).

Smiderle, Perry, and Cronshow (1994) presented the results of a concurrent validity study for a video SJT that had already been widely used as an interpersonal skills predictor to select mass transit operators in the United States and Canada. Originally developed with critical incidents generated from SMEs and scored by SME ratings of response options, the video SJT had not previously been empirically examined. Smiderle et al. described content-validity support for the video SJT, but found low reliability and weak (but significant) empirical support for one of the criteria (number of complaints). There were no significant mean differences in test score between majority group members (White males) and women or African Americans. However, the mean score for women was significantly higher than it was for African Americans. Given the low reliability of the test score and fairly small sample sizes, these results should be interpreted with caution. Perhaps more encouraging criterion-related results would be found if additional SMEs were used to develop the scoring key or if empirical scoring alternatives were examined.

D. Chan and Schmitt (1997) compared undergraduate reactions to a paper-and-pencil version of an SJT to a video-based version of the SJT. The video-based SJT was a pilot version of an assessment developed by a human resources firm to be used for skilled and semi-skilled blue-collar employees. Designed to measure four factors (work commitment, work quality, conflict management, and empathy), the SJT included 12 scenarios. The scoring was by a rational key derived from 25 SMEs. Chan and Schmitt found undergraduates responded more favorably to the video-based version (higher face validity) and found significantly smaller mean differences in performance on the video SJT between African Americans and whites.

Lievens and Coetsier (2002) described the development of two video-based SJTs that were part of a medical and dental school admission battery in Belgium. The content for the "physician–patient interaction" SJT and "medical expert discussion" SJT was developed with a critical-incident procedure. The scripts were written and verified by SMEs (professors in the consulting physician discipline) for realism and the video was filmed in a recording studio with outside "semi-professional" talent playing the roles in the scenarios. To ensure the scenes were realistic, an experienced physician was on the set during taping. Lievens and Coestsier used expert scoring for both SJTs. Although the physician–patient SJT was statistically related to the criterion measure (first-year performance in medical school), neither SJT provided incremental validity. The authors noted this criterion is heavily $g$-loaded and suggest that different results may be found for different criteria. A more recent study by Lievens, Buyse, and Sackett (2005) supports this explanation. Lievens et al. conducted a longer term predictive study of the physician–patient SJT and found incremental validity, above the cognitively loaded predictors, for predicting performance in medical schools that place greater emphasis on interpersonal skills. Moreover, the SJT validity became increasingly higher over time (i.e., it is higher for later medical school performance). This research underscores the importance of SJT predictor-criterion alignment.

Researchers at U.S. Customs and Border Protection (CBP) have developed an innovative MMSJT to aid in the selection of border patrol officers (Walker & Goldenberg, 2004). Here, candidates are shown video clips depicting highly realistic and important situations faced by border patrol officers; these scenarios were obtained from critical-incidents reported by experienced officers. At a critical juncture, the video freezes and the word "RESPOND" is displayed. The candidate must then orally react to the situation and this response is videotaped. Note that there can be no response cuing when this format is used because the responses are completely constructed by the assessee.

To score the videotaped responses, CBP researchers worked with experienced supervisory-level border patrol officers. Rubrics for scoring responses were developed for four core competencies: interpersonal skills, judgment and decision making, emotional maturity, and sensitivity to others. In addition, rubrics for a global rating of performance were developed. After the rubrics were developed, CBP researchers developed a training program for the raters who grade videotaped responses. The rubrics and training program seem to work well; Walker and Goldenberg (2004) reported interrater reliabilities ranging from .67 to .78 for the competencies just described.

The most innovative feature of this assessment lies in its open-ended response format. Test-wise candidates cannot scrutinize multiple-choice options and deduce the option that the test developer will score as correct; instead, candidates must create their own answer in real time. Much interesting research can be conducted on this response format. For example, what is the validity of this assessment? Does the use of a constructed response format provide incremental validity over that provided by a multiple-choice format? Are the latent traits assessed by the open-ended response format the same as those assessed by a multiple-choice format?

## Computer-Based SJTs

Some of the earliest MMSJTs used a videocassette recording in combination with a personal computer. Allstate's Multimedia In-Basket (Ashworth & Joyce, 1994; Ashworth & McHenry, 1993) is a good example of such an approach. Designed to measure problem solving, decision making, managing multiple priorities, and planning and prioritizing, it required assessees to take on a customer service role for a fictitious airline. In that capacity, assessees were directed to prioritize and attend to a multitude of tasks related to arranging or rearranging customer travel plans while adhering to appropriate policies and regulations. The authors discussed its development (Ashworth & McHenry, 1994) and complex SME-based scoring system (Ashworth & Joyce, 1994) at Society for Industrial and Organizational Psychology conferences. Additional information about its validity and psychometric properties has not been disseminated. Similarly, Kleinmann and Strauß (1998) reported encouraging validities for several "computer-simulated scenario" research projects that require assessees to take on the role of a manager and address complex problems.

The ability to present video via computer, rather than via a videocassette recording has changed considerably since it first became widely available in the late 1980s. Initially, video was stored on a laserdisc—a silvery disk about 12 inches in diameter. This technology required the professional (and expensive) pressing of specially prepared video input to the laserdisc; despite its large size, a laserdisc could hold no more than 30 minutes of video. Input from the laserdisc could then be shown on the computer via a dedicated (and expensive—about $1,200) adaptor card. The next generation of video technology involved the use of compact discs (CDs). Video was digitized and compressed according to the Moving Picture Experts Group (MPEG) format. When this technology was introduced, test developers could expect to pay about $100 per minute to convert their video clips to MPEG files and a special adaptor card was needed to decompress the files and play the video in real time. By the late 1990s, mainstream video adaptor cards had become capable of decompressing and playing full-motion video without obvious artifacts. In the mid-2000s, DVDs can be easily developed with digital camcorders and played on PCs. Next we discuss a range of MMSJTs that have employed these different generations of multimedia technology.

**The Illinois Project.** A group of Illinois researchers developed a comprehensive assessment battery (the COMPAS program) that includes several MMSJTs. For example, the Conflict Resolution Skills Assessment (CRSA; Olson-Buchanan et al., 1998) is an interactive SJT designed to measure managers' skill in addressing and resolving conflict in the workplace. The assessment consists of nine main scenes that depict work-related conflicts. The scene freezes at a critical decision point and the assessees are given four multiple-choice options for how they could proceed if they were in that situation. The assessment is interactive in that the test taker's response to the main scene determines which branch scene is shown. After the branch scene, the assessee is again given four multiple-choice options and he or she must pick the option that best describes how he or she would proceed. The assessment then moves to the next main scene.

The conflict scenarios were developed through a seven-step process. The first two steps were closely modeled after Motowidlo, Dunnette, and Carter's (1990) method and consisted of (a) gathering critical-incident information from managers via structured interviews and (b) generating realistic multiple-choice options for scenarios developed from the Step 1 critical incidents. The remaining steps were designed to allow model-based scoring according to a prescriptive conflict model (Olson-Buchanan et al., 1998) while maintaining realism. In Step 3, the options generated in Step 2 were narrowed down to four that were comparable in terms of social desirability. In Step 4, the conflict summaries were classified in terms of the theoretical model and modified to ensure all aspects of the model were covered. In Step 5, scripts for the main conflict and branch scenes were developed and verified for content accuracy against the original conflict summaries, modified accordingly, and reclassified in terms of the theoretical model. In Step 6, the scenes were videotaped by the researchers using local talent. In Step 7, the video was edited and converted to laserdisc.

The CRSA was originally developed for use with a laserdisc player and M-motion adapter card. A program written in Pascal was developed to play the video clips, present the multiple-choice options, and record the assessee's response (Mead, 1991). This combination of exotic hardware and custom-designed software was expensive and cumbersome, which made it difficult to administer the assessment and collect validity data (Drasgow et al., 1999). The second version of the assessment used video clips compressed in the MPEG format, software written with Asymmetrix's Multimedia Toolbook, CBT edition, and Sigma Design's RealMagic adaptor card. The most recent version uses Microsoft's Access to play MPEG videos, present multiple-choice options, and record answers. It should be noted that ordinary video adaptor cards manufactured since then can easily present the video and consequently specialized hardware is no longer needed. Moreover, the Access software is much more stable than earlier implementations.

To address the scoring issue, the researchers examined three scoring methods: model-based, empirical, and a hybrid of the model- and empirical-based methods. To minimize capitalization on chance when empirical keying was used, Breiman, Friedman, Olshen, and Stone's (1984) N-fold cross-validation was used to estimate validity. Although all three scoring approaches were significantly related to the criterion (a supervisor rating of how well the assessee dealt with conflict), the empirical and hybrid scores had the highest cross-validity ($r = .26$, $p < .01$). The conflict-resolution scores were not significantly related to verbal or quantitative ability measures. Interestingly, although the verbal and quantitative scores of African Americans were significantly lower than Whites, the reverse was true for the conflict-resolution scores. That is, African Americans scored significantly higher on the CRSA than Whites.

Richman-Hirsch, Olson-Buchanan, and Drasgow (2000) used a between-subjects design to compare managers' reactions to three versions of the CRSA SJT: the original multimedia version, a computerized page-turner version of the script, and a paper-and-pencil version of the script. Consistent with the hypothesized benefits of multimedia assessments, managers considered the MMSJT to be higher in face validity and had generally more favorable attitudes toward this form of the assessment.

***IBM's Workplace Situations.***   IBM researchers developed an assessment battery for manufacturing employees that included an MMSJT, the Workplace Situations test (Barbera, 1996; Desmarais et al., 1992; Dyer et al., 1992; Midkiff et al., 1992). The test consists of 30 short video/audio scenarios that present work-related issues such as conflict among co-workers, organizational citizenship problems, and low-quality or late work. The scenarios were developed from a number of critical incidents gathered from roundtable discussions with SMEs (IBM manufacturing employees). Following the scenes are five multiple-choice options (also developed through an iterative, SME-driven process). The scenarios were filmed by a professional production group with the researchers on hand to ensure that the fidelity of the script to the workplace was maintained.

The Workplace Situations assessment was developed for use with a laserdisc player, M-motion video adaptor, and PC. Given the scarcity of such equipment at manufacturing sites, the validation data were collected on board a specially outfitted bus complete with multiple testing workstations. The scoring system was not empirically based, but instead was derived from managers' judgments about what their best employee would do in each situation (Barbera, 1996). Barbera reported a moderate, but significant correlation between performance on the SJT and performance on the job in a nationwide concurrent validity ($N = 713$). Interestingly, unlike the other, more cognitively based assessments in the battery, the SJT had weak (but significant) relations with attitudinal measures (towards test-taking and computers), but experience with test-taking and computers was not related to SJT performance.

***Federal Aviation Administration (FAA).***   The FAA's Computer-Based Performance Measure (CBPM; Hanson, Borman, Mogilka, Manning, & Hedge, 1999) is an MMSJT that was developed to serve as a criterion measure for air traffic control specialists' job performance in a concurrent validation study. The CBPM consists of 29 air traffic scenarios and 84 multiple-choice questions. It requires a CD drive, PC, and a 17-inch monitor. Each scenario presents a simulated radar screen for a generic air sector on the computer screen; additional information (e.g., flight strips, status information) is provided in written form adjacent to the screen. After the assessee familiarizes him or herself with the situation, the scenario unfolds with audio (e.g., pilot communication) and visual input (e.g., screen updates). The scenario freezes at various points and presents multiple-choice questions that ask the assessee how he or she would proceed.

The scenarios and questions were developed in an iterative process with various groups of SMEs to develop, refine, and revise scenarios and response options. Initially, scenarios were written in paper-and-pencil script format and then later programmed with both proprietary (FAA) software to present the radar screen and publically available software (Authorware) to incorporate additional elements (e.g., graphics and audio).

After the (nearly) final version of the CBPM was developed, a 12-person team of SMEs (not previously involved in its development) developed the scoring key for the SJT. Of the 84 items, only 20 had one correct answer. The remaining items had options that varied in terms of effectiveness. The overall reliability of the SME ratings of option effectiveness was high with most interclass coefficients above .80 (Hanson et al., 1999).

Hanson et al. presented compelling construct-validity evidence for the full version of the CBPM. The assessment was significantly related to multi-rater performance evaluations of 1,046 assessees (e.g., $r = .24$, $p < .01$, with technical effort) and was strongly related to performance in a high-fidelity simulation for a sample of 107 assessees ($r = .50$, $p < .01$). Using content-validity ratings and item-total correlations, the authors shortened the CBPM to 38 items. The shortened version resulted in stronger correlations with the other performance measures (e.g., $r = .60$ for the high-fidelity simulation). The researchers reported that their goal of creating a "practical, economical measure of technical proficiency" (p. 218) was met. Indeed, a shortened version of the CBPM is highly efficient and inexpensive compared to the alternative high-fidelity simulation that requires assessees to travel to a single location, be trained for 1.5 days, and then participate in a full day of assessment.

***Clinical Nursing Skills.*** Haak (1993) developed a unique interactive MMSJT to measure clinical nursing judgment skills. The SJT presents a patient who has arrived for treatment. The patient initially complains of chest pain and the assessee is directed to identify how to proceed with that patient. That is, the nurse must determine the patient's most urgent problem and what should be done about it. To that end, the assessee can ask the patient questions and order tests and procedures through the computer. The SJT branches to the appropriate video feedback based on the procedures ordered by the nurse or the questions posed to the patient by the nurse.

The branching was programmed with the use of a verbal protocol technique. The assessee's responses are recorded by the computer and later scored by a group of experts. Haak (1993) demonstrated criterion-related validity for the SJT as well as content and construct validity.

***Computer-Based Case Simulation (CCS).*** The National Board of Medical Examiners (NBME) has adopted one of the most sophisticated MMSJTs as part of the medical licensing exam (Clyman, Melnick, & Clauser, 1999). Similar to the Clinical Nursing Skills assessment, the CCS presents the candidate physician with presenting symptoms of a hypothetical patient. To diagnose and treat the patient, the examinee can do virtually anything that practicing physicians do. The examinee can order tests, request a medical history, perform an examination, or order a treatment; thousands of actions are available. To obtain the results from any of these actions, the examinee must move a clock forward. So, for example, a test may take 2 hours to complete; to obtain the results of the test, the examinee must move the clock forward by that amount of time. Interestingly, the hypothetical patient's condition progresses as it would in the real world over the course of 2 hours.

Clauser, Margolis, Clyman, and Ross (1997) described an automated scoring algorithm for the CCS. Prior to implementing the algorithm for a particular case, SMEs must rate each of the thousands of possible actions on a 7-point scale: *nonindicated and extremely risky, nonindicated and risky or intrusive, nonindicated but of minimal risk or intrusiveness, neutral, appropriate but of modest importance, important for optimal care, essential for adequate care.* The CCS records each action taken by the candidate physician in a transaction list, and a score is obtained by evaluating the actions according to the SME ratings.

Diagnostic skills as assessed by the CCS are only modestly related to the declarative knowledge of medicine measured by the multiple-choice portion of the medical licensing examination. Clyman et al. (1999) report that the disattenuated correlations between the CCS and the multiple-choice tests range between .35 and .55. Thus, it is clear that diagnostic *skill* is only modestly related to declarative medical *knowledge*. Further research on criterion-related validity would be illuminating.

*Social Quotient (SQ).*  Born, Van der Maesen de Sombreff, and Van der Zee (2001) developed an MMSJT to measure social intelligence. Designed to be used as a selection tool for entry-level workers, the 18 primary scenes were developed by experts (industrial and organizational psychologists with experience in the area) rather than via a critical incident method. The participants were 180 volunteers from the Dutch Tax and Revenues Department. The test requires assessees to rate the effectiveness of all four response options (in video format) for the 18 main scenes, resulting in 72 ratings. The scenarios were classified according to the Leary (1957) model and seven experts were used to develop the scoring key. The authors concluded the results from the MMSJT provides construct validity support for Leary's model and participant ratings indicate high face validity, satisfaction with the MMSJT, and high user-friendliness.

*Call Center Aptitude Test (C-A-T).* Konradt, Hertel, and Joder (2003) reported the validation of an Internet-based screening battery for call center agents. The C-A-T consists of a "short biographical form, a cognitive speed test, a personality inventory, and a multimedia situational judgement test" (p. 184). Little descriptive information about the MMSJT is available except that it included four different caller situations that a call center agent would typically have to face (e.g., impolite caller). The assessee responses to the MMSJT were not included in the empirical validation study. Instead, the authors reported that they were recorded and used qualitatively for further examination in a follow-up interview.

## EVALUATION OF MMSJTs

### Benefits

*Face Validity and Motivation.* Some of the presumed benefits of MMSJTs such as heightened face validity and motivation (e.g., Drasgow et al., 1993; Weekley & Jones, 1997) have been empirically supported. For example, Richman-Hirsch et al., (2000) randomly assigned assessees to one of three versions of the CRSA: the multimedia version, a computer-administered text version, and a paper-and-pencil version. As noted previously, managers reported greater face validity for the multimedia version, enjoyed the multimedia version more, and had generally more positive views toward this version. Similarly, D. Chan and Schmitt (1997) found test takers who completed the video version of their SJT reported greater face validity.

Although we are not aware of other randomized experiments comparing MMSJTs to text-based alternatives, we have little doubt that assessees generally enjoy well crafted MMSJTs. Drasgow (2005) argued that innovative computerized assessments can lead to greater *authenticity*; traditional paper-and-pencil multiple-choice tests measure declarative knowledge, whereas innovative assessments can be designed to test skills essential for competent practice in a profession.

Many of the MMSJTs reviewed in this chapter provide higher fidelity simulations of interpersonal situations that are important for the workplace than are possible with paper and pencil. Walker and Goldenberg's (2004) video assessment for CBP officers, for example, includes a scene depicting a hostage situation. The assessee experiences an adrenalin-inducing video clip that culminates in a scene where the criminal puts a gun to the head of a young woman and says to the assessee, "Drop your gun or I'll shoot." At this point, the video stops and the candidate officer must respond. For individuals interested in careers as CBP officers, this video clip provides a realistic preview of their desired occupation and there can be little serious doubt that they will find it compelling. In addition, because it is so emotion and adrenalin inducing, it may also provide a better assessment of how applicants will respond in similar situations on the job.

*Validity.* Regardless of whether MMSJTs are more interesting to assessees, does the increased fidelity add to criterion-related validity? Clearly, there is evidence of their validity; in fact, nearly all of the video-based SJTs and MMSJTs discussed in this chapter have some compelling evidence of criterion-related, construct, or content validity. But less is known about the incremental value of the multimedia format. Research is needed that compares text versions of SJTs to their multimedia alternatives while controlling for general cognitive ability.

Both paper-and-pencil SJTs (McDaniel et al., 2001) and MMSJTs have been found to be valid. We speculate that the mediating processes may differ because these two formats seem to have different relations to $g$. Whereas paper-and-pencil SJTs often have a moderate to strong relation with cognitive ability (McDaniel et al., 2001, found $\hat{\rho} = .46$), D. Chan and Schmitt (1997) and Olson-Buchanan et al. (1998) found much weaker relations for MMSJTs. Thus, paper-and-pencil SJTs that have strong correlations with cognitive ability may be valid, in part, because they indirectly assess cognitive ability. A study that compares the incremental validity of paper-and-pencil and MMSJTs after controlling for cognitive ability would test this hypothesis.

*Subgroup Differences.* MMSJTs with little relation to cognitive ability would be expected to have smaller subgroup differences and subsequently lower adverse impact. This is exactly what D. Chan and Schmitt (1997) and Olson-Buchanan et al. (1998) found. Although more research is needed to determine the generality of this finding, it is clear that reading comprehension is unnecessary for video presentation. Tests of reading comprehension have substantial subgroup differences (effect sizes of approximately $d = 1.0$) and consequently eliminating this source of variance in test scores should have salutary effects on the performance of underrepresented minorities.

## Challenges

In addition to all of the usual difficulties and dilemmas encountered in the development and use of tests for selection, placement, and counseling, developers and users of MMSJTs face further complexities. In this section, we outline some of the issues that must be confronted.

*Test Development.* MMSJT content is frequently developed from interviews and focus groups that discuss critical incidents. This approach has been used since the mid-1950s (Flanagan, 1954) and is frequently used for paper-and-pencil SJTs. The development of MMSJTs is more complex than paper-and-pencil SJTs, even when both types of tests are based on critical incidents, because multimedia assessments require several additional steps that can compromise item integrity.

First, after critical incidents have been used to determine test content, scripts for MMSJTs must be written. They can be written by either the test developers or by a professional production company. Our experience is that psychologists are not necessarily natural script writers; the dialogue can be stilted and overly complex. The alternative, hiring a production company to write the scripts, will result in superior dialogue, but the writers' literary license may yield scenes that depart greatly from what was identified in the critical incidents. In either case, several iterations may be required before plausible dialogue is developed that faithfully reflects the content of the critical incidents.

The costs of MMSJT video production have varied considerably. Several researchers have kept production costs to a reasonable level by using preexisting video (Dalessio, 1994) or using their own talent or inexpensive community talent to create new video (e.g., the Illinois group; Haak, 1993). Although professionally developed video is arguably higher quality, it is clear that valid MMSJTs can be developed with lower costs.

Regardless of whether researchers produce video in house or use an outside vendor, the creative talent of the production—the actors—still presents a challenge. Do the actors present the dialogue in the way the test developer intended? Or do their unique interpretations make the scene very different from what was identified in the critical incident? The test developer must be vigilant in this phase of the production process. It is interesting that nearly all the MMSJTs reviewed indicated that SMEs or researchers were on site for videotaping/filming to ensure realism. Additional verification (i.e., systematic comparisons between the video and the initial script) may also be warranted.

An issue that has not yet been researched concerns the shelf life of an MMSJT. Cognitive-ability tests appear to have a substantial shelf life (K. -Y. Chan, Drasgow, & Sawin, 1999). But clothing styles, hairstyles, and even accessories such as glasses and jewelry change all too rapidly. How long can an MMSJT be used before it looks dated? We expect that even the best MMSJT will need to be refilmed periodically.

*Scoring.* The major approaches to scoring MMSJTs have used expert judgment, empirical keying, model-based scoring, or hybrid keying that combines expert judgment or model-based scoring with empirical keying. Bergman, Drasgow, Donovan, Juraska, and Nejdlik (2004) provide an extended review of scoring methods and, unfortunately, conclude that substantially more research is needed to determine which approach is best under what type of conditions.

Scoring interactive MMSJTs presents even greater challenges. Consider the branching that occurs in computerized adaptive tests (CATs) of cognitive ability: The computer branches to an easier item following an incorrect response and to a more difficult item following a correct response. An approach to scoring that simply counts the number of correct responses is inappropriate because more able examinees are deliberately branched to a set of items that are systematically more difficult. Consequently, item response theory scoring (Hulin, Drasgow, & Parsons, 1983; Lord, 1980) is required because it takes item difficulty into account.

MMSJTs do not deliberately branch an assessee to a more difficult scene following a correct response; instead they branch to a scene that shows events that might well occur as a result of the way the assessee chose to respond. Are all the branch scenes equally difficult? If there are differences in difficulty, then the number correct scoring used by MMSJTs is inappropriate. To date, few sophisticated psychometric analyses of MMSJT data sets have been conducted. Such work should be conducted to determine whether improvements in scoring are possible by using item response theory to adjust for the difficulty of the scenes presented to each individual assessee.

***Choosing a Platform.***    The concern about rapidly changing technology was well founded. In fact, the technology used to develop the earliest MMSJTs is no longer even available. As noted previously, multimedia capabilities of PCs have evolved greatly since the early 1990s: from 16 MHz 386 microprocessors with M-motion adaptor cards to 486 microprocessors with RealMagic cards to Pentium microprocessors with mainstream video adaptor cards. Concurrently, the usability of software has improved, from customized Pascal to Asymmetrix's Toolbook to Microsoft's Access. Since about 2000, stand-alone PCs—whether desktop or laptop—have generally been able to present full-motion video satisfactorily. The major remaining challenge is presentation via networks. Satisfactory video requires a throughput of approximately 200 KB per second, which greatly exceeds the capability of telephone dial-in connections. High-speed dedicated networks can provide this level of throughput, provided that the number of users requesting data simultaneously is not too great.

We expect that the major impact of changes in technology for multimedia applications will lie in improved network capability. Individual users at remote locations and multiple users on local area networks can still exceed system capabilities, so greater throughput is needed. Currently available video adaptor cards for desktops and laptops are satisfactory for multimedia and Access provides a very stable and reasonably convenient programming environment.

Computer systems inevitably malfunction and so disaster recovery is an important consideration. A disk failure on a stand-alone PC can mean that an entire testing session is irretrievably lost (as well as any prior testing sessions that have not been backed up). For this reason (as well as many others), networked systems provide a superior test-taking environment, even if the multimedia application resides on each PC's hard disk. In this situation, information about each testing session can be saved on the server as well as the examinee's PC; in case of malfunction, the exam session can be restarted where it left off. When the multimedia application runs from a server, multiple servers should be used so that a failure by one will not be noticed by examinees.

## Security

Security of networked systems has become a tremendously important issue (Naglieri et al., 2004). For a high-stakes test, a three-tier server model is essential. Here, the system includes an Internet server, a test application server, and a database server. The database server should, of course, be maintained behind a secure firewall. Backups of all data should be made on a regular and frequent basis. If a network vendor is used, a detailed disaster recovery plan should be available and redundancy of all system components (including incoming and outgoing communication lines) is essential.

Security on the test-taker side is very important for high-stakes tests. Vigilant proctors are required. In addition, test security software should be installed on each desktop or laptop PC (Naglieri et al., 2004). This software prevents examinees from leaving the multimedia application while it is in progress. Moreover, it prevents screen recorders and any other application that might compromise test security.

## FUTURE RESEARCH NEEDS

MMSJTs have moved into the mainstream of testing for selection, placement, licensing, and counseling. There are test development companies that specialize in this type of assessment (e.g., Ergometrics) and both public and private sector employers are increasingly using multimedia. Despite

the growing popularity of this assessment format, too little systematic research is available.

The lack of research on MMSJTs is striking when considered in the
context of the extensive program of research comparing paper-and-pencil
cognitive-ability tests to computerized versions of the same textual material (e.g., Mead & Drasgow, 1993). On the face of it, one would expect
less of an administrative medium effect for, say, an algebraic word problem when comparing paper-and-pencil versus computer than for an SJT
presented via written text versus full-motion video with stereo sound.
Yet, there have been hundreds of paper-and-pencil to computerized comparisons (e.g., Mcad & Drasgow's, 1993, meta-analysis) relative to only
a few studies that have compared text-based SJTs to multimedia-based
SJTs (D. Chan & Schmitt,1997; Richman-Hirsch et al., 2000). Both of these
studies found important medium of administration effects. Would similar
results be found today now that multimedia presented on computers is so
much more commonplace? What is driving the medium of administration
effects—is it that multiple senses are engaged in the assessment process
(vision, hearing) or perhaps because the SJT is more compelling? Are there
generational effects? Clearly, more research is needed to systematically ex-
plicate the generality of these findings and to explore the conditions under
which such effects will be found.

There is clear evidence to support the use of both high-fidelity work
samples and assessment centers (e.g., J. Hunter & Hunter, 1984) and low-
fidelity SJTs (e.g., McDaniel et al., 2003; Motowidlo et al., 1990). It is not
clear, however, whether the increased fidelity of MMSJTs is meaningful
enough to justify their development and maintenance expenses. One way
that future research could explore this question is by integrating relevant
situation perception literature (e.g., Mischel & Shoda, 1998) into the systematic investigation of MMSJTs. That is, do MMSJTs create meaningful
differences in scores among assessees as a result of differential abilities to
"read" or perceive situations?

The range of MMSJT content is encouraging but needs to be pushed in
further directions in future research. Similar to SJTs in general, several of
the assessments measure interpersonal skills (e.g., Desmarais et al., 1992;
Smiderle et al., 1994). However, other MMSJTs are designed to measure
judgment and decision making (Walker & Goldenberg, 2004), organization
and prioritization (e.g., Asworth & McHenry, 1993), medical diagnostic skills (Clyman et al., 1999), and even specialized task performance
(Hanson et al., 1999). Further research is needed to develop MMSJTs that
focus on other innovative content areas. For example, the role of ethics in
managerial decision making has become an increasingly important consideration in organizations. An MMSJT could be carefully developed to

present ethically ambiguous situations that require assessees to recognize and respond to subtle cues. This unobtrusive measure of ethical decision making would be especially valuable for administrative-level positions, but could be developed for all levels of jobs. Also, an MMSJT of cultural sensitivity would be an innovative way to measure a highly desirable quality for jobs that involve effectively working with diverse populations (e.g., teachers, medical professionals).

One of the most intriguing benefits of multimedia technology is the ability to create interactive assessments. A handful of interactive MM-SJTs have already been successfully developed (e.g., Ashworth & Jones, 1994; Ashworth & McHenry, 1993; Clyman et al., 1999; Haak, 1993; Olson-Buchanan et al., 1998). Today, video technology is even more accessible and can store more video information on smaller devices, thereby eliminating one of the early barriers to creating interactive MMSJTs (not having enough room for the branching, etc.). The possibilities for leveraging the power of MMSJTs through interactivity are exciting. For example, consider how an interactive MMSJT might be developed to measure an assessee's responses to individualized feedback. That is, the assessee would see the consequences of his or her initial choice(s) and have an opportunity to respond to the situation with this additional information. An MMSJT could also be tailored to an assessee's responses to an earlier assessment (e.g., a personality measure). That is, the characters in the SJT would address the assessee differently based on their personality profile. Future research is needed to examine such features: Does interactivity serve to increase the criterion-related validity of MMSJTs? If so, is it a result of enhanced fidelity? Similarly, does the increased realism result in higher construct validity?

To enhance the veridicality of the SJT even further, the technological capacity of computers could be harnessed to increase the fidelity of the test takers' responses. That is, instead of using a low-fidelity multiple-choice format, the test taker could react in a free-response format to the characters depicted in the video (e.g., Walker & Goldenberg, 2004). Although Walker and Goldenberg recorded and hand-scored the responses, the administrative scoring burden could be reduced or eliminated by taking advantage of voice-recognition software and theoretical developments with automatic scoring of open-ended responses (e.g., Powers, Burstein, Chodorow, Fowles, & Kukich, 2002). Future research could also examine the use of such open-ended responses as it relates to validity and user acceptance. Another possibility is to consider measuring nonverbal responses as well through automated processes. For example, facial and other nonverbal responses could be recorded and examined as an additional assessment measure in future research.

Several researchers have developed and validated Internet-based computerized assessment tools such as biodata forms (Reynolds, Sinar, Scott, & McClough, 2000), recruiting and screening instruments (Vlug, Furcon, Mondragon, & Mergen, 2000), and even Internet-based SJTs (D. Hunter, 2003). Yet, to date, only one Internet-based MMSJT has been reported (Konradt et al., 2003) and, unfortunately, the assessment was not included in a validation study. Internet-based administration has several potential benefits. Organizations need less hardware (e.g., personal workstations) and space for administering the assessment, proctors are not used, scores are available immediately and can be uploaded to a central data base, and a larger pool of applicants may be available. From the perspective of the job applicant, travel is not required to complete an MMSJT on site (Olson-Buchanan, 2001) and little or no scheduling is needed prior to taking the test.

There are also serious concerns about Internet assessment. For example, how do we ensure that the person completing the assessment is the one given credit for completing it? Sinar, Reynolds, and Paquet (2003) identified the importance of system speed and user-friendliness of Internet-based selection tools for creating positive impressions of the organization. Such features may be similarly important to the psychometric properties of MMSJTs. Future research attention is needed to examine whether the reliability of a MMSJT is affected by varying connectivity speeds or environmental distractions in the test taker's computer workstation area. Specifically, could the validity of an MMSJT be threatened by slow connectivity speeds because slow delivery mitigates the realism of the assessment?

Animation, particularly computer-generated animation, has reached an unprecedented level of sophistication and acceptance by movie-goers. Could such technology be used to create MMSJTs? The flexibility of computer-generated animation would be a powerful tool for creating interactive MMSJTs. It could also help to minimize concerns about the shelf life of MMSJTs because the video could be more easily modified to reflect current styles. Test-taker responses to animation is an important topic for future research.

D. Chan and Schmitt (1997) and Olson-Buchanan et al. (1998) both found subgroup differences greatly reduced or eliminated in their video assessments. These results are important because the standardized mean difference statistic *d* for cognitive ability tests shows remarkably little change over item types and test conditions. Interestingly, Olson-Buchanan et al. found that their African-American research participants' scores were significantly *higher* than Whites on the CRSA. Future research to examine the generality of this finding is needed. Are there certain types of SJTs that consistently reduce subgroup differences when administered via multimedia?

Will similar results be found for other underrepresented minority groups? Relatedly, another important question to examine in future research is whether subgroup differences could be similarly minimized with lower technology alternatives, such as an audiorecording of dialogue. Besides lower expense, audiorecordings would have the additional benefit of not quickly becoming outdated (if slang, etc., is minimized).

## CONCLUSIONS

More than 50 years ago, the Tavistock studies resulted in the notion that organizations are sociotechnical systems (Trist, 1981; Trist & Bamforth, 1951). Individual differences in facilitating the social context of work organizations, however, received little attention until the work of Borman and Motowidlo (1993, 1997), who differentiated the notion of contextual performance (e.g., helping others, supporting the organization) from task performance. It seems natural to speculate that interpersonal skills, as measured by MMSJTs, would be among the most valid predictors of performance in facilitating the social context of organizations.

J. Hunter (1986) proposed a theory of job performance that has general cognitive ability as a direct antecedent of job knowledge and job knowledge as a direct antecedent of job performance (with a weaker direct link between cognitive ability and job performance). Motowidlo, Borman, and Schmit (1997) elaborated this model by suggesting that cognitive ability predicts task-related knowledge and skills and proposing a parallel system for contextual performance. They envisioned personality variables as the direct antecedents of contextual knowledge and skills, which in turn are the proximal antecedents of contextual performance. In light of the Tavistock studies and the work of Borman and Motowidlo, it seems reasonable to separate job performance into a technical aspect and a social aspect. As job knowledge is the proximal antecedent of technical/task job performance, situational judgment concerning interpersonal relations appears to be the proximal antecedent of performance in the social domain of work.

A broad theory of job performance and its antecedents gives rise to questions about the dimensionality of interpersonal skills. Is there a strong general factor as in the cognitive domain? Or distinct multiple skills as in personality? And what are the antecedents of interpersonal skills? Cognitive ability seems like a poor candidate, given the findings of D. Chan and Schmitt (1997) and Olson-Buchanan et al. (1998). Motowidlo et al. (1997) suggested personality and indeed Lievens and Coetsier (2002) found evidence of a relation between openness and two video-based SJTs. However, another attempt to relate personality to interpersonal skills was relatively unsuccessful (Bergman, Donovan, & Drasgow, 2001). Clearly, more research is needed on this topic.

In summary, the multimedia approach to assessment has grown rapidly. Its development as a practical job selection tool has clearly outstripped our theoretical understanding of this important domain of individual differences. Research on MMSJT assessment tools and their links to aspects of job performance is greatly needed.

## REFERENCES

Ashworth, S. D., & Joyce, T. M. (1994, April). *Developing scoring protocols for a computerized multimedia in-basket exercise.* Paper presented at the annual conference of the Society for Industrial and Organizational Psychology, Nashville, TN.

Ashworth, S. D., & McHenry, J. J. (1992, April). *Developing a multimedia in-basket: Lessons learned.* Paper presented at the annual conference of the Society for Industrial and Organizational Psychology, San Francisco, CA.

Barbera, K. M. (1996). *Multimedia employment tests: The influence of attitudes and experiences on validity.* Unpublished doctoral dissertation, Department of Psychology, Bowling Green State University, Bowling Green, Ohio.

Bergman, M. E., Donovan, M. A., & Drasgow, F. (2001, April). *Situational judgment, personality, and cognitive ability: Are we really assessing different constructs?* Paper presented at the annual conference of the Society for Industrial and Organizational Psychology, San Diego, CA.

Bergman, M. E., Drasgow, F., Donovan, M. A., Juraska, S. E., & Nejdlik, J. B. (2004). *Scoring situational judgment tests.* Manuscript under review.

Borman, W. C., & Motowidlo, S. J. (1993). Expanding the criterion domain to include elements of contextual performance. In N. Schmitt & W. C. Borman (Eds.), *Personnel selection* (pp. 71–98). San Francisco, CA: Jossey-Bass.

Borman, W. C., & Motowidlo, S. J. (1997). Task performance and contextual performance: The meaning for personnel selection research. *Human Performance, 10,* 99–109.

Born, M. Ph., Van der Maesen de Sombreff, P. E. A. M., & Van der Zee, K. I. (2001, April). *A multimedia situational judgment test for social intelligence.* Paper presented at the annual conference of the Society for Industrial and Organizational Psychology, San Diego, CA.

Breiman, L. Friedman, J. H., Olshen, R. A., & Stone, C. J. (1984). *Classification and regression trees.* Belmont, CA: Wadsworth.

Broadus, M. (1990). Multimedia in post secondary education. *ComputerData, 15,* 43.

Chan, D., & Schmitt, N. (1997). Video-based versus paper-and-pencil method of assessment in situational judgment tests: Subgroup differences in test performance and face validity perceptions. *Journal of Applied Psychology, 82,* 300–310.

Chan, K.-Y., Drasgow, F., & Sawin, L. L. (1999). What is the shelf life of a test? The effect of time on the psychometrics of a cognitive ability test battery over 16 years. *Journal of Applied Psychology, 84,* 610–619.

Chiu, C.-Y., Hong, Y.-Y., Mischel, W., & Shoday, Y. (1995). Discriminative facility in social competence: Conditional versus dispositional encoding and monitoring-blunting of information. *Social Cognition, 13,* 49–70.

Clauser, B. E., Margolis, M. J., Clyman, S. G., & Ross, L. P. (1997). Development of auto-mated scoring algorithms for complex performance assessments: A comparison of two approaches. *Journal of Educational Measurement, 34,* 141–161.

Clyman, S. G., Melnick, D. E., & Clauser, B. E. (1999). Computer-based case simulations from medicine: Assessing skills in patient management. In A. Tekian, C. H. McGuire, & W. E. McGahie (Eds.), *Innovative simulations for assessing professional competence* (pp. 29–41). Chicago: Department of Medical Education, University of Illinois.

Dalessio, A. T. (1994). Predicting insurance agent turnover using a video-based situational judgment test. *Journal of Business and Psychology, 9,* 23–32.

Desmarais, L. Burris, Dyer, P. J., Midkiff, K. R., Barbera, K. M., Curtis, J. R., Esrig, F. H., & Masi, D. L. (1992, May). *Scientific uncertainties in the development of a multimedia test: Trade-offs and decisions.* Paper presented at the annual conference of the Society for Industrial and Organizational Psychology, Montreal, Quebec.

Desmarais, L. Burris, Masi, D. L., Olson, M. J., Barbara, K. M., & Dyer, P. J. (1994, April). *Scoring a multimedia situational judgment test: IBM's experience.* Paper presented at the annual conference of the Society for Industrial and Organizational Psychology, Nashville, TN.

Drasgow, F. (2005). Innovative computerized test items. In K. Kempf-Leonard (Ed.), *Encyclopedia of social measurement* (Vol. 2, pp. 283–290). San Diego, CA: Academic Press.

Drasgow, F., & Olson-Buchanan, J. B. (Eds.). (1999). *Innovations in computerized assessment.* Mahwah, NJ: Lawrence Erlbaum Associates.

Drasgow, F., Olson-Buchanan, J. B., & Moberg, P. J. (1999). Development of an interactive video assessment: Trials and tribulations. In F. Drasgow & J. B. Olson-Buchanan (Eds.), *Innovations in computerized assessment* (pp. 177–196). Mahwah, NJ: Lawrence Erlbaum Associates.

Drasgow, F., Olson, J. B., Keenan, P. A., Moberg, P. J. , & Mead, A. D. (1993). Computerized assessment. In G. R. Ferris & K. M. Rowland (Eds.), *Research in personnel and human resources management,* (Vol. 11, pp. 163–206). Greenwich, CT: JAI Press.

Dyer, P. J., Desmarais, L. B., Midkiff, K. R., Colihan, J. P, & Olson, J. B. (1992, May). *Designing a multimedia test: Understanding the organizational charge, building the team, and making the basic research commitments.* Paper presented at the annual conference of the Society for Industrial and Organizational Psychology, Montreal, Quebec.

Flanagan, J. C. (1954). The critical incident technique. *Psychological Bulletin, 51,* 327–358.

Haak, S. W. (1993). *Development of a computer tool including interactive video simulation for eliciting and describing clinical nursing judgment performance.* Unpublished doctoral dissertation, The University of Utah, College of Nursing, Salt Lake City, Utah.

Hanson, M. A., Borman, W. C., Mogilka, H. J., Manning, C., & Hedge, J. W. (1999). Computerized assessment of skill for a highly technical job. In F. Drasgow & J. B. Olson-Buchanan (Eds.), *Innovations in computerized assessment* (pp. 197–220). Mahwah, NJ: Lawrence Erlbaum Associates.

Hulin, C. L., Drasgow, F., & Parsons, C. K. (1983). *Item response theory: Applications to psychological measurement.* Homewood, IL: Dow Jones—Irwin

Hunter, D. R. (2003). Measuring general aviation pilot judgment: Using a situational judgment technique. *The International Journal of Aviation Psychology, 13,* 373–386.

Hunter, J. E. (1986). Cognitive ability, cognitive aptitudes, job knowledge, and job performance. *Journal of Vocational Behavior, 29,* 340–362.

Hunter, J. E., & Hunter, R. F. (1984). Validity and utility of alternative predictors of job performance. *Psychological Bulletin, 96,* 72–98.

Interactive video training. (1991). *IBM Directions, 5,* 8–9.

Johnson, D. F. (1983). Things we can measure through technology that we could not measure before. In *New directions for testing and measurement: Measurement, technology, and individuality in education* (Proceedings of the 1982 Educational Testing Services Invitational Conference, pp. 13–18). Princeton, NJ: Educational Testing Service.

Jones, C., & DeCotiis, T. A. (1986, August). Video-based selection of hospitality employees. *The Cornell Hotel and Restaurant Administration Quarterly*, pp. 67–73.

Keenan, P. A., & Olson, J. B. (1991, April). *A model-based multi-media technique for assessing conflict management skills.* Paper presented at the annual conference of the Society for Industrial and Organizational Psychology Conference, St. Louis, MO.

Kleinmann, M., & Strauß, B. (1998). Validity and application of computer-simulated scenarios in personnel assessment. *International Journal of Selection and Assessment, 6,* 97–106.

Konradt, U., Hertel, G., & Joder, K. (2003). Web-based assessment of call center agents: Development and validation of a computerized instrument. *International Journal of Selection and Assessment, 11,* 184–193.

Leary, T. (1957). *Interpersonal diagnosis of personality.* New York: Ronald.

Lievens, F., Buyse, T., & Sackett, P. R. (2005). The operational validity of a video-based situational judgment test for medical college admissions: Illustrating the importance of matching predictor and criterion construct domains. *Journal of Applied Psychology, 90*(3), 442–452.

Lievens, F., & Coetsier, P. (2002). Situational tests in student selection: An examination of predictive validity, adverse impact, and construct validity. *International Journal of Selection and Assessment, 10,* 245–257.

Lord, F. M. (1980). *Applications of item response theory to practical testing problems.* Hillsdale, NJ: Lawrence Erlbaum Associates.

McDaniel, M. A., Morgeson, F. P., Finnegan, E. B., Campion, M. A., & Braverman, E. P. (2001). Use of situational judgment tests to predict job performance: A clarification of the literature. *Journal of Applied Psychology, 86,* 730–740.

McHenry, J. J., & Schmitt, N. (1994). Multimedia testing. In M. G. Rumsey & C. B. Walker (Eds.), *Personnel selection and classification* (pp. 193–232). Hillsdale, NJ: Lawrence Erlbaum Associates.

Mead, A. (1991, April). *Hardware and software for multi-media computerized assessments.* Paper presented at the annual conference of the Society for Industrial and Organizational Psychology, St. Louis, MO.

Mead, A. D., & Drasgow, F. (1993). Equivalence of computerized and paper-and-pencil cognitive ability tests: A meta-analysis. *Psychological Bulletin, 114,* 449–458.

Midkiff, K. R., Dyer, P. J., Desmarais, L. B., Rogg, K., & McCusker, C. R. (1992, May). *The multimedia test: Friend or foe?* Paper presented at the annual conference of the Society for Industrial and Organizational Psychology Conference, Montreal, Quebec.

Mischel, W., & Shoda, Y. (1998). Reconciling processing dynamics and personality dimensions. *Annual Review of Psychology, 49,* 229–258.

Motowidlo, S. J., Borman, W. C., & Schmit, M. J. (1997). A theory of individual differences in task and contextual performance. *Human Performance, 10,* 71–83.

Motowidlo, S. J., Dunnette, M. D., & Carter, G. W. (1990). An alternative selection procedure: The low-fidelity simulation. *Journal of Applied Psychology, 75,* 640–647.

Naglieri, J. A., Drasgow, F., Schmit, M., Handler, L., Prifitera, A., Margolis, A., & Velasquez, R. (2004). Psychological testing on the Internet: New problems, old issues. *American Psychologist. 59,* 150–162.

Olson-Buchanan, J. B. (2001). Computer-based advances in assessment. In F. Drasgow & N. Schmitt (Eds.), *Measuring and analyzing behavior in organizations* (pp. 44–87). San Francisco, CA: Jossey-Bass.

Olson-Buchanan, J. B., Drasgow, F., Moberg, P. J., Mead, A. D., Keenan, P. A., Donovan, M. A. (1998). Interactive video assessment of conflict resolution skills. *Personnel Psychology, 51,* 1–24.

Olson, J. B., & Keenan, P. A. (1994, April). *Scoring interactive video assessments: A model-based approach.* Paper presented at the annual conference of the Society for Industrial and Organizational Psychology Conference, Nashville, TN

Petty, L. C., & Rosen, E. F. (1987). Computer-based interactive video systems. *Behavior Research Methods, Instruments, and Computers, 19,* 160–166.

Pine, D. E. (1994, April). *The development and validation of a video-based situational response test.* Paper presented at the annual conference of the Society for Industrial and Organizational Psychology, Nashville, TN.

Powers, D. E., Burstein, J. C., Chodorow, M. S., Fowles, M. E., & Kukich, K. (2002). Comparing the validity of automated and human scoring of essays. *Journal of Educational Computing Research, 26,* 407–425

Reynolds, D. H., Sinar, E. F., Scott, D. R., & McClough, A. C. (2000, April). *Evaluation of a Web-based selection procedure.* Paper presented at the annual conference of the Society for Industrial and Organizational Psychology, New Orleans, LA.

Richman-Hirsch, W. L., Olson-Buchanan, J. B., & Drasgow, F. (2000). Examining the impact of administration medium on examinee perceptions and attitudes. *Journal of Applied Psychology, 85,* 880–887.

Schmitt, N., Gilliland, S. W., Landis, R. S., & Devine, D. (1993). Computer-based testing applied to selection of secretarial applicants. *Personnel Psychology, 46,* 149–165.

Shoda, Y., Mischel, W., & Wright, J. C. (1993). The role of situational demands and cognitive competencies in behavior organization and personality congruence. *Journal of Personality and Social Psychology, 65,* 1023–1035.

Sinar, E. F., Reynolds, D. H., & Paquet, S. L. (2003). Nothing but 'net'? Corporate image and web-based testing. *International Journal of Selection and Assessment, 11,* 150–157

Smiderle, D., Perry, B. A., & Cronshaw, S. F. (1994). Evaluation of video-based assessment in transit operator selection. *Journal of Business and Psychology, 9.* 3–22.

Thorndike, R. L. (1949). *Personnel selection.* New York: Wiley.

Trist, E. L. (1981). *The evolution of sociotechnical systems: A conceptual framework and an action research program.* Toronto: Ontario Quality of Working Life Centre.

Trist, E. L., & Bamforth, K. W. (1951). Some social and psychological consequences of the longwall method of coal-getting. *Human Relations, 4,* 1–38.

Walker, D., & Goldenberg, R. (2004, June). *Bringing selection into the 21st century: A look at video-based testing within U.S. Customs and Border Protection.* Paper presented at the annual conference of the International Public Management Association—Assessment Council, Seattle, WA.

Vlug, T., Furcon, J. E., Mondragon, N., & Mergen, C. Q. (2000, April). *Validation and implementation of Web-based screening system in the Netherlands.* Paper presented at the annual conference of the Society for Industrial and Organizational Pscyhology, New Orleans, LA.

Weekley, J. A., & Jones, C. (1997). Video-based situational testing. *Personnel Psychology, 50,* 25–49.

# 13

# International Situational Judgment Tests

## Filip Lievens
### *Ghent University, Belgium*

*Your sports club is planning a trip to Berlin to attend the Germany-England football game, which will take place in 2 weeks. You have been entrusted with the preparations and entire management of the trip. What do you intend to do?*
—Ansbacher (1941, p. 381, cited in Highhouse, 2002)

The above item was given in the late 1930s to German employees to measure something else other than cognitive ability (e.g., planning and organizing). It illustrates that situational judgment tests (SJTs) have been used outside the United States for quite some time. Early international applications of SJTs can also be found in the so-called cultural assimilators in cross-cultural training programs (Bhawuk & Brislin, 2000). In these cultural assimilators, future expatriates are presented with written situations of an expatriate interacting with a host national and are asked to indicate the most effective response alternative.

Recently, there has been a renewed interest in the use of SJTs in an international selection context. One of the key reasons is that the globalization of the economy necessitates organizations to view the labor market in an international scope and to develop selection procedures that can be used across multiple countries. However, there is a dearth of research on international selection in general and on international SJTs in particular. This leaves many questions unanswered. Most importantly, a key issue is

279

whether SJTs developed in one culture can be transported to and used as a valid predictor in another culture?

The purpose of this chapter is to explore the limits of the generalizability of SJTs and their criterion-related validity across cultural boundaries. The chapter begins with a brief review of personnel selection in an international context. Next, I focus on the criterion-related validity of SJTs across cultures. Specifically, I delineate the factors under which the criterion-related validity of SJTs might generalize to foreign countries and across-country applications. Finally, I offer insights into best practices.

## A BRIEF OVERVIEW OF INTERNATIONAL SELECTION RESEARCH

Despite the growing importance of selection in an international context, there is a paucity of internationally oriented selection research (see Lievens, in press, for a review). Most prior studies were descriptive in nature and compared selection practices from one country to another. Generally, considerable variability in selection procedure usage across countries was found (see Newell & Tansley, 2001; Shackleton & Newell, 1997). More recent studies have started to examine why selection procedures are used differentially across countries. In particular, the multi-country study of Ryan, McFarland, Baron, and Page (1999) found some evidence that one of Hofstede's (1991) dimensions (i.e., uncertainty avoidance) could explain some of the variability in selection practices. For example, organizations in cultures high in uncertainty avoidance used more selection methods, used them more extensively, and conducted more interviews.

Other internationally oriented selection studies focused on the perceptions of selection procedures across different countries. Steiner and Gilliland (2001) reviewed these studies and concluded that a fairly consistent picture emerged as the same selection procedures (interviews, resumes, and work samples) received favorable reactions across various countries. In all countries, job-relatedness also emerged as the key determinant of favorable perceptions. Steiner and Gilliland (2001) explained these similarities on the basis of the shared European heritage of the countries reviewed (Belgium, France, Spain, South Africa, and the United States).

Finally, a limited amount of studies has tackled the fundamental question as to whether the criterion-related validity of a selection procedure will differ when used in other countries and cultures. Essentially, two hypotheses have been proposed, namely the validity generalization hypothesis and the situational specificity hypothesis (Salgado & Anderson, 2002). The validity generalization hypothesis states that observed criterion-related validity coefficients will vary because of statistical artifacts (such as sampling error, range restriction, criterion unreliability). When these statistical artifacts are accounted for, criterion-related validity coefficients will generalize across different situations (jobs, occupational groups, organizations; F. Schmidt & Hunter, 1984). In an international context, this means that criterion-related validity coefficients associated with a specific selection procedure obtained in one country will generalize to another country. Exactly the opposite is posited by the situational specificity hypothesis. According to this hypothesis, there should be high variability in the observed criterion-related validity coefficients obtained in different situations (jobs, occupational groups, organizations). Whenever the situation changes, the observed criterion-related validity coefficient might also change (F. Schmidt & Hunter, 1984). Applied to an international context, this means that selection procedures might be valid in one country but not in another country.

Few empirical studies have tested these competing hypotheses. To our knowledge, only the generalizability of the criterion-related validity of cognitive-ability tests and personality inventories has been put to the test in an international context. Generally, results have provided support for the validity generalization hypothesis. For example, Salgado Anderson, Moscoso, Bertua, and De Fruyt (2003), and Salgado, Anderson, et al. (2003) found evidence for validity generalization for cognitive ability tests across seven European countries. In addition, the magnitude of the criterion-related validity coefficients found conformed to previous U.S. meta-analyses (F. Schmidt & Hunter, 1998), underscoring that cognitive-ability validities generalized across jobs, occupations, and borders. In the domain of personality tests, fairly consistent results have also been found across American (Barrick & Mount, 1991; Tett, Jackson, & Rothstein, 1991) and European (Salgado, 1997) meta-analyses, with mainly Conscientiousness emerging as a consistent predictor across jobs, occupations, and cultures.

## THE CRITERION-RELATED VALIDITY OF SJTs ACROSS CULTURES

Our overview of prior international selection research showed that the criterion-related validity of cognitive ability tests and personality inventories generalized across countries. Does this mean that the same consistent results in terms of criterion-related validity will be found for SJTs across countries and cultures? Equally important, which factors can be expected to impact on the potential generalizability of SJTs across cultures? The remainder of this chapter focuses on these issues. Specifically, I discuss three influencing factors: (a) the cultural transportability of SJT item characteristics, (b) the point-to-point correspondence between predictor and criterion, and (c) the type of constructs measured by SJTs.

## The Cultural Transportability of SJT Item Characteristics

*SJT Item Characteristics.* SJT items are highly contextualized because they are embedded in a particular context or situation. The contextualized nature of SJT items makes them particularly prone to cultural differences because the culture wherein one lives acts like a lens, guiding the interpretation of events and defining appropriate behaviors (Cropanzano, 1998; Lytle, Brett, Barsness, Tinsely, & Janssens, 1995). Table 13.1, presents a matrix in which SJT item characteristics are cast in terms of Hofstede's (1991) cultural dimensions (i.e., individualism/collectivism, power distance, uncertainty avoidance, and masculinity/femininity). Note that I use Hofstede's (1991) framework, although I acknowledge it is also possible to construct this matrix with other cultural frameworks (House, Hanges, Javidan, Dorfman, & Gupta, 2004; Kluckhohn & Strodtbeck, 1961; Schwartz & Bardi, 2001; Schwartz & Sagiv, 1995; Trompenaars & Hampden-Turner, 1997).

The problem situations (as reflected in the item stems of SJTs) that are presented to candidates in a written or video-based format are a first characteristic of SJTs. These problem situations are generated from a job analysis and from critical incidents provided by high and low performers on a specific criterion (job). When SJTs are used in an international context, the issue then becomes whether there are cultural differences in terms of the situations (critical incidents) generated (holding the type of job constant). According to value orientations theory (Kluckhohn & Strodtbeck, 1961), all cultures encounter very common problem situations. Applied to SJTs, this would mean that for a given job the situations encountered might be fairly similar across various cultures. However, we believe a lot also depends on the type of situations studied. In cross-cultural psychology, generalizability

TABLE 13.1

Matrix of Relevant SJT Item Characteristics and Cultural Dimensions

| Hofstede's (1991) Cultural Dimensions | Items Situations (Item Stems) | Response Options | Response Option Effectiveness (Scoring Key) | Response Option–Construct Relationship |
|---|---|---|---|---|
| Individualism/collectivism | | | | |
| Masculinity/femininity | | | | |
| Power distance | | | | |
| Uncertainty avoidance | | | | |

has typically been studied and found for major situations such as situations of joy, fear, anger, sadness, disgust, shame, and guilt (Scherer & Wallbott, 1994; Scherer, Wallbott, & Summerfield, 1986). Such basic configurations are different from many of the work-related situations included in SJTs. Therefore, we do not expect the situations and response options of SJTs to generalize across cultures. Some situations will simply not be relevant in one culture, whereas they might be very relevant in another culture. Think about the differences in organizing meetings across countries. Or think about applicants in a culture high on power distance who have trouble answering a situation about a party off hours between employees and their boss. If one does not take account of these cultural differences, it might well be that applicants are presented with an SJT item stem that is simply not relevant in their culture. To our knowledge, no empirical studies have tested whether similar situations are generated across cultures.

A second item characteristic of SJTs are the response alternatives. These are taken from possible ways of dealing with a given situation as provided by high and low performers on a specific criterion (job). In an international context, one might question whether the response alternatives given to applicants are transportable from one culture to another. Value orientations theory (Kluckhohn & Strodtbeck, 1961) posits that all cultures encounter similar problems and that all cultures discovered similar responses to these problems. Yet, the same argument as earlier applies here. The possible responses to the basic configurations studied in cross-cultural psychology do not echo the specific responses to the work-related situations depicted in SJTs. Thus, we expect that the possible range of relevant response options might differ from one culture (holding the type of situations and the type of job constant) to another. If one does not take account of these differences, the SJT might present applicants with response options that are not relevant in a given culture. This also means that the response endorsement frequencies might differ from one culture to another. So, what might be a good distractor (e.g., yelling in a meeting when no one is listening to your opinion) in one culture (e.g., culture low in power distance) might not be endorsed by many applicants in another (e.g., culture high in power distance).

Apart from item stems and response alternatives, the SJT scoring key is a third component of all SJTs (McDaniel & Nguyen, 2001). The correct answer on an SJT is determined either empirically (by comparing low and high performers) or rationally (by experts), although a hybrid of these two approaches is sometimes followed. It is expected that cultural differences will affect the effectiveness of response options and therefore the scoring key of SJTs. This expectation is based on value orientations theory (Kluckhohn & Strodtbeck, 1961) and attribution theory (Bond, 1983; Morris & Peng, 1994).

According to value orientations theory (Kluckhohn & Strodtbeck, 1961), cultures differ in terms of their preference for specific responses to problem situations. This is illustrated by linking Hofstede's dimensions with the effectiveness of response alternatives to SJT items. For instance, in a culture high on uncertainty avoidance, the effective response to a specific written SJT situation (e.g., supervising a group of young employees) might be to impose rules and structure. However, the same reply to the same situation might be valued as ineffective in a culture low on uncertainty avoidance because ambiguity is not perceived as a threat. The individualism–collectivism might also affect SJT response effectiveness. In fact, we expect that answers that promote group harmony might be considered more effective in cultures high in collectivism, whereas the reverse might be true in cultures low on individualism. The masculinity–femininity dimension might affect SJT responses, such that answers that involve competition might be preferred in cultures high on masculinity. Finally, answers that minimize ambiguity and appear decisive might be considered most effective in a culture high on uncertainty avoidance.

Attribution theory also posits that the effectiveness of responses to situations might differ from one culture to another. This is because attribution patterns reflect implicit theories acquired from socialization in a specific culture. Therefore, they are differentially distributed across human cultures (Bond, 1983; Morris & Peng, 1994). For example, Morris and Peng's study revealed that American people attributed social events more to personal dispositions (i.e., attributions based on the belief that social behavior expresses stable, global, and internal dispositions), whereas Chinese people attributed more to situational factors (attributions based on the belief that social behavior is shaped by relationships, roles, and situational pressures). The evidence that attribution patterns are differentially distributed across human cultures serves as the foundation of the so-called cultural assimulators that are often used in cross-cultural training (Bhawuk & Brislin, 2000). Cultural assimulators share similarities with SJTs because they also present written or video-based situations to individuals. A difference is that the situation is always a social situation in another culture and that the response alternatives given are essentially possible attributions associated with the event depicted. According to Bhawuk and Brislin, cultural assimilators aim to teach expatriates to make isomorphic attributions. This means that individuals attribute a social event in a specific culture in the same way as is done in that specific culture.

A fourth item characteristic that might be prone to cultural differences is the link between response options as indicators for a given construct. Unlike cognitive-ability tests, we expect that the item-construct relationship in SJTs is more susceptible to deficiency and contamination because of possible cross-cultural differences in the meaning/interpretation of the same situation content or same response to the same situation. For example, given the same written situation (e.g., a situation depicting a meeting between an older supervisor and a group of employees), the same behavior (e.g., clearly and openly defending one's views about work standards in front of the supervisor with all employees being present) might be linked to a specific construct (e.g., assertiveness) in one culture (culture low in power distance), whereas it might be an indicator for another construct (e.g., rudeness, impoliteness) in another culture (culture high in power distance).

*Empirical Research.* Studies that have examined the cultural transportability of SJT item characteristics are very scarce. As noted, no studies have explored cultural differences in terms of the situations, response options, or response option–construct linkages. We retrieved only one empirical study that examined whether the preference (effectiveness) for response alternatives differs across cultures. Nishii, Ployhart, Sacco, Wiechmann, and Rogg (2001) conducted a study among incumbents of a multinational food chain in different countries (Canada, Germany, Korea, Mexico, Spain, the United Kingdom, and Thailand). They investigated whether the endorsement of response options to five SJT items was affected by culture. Cultural dimensions were operationalized in terms of Hofstede's cultural dimensions. Results revealed that people of different cultural backgrounds were differentially attracted to specific response alternatives, and that these differences were consistent with theoretical expectations. As a matter of fact, people from individualistic cultures chose response options that were task-oriented and that involved communicating directly with others. However, for the same item, people from collectivistic cultures tended to choose response options with a focus on group harmony and protecting others' face.

On a more general level, a wide variety of empirical research in cross-cultural psychology (e.g., Smith, Dugan, Peterson, & Leung, 1998; Smith et al., 2002) has also shown that the effectiveness of work-related behaviors in response to a given situation might drastically differ across cultures. As there are numerous examples are, we cite only two studies. Adler, Doktor, and Reddin (1986) showed that there were differences in decision making and information processing across cultures and countries. As an example, they mentioned that Japanese people like to go from general to specific, whereas Western people prefer to get rid of details before talking about larger issues. S. Schmidt and Yeh (1992) drew similar conclusions with regard to differences in leadership behaviors and styles across cultures.

## The Point-to-Point Correspondence Between Predictor and Criterion

*SJTs as Externally Constructed Measures.*  SJTs are fundamentally different measures than cognitive-ability or personality tests. Cognitive-ability tests and to a certain extent also personality inventories are internally constructed predictor measures (Mount, Witt, & Barrick, 2000). These predictor measures are typically decontextualized and are developed to have generalizability across a wide variety of situations. Accordingly, it is expected that the criterion-related validity of these measures will generalize across jobs, occupations, and cultures. As noted earlier, this expectation has been confirmed so far.

Conversely, contextualized measures such as SJTs are externally constructed because they are also developed for a very specific criterion. In fact, SJT items are directly developed or sampled from the criterion behaviors that the test is designed to predict (Chan & Schmitt, 2002). Apart from SJTs, other examples of externally constructed measures include situational interviews, behavior-description interviews, work samples, and assessment center exercises.

For externally constructed predictors such as SJTs, the point-to-point correspondence between the predictor and the criterion domain is of paramount importance as it gives them their criterion-related validity. This contrasts to internally oriented measures such as cognitive ability tests whose criterion-related validity is expected to generalize across a wide variety of jobs and occupations. When framed in this way, it should be clear that using an SJT in a different culture than originally intended is conceptually not different from using an SJT for another job or occupation than originally intended. In other words, the fact that an SJT is used in another culture does not make it invalid per se. As long as one ensures that the predictor and criterion domains match, criterion-related validity might be high. Conversely, when the predictor and criterion domains do not overlap, criterion-related validity will be low. All of this is based on the well-known notion that validity is about matching predictor and criterion domains (Binning & Barrett, 1989).

To examine these expectations, we categorized possible international applications of SJTs along these two dimensions (predictor and criterion). A further distinction is made between "national" (original culture) and "international" (host culture). As the vast majority of SJT practice and research has been conducted in the United States, we take the United States

| | Criterion | |
|---|---|---|
| | National | International |
| **Predictor (SJT)** National | A | B |
| International | C | D |

FIG. 13.1. Overview of international applications of situational judgment tests.

as point of reference. This means that "national" applications refer to the use of SJTs in the United States. International applications, in turn, refer to the use of SJTs outside the United States.

The "predictor–criterion" distinction and the "national–international" distinction lead to four quadrants. These quadrants are presented in Fig. 13.1. The following section discusses the main criterion-related validity issues for each of these four quadrants. When available, prior SJT criterion-related validity studies are reviewed.

***Within-Culture Applications.***   Quadrant A of Fig. 13.1 does not really deal with SJT research in an international context because it consists of studies wherein the predictor (SJT) was developed and used in the United States. Afterward, the criterion data (job-performance data) were also gathered in the United States.

Given that most prior SJT studies have been conducted in the United States, this quadrant consists of the majority of SJT research. In fact, McDaniel, Morgeson, Finnegan, Campion, and Braverman (2001) meta-analyzed 39 prior SJT studies (that generated 102 criterion-related validity coefficients) conducted in the United States. Results showed that SJTs were valid predictors, with an estimated population validity of .34. Other studies conducted in the United States (e.g., Clevenger, Pereira, Wiechmann, Schmitt, & Schmidt Harvey, 2001) have further shown that SJTs have incremental validity over and above cognitive ability and personality tests.

Quadrant D of Fig. 13.1 also entails within-culture applications of SJTs. In studies in Quadrant D, the predictor (SJT) was developed and used outside the United States. Afterward, the criterion data were also gathered outside the United States. Studies in Quadrant D used a so-called *emic approach* (Berry, 1969). This means that SJTs are developed and validated with the own culture as the point of reference. One example is the study of Chan and Schmitt (2002). These researchers developed an SJT for civil service positions in Singapore. Although the development of the SJT conformed to the procedures used in U.S. SJTs (see Motowidlo, Hanson, & Crafts, 1997), the job analysis, the collection of situations, the derivation of response alternatives, the development of the scoring key, and the validation took place in Singapore. Another example is the development of a video-based SJT for use in the Belgian admission exam "Medical and Dental Studies" (Lievens, Buyse, & Sackett, 2005; Lievens & Coetsier, 2002). Again, the development of the SJT closely followed U.S. studies, while at the same time ensuring that the job-relevant scenarios were derived from input of local experts. Although SJTs seem to be less popular outside the United States, we found other examples of SJT studies in Quadrant D in Germany (Behrmann, 2004; Funke & Schuler, 1998; Kleinmann & Strauss, 1998; Schuler, Diemand, & Moser, 1993), the Netherlands (Born, 1994; Born, Van der Maesen de Sombreff, & Van der Zee, 2001; Van Leest & Meltzer, 1995), Korea (Lee, Choi, & Choe, 2004), and China (Jin & Wan, 2004).

Given the clear overlap between predictor and criterion contexts, we see no reason why carefully developed SJTs would not be valid in the applications mentioned in Quadrant D. Empirical research attests to this. Chan and Schmitt (2002) found that their SJT was a valid predictor for overall performance. In addition, their SJT application in Singapore had incremental validity over cognitive ability, personality, and job experience. This corresponds to the aforementioned studies in the United States. Similarly, Lievens et al. (2005) found that a video-based SJT was a valid predictor of Belgian medical students' performance on interpersonally oriented courses and had incremental validity over cognitive ability for predicting these courses. Funke and Schuler (1998) showed that their SJT was predictive for German students' performance on interpersonally oriented roleplays. Finally, Behrmann's (2004) study revealed that the initial criterion-related validity results of an SJT developed for German call center agent incumbents were promising.

***Across-Culture Applications.*** Quadrant B of Fig. 13.1 consists of studies wherein the SJT was developed in the United States. However, it was used and validated in a different culture. Thus, contrary to Quadrants A and D, Quadrant B involves across-country applications of SJTs. The studies in Quadrant B are also examples of an imposed etic approach (Berry, 1969) as it is assumed that pre-existing assessment techniques (e.g., an SJT developed in the United States) can be adapted to different countries. For example, an SJT designed for a particular job in the United States might be used in other countries where the organization operates. Another example is the selection of people in the United States for international assignments. Once selected, these expatriates might be evaluated in the host culture (outside the United States).

Empirical research in Quadrant B is scarce. Such and Schmidt (2004) validated an SJT in four countries. The SJT and its scoring key were developed on the basis of a "cross-cultural" job analysis across multiple countries. Results in a cross-validation sample showed that the SJT was valid in half of the countries, namely the United Kingdom and Australia. Conversely, it was not predictive in Mexico. These results illustrate that the criterion-related validity of an SJT might be undermined when the predictor and criterion domains do not overlap. As noted previously, given the substantial cultural differences in what is considered effective behavior in a given situation, it seems impossible to determine a universal scoring key. So, although attempts were made to ensure that the scoring key was cross-culturally oriented, we believe that the results indicate that effective behavior on the SJT was mainly determined in terms of what is considered effective behavior in two countries with a similar heritage (the United Kingdom and Australia). Hence, the SJT was predictive only for job performance as rated in the United Kingdom and Australia but not in Mexico. In general, Nishii et al. (2001) succinctly summarized the problem as follows:

> If a scoring key for a SJT is developed in one country and is based on certain cultural assumptions of appropriate or desirable behavior, then people from countries with different cultural assumptions may score lower on these tests. Yet these lower scores would not be indicative of what is considered appropriate or desirable response behavior in those countries. (p. 10)

Applications of SJTs in Quadrant C of Fig. 13.1 are even more scarce. This quadrant is comprised of applications wherein the SJT was developed outside the United States. However, it was used and validated in the United States. The selection of impatriates (people from foreign countries that are assigned to work in the corporate headquarters in the United States) on the basis of an SJT might be an example of such a cross-country application of SJTs. In a similar vein, international personnel might be selected on the basis of SJTs in a European country. Afterward, they are sent to the United States where U.S. managers evaluate them. We were not able to retrieve criterion-related validity studies of SJTs in such contexts. On the basis of the logic just explained, we expect that the criterion-related validity of the SJT will suffer in case of a lack of predictor and criterion overlap.

The difficulties related to predictor and criterion match that might be encountered in across-culture applications of SJTs are further exemplified when one takes into consideration that cultural differences might affect the criterion itself (Ployhart, Wiechmann, Schmitt, Sacco, & Rogg, 2003). In fact, in individualistic cultures, task performance is typically given more importance than contextual performance in global job performance ratings (Johnson, 2001; Rotundo & Sackett, 2002). However, it might well be that the relative importance attached to task performance vis-à-vis contextual performance when combining ratings into a summary job-performance rating might be different in other cultures (Arthur & Bennett, 1997). For example, in collectivist cultures, job-performance ratings may resemble more closely measures of contextual performance—at least as those concepts are defined in these cultures. The key point here is that the criterion-related validity of an SJT in a host culture (country) might vary considerably depending on the relative weights given to specific performance components (task vs. contextual performance) when defining the construct of job performance in that specific culture (country) (Murphy & Shiarella, 1997).

***Possible Moderators.*** The importance of the point-to-point correspondence between SJT and the criterion might be moderated by at least two factors. First, careful attention to matching predictor and criterion domains in international use of selection procedures might be less important for cognitively loaded SJTs than for noncognitive SJTs. As discussed here, cognitive constructs seem to be less susceptible to cultural variation. Second, the validity of cross-cultural applications is dependent on the culture specificity of the job in question. This refers to the issue as to what extent the same job-relevant behaviors on this same job are evaluated differently between cultures. If a job is not very culture-dependent/susceptible, it should not matter to validity whether SJT test development, scoring key development (expert's judgments), and criterion-domain judgments (performance ratings) were done in the same or a different culture from the culture that the test is used. Conversely, it should matter if the job is culture-dependent/susceptible. As argued by Furrer, Liu, and Sudharshan (2000), customer service quality might be an example of a job dimension that is especially susceptible to cultural differences (see also Ployhart et al., 2003).

## The Type of Constructs Measured by SJTs

In recent years, an increasing amount of studies have tried to uncover which are the constructs underlying SJTs. Most studies *a posteriori* correlated SJT scores with measures of cognitive ability or personality. The meta-analysis of McDaniel et al. (2001) examined the relationship between cognitive ability and SJT scores. Correlations varied considerably (between .17 and .75), with an average correlation of .46. Another meta-analysis concentrated on noncognitive correlates of SJT scores. McDaniel and Nguyen (2001) found that SJTs correlated with most of the Big Five personality traits. Apart from cognitive ability and personality, SJTs have also been found to correlate with experience and job knowledge. Although the debate about the constructs underlying SJTs is still ongoing, there is general consensus that—similar to assessment center exercises or structured interviews—SJTs are basically methods that can be designed to measure a variety of cognitive and noncognitive constructs. This notion is best exemplified by recent efforts to a priori build constructs into SJTs (Motowidlo, Diesch, & Jackson, 2003; Ployhart & Ryan, 2000)

Why might the nature of the constructs (cognitive vs. noncognitive) measured by SJTs have important implications on the generalizability of their criterion-related validity across cultures? The main reason relates to the finding that cognitive constructs are more robust to cultural variation. In fact, cognitive ability has emerged as the best stand-alone predictor whose validity generalizes across jobs, occupations, and countries (Salgado et al., 2003a, b). The key advantage of working with constructs is that it provides a basis for predicting the criterion-related validity of specific constructs measured by other methods (Hattrupp, Schmitt, & Landis, 1992; Schmitt & Chan, 1998). In particular, applied to SJTs, this would mean that SJTs that are cognitively loaded would exhibit more cross-cultural validity than SJTs that are not cognitively loaded, all other things being equal. According to Chan and Schmitt (2002), the $g$-loadedness of an SJT is dependent on the nature of the SJT test content. Thus, the more the SJT content is loaded with cognitive ability, the more likely it will exhibit cross cultural validity, all other things being equal.

## DIRECTIONS FOR FUTURE RESEARCH

One of the common threads running through this chapter is that research on SJTs in an international context is scarce. Therefore, it was no surprise that throughout this chapter, future research needs have been suggested. In this section, I summarize these various research needs in six key directions for future research regarding the use of SJTs in an international context.

First, studies are needed that examine how culture affects the various steps in SJT development. In the matrix of Table 13.1, prior research (Nishii et al., 2001) has concentrated only on the fifth column, namely how cultural differences impact on response-choice effectiveness. Granted, this is important because both value orientations theory and attribution theory show that the effectiveness and thus the scoring key of for SJT response alternatives will differ across cultures. Yet, SJT design also entails gathering job-related situations and possible response options to these situations. It would be interesting to investigate whether SMEs in different countries provide the same critical situations and response alternatives. This can be easily done by presenting a given job to SMEs in different countries and asking them to generate critical incidents. Such research can shed light on whether the same types of situations occur across cultures. As noted, we expect that cultural inhibitions are often so strong that specific situations and responses in one culture would never occur in another. Apart from scrutinizing the relevance of problem-situations and response options across cultures, the frequency of response-option endorsement should also be compared across cultures. Finally, it should be examined whether the relationship linking SJT items and SJT intended constructs is transportable across cultures. It might be important to investigate the cultural transportability of the item–construct relationship because it suggests that the extent to which an SJT can successfully be used across cultures is dependent on the nature of the test content vis-à-vis the similarities and differences between cultures with respect to that content. If the aforementioned is correct, then within one SJT, some SJT responses will be more cross-culturally valid than others depending on the (dis)similarity between cultures in item content.

Second, very little is known about which SJT features increase or reduce cultural differences. McDaniel and colleagues (chap. 9, this volume) provides a good review of various item characteristics that might impact on the criterion-related validity of SJTs in a national context. Yet, virtually none of these characteristics have been investigated in an international context. One exception is the presentation format of SJT items. Chan and Schmitt (1997) showed that a video-based presentation format significantly reduced Black–White subgroup differences as compared with a written format. Therefore, similar to research on cognitive-ability tests (Cole, 1981; Scheuneman & Gerritz, 1990), future studies should identify specific types of item characteristics that may moderate differential item functioning across cultures.

Third, future studies should go beyond examining the effects of culture on response-option choice and include the effects on criterion-related validity. As already noted, we retrieved only one study (Such & Schmidt, 2004) that examined the criterion-related validity of SJTs in a variety of countries. In that specific study, the SJT development and scoring followed an imposed etic approach as the SJT was developed in one country and then used in other countries, with the result being that the SJT was predictive in only half of the countries. Probably, there was a lack of overlap between the SJT and the criterion in the other half of the countries. In this chapter, we posited that future studies should use an emic approach so that the SJT scoring key is tailored to the specific countries where the criterion data are gathered, guaranteeing sufficient overlap between predictor and criterion domains. Future research should be conducted to test these ideas.

In a similar vein, there is a clear need for studies that examine how the criterion-related validity of SJTs might be influenced by differences across cultures in how the various performance dimensions are weighted and combined into an overall job-performance rating. For instance, if managers in a particular culture (country) value that people get along (a contextual performance dimension), the fact that an SJT in another culture (country) predicts well individual task performance does not say much about the relevance of this SJT for hiring the best personnel in that specific culture (country). To our knowledge, no studies have investigated these issues.

Fourth, there is a need for a priori theory-driven examinations of the impact of cultural differences on SJT performance and criterion-related validity. So far, previous investigations (i.e., Nishii et al., 2001) have correlated SJT responses that had already been gathered across various countries with country scores on Hofstede's (1991) dimensions. Apart from its a posteriori nature, another limitation of this approach is that individual and country levels of analysis are confounded because an individual in a given country is equated with the score of his or her country. Clearly, such a country score on a cultural dimension such as individualistic serves at best as only a proxy of an individual's standing on this cultural dimension. A better approach would consist of determining a priori which items might be prone to cultural differences. In addition, respondents' individual scores on Hofstede's (1991) scales or similar scales (e.g., the GLOBE project; House et al., 2004) should be gathered. Whitney and Schmitt (1997) published an excellent example of such an a priori theory-driven approach for examining the influence of culture on selection procedures. On the basis of prior theory about value differences between Blacks and Whites, they a priori determined biodata items that would be vulnerable to cultural differences between Blacks and Whites. Next, they measured the cultural values of the individual respondents and correlated them with the individuals' response selection on these items. Some support was found for the hypothesis that cultural values were associated with the observed difference in Black–White response choices.

Fifth, no studies have used a construct-driven approach for examining the cross-cultural validity of SJTs. As already mentioned, it would be particularly interesting to examine whether $g$-loaded SJTs (i.e., SJTs whose content is loaded with cognitive ability) are more likely to exhibit cross cultural validity, all other things being equal, than SJTs that are less $g$-loaded. Future studies can test this proposition at various levels. In particular, researchers might test this proposition at the overall score level (e.g., by comparing a "cognitive" SJT with a "noncognitive" SJT) and/or at the item level (e.g., by comparing "cognitive" SJT items with "noncognitive" SJT items).

Finally, it should be noted that virtually all "international" SJT applications discussed in this chapter were conducted in the United States and/or in western Europe. Future studies should be conducted in other parts of the world. Only in that case, we can obtain a full understanding of the cultural influences on SJTs.

## IMPLICATIONS FOR PRACTICE

A first practical lesson to be learned is that general statements such as "SJTs are useful [or not useful] in other cultures" are not warranted. Instead, the specific application should be taken into account. We showed that SJTs carefully developed in Singapore, Belgium, or Germany for predicting job performance in these countries might have validities in the same range as SJTs developed in the United States. So, practitioners should be aware of the type of international application of SJTs. If the SJT is used for within-culture applications (predictor and criterion data are gathered in the same culture, e.g., an organization in Korea hires Korean individuals for a given job in Korea, see Quadrants A and D in Fig. 13.1), cultural differences do not seem to be a major threat. The reverse is true for cross-cultural applications of SJTs (predictor and criterion data are gathered in different cultures, e.g., a multinational hires individuals for a given job in a host culture, see Quadrants B and C). In these applications, the cultural transportability of SJT item characteristics might be at risk. Hence, their criterion-related validity might suffer if practitioners do not ensure predictor and criterion overlap.

How might practitioners ensure predictor and criterion overlap in cross-cultural applications of SJTs? Generally, there are two solutions possible. One solution might consist of changing the criterion. For example, one might consider evaluating the expatriates by corporate personnel in the original culture. However, this solution is both practically and conceptually debatable. From a conceptual point of view, this would mean that the criterion is changed on the basis of the predictor. One should always take the primacy of the criterion into account. From a practical point of view, it does not seem very acceptable that corporate headquarters determine what is good and bad performance in a specific host country. Instead, inspection of expatriate success criteria indicate that good performance implies that the expatriate is evaluated positively in the host culture in terms of task and interpersonal performance domains.

Another solution might be to change the predictor (the SJT) and to tailor the SJT to each specific culture (country). This means that both item stems and response alternatives should be carefully scrutinized for clarity and relevance in the host culture. In addition, it does not make sense to use or develop a "universal" scoring key as the same response option might be effective in one culture and ineffective in another culture. Instead, organizations should invest time and money to determine the effectiveness of the various response options in different cultures. Accordingly, it should be possible to tailor the scoring key to the specific host culture so that the key is consistent with the specific cultural norms.

On a more general level, our recommendations to scrutinize the content of item stems and response alternatives and to develop culture-specific scoring keys question the utility of an imposed etic approach when developing SJTs. Instead, our recommendations are in line with an emic approach. Ascalon, Schleicher, and Born (2004) provided an example of such a tailored country-specific approach. They developed an SJT for selecting expatriates targeted to five countries (The Netherlands, China, Germany, the United States, and Spain). Their SJT consisted of written scenarios representing the interaction of the five nationalities with one another. The SJT was designed to measure empathy and ethnocentrism; two dimensions that were posited to be related to cross-cultural social intelligence. People from these five countries served as experts to determine how the response options would be scored on these two dimensions.

## EPILOGUE

Recently, organizations have started to use SJTs in an international context. The use of contextualized measures such as SJTs in an international context puts some challenges for organizations on the table. This chapter posited that three factors might determine the cross-cultural validity of SJTs, namely the transportability of the SJT items characteristics, the matching of predictor and criterion domains, and the type of constructs measured.

One of the key premises was that using an SJT in a different culture than originally intended is conceptually not different from using an SJT for another job or occupation than originally intended. This meant that the generalizability of SJTs to other contexts might be jeopardized if these measures were used in a different context (e.g., job, organization, culture) and for a different criterion than originally intended. This leads to two implications. First, the interpretation of the correct or appropriate behavioral response to a specific situation might differ as a function of cultural values. In other words, the scoring key might differ from one culture to another. Second, SJTs might have differential validity across cultures if SJT scores do not match the criterion data gathered in another culture. In cross-cultural applications of SJTs, tailoring the scoring key to the host culture might be a way of matching predictors and criteria.

## ACKNOWLEDGMENT

I would like to thank David Chan for his valuable suggestions on an earlier version of this chapter.

## REFERENCES

Adler, N. J., Doktor, R., & Redding, S. G. (1986). From the Atlantic to the Pacific century: Cross-cultural management reviewed. *Journal of Management, 12,* 295–318.

Ansbacher, H. L. (1941). German military psychology. *Psychological Bulletin, 38,* 370–392.

Arthur, W. Jr., & Bennett, W. Jr. (1997). A comparative test of alternative models of international assignee job performance. In D. M. Saunders (Series Ed.) & Z. Aycan (Vol. Ed.), *New approaches to employee management, Vol. 4: Expatriate management: Theory and research* (pp. 141–172). Stanford, CT: JAI Press.

Ascalon, M. E., Schleicher, D. J., & Born, M. P. (2004). *Cross-cultural social intelligence: The development of a theoretically-based measure.* Manuscript in preparation.

Barrick, M. R., & Mount, M. K. (1991). The big five personality dimensions and job performance: A meta-analysis. *Personnel Psychology, 44,* 1–26.

Behrmann, M. (2004). *Entwicklung und Validierung eines Situational Judgment Tests für Call Center Agents—CalCIUM25: Baustein für die Personalauswahl.* [Development and validation of an Situational Judgment Test for call center agents]. Unpublished dissertation, Universität Mannheim, Germany.

Berry, J. (1969). On cross-cultural comparability. *International Journal of Psychology, 4,* 119–128.

Bhawuk, D. P. S., & Brislin, R. W. (2000). Cross-cultural training: A review. *Applied Psychology: An International Review, 49,* 162–191.

Binning, J. F., & Barrett, G. V. (1989). Validity of personnel decisions: A conceptual analysis of the inferential and evidential bases. *Journal of Applied Psychology, 74,* 478–494.

Bond, M. H. (1983). A proposal for cross-cultural studies of attribution processes (pp. 157–170). In M. H. Hewstone (Ed.), *Attribution theory: Social and applied extensions.* Oxford: Basil Blackwell.

Born, M. P. (1994). Development of a situation-response inventory for mangerial selection. *International Journal of Selection and Assessment, 2,* 45–52.

Born, M. P., Van der Maesen de Sombreff, P., & Van der Zee, K. I. (2001, April). *A multimedia situational judgment test for the measurement of social intelligence.* Paper presented at the 16th annual conference of the Society for Industrial and Organizational Psychology, San Diego, CA.

Chan, D., & Schmitt, N. (1997). Video-based versus paper-and-pencil method of assessment in situational judgment tests: Subgroup differences in test performance and face validity perceptions. *Journal of Applied Psychology, 82,* 143–159.

Chan, D., & Schmitt, N. (2002). Situational judgment and job performance. *Human Performance, 15,* 233–254.

Clevenger, J., Pereira, G. M., Wiechmann, D., Schmitt, N., & Schmidt Harvey, V. S. (2001). Incremental validity of situational judgment tests. *Journal of Applied Psychology, 86,* 410–417.

Cole, N. (1981). Bias in testing. *American Psychologist, 36,* 1067–1077.

Cropanzano, R. (1998, April). *Organizational justice and culture.* Paper presented at the 13th annual conference of the Society for Industrial and Organizational Psychology, Dallas, TX.

Funke, U., & Schuler, H. (1998). Validity of stimulus and response components in a video test of social competence. *International Journal of Selection and Assessment, 6,* 115–123.

Furrer, O., Liu, B. S., & Sudharshan, D. (2000). The relationship between culture and service quality perceptions: Basis for international market segmentation and resource allocation. *Journal of Service Research, 2,* 355–371.

Hattrup, K., Schmitt, N., & Landis, R. S. (1992). Equivalence of constructs measured by job-specific and commercially available aptitude tests. *Journal of Applied Psychology, 77,* 298–308.

Highhouse, S. (2002). Assessing the candidate as a whole: An historical and critical analysis of individual psychological assessment for personnel decision making. *Personnel Psychology, 55,* 363–396.

House, R. J., Hanges, P. J., Javidan, M., Dorfman, P. W., & Gupta, V. (2004). *Culture, leadership, and organizations: The GLOBE study of 62 societies.* Thousand Oaks, CA: Sage.

Jin, Y., & Wan, Z. (2004, August). *Managerial competence oriented situational judgement tests and construct validation.* Paper presented at the 28th International Congress of Psychology, Beijing, China.

Johnson, J. W. (2001). The relative importance of task and contextual performance dimensions to supervisor judgments of overall performance. *Journal of Applied Psychology, 86,* 984–996.

Kleinmann, M., & Strauss, B. (1998) Validity and application of computer-simulated scenarios in personnel assessment. *International Journal of Selection and Assessment, 6,* 97–106.

Hofstede, G. (1991). *Culture and Organizations: Software of the mind.* London: McGraw-Hill.

Kluckhohn, F. R., & Strodtbeck, F. L. (1961). *Variations in value orientations.* Evanston, IL: Row, Peterson.

Lee, S., Choi, K. S., & Choe, I. S. (2004, July). *Two issues in situational judgment tests.* Paper presented at the annual convention of the American Psychological Association, Honolulu, HI.

Lievens, F. (in press). Personnel selection research in an international context. In M. M. Harris (Ed.). *Handbook of research in international human resource management.* Mahwah, NJ: Lawrence Erlbaum Associates.

Lievens, F., Buyse, T., & Sackett, P. R. (2005). The operational validity of a video-based situational judgment test for medical college admissions: Illustrating the importance of matching predictor and criterion construct domains. *Journal of Applied Psychology, 90,* 442–452.

Lievens, F., & Coetsier, P. (2002). Situational tests in student selection: An examination of predictive validity, adverse impact, and construct validity. *International Journal of Selection and Assessment, 10,* 245–257.

Lytle, A. L., Brett, J. M., Barsness, Z. I., Tinsley, C. H., & Janssens, M. (1995). A paradigm for confirmatory cross-cultural research in organizational behavior. *Research in Organizational Behavior, 17,* 167–214.

McDaniel, M. A., Morgeson, F. P., Finnegan, E. B., Campion, M. A., & Braverman, E. P. (2001). Use of situational judgment tests to predict job performance: A clarification of the literature. *Journal of Applied Psychology, 86,* 730–740.

McDaniel, M. A., & Nguyen, N. T. (2001). Situational judgment tests: A review of practice and constructs assessed. *International Journal of Selection and Assessment, 9,* 103–113.

Morris, M. W., & Peng, K. (1994). Culture and cause: American and Chinese attributions for social and physical events. *Attitudes and Social Cognition, 67,* 949–971.

Motowidlo, S. J., Diesch, A. C., & Jackson, H. L. (2003, April). *Using the situational judgment test format to measure personality characteristics.* Paper presented at the 18th Annual Conference of the Society for Industrial and Organizational Psychology, Orlando, FL.

Motowidlo, S. J., Hanson, M. A., & Crafts, J. L. (1997). Low-fidelity simulations. In D. L. Whetzel & G. R. Wheaton (Eds.), *Applied measurement methods in Industrial Psychology* (pp. 241–260). Palo Alto, CA: Davies-Black Publishing.

Mount, M. K., Witt, L. A., & Barrick, M. R. (2000). Incremental validity of empirically keyed biodata scales over GMA and the five factor personality constructs. *Personnel Psychology, 53,* 299–323.

Murphy, K. R., & Shiarella, A. H. (1997). Implications of the multidimensional nature of job performance for the validity of selection tests: multivariate framework for studying test validity. *Personnel Psychology, 50,* 823–854.

Newell, S. & Tansley, C. (2001) International uses of selection methods. In C.L. Cooper & I.T. Robertson (eds.) International Review of Industrial and Organizational Psychology, vol 21. pp. 195-213. Chichester, Wiley: UK.

Nishii, L. H., Ployhart, R. E., Sacco, J. M., Wiechmann, D., & Rogg, K. L. (2001, April). *The influence of culture on situational judgment test responses.* Paper presented at the 16th Annual Cnference of the Society for Industrial and Organizational Psychology, San Diego, CA.

Ployhart, R. E., & Ryan, A. M. (2000, April). *A construct-oriented approach for developing situational judgment tests in a service context.* Paper presented at the 15th Annual Conference of the Society for Industrial and Organizational Psychology, New Orleans, LA.

Ployhart, R. E., Wiechmann, D., Schmitt, N., Sacco, J. M., & Rogg, K. L. (2003). The cross-cultural equivalence of job performance ratings. *Human Performance, 16,* 49–79.

Rotundo, M., & Sackett, P.R. (2002). The relative importance of task, citizenship, and counterproductive performance to global ratings of job performance: A policy capturing approach. *Journal of Applied Psychology, 87,* 66–80.

Ryan, A. M., McFarland, L., Baron, H., & Page, R. (1999). An international look at selection practices: Nation and culture as explanations for variability in practice. *Personnel Psychology, 52,* 359–391.

Salgado, J. F. (1997). The Five-Factor model of personality and job performance in the European Community. *Journal of Applied Psychology, 82,* 30–43.

Salgado, J. F., & Anderson, N. R. (2002). Cognitive and GMA testing in the European Community: Issues and evidence. *Human Performance, 15,* 75–96.

Salgado, J. F., Anderson, N., Moscoso, S., Bertua, C., & De Fruyt, F. (2003). International validity generalization of GMA and cognitive abilities: A European community meta-analysis. *Personnel Psychology, 56*, 573–605.

Salgado, J. F., Anderson, N., Moscoso, S., Bertua, C., De Fruyt, F., & Rolland, J. P. (2003). A meta-analytic study of general mental ability validity for different occupations in the European Community. *Journal of Applied Psychology, 88*, 1068–1081.

Scherer, K. R., & Wallbott, H. G. (1994). Evidence for universality and cultural variation of differential emotion response patterning. *Journal of Personality and Social Psychology, 66*, 310–328.

Scherer, K. R., Wallbott, H. G., & Summerfield, A. B. (Eds.). (1986). *Experiencing emotion: A cross-cultural study*. Cambridge: Cambridge University Press.

Scheuneman, J., & Gerritz, K. (1990). Using differential item functioning procedures to explore sources of item difficulty and group performance characteristics. *Journal of Educational Measurement, 27*, 109–131.

Schmidt, F. L., & Hunter, J. E. (1984). A within setting test of the situational specificity hypothesis in personnel selection. *Personnel Psychology, 37*, 317–326.

Schmidt, F. L., & Hunter, J. E. (1998). The validity and utility of selection methods in personnel psychology: Practical and theoretical implications of 85 years of research findings. *Psychological Bulletin, 124*, 262–274.

Schmidt, S. M., & Yeh, R. S. (1992). The structure of leader influence: A cross-national comparison. *Journal of Cross-Cultural Psychology, 23*, 251–264.

Schmitt, N., & Chan, D. (1998). *Personnel selection: A theoretical approach*. Thousands Oaks, CA: Sage.

Schuler, H., Diemand, A. & Moser, K. (1993). Film scenes: development and construct validity of a new aptitude assessment method [In German]. Filmszenen: Entwicklung und Konstruktvalidierung eines neuen eignungsdiagnostischen Verfahrens. *Zeitschrift für Arbeits- und Organisationspsychologie, 37*, 3–9

Schwartz, S. H., & Bardi, A. (2001). Value hierarchies across cultures: Taking a similarities perspective. *Journal of Cross Cultural Psychology, 32*, 268–290.

Schwartz, S. H., & Sagiv, L. (1995). Identifying culture-specifics in the content and structure of values. *Journal of Cross-Cultural Psychology, 26*, 92–116.

Shackleton, V., & Newell, S. (1997). International assessment and selection. In N. Anderson & P. Herriot (Eds.), *International handbook of selection and assessment*. New York: Wiley.

Smith, P. B., Dugan, S., Peterson, M. F., & Leung, K. (1998). Individualism/collectivism and the handling of disagreement: A 23 country study. *International Journal of Intercultural Relations, 22*, 351–368.

Smith, P. B., Peterson, M. F., Schwartz, S. H., Ahmad, A. H., Akande, D., Andersen, J. A., et al. (2002). Cultural values, sources of guidance, and their relevance to managerial behavior: A 47-nation study. *Journal of Cross-Cultural Psychology, 33*, 188–208.

Steiner, D. D., & Gilliland, S. W. (2001). Procedural justice in personnel selection: International and cross-cultural perspectives. *International Journal of Selection and Assessment, 9*, 124–137.

Such, M. J., & Schmidt, D. B. (2004, April). *Examining the effectiveness of empirical keying: A cross-cultural perspective*. Paper presented at the 19th annual conference of the Society for Industrial and Organizational Psychology, Chicago, IL.

Tett, R. P., Jackson, D. N., & Rothstein, M. G. (1991). Personality measures as predictors of job performance: A meta-analytic review. *Personnel Psychology, 44*, 703–742.

Trompenaars, F., & Hampden-Turner, C. (1997). *Riding the waves of culture: Understanding cultural diversity in business*. London: Nicholas Brealey.

Van Leest, P. F., & Meltzer, P. H. (1995). *Videotesting of social, leadership, and commercial competencies.* Paper presented at the 7th European Congress on Work and Organizational Psychology, Györ, Hungary.

Whitney, D. J., & Schmitt, N. (1997). Relationship between culture and responses to biodata employment items. *Journal of Applied Psychology, 82,* 113–129.

# 14

# Enhancing the Design, Delivery, and Evaluation of Scenario-Based Training: Can Situational Judgment Tests Contribute?

Barbara A. Fritzsche
Kevin C. Stagl
Eduardo Salas
C. Shawn Burke
*University of Central Florida*

Situational judgment tests (SJTs) have been developed to assess a wide range of constructs (Chan & Schmitt, 1997) including job knowledge (Schmidt & Hunter, 1993), tacit knowledge (Sternberg et al., 2000), cognitive ability (Weekley & Jones, 1997), interpersonal skills (Hedge, Borman, & Hanson, 1996), and personality characteristics (Ployhart, Porr, & Ryan, 2004). Typically, SJTs have been utilized as human resource selection tools. Presumably, job applicants who can identify more effective and less effective responses to job-related situations have greater job-relevant knowledge or better job-related judgment and reasoning skills and are thus, expected to have higher levels of job performance than those who are less able to identify appropriate responses to job-related situations (Hedge et al., 1996). In fact, a recent meta-analysis reported an average validity coefficient of .34 for SJTs as predictors of job performance (McDaniel, Morgeson,

Finnegan, Campion, & Braverman, 2001). McDaniel et al.'s findings suggest that SJTs can predict a moderate amount of variance in job performance, and research suggests that SJTs can add incremental validity over other widely used selection tools (Chan & Schmitt, 2002; Clevenger, Pereira, Wiechmann, Schmitt, & Harvey, 2001; Schmitt & Mills, 2001). Moreover, SJTs are attractive as selection tools because they tend to show less adverse impact than cognitive ability measures (Clevenger et al., 2001; Hanson & Borman, 1995) and have high face validity (Rosen, 1961).

Not only can SJTs be utilized in human resource selection, but we also suggest they can be used successfully in workplace training contexts. The idea of using SJTs in training and development is not completely novel. For example, Hedge et al. (1996) suggested the application of their SJT to crew resource management team training for the U.S. Air Force. Mullins (2000) used an SJT in training evaluation to measure adaptive knowledge. Moreover, Hanson, Horgen, and Borman (1996) suggested that SJTs could be used for training needs analysis and training evaluation. SJTs could be used to train expatriate managers to understand that what is appropriate in their home culture might be inappropriate in other cultures, or to train sales professionals on when to use various closing strategies. SJTs have been utilized to train supervisors and managers in both individual and team-based organizations (www.alignmark.com). Similarly, SJTs have been used as leader and team member diagnostic tools in organizational retention efforts (www.talentkeepers.com).

Given their popularity in training contexts, it is surprising that research is sparse on the topic of using SJTs in training contexts. In this chapter, we suggest ways in which SJTs could be used in the design, delivery, and/or evaluation of scenario-based training and propose a research agenda on this topic. Scenario-based training seems well-suited for exploring how lower fidelity work simulations, such as SJTs, could be incorporated into training, as work simulations are the basic training tools used in scenario-based training. We conclude with a research agenda that is designed to evaluate the effectiveness of SJTs in scenario-based training and discuss how it is expected to contribute to the current body of literature on the validity of SJTs.

## WHAT IS SCENARIO-BASED TRAINING?

*Scenario-based training* "relies on controlled exercises or vignettes, in which the trainee is presented with cues that are similar to those found in the actual task environment and then given feedback regarding his or her responses" (Cannon-Bowers, Burns, Salas, & Pruitt, 1998, p. 365).

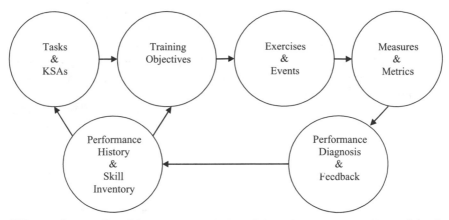

FIG. 14.1. Scenario-Based Team Training. (Adapted from Cannon-Bowers, Burns, Salas & Pruitt, 1998)

Scenario-based training is designed to facilitate learning by closely linking job knowledge, skills, attitudes, requisite training objectives, scenarios, training performance, and feedback (see Fig. 14.1).

Scenarios represent naturalistic environments characterized by psychological safety, allowing participants to practice actions considered too costly or risky to perform in their actual operational context (Edmondson, Bohmer, & Pisano, 2001). A defining characteristic of scenario-based training is that scenario "events" are presented that require trainees to practice using critical job-related skills (Oser, Cannon-Bowers, Salas, & Dwyer, 1999). In other words, the goal of scenario-based training is to present embedded events that provide trainees with guided practice and performance feedback in scripted work simulations (Cannon-Bowers et al., 1998; Oser et al., 1999).

Scenario-based training has been used to develop complex skills in individual and team training contexts. For example, some commercial airlines utilize rapidly reconfigurable line-oriented evaluations, a process grounded in embedded events, to provide training to cockpit crews (Bowers, Jentsch, Baker, Prince, & Salas, 1997). An event-based approach has also been adopted to evaluate the decision making and coordination skills of U. S. Navy combat information center teams (Johnston, Cannon-Bowers, & Jentsch, 1995) and to develop performance measures for decision-making training (Johnston, Smith-Jentsch, & Cannon-Bowers, 1997). Furthermore, elements of a scenario-based approach have been effectively coupled with crew resource management training (Salas, Fowlkes, Stout, Milanovich, & Prince, 1999), aircrew coordination training (Fowlkes, Lane, Salas, Franz, &

Oser, 1994), team self-correction training (Smith-Jentsch, Zeisig, Acton, & McPherson, 1998), joint military training (Dwyer, Oser, & Fowlkes, 1995), and teamwork training (Stout, Salas, & Fowlkes, 1997).

"How-to" guides developed for the design and delivery of scenario-based training (e.g., Fowlkes & Burke, 2004) suggest that scenario-based training is generally more costly and time-consuming to use than other forms of training, such as lecture-based training. However, technological advances have enabled training developers to automate several aspects of scenario-based training, thereby increasing the flexibility of this training method and reducing staffing needs and training time (Cannon-Bowers et al., 1998). In other words, scenario-based training can be characterized by distributed simulation, automated performance monitoring, automated performance assessment, dynamic real-time feedback, and expert performance modeling (Cannon-Bowers et al., 1998).

For example, the Army Research Institute currently utilizes Simulation Training Advanced Testbed for Aviation (STRATA). STRATA is comprised of a set of high-fidelity simulations and simulation tools such as the Kiowa Warrior aircraft simulator. The STRATA system can be accessed almost anywhere because it utilizes distributed interactive simulation/high-level architectural protocols via fiber optic connections over the Defense Simulation Internet. The STRATA system has been utilized to help train both FORSCOM units for deployment to Bosnia and Apache helicopter pilots. Similar to the U.S. Army's efforts, the U.S. Navy utilizes the Synthetic Cognition for Operational Team Training (SCOTT) system to conduct event-based aircrew training (Scolaro & Santarelli, 2002). The SCOTT system is characterized by interactive synthetic team members embedded in training exercises.

Scenario-based training has also been delivered via moderate fidelity desktop-based computer work simulations (e.g., see Streufert, Pogash, & Piasecki, 1988). Desktop-based computer work simulation offers an attractive alternative to delivering scenario-based training via high-fidelity simulators in terms of cost, accessibility by both co-located and distributed trainees, portability, usability, and flexibility of programmable content.

Aptima's Distributed Dynamic Decision Making (DDD) platform is an example of a desktop computer-delivered work simulation that has been utilized as a scenario-based approach to developing the competencies of team members and team leaders (Ellis, Ilgen, Hollenbeck, & Porter, 2001). In its most recent iteration, DDDIII Stability and Support Operations, it has been utilized to train soldiers who have been deployed to peace-keeping missions in Bosnia-Herzegovina and Afghanistan (Paley, Baker, Entin, Serfaty, & Salas, 2002). Swezey, Hutcheson, and Swezey (2000) suggested the desktop computer-based Team Performance Assessment Technology can be utilized to develop teams and their members in virtually any human–computer interface situation. Other desktop computer-based work simulations that can be utilized for training include the Strategic Management Simulations (see Breuer & Streufert, 1995), Airport (see Obermann, 1988), Manage! (see Kreuzig, 1995), Disko (see Funke, 1992), and Textilfabrik (see Hasselmann & Straub, 1995). For comprehensive reviews of the advantages and disadvantages of computer-based training simulations see Kleinmann and Straub (1998), Funke (1998), and Graf (1992).

As individuals, teams, and organizations focus more on employee development and life-long learning (see Day, Zaccaro, & Halpin, 2004; Rutkowski, Steelman, & Griffith, 2004) the use of formal training programs, including scenario-based training, will likely increase (Salas, Stagl, & Burke, 2004). This may be especially true if scenario-based training can be designed and delivered in a more cost-effective manner without sacrificing the learning that accrues from the training. In conjunction with capitalizing on technological advances that allow greater automation and flexibility of use, this goal may be accomplished by incorporating SJTs into scenario-based training.

## WHY SJTs IN TRAINING?

SJTs have already been used to screen candidates prior to participation in managerial assessment centers (Motowidlo, Hanson, & Crafts, 1997) and as low-fidelity assessment center exercises (Joiner, 2002). Because as many as 20 scenarios can be presented to candidates in the time that it takes to conduct one high-fidelity assessment center exercise (Joiner, 2002), the use of SJTs can greatly reduce the cost and increase the efficiency of assessment centers.

Like high-fidelity assessment center exercises, scenario-based training exercises are costly to develop and administer. Thus, the use of SJTs in scenario-based training also has the potential to greatly increase the efficiency and cost-effectiveness of scenario-based training. Furthermore, SJTs can be group administered, which is a practical limitation of some types of scenario-based training. SJTs can also provide trainees with far more practice than could be otherwise offered, practically speaking, in scenario-based training.

Moreover, SJTs can be highly flexible training tools for self-directed training that requires on-demand, anytime, anywhere access. Thus, the portion of scenario-based training that includes the SJT can not only be administered via paper-and-pencil methods or traditional videotaped methods, but it can also be administered via computer or hand-held personal digital assistants (PDAs). Thus, trainees can access the test items at their convenience, whether they are in a traditional training environment, at their desk participating in distributed training, or in the field where they need to assess their skills prior to starting a new assignment. SJT items are also more flexible because they can be easily updated as training content changes. Furthermore, normative data can be continuously updated from a remote data warehouse.

In our review, we found examples of SJTs already being used in training contexts. For example, AIMM Consulting has used SJTs for certification, training needs assessment and leader development in the manufacturing, health care, transportation, and information technology industry (www.aimmconsult.com). Moreover, the Federal Aviation Administration has used an SJT as part of a computer-based developing leadership skill module (www.academy.faa.gov). Hedge et al. (1996) found that their SJT, originally designed for a human resource selection application, was in demand as a training tool. They stated:

> At virtually every unit that we visited to conduct workshops, we were approached by training officers, flight safety officers, or squadron commanders, who were excited about the possibility of using these items as training stimulus materials, whereby junior and senior crewmembers could discuss how to apply good CRM [crew resource management] skills to difficult situations. (p. 2)

Despite the practical advantages of SJTs, higher efficiency, lower cost, and greater flexibility do not come without drawbacks. The largest drawback is that SJT test takers do not necessarily provide behavioral responses, as they do in other high-fidelity simulations. Thus, SJTs are not *true* job simulations (Joiner, 2002). The challenge is to create SJT items that can induce similar psychological processes as those occurring in the trainees' typical operational context (see Marks, 2000).

In the following sections, we describe how SJTs might be used as scenario-based training needs analysis measures, as training content, and as training outcomes assessments. We do not expect that any given training program would try to incorporate SJTs into all three of these phases of the training process. Instead, we present possible alternative uses of SJTs in scenario-based training.

## SJTs IN TRAINING NEEDS ANALYSIS

Like other forms of training, scenario-based training starts with a training needs analysis (Cannon-Bowers et al., 1998). Training needs analysis includes examining organizational, job/task, and person needs (Salas & Cannon-Bowers, 2001). Person-level needs assessment consists of a description of the performance domain, delineation of the determinants of performance, and identification of the competencies most likely to benefit from training (Campbell & Kuncel, 2002). Thus, person-level training needs analysis is essential for deciding when training is needed, what competencies need to be targeted, and who needs to be trained.

As individual differences measures, SJTs can complement other forms of training needs analysis to assess pretraining knowledge or skill. Based on trainees' SJT scores, instruction can be tailored to trainees' developmental needs. For example, high scorers may be routed to a more advance training session than their lower scoring peers. Alternatively, only those trainees who scored high on SJT knowledge questions would proceed immediately to scenario-based training. Others would be given the chance to remediate prior to formal training. When SJTs are used in this way, they could help reduce the number of high-fidelity scenarios necessary for training because only trainees who have demonstrated knowledge on the low-fidelity SJTs are admitted to the higher fidelity training.

## SJTs AS LEARNING TOOLS

For many skills trained via scenario-based training, SJT items could be used as part of the training itself. Depending on how SJTs are conceptualized, there can be different ways to include SJTs as training content in scenario-based training. We offer suggestions for how SJTs might be used if they are conceptualized as low-fidelity simulations or if they are conceptualized as measures of job or tacit knowledge.

According to Motowidlo, Dunnette, and Carter (1990), SJTs are low-fidelity job simulations. They predict future performance because simulations are behavioral samples, and the best predictor of future performance is past behavior (see Wernimont & Campbell, 1968). Low-fidelity simulations are expected to be somewhat poorer predictors of future performance than high-fidelity simulations that better mimic real-world job-performance conditions (Motowidlo et al., 1990). Yet, moderate correlations have been found between an SJT and a comparison high-fidelity assessment center (Motowidlo et al., 1990).

As low-fidelity simulations, SJTs might be expected to *replace* high-fidelity scenarios in training (Hedge et al., 1996). The challenge is to develop and use them in such a way that learning and skill acquisition is not negatively impacted but costs and efficiency are improved. This is the same challenge faced in human resource selection contexts when SJTs are designed and used as replacements for high-fidelity assessment center exercises. SJTs that replace other higher fidelity scenarios should be designed to model real-world situations, provide enough items to cover a representative sample of the performance domain represented, and use "would do" instructions (Ployhart & Ehrhart, 2003).

SJTs may be particularly useful as substitutes for scenario-based training when training focuses on developing complex decision-making skills. In these situations, SJTs may be superior to lecture-based training and may also be an appropriate alternative to traditional scenario-based training (Hunter, Martinussen, & Wiggins, 2003). Complex judgment tasks, such as those faced by executives, medical doctors, military personnel, and pilots, for example, can be modeled in SJT items. Thus, the SJT items can provide a relatively high-fidelity way to train judgment and decision-making skills. This is the training application suggested by Hedge et al. (1996) for their SJT called the Situational Test of Aircrew Response Styles (STARS). STARS was designed to measure crew resource management interpersonal problem-solving and decision-making skills of U.S. Air Force pilots.

Moreover, the training of judgment and decision-making skills can be delivered via portable devices such as PDAs to deliver just-in-time training for operational assignment preparation or to conduct self-development training to identify knowledge and judgment deficiencies. For example, Special Forces personnel deployed on a moments notice may benefit from completing an SJT in route to their mission. In this example, SJT content can be tailored a priori to the specific contingencies likely to be faced and delivered via wireless technology in a just-in-time fashion. This may be an effective way to improve situation awareness, "the perception of the elements in the environment within a volume of time and space, the comprehension of their meaning and the projection of their status in the near future" (Endsley, 1988, P. 97). Research suggests that situation awareness skills can be trained in high-fidelity simulations using techniques such as Endsley's (1995) Situation Awareness Global Assessment Technique (SAGAT). Perhaps lower fidelity SJT items can be developed that are specifically designed to improve the situation awareness of military forces prior to a mission.

SJTs conceptualized as low-fidelity work simulations can also be developed to train interpersonal skills, such as negotiation and conflict resolution. One such tool, the Conflict Resolution Skills Assessment (CRSA; Olson-Buchanan et al., 1998), was advanced as an interactive, video-based SJT for the assessment of conflict-resolution skills. Multi-sample evidence suggests that CRSA scores were related to supervisory ratings of the effectiveness with which job-related conflict was managed and showed no adverse impact against women (Olson-Buchanan et al., 1998). Although further investigation of the psychometric properties of the CRSA is warranted, these findings suggest that the CRSA may provide a useful means of training conflict resolution skills via work-related simulation.

In contrast to viewing SJTs as low-fidelity simulations, SJTs have also been conceptualized as a method by which job knowledge, tacit knowledge, cognitive ability, or personality can be measured (see Ployhart & Ehrhart, 2003; Schmidt & Hunter, 1993). There is empirical support for this conceptualization, as SJTs have been found to correlate modestly with independent measures of job knowledge, cognitive ability, and emotional stability (McDaniel & Nguyen, 2001).

As knowledge measures, SJTs could be used prior to the administration of higher fidelity scenarios to develop the declarative or procedural knowledge necessary to facilitate skill development. In other words, SJTs may be excellent supplements to scenario-based training of complex skills, as most theories of skill acquisition suggest that knowledge acquisition precedes skill development (see Anderson, 1985; Campbell, 1990). SJTs used as supplements to scenario-based training should be designed to measure the construct of interest, and "should do" response instructions (rather than "would do" response options) may better focus test takers on demonstrating their knowledge (Ployhart & Ehrhart, 2003).

Rather than administering and scoring the SJTs as individual differences measures, SJT items used as training tools would be administered one at a time. Before proceeding to the next SJT item, a trainer could guide a discussion about the most and least effective response options and why they are appropriate. Also, guided by a trainer, more advanced trainees can offer insights to less advanced trainees. If video-based SJT items are used, following discussion and analysis of the situation, the scenario could be allowed to play out so that trainees could see the appropriate behaviors in action. Similarly, desktop-based expert systems could be developed to automatically administer SJT content, score responses, and provide respondents with customized feedback reports for remediation.

Following successful training on the SJT items, trainees can be given high-fidelity scenario-based training. Thus, the SJT portion of the training can focus on the development of knowledge (using an active learning approach) and the high-fidelity scenario-based training can focus on skill mastery alone. In this case, SJTs are expected to positively affect training outcomes, as the SJTs provide more scenario-based practice than may be practical to offer using high-fidelity scenario-based training alone. Buch and Diehl (1984) showed, for example, that judgment training that is used prior to conventional training can significantly improve job performance.

## SJTs IN TRAINING EVALUATION

Training evaluation is the systematic collection of descriptive and judgmental information necessary to make effective training decisions

(Goldstein, 1991). Training must be systematically evaluated (a) to make decisions about the future use of a training program or technique, (b) to make decisions about trainees, (c) to contribute to the science of training and (d) for political or public relations purposes. Summative evaluation is necessary to help ensure that performance transfers to the operating environment, and formative evaluation is important for diagnosing the strengths and weaknesses of training design and delivery (Brown & Gerhardt, 2002).

Kirkpatrick's (1959) taxonomy of training evaluation is a widely utilized framework for understanding the outcomes of training. Kirkpatrick suggested that training can be evaluated at four levels including reactions, learning, behavior, and results. Kirkpatrick conceptualized (a) reactions as how well the trainees liked a particular training program; (b) learning as the principles, facts, and skills that were learned by the trainees; (c) behavior as changes in on-the-job behavior; and (d) results as the organization-level changes that result from the training. SJTs, as knowledge measures, could provide training evaluation that is targeted at the learning level of Kirkpatrick's taxonomy.

Declarative knowledge tests, which are designed to measure cognitive changes that result from training, are commonly used as learning-level measures. Because learning refers to changes in cognitive, affective, and/or skill-based outcomes (Kraiger, Ford, & Salas, 1993), SJTs can be designed to gather learning-level data that compliments declarative knowledge tests. For example, SJTs can be designed with an extended case study and constructed response format, instead of a forced-choice format, to better understand learning outcomes (Cianciolo, Antonakis, & Sternberg, 2004). Cianciolo et al. suggested that SJTs with extended case studies may help in "assessing not only the outcome of possessing and applying tacit knowledge but also the cognitive processes employed by the individual during the application of tacit knowledge" (p. 223).

Hunter (2003) found that pilots who scored higher on an SJT designed to measure pilot judgment and decision-making skills were less likely to have experienced hazardous flight events. Thus, he argued:

> particularly, for trainers, the use of SJT methodology would provide a means of quantitatively evaluating the impact of training whose purpose was to improve the judgment or ADM [aeronautical decision making] skills of pilots using pre- and posttest design and parallel forms of SJT measures. (p. 383)

In another study (Mullins, 2000), an SJT was designed as a training evaluation measure of adaptive knowledge. Mullins developed an SJT that was used to measure trainees' ability to transfer knowledge from a training context to more complex job contexts. He found that declarative knowledge, self-regulatory behavior, and strategic performance during training (but not self-efficacy) related to post-training SJT scores. This study suggests that SJTs may have a use in training evaluation to examine whether trainees have the knowledge required to generalize and adapt what they learned during scenario-based training to novel situations.

## WHEN TO USE SJTs IN SCENARIO-BASED TRAINING

Although we presented SJTs as potentially useful measures during needs analysis, training, and the evaluation of scenario-based training, it is not desirable to use SJTs in all three phases of training for any given training program. Instead, SJTs are expected to be useful to the extent that they can reduce the costs associated with training or increase its efficiency without sacrificing desired training outcomes. SJTs will also be useful if their addition to scenario-based training results in better training outcomes such as what might be expected if SJTs are added as supplements to scenario-based training to provide additional practice. These are empirical questions, which leads us to a discussion of a research agenda for using SJTs with scenario-based training.

## A RESEARCH AGENDA

Most research on SJTs has focused on their criterion-related (Clevenger et al., 2001; McDaniel et al., 2001) and construct validity (e.g., McDaniel & Nguyen, 2001) as human resource selection tools. Much less empirical work has focused on the use of SJTs in training contexts. We offer a future research agenda designed to advance our understanding of SJTs in scenario-based training. Specifically, we discuss the usefulness of SJTs in training contexts, aptitude by treatment interactions, and new ways to explore the construct validity of SJTs that result from their use in training contexts.

The most obvious research questions relate to the value added of using SJTs in scenario-based training. When SJTs are used in training needs assessment or as training evaluation measures, do they accurately assess individual training needs or training outcomes? An important question is whether they are better needs assessment or outcome measures than traditional declarative or procedural knowledge measures.

Campbell, McCloy, Oppler, and Sager (1993) suggested that individual performance can be represented via eight broad factors: job-specific task proficiency, non-job-specific task proficiency, written and oral communication proficiency, demonstration of effort, maintenance of personal discipline, facilitation of peer and team performance, supervision/leadership, and management/administration. Moreover, Campbell and colleagues suggested the direct determinants of on-the-job performance are declarative knowledge, procedural knowledge and skill, and motivation.

Of particular interest is whether SJTs designed to measure procedural knowledge, and skill are better predictors of some types of job performance than SJTs designed to measure declarative knowledge. For example, procedural knowledge and skill in facilitating peer and team performance may be more important to actually engaging in on-the-job dyadic role exchanges than simply having declarative knowledge of this domain. Likewise, SJTs designed to measure the procedural knowledge and skill underlying leadership may be more predictive of demonstrable leadership in the workplace than scores obtained from SJTs designed to measure the declarative knowledge requisite to effective leadership.

This issue may be one of aligning the specific types of antecedents (e.g., declarative knowledge, procedural knowledge, and skill) critical to job performance with the specific types of knowledge targeted for development by scenario-based training and with the specific types of knowledge assessed by SJTs in training evaluation. Aligning the type of knowledge identified in job analysis, targeted by training, and assessed during training evaluation, should serve to maximize the predictive validity of SJTs administered used during training evaluation.

Another value-added question is as follows: When SJTs are used during training, does adding lower-fidelity assessments to scenario-based training result in better learning outcomes than traditional scenario-based training alone? As knowledge measures, it is important to test whether SJTs facilitate the development of declarative, procedural, or tacit knowledge that would help prepare trainees for skill development during the high-fidelity simulations they encounter in scenario-based training. We hypothesize that the knowledge developed through the use of SJTs as training tools may free cognitive resources during scenario-based training that would allow trainees to better focus specifically on developing complex skills, rather than focusing on knowledge and skill, during the high-fidelity simulations. We also expect that transfer of training will be improved because SJTs allow trainees to be exposed to a greater number and wider range of situations than would be practical in traditional scenario-based training. When SJTs are used as alternatives to high-fidelity training, it is important to understand how much learning is sacrificed, if any, by using lower fidelity scenarios.

In addition to examining the value added of using SJTs in training contexts, another important set of research questions relate to the examination of aptitude-by-treatment interactions (ATIs). An ATI occurs when training differentially impacts trainees because of individual differences in trainee aptitude (Cronbach, 1957). Research suggests SJT performance relates to individual differences in general cognitive ability, neuroticism, conscientiousness, agreeableness, and job experience (McDaniel & Nguyen, 2001). Thus, it is important to examine how training, using SJTs, will impact learning outcomes differently for different trainees. Significant ATIs would suggest training should be tailored to the specific needs of different trainees (Day, 2000). Moreover, research is needed to examine the nature of the interactions between SJT scores and design features of scenario-based training when predicting training outcomes.

Finally, using SJTs in scenario-based training provides a unique opportunity to further examine the criterion-related and construct validity of SJTs. If SJTs are developed to measure the same constructs that will be trained in scenario-based training, predictive validity studies can be conducted. Specifically, researchers can administer trainees the SJT (without using the scores for needs assessment or training) and then relate those scores to performance in scenario-based training. In other words, performance in scenario-based training would be the criterion of interest. This should establish the upper bound for the validity coefficients associated with SJTs utilized in human resource selection contexts. For example, an SJT designed to measure cockpit crew resource management skills should predict performance in simulations designed to assess cockpit crew resource management skills. It is expected that "should do" responses would better predict tightly controlled simulations that represent "can do" behavior of the same skill than they would predict other aspects of job performance or less tightly controlled on-the-job measures of crew resource management performance.

Studies that directly compare low-fidelity SJTs with scenario-based training of the same constructs or skills will also generally advance our understanding of the relation between SJT responses and "can do" assessments. Ployhart and Ehrhart (2003) found that different SJT instructions affected their reliability and validity. Specifically, they found the greatest support for "would do" instructions in predicting self- and peer-skill ratings and other test scores. It would be interesting to determine if the same results occur using scenario-based training performance as the criterion.

As Ployhart and Ehrhart (2003) mentioned, different response instructions might be useful when SJTs are used to demonstrate knowledge and when they are used to predict future behavior. In other words, "would do" instructions focus test takers on their typical or likely performance, whereas "should do" instructions focus test takers on their knowledge of best practice or ideal, maximum performance. Thus, when SJTs are used in human resource selection contexts, "would do" instructions may be more useful because criterion measures are generally designed to measure typical job performance. However, different outcomes might be expected in training contexts because training focuses on developing maximal performance or "should do" knowledge. In other words, SJTs might be used to identify training needs because trainees do not have "should do" knowledge. Alternatively, SJTs might be used as training tools to teach trainees "should do" behaviors. Or, they might be used in training evaluation to demonstrate that trainees have learned "should do" behaviors during training. Thus, research should explore whether "should do" SJT instructions are more useful than "would do" instructions in this context.

## CONCLUSION

Organizations spend in excess of $55 billion annually on training and development (Bassi & Van Buren, 1998) because it is widely understood that "the people make the place" (Schneider, 1987). As organizations grapple with the realities of increasing global interdependencies, empowerment at the lowest of system levels, co-dependent employment relationships, mounting domestic and foreign competition, the emergence of teams as an organizing structure, changing demographics, and the startling deficit of domestic human capital that will result from the retirement of baby boomers, they are expected to spend even more on interventions to develop their human capital such as scenario-based training.

The systematic development of human capital is a source of sustained competitive advantage when such activities result in knowledge, skills, and attitudes that are (a) not easily duplicated, (b) distinguishable from ones' competitors, and (c) add positive economic benefit to the production of goods or the rendering of services (see Cascio, 1998). Thus, the wisdom of this growing multibillion dollar investment is predicated on interventions such as scenario-based training being an effective medium via which organizations can better execute their strategy and obtain their goals (see Jackson & Schuler, 1990; Kozlowski, Brown, Weissbein, Cannon-Bowers, & Salas, 2000).

In this chapter, we have suggested that SJTs may enhance the effectiveness and increase the efficiency of the design, delivery and/or evaluation of scenario-based training. Mounting evidence suggests that SJTs can be useful predictors of future job performance. Our objective was to extend current thinking about SJTs beyond their traditional use in selection systems and managerial assessment centers. We hope that future research will be conducted to examine the many yet unanswered questions about the use of SJTs in training contexts.

## REFERENCES

Anderson, J. P. (1985). *Cognitive psychology and its implications* (2nd ed.). New York: Freeman.

Bassi, L. J., & Van Buren, M. E. (1998). *The 1998 ASTD state of the industry report* [on-line]. Available http://www.astd.org

Bowers, C., Jentsch, F., Baker, D., Prince, C., & Salas, E. (1997). Rapidly reconfigurable event-set based line operational evaluation scenarios. *Proceedings of the Human Factors and Ergonomics Society 41st Annual Meeting* (pp. 912–915). Santa Monica, CA: Human Factors and Ergonomics Society.

Breuer, K., & Streufert, S. (1995). Strategic management simulations: The German case. In M. Mulder & W. J. Nijhof (Eds.), *Corporate training for effective performance* (pp. 195–208). Boston, MA: Kluwer

Brown, K., & Gerhardt, M. (2002). Formative evaluation: An integrated practice model and case study. *Personnel Psychology, 55*, 951–983.

Buch, G., & Diehl, A. (1984). An investigation of the effectiveness of pilot judgment training. *Aviation Psychology, 2*, 557–564.

Campbell, J. P. (1990). The role of theory in industrial and organizational psychology. In M. D. Dunnette & L. M. Hough (Eds.), *Handbook of industrial and organizational psychology* (Vol. 1, pp. 39–74). Palo Alto, CA: Consulting Psychologists Press.

Campbell, J. P., & Kuncel, N. R. (2002). Individual and team training. In N. Anderson, D. S. Ones, H. K. Sinangil, & C. Viswesvaran (Eds.), *Handbook of industrial, work and organizational psychology* (pp. 272–312). London: Sage.

Campbell, J. P., McCloy, R. A., Oppler, S. H., & Sager, C. E. (1993). A theory of performance. In N. Schmitt & W. C. Borman (Eds.), *Personnel selection in organizations* (pp. 35–70). San Francisco: Jossey-Bass.

Cannon-Bowers, J. A., Burns, J. J., Salas, E., & Pruitt, J. S. (1998). Advanced technology in scenario-based training. In J. A. Cannon-Bowers & E. Salas (Eds.), *Making decisions under stress: Implications for individual and team training* (pp. 365–374). Washington, DC: American Psychological Association.

Cascio W. F. (1998). *Applied psychology in human resource management* (5th ed.) Upper Saddle River, NJ: Prentice-Hall.

Chan, D., & Schmitt, N. (1997). Video based versus paper-and-pencil method of assessment in situational judgment tests: Subgroup differences in test performance and face validity perceptions. *Journal of Applied Psychology, 82*, 143–159.

Chan, D., & Schmitt, N. (2002). Video-based versus paper-and-pencil method of assessment in situational judgment tests. *Journal of Applied Psychology, 82*, 143–159.

Cianciolo, A. T., Antonakis, J., & Sternberg, R. J. (2004). Practical intelligence and leadership: Using experience as a mentor. In D. Day, S. J. Zaccaro, & S. M. Halpin (Eds.), *Leader development for transforming organizations* (pp. 211–236). Mahwah, NJ: Lawrence Erlbaum Associates.

Clevenger, J., Pereira, G. M., Wiechmann, D., Schmitt, N., & Harvey, V. S. (2001). Incremental validity of situational judgment tests. *Journal of Applied Psychology, 86*, 410–417.

Cronbach, L. J. (1957). The two disciplines of scientific study. *American Psychologists, 12*, 671–684.

Day, D., Zaccaro, S. J., & Halpin, S. M. (2004) (Eds.), *Leader development for transforming organizations*. Mahwah, NJ: Lawrence Erlbaum Associates.

Day, D. V. (2000). Leadership development: A review in context. *Leadership Quarterly, 11,* 581–613.

Dwyer, D. J., Oser, R. L., & Fowlkes, J. E. (1995). A case study of distributed training and training performance. *Proceedings of the Human Factors and Ergonomics Society 39th Annual Meeting* (pp. 1316–1320). Santa Monica, CA: Human Factors and Ergonomics Society.

Edmondson, A., Bohmer, R., & Pisano, G. (2001). Disrupted routines: Team learning and technology implementation in hospitals. *Administrative Sciences Quarterly, 46,* 685–716.

Ellis, A. P. J., Ilgen, D. R., Hollenbeck, J. R., & Porter, C. O. L. H. (2001). *Capacity collaboration, and commonality: A framework for understanding team learning.* Paper presented at the annual conference of the Academy of Management, Washington, DC.

Endsley, M. R. (1988). Design and evaluation for situation awareness enhancement. In *Proceedings of the Human Factors Society 32nd Annual Meeting* (pp. 97–101). Santa Monica, CA: Human Factors Society.

Endsley, M. R. (1995). Toward a theory of situation awareness. *Human Factors, 1,* 32–64.

Fowlkes, J. E., & Burke, C. S. (2004). Event-Based Approach to Training (EBAT). In N. Stanton, H. Hendrick, S. Konz, K. Parsons, & E. Salas (Eds.), *Handbook of human factors and ergonomics methods* (pp. 47-1–47-5). London: Taylor & Francis.

Fowlkes, J. E., Lane, N. E., Salas, E., Franz, T., & Oser, R. (1994). Improving the measurement of team performance: The TARGETS methodology. *Military Psychology, 6,* 47–61.

Funke, J. (1992). The validity of a personnel assessment simulation on complex problem solving. *Kongre der Deutschen Gesellschaft fur Psychologie, Trier.*

Funke, J. (1998). Computer-based testing and training with scenarios from complex problem-solving research: Advantages and disadvantages. *International Journal of Selection and Assessment, 2,* 90–96.

Goldstein, I. L. (1991). Training in work organizations. In M. D. Dunnette & L. M. Hough (Eds.), *Handbook of industrial and organizational psychology* (Vol. 2, pp. 507–619). Palo Alto, CA: Consulting Psychologist Press.

Graf, J. (Ed.). (1992). *Scenarios—simulated realities for tomorrows' manager.* Speyer: GABAL-Verlag.

Hanson, M. A., & Borman, W. C. (1995, April). *Construct validation of a measure of supervisory job knowledge.* Poster presented at the 10th annual conference of the Society for Industrial and Organizational Psychology, Orlando, FL.

Hanson, M. A., Horgen, K. E., & Borman, W. C. (1996, November). *Situational judgment: An alternative approach to selection test development.* Paper presented at the 38th annual conference of the International Military Testing Association.

Hasselmann, D., & Straub, B. (1995, November). *Challenge complexity, Element 2: textile factory.* Hamburg, Germany: Windmuhle.

Hedge, J. W., Borman, W. C., & Hanson, M. A. (1996). *Videotaped crew resource management scenarios for selection and training applications.* Paper presented at the 38th annual conference of the International Military Testing Association.

Hunter, D. R. (2003). Measuring general aviation pilot judgment using a situational judgment technique. *The International Journal of Aviation Psychology, 13,* 373–386.

Hunter, D. R., Martinussen, M., & Wiggins, M. (2003). Understanding how pilots make weather-related decisions. *The International Journal of Aviation Psychology, 13,* 73–87.

Jackson, S. E., & Schuler, R. S. (1990). Human resource planning: Challenges for industrial/organizational psychologists. *American Psychologist, 45,* 223–239.

Johnston, J., Cannon-Bowers, J. A., & Jentsch, K. A. S. (1995). Event based performance measurement system for shipboard command teams. *Proceedings of the first International Symposium on Command and Control Research and Technology* (pp. 274–276). Washington, DC: The Center for Advanced Command and Technology.

Johnston, J., Smith-Jentsch, K. A., & Cannon-Bowers, J. A. (1997). Performance measurement tools for enhancing team decision-making. In M. T. Brannick, E. Salas, & C. Prince (Eds.), *Team performance assessment and measurement: Theory, methods and applications* (pp. 311–327). Hillsdale, NJ: Lawrence Erlbaum Associates.

Joiner, D. A. (2002). Assessment centers: What's new? *Public Personnel Management, 31,* 179–185.

Kirkpatrick, D. L. (1959). Techniques for evaluating training programs. *Journal of ASTD, 13,* 3–9.

Kleinmann, M., & Straub, B. (1998). Validity and application of computer- simulated scenarios in personnel assessment. *Validity and Implementation of Computer-Simulated Scenarios, 2,* 97–106.

Kozlowski, S. W. J., Brown, K. G., Weissbein, D. A., Cannon-Bowers, J. A., & Salas, E. (2000). A multilevel approach to training effectiveness: Enhancing horizontal and vertical transfer. In K. Klein & S. W. J. Kozlowski (Eds.), *Multilevel theory, research and methods in Organization* (pp. 157–210). San Francisco, CA: Jossey-Bass.

Kraiger K., Ford, J. K., & Salas, E. (1993). Application of cognitive, skill-based, and affective theories of learning outcomes to new methods of training evaluation. *Journal of Applied Psychology, 78,* 311–328.

Kreuzig, H. W. (1995). The computer simulation Manage!. In T. Geilhardt & T. Muhlbradt (Eds.), *Planspiele im Personal- und Organizations Management* (pp. 387–400). Gottingen, Germany: Verlag fur Angewandte Psychologie.

Marks, M. A. (2000). A critical analysis of computer simulations for conducting team research. *Small Group Research, 31,* 653–675.

McDaniel, M. A., Morgeson, F. P., Finnegan, E. B., Campion, M. A., & Braverman, E. P. (2001). Use of situational judgment tests to predict job performance: A clarification of the literature. *Journal of Applied Psychology, 86,* 730–740.

McDaniel, M. A., & Nguyen, N. T. (2001). Situational judgment tests: A review of practice and constructs assessed. *International Journal of Selection and Assessment, 9,* 103–113.

Motowidlo, S. J., Dunnette, M. D., & Carter, G. W. (1990). An alternative selection procedure: The low-fidelity simulation. *Journal of Applied Psychology, 75,* 640–647.

Motowidlo, S. J., Hanson, M. A., & Crafts, J. L. (1997). Low-fidelity simulations. In D. L. Whetzel, & G. R. Wheaton (Eds.), *Applied measurement methods in industrial psychology* (pp. 241–260). Palo Alto, CA: Consulting Psychologists Press.

Mullins, M. E. (2000). *The effects of practice variability and velocity feedback on the development of basic and strategic training skills.* Unpublished doctoral dissertation, Michigan State University, Ann Arbor.

Obermann, C. (1988). *Development of a personnel assessment instrument based on the complex problem solving paradigm.* Mannheim: Institut fur Psychologie.

Olson-Buchanan, J. B., Drasgow, F., Moberg, P. J., Mead, A. D., Keenan, P. A., & Donovan, M. A. (1998). Interactive video assessment of conflict resolution skills. *Personnel Psychology, 51,* 1–24.

Oser, R. L., Cannon-Bowers, J. A., Salas, E., & Dwyer, D. J. (1999). Enhancing human performance in technology-rich environments: Guidelines for scenario based training. *Human Technology Interaction in Complex Systems, 9,* 175–202.

Paley, M., Baker, K., Entin, E., Serfaty, D., & Salas, E. (2002). *Scenario-based training for stability and support operations (SASO) with the distributed dynamic decision-making (DDD) simulation (AP-R-1200)*. Woburn, MA: Aptima, Inc.

Ployhart, R. E., & Ehrhart, M. G. (2003). Be careful what you ask for: Effects of response instructions on the construct validity and reliability of situational judgment tests. *International Journal of Selection & Assessment, 11*, 1–16.

Ployhart, R. E., Porr, W. B., & Ryan, A. M. (2004). A construct oriented approach for developing situational judgment tests in a service context. In P. R. Sackett (Chair), *New developments in SJTs: Scoring, coaching, and incremental validity*. Paper presented at the 19th annual conference of the Society for Industrial and Organizational Psychology, Chicago, IL.

Rosen, N. A. (1961). How to supervise? *Personnel Psychology, 14*, 87–99.

Rutkowski, K. A., Steelman, L. A., & Griffith, R. L. (2004, April). *An empirical examination of accountability for performance development*. Paper presented at the 19th annual meeting for the Society of Industrial Organizational Psychology

Salas, E., & Cannon-Bowers, J. A. (2001). The science of training: A decade of progress. *Annual Review of Psychology, 52*, 471–499.

Salas, E., Fowlkes, J. E., Stout, R. J., Milanovich, D. M., & Prince, C. (1999). Does CRM training improve teamwork skills in the cockpit?: Two evaluation studies. *Human Factors, 41(2)*, 326–343.

Salas, E., Stagl, K. C., & Burke, C. S. (2004). 25 years of team effectiveness in organizations: Research themes and emerging needs. In C. L. Cooper & I. T. Robertson (Eds.), *International review of industrial and organizational psychology* (pp. 47–91). New York: Wiley.

Schneider, B. (1987). The people make the place. *Personnel Psychology, 40*, 450–467.

Schmidt, F. L., & Hunter, J. E. (1993). Tacit knowledge, practical intelligence, general mental ability and job knowledge. *Current Directions in Psychological Science, 2*, 8–9.

Schmitt, N., & Mills, A. E. (2001). Traditional tests and job simulations: Minority and majority performance and test validities. *Journal of Applied Psychology, 3*, 451–458.

Scolaro, J., & Santarelli, T. (2002). Cognitive modeling teamwork, taskwork, and instructional behavior in synthetic teammates. *Proceedings of the 11th Conference on Computer Generated Forces and Behavioral Representation*. Orlando, FL: Institute for Simulation and Training.

Smith-Jentsch, K. A., Zeisig, R. L., Acton, B., & McPherson, J. A. (1998). Team dimensional training: A strategy for guided team self-correction. In J. A. Cannon-Bowers & E. Salas (Eds.). *Making decisions under stress* (pp. 271–297).Washington, DC: American Psychological Association.

Sternberg, R. J., Forsythe, G. B., Hedlund, J., Horvath, J. A., Wagner, R. K., Williams, W. M., Snook, S. A., & Grigorenko, E. L. (2000). Practical intelligence: An example from the military workplace. In *Practical intelligence in everyday life*. Cambridge: Cambridge University Press.

Stout, R. J., Salas, E., & Fowlkes, J. E. (1997). Enhancing teamwork in complex environments through team training. *Group Dynamics: Theory, Research and Practice, 1*, 169–182.

Streufert, S., Pogash, R., & Piasecki, M. (1988). Simulation-based assessment of managerial competence: Reliability and validity. *Personnel Psychology, 41*, 537–557.

Swezey, R. W., Hutcheson, T. D., & Swezey, L. L. (2000). Development of a second-generation computer-based team performance assessment technology. *International Journal of Cognitive Ergonomics, 4*, 163–170.

Weekley, J. A. & Jones, C. (1997). Video-based situational testing. *Personnel Psychology, 50*, 25–49.

Wernimont, P., & Campbell, J. P. (1968). Sign, sample and criteria. *Journal of Applied Psychology, 52*, 372–376.

# 15

# Situational Judgment in Work Teams: A Team Role Typology

Troy V. Mumford
*Utah State University*

Michael A. Campion
*Purdue University*

Frederick P. Morgeson
*Michigan State University*

As work teams become more prevalent in organizations, it becomes more important to better understand and predict effective team member contributions. Functional team roles are a potentially important tool for understanding the contributions made by individuals to teams. This chapter develops a typology of team roles and discusses how they can be used to develop a situational judgment test (SJT).

The contributions made by individuals to the requirements of the team environment can be understood by considering the roles that team members play in executing critical team functions. These functional team roles represent clusters of related behaviors that perform critical functions within the team. These functions are necessary for effective internal execution of the team's work, effective management of the team's relationship with its environment, and preserving the team's vitality through meeting the social needs of members (Hackman, 1987; McGrath, 1984; Sundstrom, De Meuse, & Futrell, 1990).

This chapter makes two primary contributions. The first is furthering the understanding of functional roles in teams. The chapter draws on the past research on team roles to create a comprehensive and parsimonious typology of functional team roles. Although past research has referred to roles as being a valuable focus of research (Ancona & Caldwell, 1988), and roles often appear in textbook discussions of group dynamics (Steers, 1991), surprisingly little attention has been given to evaluating extant typologies such as Benne and Sheat's (1948) seminal typology of work-group roles (Mudrack & Farrell, 1995), or integrating the more recent research by Ancona (Ancona & Caldwell, 1992) dealing with boundary-spanning roles or Belbin's (1981, 1993) work using individual differences to predict team-role behavior. This chapter lays the foundation for knowledge about team roles by reviewing the extant literature and creating an integrated typology of functional team roles.

The second contribution is to integrate team roles with situational judgment. This will enhance understanding of how team members' knowledge of when a particular team role should be adopted impacts their performance of that role within the team. This diagnostic ability to assess team situations and determine which role is required is critical to being an effective team member because it allows the team member to be flexible and assume different roles depending on the demands of the situation and the roles taken by other team members. This chapter outlines how the situational judgment perspective can be used effectively to assess these team-role abilities.

## PREVIOUS RESEARCH ON TEAM ROLES

One way to conceptualize the behavior of team members is to consider the different roles that team members take while interacting as a team. A *role* is generally defined as a cluster of related and goal-directed behaviors characteristic of a person within a specific situation (Stewart, Manz, & Sims, 1999). It is often considered to be one of the fundamental and defining features of organizations (Katz & Kahn, 1978) and teams (Hackman, 1990b). Early research attempted to outline typologies of roles that team members take in interacting with their teammates (e.g., Benne & Sheats, 1948). The fulfillment and coordination of these roles by team members was hypothesized to be necessary in order for the team to perform effectively and avoid process losses associated with dysfunctional conflict, role ambiguity, and social loafing (Steiner, 1972).

The use of the role construct provides several advantages for understanding how individuals contribute to the group. First, roles have been considered one of the defining features of work groups (Hackman, 1990a; Sundstrom et. al., 1990), and are often cited as important determinants of team performance (Belbin, 1993). Second, the concept of a role is well suited to capture the notion that team members play different, but complementary, parts in the team. This includes the importance of taking situational and social cues into account, and enacting an appropriate role. Third, the concept of a role is more dynamic and flexible than the concepts of jobs. The specific allocation of tasks among employees is often done in a more real-time and changing manner, which is better captured with the role construct. Fourth, the role-knowledge construct provides a useful alternative to personality for understanding the contributions that team members make to teams. The link between personality and the team's work requirements is often distal and emphasizes only the social functions within the team. Roles provide a more proximal description that corresponds to the needs of the team with respect to social, task, and boundary-spanning functions.

Previous research has made several contributions to the understanding of team roles. Benne and Sheats (1948) and Bales (1950) provided insight into two critical functions that roles are instrumental in performing—task execution and the maintenance of the social viability of the team. Another primary contribution made by Benne and Sheats and Bales is that their research showed the utility of using the role construct to cluster behaviors exhibited in groups. The work by Belbin (1981, 1993), McCann and Margerison (1989), and Parker (1996) highlights the utility of using individual differences as predictors of which roles individuals are likely to take within teams. All three typologies are built on the classic personality model of Carl Jung (1923), and categorize individuals according to their "role preferences." Finally, the work by Ancona addresses the functions that team members must execute outside of the team context in terms of interactions, exchanges, and behavior interfacing with constituents outside the team.

There are also several limitations in the previous research on team roles. First, although Benne and Sheats is the theory of choice for most current discussions of team roles (Forsyth, 1990; Stewart et al., 1999), there has been only scant empirical testing to justify its acceptance (Mudrack & Farrell, 1995). Second, this typology, like that of Bales (1950), was created out of research on ad hoc groups working in laboratory settings, with uncertain generalizability to work teams in organizations. Third, as illustrated by Ancona's (Ancona & Caldwell, 1988, 1992) work, there is a need to integrate both internal and external team roles into the typologies. Fourth, the theories that attempt to predict the adoption of team roles using individual differences are all personality-based measures (Belbin, 1993; McCann &

Margerison, 1995). They assume that the role a person takes is determined by preference, neglecting the possibility that there is a knowledge component that determines role enactment. Finally, the primary focus of research on functional team roles has been the creation of descriptive typologies of roles with less attention paid to applying this knowledge to organizational issues.

## An Integrated Team-Role Typology

The purpose of this chapter is to overcome the fragmentation in the team-role literature by integrating the existing typologies of roles. The team-role literature was thoroughly reviewed, and the roles from the various typologies were catalogued. Each of the roles was recorded and given a descriptive label, yielding 120 team roles. The roles were then sorted independently into homogeneous groups by two researchers using a Q-sort methodology. The percentage of time that roles were placed in the same category was 83% and Cohen's kappa, which indicates the level of agreement after correcting for chance agreement, was .80. The researchers then met to discuss the groupings and reconcile any discrepancies. The resulting team roles and their relationship with previous roles in the literature are presented in Table 15.1.

This typology is considered exhaustive because it inductively incorporated all roles from the extant team-role literature. It is also considered parsimonious because the behaviors are functionally grouped into 10 team roles and further organized into three broad categories suggested by the literature—task roles, socioemotional roles, and boundary-spanning roles. In the discussion that follows, these roles are described in terms of their definitions, behaviors, and situations in which they are most appropriate based on previous research. Each of these elements plays a part in the development of the SJT. Table 15.2 presents a summary.

## TASK ROLES

The existence of teams within organizations is, to a large extent, driven by their utility in accomplishing work. The review of the literature suggested that task roles could be further broken down into the following six team roles.

### Contractor

Teams exist in an environment that is interdependent (Campion, Medsker, & Higgs, 1993; Hackman, 1987) and, to varying degrees, autonomous

(Wellins, Byham, & Wilson, 1991). Because the behaviors of one team member influence those of another, there is a need for team members to coordinate their actions by sequencing tasks, synchronizing schedules, and harmonizing actions. In addition, if the team is accountable, it creates a degree of ambiguity in terms of which team member is responsible for which behaviors, because now the team is responsible for allocating tasks.

***Definition.***   The task organization and coordination is accomplished by team members taking a contractor role. This role serves to provide structure to the team's task and the task-related behaviors. Behaviors related to the contractor role include attempts at (a) organizing and coordinating the actions of group members relative to the task by suggesting task allocations, deadlines, task sequencing, follow-ups, and motivating members to achieve team goals; and (b) clarifying team member abilities, resources, and responsibilities, summarizing the team's task accomplishments to date, and providing task focus to meeting time. The focus here is on efficiency.

***Appropriate Situations.***   There are several situational characteristics that call for the contractor role. Among the most prominent are the complexity and ambiguity surrounding the work in which the team is engaged. Work complexity represents the number of informational cues and actions required, the dynamism of the requirements, and the relationship among them (Campbell, 1988; Wood, 1986). Ambiguity represents the clarity of the information and action requirements. To the degree that these conditions are present in the situation, the contractor role is helpful to clarify, segment, and assign the work among the team members.

Work complexity and ambiguity are often present in teams because of the shared and interdependent nature of the work. Another source of ambiguity is the level of task-based experience possessed by the team members. Leadership research suggests that more organizing and directive leadership behaviors increase in importance when team members have little experience with the task (Hersey & Blanchard, 1993; Vecchio, 1987). Ambiguity can also be created in situations where team members are familiar with the task, but have never worked with the other team members (McIntyre & Salas, 1995). For example, this situation exists in cockpit crews, where the teams are formed literately hours before they must perform and members often have not even met each other (Ginnett, 1990; Hughes, Ginnett, & Curphy, 1996). In such situations, effective captains are those who explicitly discuss the tasks that need to be coordinated within the team (Ginnett, 1990), thus fulfilling a contractor role.

TABLE 15.1

Previous Literature Related to the Integrated Team-Role Typology

**Task Roles**

| This Chapter | Benne and Sheats (1948) | Bales (1950) | Belbin (1981, 1993) | Ancona and Caldwell (1988, 1992) | McCann and Margerison (1989, 1995) | Barry (1991) | DuBrin (1995) | Parker (1994, 1996) |
|---|---|---|---|---|---|---|---|---|
| **Contractor** | Coordinator<br><br>Initiator-contributor<br>Opinion Seeker<br>Information seeker<br>Orientor<br>Energizer | Gives orientation<br>Asks for orientation<br>Asks for opinion<br>Asks for suggestion | Coordinator<br><br>Shaper | | Assessor<br><br>Thruster | Organizing | Collaborator<br><br>Summarizer | Collaborator |
| **Creator** | | | Plant | | Creator | Envisioning | | |
| **Contributor** | Opinion giver<br>Information giver<br>Elaborator | Gives opinion<br>Gives suggestion | Specialist | | | | | |
| **Completer** | Procedural technician<br>Recorder | | Completer<br><br>Implementer | | Concluder<br><br>Controller Reporter | | Knowledge contributor | Contributor |

|  |  |  |  | **Socioemotional Roles** |  |  |  | **Boundary-Spanning Roles** |  |  |  |
|---|---|---|---|---|---|---|---|---|---|---|---|
| **Critic** | Evaluator-critic | Disagrees<br>Shows tension<br>Shows antagonism | Monitor Evaluator |  | Upholder Social |  | Challenger Challenger |  | Explorer Spanning |  | Communicator |
| **Communicator** | Encourager | Shows solidarity<br>Tension release<br>Agrees | Team worker |  |  | People supporter<br>Listener |  |  |  |  |  |
| **Cooperator** | Follower<br>Compromiser |  |  |  |  |  |  |  |  |  |  |
| **Calibrator** | Harmonizer<br><br>Gate keeper<br>Group observer<br>Standard Setter |  |  |  |  | Process observer<br>Conciliator<br>Mediator<br>Gatekeeper |  |  |  |  |  |
| **Collector** |  | Resource investigator | Task coordinator<br>Scout |  |  |  |  |  |  |  |  |
| **Consul** | Ambassador<br>Guard |  |  |  |  |  |  |  |  |  |  |

## TABLE 15.2

Definitions, Examples, and Situations for the Integrated Team-Role Typology

| Role | | Definition | Examples | Situations in Which Role is Appropriate |
|---|---|---|---|---|
| Task | Contractor | Behaviors that function to structure the task-oriented behaviors of other group members. Organizes and coordinates the actions of group members relative to the task by suggesting task allocations, deadlines, task sequencing, follow-ups, and motivating members to achieve team goals. Summarizes the team's task accomplishments to date, and assures that team meeting time is spent efficiently focusing on task issues. | Organizer Orientor Energizer | **Work Ambiguity**<br>Work ambiguity represents uncertainty surrounding the work to be accomplished or the strategy for accomplishing it. It includes the following:<br><br>• When task demands are technically complex (Herold, 1978, 1980)<br>• When team members have little task experience (Vecchio, 1987)<br>• When team members have little experience working together (Bettenhausen & Murnighan, 1985; Ginnett, 1990) |
| Task | Creator | Behaviors that function to change or give original structure to the task processes and strategies of the team. Provides new, innovative, or compelling visions of the team objective and approaches to the task, or strategies for accomplishing the task. These behaviors may involve a "reframing" of the teams objective, the means that should be used to accomplish it, and looking at the big picture, as well as providing creative solutions to the tasks problems. | Envisioner Creator Plant | **Creative and Strategic Stagnation**<br>Creative and strategic stagnation is when the team needs creativity in terms of task strategy or task ideas and solutions. It includes the following:<br><br>• When team is new and members have little task experience (Gersick & Hackman, 1990)<br>• When the work is predominantly "creative" in nature (Hackman & Morris, 1975; McGrath, 1984)<br>• When the team's purpose is unclear or current strategy is failing (Gersick, 1988, 1989)<br>• When the team is in its initial meeting, or at its developmental midpoint transition (Gersick, 1988; 1989; Hackman & Walton, 1986) |

| | | | | |
|---|---|---|---|---|
| Task | Contributor | Behaviors that function to contribute critical information or expertise to the team. These include being assertive when dealing with areas that are within the domain of the team member's expertise, sharing critical knowledge within the team, and may involve enough self-promotion to convey his or her credentials to the team. Clarifying team member abilities, resources, and responsibilities, and training individual team members, as well as the team in general. | Information giver Specialist Elaborator | **Distributed Expertise**<br>Distributed expertise represents situations in which task required resources are heterogeneously distributed among the members. It includes the following:<br><br>• When the work is predominantly "choice"-oriented (McGrath, 1984)<br>• When team members have little experience working together (Ginnett, 1990)<br>• When high-status differentials (Ginnett, 1990; McIntyre & Salas, 1995)<br>• When task resources are heterogeneously distributed among team members (Libby, Trotman, & Zimmer, 1987) |
| Task | Completer | Behaviors that function to execute the individual-oriented tasks within the team. May involve "doing homework" to prepare for team meetings, volunteering to take personal responsibility to complete certain tasks within the team, assisting team members with completing their tasks, and following through on commitments made within the team. | Completer-finisher Implementer Concluder | **Individual-Oriented Work**<br>Individual-oriented work represents the situations in which team effectiveness depends on the performance of behaviors by individuals working alone outside the team environment.<br><br>• When the work is predominantly "execution"-oriented (Larson & LaFasto, 1989; McGrath, 1984)<br>• When there are individual-oriented and unitary tasks that must be completed (Steiner, 1972)<br>• When the team is at its second developmental phase (Gersick, 1988, 1989; Hackman & Walton, 1986) |

(Continued)

**TABLE 15.2**
(Continued)

| Role | | Definition | Examples | Situations in Which Role is Appropriate |
|---|---|---|---|---|
| **Task** | **Critic** | Behaviors related to going against the "flow" of the group. They function to subject the ideas or decisions of the group to critical evaluation and scrutiny. Questioning the purpose or actions of the team or ideas proposed within the team, even if a formal "leader" has sponsored an idea. The role insists on evaluating "worst-case scenarios" and points out flaws or assumptions the group is making, and a willingness to present negative information to the team. | Challenger Evaluator Monitor | **Unscrutinized Concurrence**<br>Unscrutinized concurrence represents situations in which the team is approaching consensus on a task without adequately analysis of positive and negative contingencies.<br><br>• When the team is prematurely seeking concurrence (Lawrence & Lorsch, 1969)<br>• When there is a high level of trust among team members (McIntyre & Salas, 1995)<br>• When the work is predominately a "decision-making dilemma" (Katz & Kahn, 1978)<br>• When task demands are technically and/or socially complex (Herold, 1978, 1980; Longley & Pruitt, 1980)<br>• When the team is highly cohesive, insulated, and has directive leadership in a stressful environment (Janis, 1972) |
| **Social** | **Cooperator** | Behaviors functioning to conform to the expectations, assignments, and influence attempts of other team members, the team in general, or constituents to the team. This should be a proactive role where there is critical inquiry into the decision, and provision of input, but then supporting the team's decision once it has been made, allowing the team to move forward. This role involves acknowledging the expertise of others, and supporting their direction. | Compromiser Follower | **Scrutinized Concurrence**<br>Scrutinized concurrence represents situations in which the team has critically evaluated and clearly established the merits of a particular decision.<br><br>• When the team has had adequate differentiation before seeking concurrence (Lawrence & Lorsch,1969)<br>• When the work is predominantly "negotiation"-oriented (McGrath, 1984)<br>• Distributed expertise and high-status differentials (Ginnett, 1990; Libby, Trotman, & Zimmer, 1987; McIntyre & Salas, 1995) |

| Social | | | |
|---|---|---|---|
| **Communicator** | Behaviors functioning to create a social environment that is conducive to collaboration. Including paying attention to the feelings of team members, listening to the opinions/contributions of others, communicating effectively, or injecting humor into tense situations. This role does not deal with direct "influence attempts" as does the calibrator. | Encourager<br>Team worker<br>Listener | **Social Sensitivity**<br>Social sensitivity represents situations in which team effectiveness is elastic with regard to social processes.<br><br>• When the work is predominantly "negotiation"-oriented (McGrath, 1984)<br>• When task demands are socially complex (Herold, 1978, 1980)<br>• When team context is emotionally demanding or stressful (McIntyre & Salas, 1995; Morgan & Bowers, 1995)<br>• When team is diverse in terms of values and attitudes (Jackson, May, & Whitney, 1995) |
| **Calibrator** | Behaviors functioning to observe the group social processes, make the group aware of them, and suggest changes to these processes to bring them in line with functional social norms. The overt creation of new group norms dealing with group process issues (not task issues). This may involve initiating discussion of power struggles or tensions in the group, settling disputes among team members, summarizing group feeling, soliciting feedback, and so on. | Harmonizer<br>Gate-keeper<br>Mediator<br>Conciliator | **Nonfunctional Group Processes**<br>Nonfunctional group process represent situations in which functional patterns of social interaction have not been established in the team, or they have been disrupted by malfunctional behavior.<br><br>• When the team is new and team members have little experience working together or there are changes in group composition (Ginnett, 1990)<br>• When there is emotional or task-based conflict or distrust in the team (Jehn, 1995, 1997)<br>• When the work is "negotiation"-oriented and the context is socially demanding (Herold, 1978, 1980; McGrath, 1984) |

(Continued)

**TABLE 15.2**
Continued

| Role | Definition | Examples | Situations in Which Role is Appropriate |
|---|---|---|---|
| **Spanning** — Consul | Behaviors that involve interactions that take place primarily outside the team setting that function to collect information and resources from relevant parties in the organization. This involves presenting the team, its goals and interests in a favorable light, influencing constituent perceptions of the likelihood of team success and willingness to provide resources. | Ambassador Explorer Resource investigator | **External Resource Dependence**<br>External resource dependence represents situations in which the existence and effectiveness of the team is dependent on support and resources from its environment.<br><br>• When team does not possess the needed information, money, personnel, and so on (Hackman & Walton, 1986)<br>• When the team is new, and somewhat experimental and constituents need status updates (Ancona, 1990) |
| Coordinator | Behaviors that involve interactions that take place primarily outside the team setting that function to interface with constituents, coordinate team efforts with other parties. It also involves soliciting timely feedback on the team's performance | Task Coordinator Spanner | **External Activity Interdependence**<br>External activity interdependence represents situations in which the activities of the team must be coordinated with the activities of teams, customers, and individuals outside the team.<br><br>• When the activities of the team are interdependent with activities of other teams (Ancona, 1990; Ancona & Caldwell, 1992; Green, McComb, & Compton, 2000)<br>• When the activities of the team are interdependent with customers or suppliers (Ancona, 1990; Ancona & Caldwell, 1992; Barry, 1991) |

## Creator

The creator role relates to creativity and leadership in teams. Teams are often used within organizations to foster innovation. However, teams also can have a tendency to form norms that limit such innovation. The creator role embodies those behaviors that create change in the group's task processes to solve problems and bring about this innovation.

*Definition.* The creator role provides new, innovative, or compelling visions of the team objective and approaches to the task, or strategies for accomplishing the task. This might include reframing the team's objectives, redesigning methods, looking at the big picture, and making sense of events in the environment. The creator role fosters creativity and adaptation within the team. The distinction between the creator and the contractor roles has parallels with the distinction between management and leadership (e.g., Bennis & Nanus, 1985; Yukl, 1994). Management focuses on the efficient execution of systems and leadership focuses on vision, innovation, and change (House & Aditya, 1997). Similarly, the creator role emphasizes taking creative approaches to the team's task that often go beyond organizing.

*Appropriate Situations.* The creator role is especially important when there is strategic ambiguity, the current team strategies are inadequate, or the work has a large creative component. Strategic ambiguity represents a lack of clarity among the team members as to the most effective way to proceed and is often accompanied by the perception among team members that their current approach is not working. Research by Gersick (1989) suggests that the most advantageous times for establishing a new strategy are in a team's first encounter, in response to poor performance, or when performance appears to be floundering. The creator role is also important when the work has a large creative component (Hackman & Morris, 1975; McGrath, 1984). Teams have a general tendency to form habitual routines for dealing with situations that they encounter frequently (Gersick & Hackman, 1990). This tendency usually helps the team save time and energy, but it reduces innovation.

## Contributor

Often the driving reason for using teams is to provide a social structure for the integration of ideas, actions, and processes from different areas or individuals in an organization (Parker, 1994). In these situations, each team member has a distinct set of knowledge, skills, and abilities, as well as different preferences and priorities. Teams are a social mechanism for integrating the expertise held by diverse individuals (Larson & LaFasto, 1989). This is increasingly important as the scope and complexity of the work increases to the point that one individual is unlikely to be able to perform it.

*Definition.* The contributor role represents those behaviors that function to contribute critical information or expertise to the team. Behaviors consistent with the contributor role include sharing knowledge, communicating ideas, and training others. To assume this role, it may be necessary to engage in sufficient self-promotion to convey credentials to the team, and hence involves a degree of assertiveness. This role is context-specific in that it is only appropriate when one has relevant expertise. The team member who correctly detects when he or she has relevant expertise and then takes steps to share that expertise is an effective team member.

*Appropriate Situations.* The contributor role is most likely to be called for under conditions of distributed expertise, high-status differentials, and choice-related tasks. With distributed expertise, the team cannot achieve optimal performance without receiving input from all members (Steiner, 1972). Taking a contributor role gives the team a clearer picture of who has the needed expertise (Libby, Trotman, & Zimmer, 1987). With high-status differentials, there is a tendency to reduce the flow of information in the team, particularly information that runs counter to the position endorsed by the high-status individuals (McIntyre & Salas, 1995). The contributor role can counteract this tendency. Finally, with choice-related tasks (McGrath, 1984), performance is sensitive to the amount and quality the information used to make the choice, thus increasing the importance of the contributor role.

## Completer

When conceptualizing the work that teams accomplish, often the implicit assumption is made that all of the work takes place in a team setting via joint collaboration. This assumption is often incorrect and ignores the fact that a large portion of the work may be performed by individual team members outside of the team context (Larson & LaFasto, 1989).

*Definition.* The completer role represents behaviors that contribute to the effectiveness of the team by individuals working alone. This may involve volunteering to take personal responsibility for a particular task, following through on commitments made in team meetings, coming to team meetings prepared, and assisting teammates.

*Appropriate Situations.* The completer role is called for any time there is a task to be completed that is relatively unitary (unable to be divided among multiple individuals; Steiner, 1972), is execution in nature (McGrath, 1984), or is relatively unassigned. As the proportion of the team's work that involves unitary or execution tasks increases, the completer role becomes more important. In a situation involving unassigned tasks, the individual volunteering to take responsibility and then following through on that commitment is taking the completer role. This role is especially important when the team is in its post-midpoint phase of development (Gersick, 1988, 1989). This is characterized by an increase in task activity in preparation for a deadline when it is critical for members to take individual responsibly (Hackman & Walton, 1986).

## Critic

Among the most cited constructs in group discussions is Janis' (1972) work on "groupthink." Janis proposed that many faulty decisions reached by teams can be traced to the groupthink phenomena, which is "a mode of thinking that people engage in when they are deeply involved in a cohesive in-group, when the members' strivings for unanimity override their motivation to realistically appraise the alternative courses of action" (p. 9). So, cohesive teams may avoid critically evaluating proposed courses of action for fear of disrupting the positive relations among team members.

*Definition.* The critic role captures behaviors that "go against the flow" of the group. They function to subject the ideas or decisions to critical evaluation and scrutiny. They may question the purpose or actions of the team or ideas proposed within the team, even if contrary to the views of the formal leader. The role insists on evaluating worst-case scenarios, pointing out flaws or assumptions the group is making, and presenting negative information.

*Appropriate Situations.* The critic role is most essential in conditions of unscrutinized consensus in the team. Unscrutinized consensus refers to situations in which the team is going forward with an idea or a decision without having considered all the potential costs of the decision, or without conducting adequate research into the problem, a situation referred to by Lawrence and Lorsch (1969) as premature concurrence seeking. In such situations, the team needs a "devil's advocate" to bring out the potential oversights and negative aspects of the team's direction.

The task can also influence the likelihood of the critic role being appropriate. When the task is a decision-making dilemma (novel and complex tasks with nonstandard solutions; Katz & Kahn, 1978) or as a decision-making task (choice tasks with no single correct answer; McGrath, 1984), or a socially complex task (high team-member involvement in the task; Herold, 1978), then it is more important for the critic role to be taken (Longely & Pruitt, 1980).

This role can also be important when there is directive leadership within the team because such status differentials tend to decrease the likelihood of bringing up alternative viewpoints (McIntyre & Salas, 1995).

Finally, this role is also most appropriately taken when a trusting relationship exists among team members (McIntyre & Salas, 1995). To accept the monitoring of the critic role, and feedback that accompanies it, requires that there is a psychological contract (McIntyre & Salas, 1995) among the team members that accepts such evaluations because they are for the good of the team.

## SOCIOEMOTIONAL ROLES

One of the most fundamental realities of work teams is that effective team members must have certain interpersonal as well as technical skills (Katzenbach & Smith, 1993; Stevens & Campion, 1994, 1999; Stewart et al., 1999).

### Communicator

Teams typically are interdependent and require communication with others to accomplish the work (Shea & Guzzo, 1987), to resolve conflicts and solve problems (Stevens & Campion, 1994, 1999), and to share information, resources, and opinions.

*Definition.* The communicator role encompasses behaviors that create a social environment that is positive, open, and conducive to collaboration. These behaviors include paying attention to the feelings of team members, listening to the opinions of others, communicating personal sentiments effectively, being friendly, or injecting humor as appropriate. This role does not deal with direct influence attempts (as does the calibrator), but instead focuses on the smoothness of interactions.

*Appropriate Situations.*   The communicator role is generally required in almost all team situations, but there are situations when it is particularly vital. One such situation is when the task is socially complex, such as a negotiation task as opposed to an execution task (McGrath, 1984). Herold (1978, 1980) categorized tasks as having complex social demands if they dealt with emotionally charged issues for which members were ego-involved and held different opinions. Another situation is high-stress environments, such as in times of change, when communication is especially important to deal with nonroutine tasks (McIntyre & Salas, 1995) and to provide social support (Hackman, 1987; Sundstrom et al., 1990). Finally, in situations where there is great diversity in the team, communication patterns can be affected (Jackson, May, & Whitney, 1995), and the communicator role becomes more important.

## Cooperator

Benne and Sheats (1948) lamented that too much research attention has focused on the leader within teams without considering the follower, a view that has been echoed by other authors (Barry, 1991; Katzenbach & Smith, 1993). The cooperator role acknowledges the importance of supporting the team through being open to influence, and not letting ego get in the way of allowing other team members to take more directive roles when appropriate (Katzenbach & Smith, 1993).

*Definition.*   The cooperator role behaviors function to support the progress of the team by conforming to the expectations and influence attempts of other team members or the team in general. Once the team has made a decision, the cooperator role reflects a willingness to support that decision independent of the individual's original position on the matter (Kelley, 1988). This role allows the team to move forward.

*Appropriate Situations.*   Situations in which the cooperator role is particularly important are conditions of scrutinized concurrence, distributed expertise, high-status differentials, and negotiation tasks. Scrutinized concurrence represents team unity in a decision that has resulted from critical evaluation of alternatives, with all dissenting opinions in the team being heard (Lawrence & Lorsch, 1969; Longely & Pruitt, 1980). Distributed expertise means that in order for the team to bring the best possible information and judgment to bear on the task, the individuals possessing that expertise must be allowed to contribute the most (Libby et al., 1987). That means other team members, especially high-status members (Ginnett, 1990; Hughes et al., 1996), need to be willing to take a cooperator role

(McIntyre & Salas, 1995). High-status differentials can result in the inappropriate weighting of ideas (Hackman & Walton, 1986).

## Calibrator

Research on teams indicates that it is important for teams to overtly address their norms for interacting (Hackman, 1987). The notion of process facilitation is grounded in the premise that by reflecting on their norms, assumptions, and patterns of interacting, teams can improve those processes and their performance. The calibrator role refers to behaviors that serve to change the social process of the team.

*Definition.* The calibrator role observes the team social processes, makes the team aware of the processes, and suggests changes to the processes to improve team functioning. It facilitates the creation of norms dealing with group-process issues. This may involve initiating discussion of power struggles or tensions in the group, settling disputes among team members, summarizing group feeling, soliciting feedback, and so forth.

*Appropriate Situations.* The calibrator role is most essential under situations of process uncertainty or conflict. Process uncertainty occurs when ambiguity surrounds the best way for team members to interact and is most common in new teams or teams with changing composition. The calibrator role is appropriate in this situation because it helps establish initial social structures and team norms for interacting. Conflict in teams can have both positive and negative consequences (Jehn, 1995, 1997). Generally, emotional conflict is always a liability to team performance, whereas task-based conflict may show some benefits for teams performing non-routine tasks (Jehn, 1997). The calibrator role is functional when conflict arises because it helps minimize the occurrence and duration of emotional conflict and bring focus to task-based conflict.

## BOUNDARY-SPANNING ROLES

Teams exist within an organizational context, and the boundaries that determine where the group begins and where that context begins are somewhat permeable. Early research on teams created typologies of roles that only occurred within the team's boundaries (Ancona & Caldwell, 1988; Sundstrom et al., 1990). Boundary-spanning roles recognize that important behaviors by team members occur outside the team.

The degree to which a team's effectiveness depends on the environment has been referred to as *external dependence* (Ancona, 1990) and is similar to Sundstrom and Altman's (1989) work-team integration and differentiation and Green, McComb, and Compton's (2000) external linkages.

## Consul

One of the most intriguing findings of Ancona (1990) was that the effectiveness of externally dependent teams is influenced by the image of the team held by external constituents. Ancona found that initial reputations of newly formed teams tended to endure in the minds of people who evaluate teams. This need to manage the team's image and relationship with important decision makers highlights the need for the consul role.

*Definition.* The consul role involves interactions that take place primarily outside the team setting that function to present the team, its goals, and its interests in a favorable light, and to influence constituent perceptions of the likelihood of team success and willingness to provide resources.

*Appropriate Situations.* The consul role is essential under conditions of external resource dependence. When the team needs money, information, training, equipment, new members, time, or other resources from outside the team, it is critical to take a consul role (Hackman & Walton, 1986). This role is especially important for new teams who need to establish their utility and reputation to the organization in order to survive.

## Coordinator

The activities of teams are often highly interdependent with other activities within the organization (Sundstrom et al., 1990). Teams, and in particular self-managed teams, must manage this interdependence in order to be truly effective in meeting customer expectations (Hackman, 1987). The key role in dealing with this interdependence is the coordinator.

*Definition.* The coordinator role involves interactions that take place primarily outside the team setting that function to interface with constituents and coordinate team efforts with other parties. This may involve visiting other departments, passing on schedule information to other teams in the organization, or communicating with customers about their specific needs. In all these interactions, it can involve soliciting timely feedback on the team's performance.

***Appropriate Situations.*** The coordinator role is most essential when the team's work is externally interdependent. That is, when the activity, product, or service that the team provides is closely related to that of other teams and functions in the organization. This role is especially important in cross-functional teams (Green et al., 2000).

Also, this role takes on added importance when formal integration structures are not in place (Ancona & Caldwell, 1992). In the absence of formal mechanisms for communication between departments, the informal execution of this role by team members is vital. This role is particularly important if the team's task involves interfacing with external clients with changing needs. Research indicates that the failure to execute this role in an externally interdependent environment is detrimental to team success (Ancona & Caldwell, 1992).

## TEAM ROLES AND SITUATIONAL JUDGMENT TESTS

SJTs are well suited for assessing team roles for several reasons. First, because SJTs are an effective tool in performance contexts with discretionary behaviors, they are likely to be well suited to predict team-role behavior. The team context provides team members greater flexibility in their behaviors and opportunity for discretionary actions such as organizational citizenship behaviors, both of which increase the importance of situational judgments. Second, SJTs tap into the capability of the individual in a context-rich manner, with judgments being informed by information about the situation. The appropriateness of team roles is also driven by their context, with the appropriateness of any given role being driven by situational factors. Thus, team roles lend themselves well to the development of SJTs that provide those contextual cues. Third, SJTs allow for the assessment of behavior in a multi-cue environment. Multi-cue assessments are those that require individuals to recognize and evaluate multiple elements of their environment and use these elements in arriving at a course of action. The team environment, in which team roles are carried out, is clearly one such environment.

Finally, an SJT based on team roles would be particularly useful for selection in team-based organizations. The SJT could be used in several ways. First, by selecting employees with the ability to discern and carry out the most appropriate roles in the team, organizations could acquire the general collaborative abilities needed throughout the workforce. Second, basic teams where formal leadership is designated (e.g., team leader), the information from the SJT could be used to assure that those given the position of leader possess the requisite team-role capabilities. Finally, organizations using more advanced team forms (e.g., self-led teams), could use the team roles to make decisions about staffing teams to assure that each team has each role capability present.

## Situational Judgment and Team Roles: Test Development

Several steps should be followed in developing an SJT for assessing team-role capabilities. The first step is to clearly define the desirable team-role behaviors. This chapter has presented one typology intended to generalize to most teams, but the relative importance of the roles and their precise definitions should be adapted to the specific context where the SJT will be used. This adaptation would best be made through the involvement of subject matter experts from the teams, management, and other experts in team dynamics.

The second step is to clearly delineate the situational contingencies that should govern taking the team role. This chapter has developed many of those contingencies based on previous research.

The third step involves the creation of the stimulus. This can take the form of a written scenario, a video enactment, or a structured interview question. The stimuli should have three characteristics. First, they should be grounded in the organizational context where they will be used. Second, they should clearly illustrate the relevant situational contingencies as defined in Step 2. Third, care should be taken to ensure that, to the extent possible, there is one clear correct role for each stimulus.

The fourth step is the creation of response alternatives. The responses alternatives should represent feasible behavioral responses to the situation. The correct responses are those with behaviors most consistent with the role suited to the situation.

## Situational Judgment and Team Roles: Future Directions

Using SJTs in the team-role context would benefit research and practice. Due to the newness of the application, however, several intriguing research questions remain unanswered. First, research needs to investigate the effectiveness of team-role based SJTs. Several questions dealing with the context of the application need to be answered. For example, is the SJT equally effective for all types of teams? One could argue that in team types allowing for greater behavioral discretion (e.g., self-directed work teams) the SJT would more effectively predict behavior. A related question is whether the nature of the work in which the team is engaged effects the usefulness of the SJT. For example, teams involved in creative work may find performance is more sensitive to team roles than teams engaged in psychomotor work (Matteson, Mumford, & Sintay, 1999).

Second, research needs to investigate the role that realism plays in the SJT. Team roles take place in multi-cue environments (e.g., task, time, social, etc.), and it represents a significant challenge to capture those environments in the stimulus material. Future research should investigate innovative methods for presenting the stimuli such as video-based presentation. Alternatively, the method could be adapted to a structured interview form. Future research should investigate the effectiveness of these alternative methods.

Finally, a challenging area for future research lies in investigating the role that team norms play in team roles. If for example, the appropriate team role depends on norms within the team, then perhaps the correctness of any team role could be defined by comparing it to these team norms. Future research should investigate the extent to which this type of norm-scoring is possible and advantageous.

## CONCLUSION

This research has attempted to make two contributions for both research and practice. First, based on a thorough review and integration of the literature, this chapter provides a framework of 10 roles that are important for effective team member performance. Second, the chapter drew on the research literature to extract situations in which each team role is most appropriate. Future research could use this information to develop various human resource systems to improve team performance including the development of an SJT for selection and development in a team context.

## REFERENCES

Ancona, D. G. (1990). Outward bound: Strategies for team survival in an organization. *Academy of Management Journal, 33*(2), 334–365.

Ancona, D. G., & Caldwell, D. F. (1988). Beyond task and maintenance: Defining external functions in groups. *Group & Organization Studies, 13*(4), 468–494.

Ancona, D. G., & Caldwell, D. F. (1992). Bridging the boundary: External activity and performance in organizational teams. *Administrative Science Quarterly, 37*(4), 634–665.

Bales, R. F. (1950). *Interaction process analysis: A method for the study of small groups.* Cambridge: Addison-Wesley.

Bales, R. F. (1958). Task roles and social roles in problem-solving groups. In E. E. Maccoby & T. M. Newcomb (Eds.), *Readings in social psychology* (3rd ed., pp. 437–447). New York: Holt, Rinhart, & Winston.

Barry, D. (1991). Managing the bossless team: Lessons in distributed leadership. *Organizational Dynamics, 20*(1), 31–47.

Belbin, R. M. (1981). *Management teams: Why they succeed or fail.* Oxford: Butterworth-Heinemann.

Belbin, R. M. (1993). *Team roles at work.* Oxford: Butterworth-Heinemann.

Benne, K. D., & Sheats, P. (1948). Functional roles of group members. *Journal of Social Issues, 4*(2), 41–49.

Bennis, W., & Nanus, B. (1985). *Leaders: The strategies for taking charge.* New York: Harper & Row.

Bettenhausen, K., & Murnighan, J. K. (1985). The emergence of norms in competitive decision-making groups. *Administrative Science Quarterly, 30*(3), 350–372.

Biddle, B. J., & Thomas, E. J. (1966). *Role theory: Concepts and research.* New York: Wiley.

Campbell, D. J. (1988). Task complexity: A review and analysis. *Academy of Management Review, 13*(1), 40–52.

Campion, M. A., Medsker, G. J., & Higgs, A. C. (1993). Relations between work group characteristics and effectiveness: Implications for designing effective work groups. *Personnel Psychology, 46*(4), 823–850.

Cloyd, J. S. (1964). Patterns of role behavior in informal interaction. *Sociometry, 27*(2), 160–173.

DuBrin, A. J. (1995). *The break through team player.* New York: American Management Association.

Forsyth, D. R. (1990). *Group dynamics.* Pacific Grove, CA: Brooks/Cole.

Gersick, C. J. (1988). Time and transition in work teams: Toward a new model of group development. *Academy of Management Journal, 31*(1), 9–41.

Gersick, C. J. (1989). Marking time: Predictable transitions in task groups. *Academy of Management Journal, 32*(2), 274–309.

Gersick, C. J., & Hackman, J. R. (1990). Habitual routines in task-performing groups. *Organizational Behavior & Human Decision Processes, 47*(1), 65–97.

Ginnett, R. C. (1990). Airline cockpit crew. In J. R. Hackman (Ed.), *Groups that work (and those that don't): Creating conditions for effective teamwork* (pp. 427–448). San Francisco, CA: Jossey-Bass.

Green, S., McComb, S. A., & Compton, D. (2000). Promoting effective linkages between cross-functional teams and the organization. *Advances in the Management of Organizational Quality* (Vol. 5, pp. 29–70). Greenwich, CT: JAI Press.

Hackman, J. R. (1987). The design of work teams. In J. W. Lorsch (Ed.), *Handbook of organizational behavior* (pp. 315–342). Englewood Cliffs, NJ: Prentice-Hall.

Hackman, J. R. (1990a). Group influences on individuals in organizations. In M. D. Dunnette & L. M. Hough (Eds.), *Handbook of industrial and organizational psychology* (Vol. 2, pp. 199–267). Palo Alto, CA: Consulting Psychologists Press.

Hackman, J. R. (Ed.) (1990b). *Groups that work (and those that don't) : Creating conditions for effective teamwork* (1st ed.). San Francisco: Jossey-Bass.

Hackman, J. R., & Morris, C. G. (1975). Group tasks, group interaction process, and group performance effectiveness: A review and proposed integration. In L. Berkowitz (Ed.), *Advances in experimental social psychology* (pp. 45–99). New York: Academic Press.

Hackman, J. R., & Walton, R. E. (1986). Leading groups in organizations. In P. S. Goodman (Ed.), *Designing effective work groups* (pp. 72–120). San Francisco, CA: Jossey-Bass.

Hare, A. P. (1976). *Handbook of small group research.* New York: The Free Press.

Herold, D. M. (1978). Improving the performance effectiveness of groups through a task-contingent selection of intervention strategies. *Academy of Management Review, 3*(2), 315–325.

Herold, D. M. (1980). The effectiveness of work groups. In S. Kerr (Ed.), *Organizational behavior* (pp. 95–118). Columbus, OH: Grid Publishing.

Hersey, P., & Blanchard, K. H. (1993). *Management of organizational behavior: Utilizing human resources* (6th ed.). Englewood Cliffs, NJ: Prentice-Hall.

House, R. J., & Aditya, R. N. (1997). The social scientific study of leadership: Quo vadis? *Journal of Management, 23*(3), 409–473.

Hughes, R. L., Ginnett, R. C., & Curphy, G. J. (1996). *Leadership: Enhancing the lessons of experience* (2nd ed.). Chicago, IL: Irwin.

Jackson, S. E., May, K. E., & Whitney, K. (1995). Understanding the dynamics of diversity in decision-making teams. In R. A. Guzzo & E. Salas (Eds.), *Team effectiveness and decision making in organizations* (pp. 204–261). San Francisco, CA: Jossey-Bass.

Janis, I. L. (1972). *Victims of groupthink: A psychological study of foreign-policy decisions and fiascos.* Boston, MA: Houghton Mifflin.

Jehn, K. A. (1995). A multimethod examination of the benefits and detriments of intragroup conflict. *Administrative Science Quarterly, 40*(2), 256–282.

Jehn, K. A. (1997). A qualitative analysis of conflict types and dimensions in organizational groups. *Administrative Science Quarterly, 42*, 530–557.

Jung, C. G. (1923). *Psychological types.* London: Routledge & Kegan Paul.

Katz, D., & Kahn, R. L. (1978). *The social psychology of organizations* (2nd ed.). New York: Wiley.

Katzenbach, J. R., & Smith, D. K. (1993). *The wisdom of teams: Creating the high-performance organization.* Boston, MA: Harvard Business School Press.

Kelley, R. E. (1988). In praise of followers. *Harvard Business Review, 88*(6), 142–148.

Larson, C. E., & LaFasto, F. M. J. (1989). *Teamwork: What must go right/what can go wrong.* Newbury Park, CA: Sage.

Lawrence, P. R., & Lorsch, J. W. (1969). *Organization and environment: Managing differentiation and integration.* Homewood, IL: Irwin.

Libby, R., Trotman, K. T., & Zimmer, I. (1987). Member variation, recognition of expertise, and group performance. *Journal of Applied Psychology, 72*(1), 81–87.

Longely, J., & Pruitt, D. G. (1980). Groupthink: A critique of Janis' theory. In L. Wheeler (Ed.), *Review of personality and social psychology* (Vol. 1, pp. 74–93). Beverly Hills, CA: Sage.

Matteson, M., Mumford, T. V., & Sintay, G. S. (1999). Taking teams to task: A normative model for designing or recalibrating work teams. In S. J. Havlovic, *Academy of Management Best Paper Proceedings.*

McCann, D., & Margerison, C. (1989, November). Managing high-performance teams. *Training and Development Journal*, 52–60.

McCann, D., & Margerison, C. (1995). *Team management: Practical new approaches.* London: Management Books 2000.

McGrath, J. E. (1984). *Groups: Interaction and performance.* Englewood Cliffs, NJ: Prentice-Hall.

McIntyre, R. M., & Salas, E. (1995). Measuring and managing for team performance: Emerging principles from complex environments. In R. A. Guzzo & E. Salas (Eds.), *Team effectiveness and decision making in organizations* (pp. 945). San Francisco: Jossey-Bass.

Morgan, B. B., & Bowers, C. A. (1995). Teamwork stress: Implications for team decision making. In R. A. Guzzo & E. Salas (Eds.), *Team effectiveness and decision making in organizations* (pp. 262–290). San Francisco, CA: Jossey-Bass.

Mudrack, P. E., & Farrell, G. M. (1995). An examination of functional role behavior and its consequences for individuals in group settings. *Small Group Research, 26*(4), 542–571.

Parker, G. M. (1994). *Cross-functional teams.* San Francisco, CA: Jossey-Bass.

Parker, G. M. (1996). *Team players and teamwork* (1st ed.). San Francisco, CA: Jossey-Bass.

Seers, A. (1996). Better leadership through chemistry: Toward a model of emergent shared team leadership. In M. Beyerlein, D. A. Johnson, & S. T. Beyerlein (Eds.), *Advances in interdisciplinary studies of work teams* (Vol. 3, pp. 145–172). Greenwich, CT: JAI Press.

Shea, G. P., & Guzzo, R. A. (1987). Groups as human resources. *Research in Personnel and Human Resources Management, 5*, 323–356.

Steers, R. M. (1991). *Introduction to organizational behavior* (4th ed.). New York: Harper-Collins.

Steiner, I. D. (1972). *Group processes and productivity.* New York: Academic Press.

Stevens, M. J., & Campion, M. A. (1994). The knowledge, skill, and ability requirements for teamwork: Implications for human resource management. *Journal of Management, 20*, 503–530.

Stevens, M. J., & Campion, M. A. (1999). Staffing work teams: Development and validation of a selection test for teamwork settings. *Journal of Management, 25*(2), 207–228.

Stewart, G. L., Manz, C. C., & Sims, H. P. (1999). *Team work and group dynamics.* New York: Wiley.

Sundstrom, E., & Altman, I. (1989). Physical environments and work-group effectiveness. *Journal of Organizational Behavior, 11*, 175–209.

Sundstrom, E., De Meuse, K. P., & Futrell, D. (1990). Work teams. *American Psychologist, 45*(2), 120–133.

Van Dyne, L., Cummings, L. L., & Parks, J. M. (1995). Extra-role behaviors: In pursuit of construct and definitional clarity (a bridge over muddied waters). *Research in Organizational Behavior, 17*, 215–285.

Vecchio, R. P. (1987). Situational leadership theory: An examination of a prescriptive theory. *Journal of Applied Psychology, 72*(3), 444–451.

Wellins, R. S., Byham, W. C., & Wilson, J. M. (1991). *Empowered teams: Creating self-directed work groups that improve quality, productivity, and participation* (1st ed.). San Francisco, CA: Jossey-Bass.

Wood, R. E. (1986). Task complexity: Definition of the construct. *Organizational Behavior & Human Decision Processes, 37*(1), 60–82.

Yukl. (1994). Perspectives on effective leadership behavior.

Yukl, G. A. (1994). Perspectives on effective leadership behavior. In *Leadership In Organizations*. Englewood Cliffs, NJ: Prentice-Hall.

# 16

## Situational Judgment: Some Suggestions for Future Science and Practice

Robert E. Ployhart
*University of South Carolina*

Jeff A. Weekley
*Kenexa*

This book and the volume of literature reviewed in these chapters attests to the importance of situational judgment in modern staffing research and practice. As noted throughout this book, situational judgment tests (SJTs) play an important role by supplying practitioners with a selection method that is fairly predictive, face valid, relatively easy to develop, flexible to administer, and has moderate to small subgroup differences. Perhaps for these reasons, practical applications of SJTs have far outpaced theoretical developments.

Throughout this book, leading SJT researchers have reviewed the current science and practice of SJTs and provided recommendations and directions for future research. We have seen that although we know a lot about SJTs, much more remains to be done to understand why and how they relate to performance. The chapters in this book help us hypothesize what the likely constructs are and how we should go about testing these hypotheses. Our intention with this final chapter is not to reiterate the many excellent ideas provided earlier. The previous chapters are thorough and detailed and offer many useful suggestions. Rather, we wish to step back from the specific programs of research and conclude with a broad examination of where SJT research and practice may be going. Specifically, we integrate the ideas raised in the chapters to identify the major research needs and offer our observations on where the major developments/movements of SJT research will occur.

## NEED TO KNOW THE CONSTRUCT VALIDITY OF SJTs

Understanding what constructs are assessed by SJTs has been a major impetus of research for the last decade, but there has been little success in understanding what SJTs really measure (other than knowing they correlate with certain personality traits, cognitive ability, experience, and knowledge; see McDaniel, Whetzel, Hartman, Nguyen, & Grubb, chap. 9, this volume). Part of the frustration in determining construct validity comes from the fact that the constructs assessed by SJTs may be dependent on the nature of the job, situations extracted, and the wording/format of the SJT itself. It might come as no surprise, for example, that SJTs primarily relate to agreeableness in customer service positions and cognitive ability in managerial positions.

Several chapters in this book offer new hope and directions for better understanding the constructs SJTs measure. Indeed, Gessner and Klimoski (chap. 2), Brooks and Highhouse (chap. 3), Motowidlo, Hooper, and Jackson (chap. 4), Ployhart (chap. 5), Stemler and Sternberg (chap. 6), and Schmitt and Chan (chap. 7) each offer a unique and important perspective on how we might infer the nature of constructs assessed with SJTs. Importantly, these chapters also highlight how we might develop SJTs a priori to target particular constructs. This latter question has sort of been the "holy grail" of SJT research, and it will be an important scientific advancement when it is answered.

If we were to bet what constructs SJTs truly measure, our bet is on judgment broadly defined. It is ironic that even though the word *judgment* appears in the title of SJTs, we have not done a good job of taking the implications of that word seriously. Judgment is likely to be influenced by cognitive ability, personality, experience, and knowledge—the very correlates of SJTs found in past research. Yet it also helps explain how a SJT can provide incremental validity over these other knowledge, skills, abilities, and other characteristics (KSAOs). That is, because the SJT taps judgment, it explains unique variance beyond these other predictors. We believe the chapter by Brooks and Highhouse (chap. 3) is going to be an important point of departure for SJT research because it articulates how we might better develop and evaluate the construct validity of SJTs. It is clear we are going to have to make much greater connections to the basic judgment and decision-making literature for this to be successful. However, doing so should not only help us understand what SJTs measure, but also improve their operational effectiveness.

## NEED TO UNDERSTAND SJT STRUCTURE

In Schmitt and Chan (chap. 7) and Weekley, Ployhart, and Holtz (chap. 8), one conclusion is clear—we know very little about how to best develop, scale, and score SJTs to target particular constructs. Furthermore, McDaniel et al. (chap. 9) indicate that different ways of structuring SJTs ("would do" vs. "should do" instructions) may produce different correlates of SJTs. It is clear we need systematic research into how to best structure SJTs to ensure construct homogeneity (or at least homogeneous subscales), and what consequences structure has on validity, subgroup differences, fakability, and user acceptability. Weekley et al. (chap. 8) found a scattering of studies on different topics related to SJT structure, but not the kind of systematic research needed to truly answer such questions.

Likewise, research on how to best develop and structure SJTs in multimedia applications is needed. Olson-Buchanan and Drasgow (chap. 12) provide a number of thoughtful insights into the issues corresponding with SJTs in non-paper applications, and it is clear there are many as yet unanswered questions that must be considered. Given the increased adoption of technology into assessment, whether through Internet administration or high-fidelity multimedia presentation, it is critical we start to understand what this does to enhance the construct and criterion-related validity of SJTs. Technology should enable us to consider complex questions more readily than before. For example, if SJTs do in fact measure a unique individual difference called "judgment," then we should find people with similar judgment profiles pursue similar branches when presented with a multistage SJT.

Although we have a good idea of how SJTs relate to cognitive ability and personality (e.g., McDaniel et al., chap. 9), research comparing SJTs to other common assessment methods would be enlightening. For example, it would be interesting to compare a situational interview to a SJT in terms of validity, subgroup differences, and fakability. Would they be similar? How comparable would an SJT score be to the overall score generated by an assessment center? Research that highlights the relationships between SJTs and a broad array of alternative predictors would certainly help practitioners determine which combination of predictors would likely yield the best results.

As noted by Schmitt and Chan (chap. 7), we need research that shows how SJTs might best target particular constructs, and we suspect that question will in part be affected by SJT structure (see McDaniel et al., chap. 9). We envision a research agenda that ultimately will provide information on how to best develop, scale, and score items to be maximally effective in different operational contexts. Related to this issue, there is a need to understand how to structure SJTs to enhance their reliability. This is an important point, because to the extent SJTs have lower reliability, their validity and observed subgroup differences will be attenuated. It is dangerous to believe SJTs have lower subgroup differences than other predictors, for example, when those lower subgroup differences are attributable only to the lower reliability of the SJT.

## NEED FOR MORE EXPERIMENTATION AND MICRO-RESEARCH

To date, nearly all SJT research has been conducted in the field, and nearly everything we know about SJT construct validity is based on correlational studies. This research has been invaluable and we now have convincing evidence that SJTs relate to job performance across jobs and that they are related to a variety of KSAOs (see McDaniel et al., chap. 9). However, we suspect that further insight into SJT construct validity will require moving beyond meta-analysis and correlational studies. Instead, it is time researchers adopt an experimental approach more amenable to inferring the underlying constructs SJTs measure. If the speculation that SJTs measure judgment is correct, then the experimental methods used in the judgment and decision-making literature should prove applicable to this situation. For example, the approaches noted by Motowidlo et al. (chap. 4) and Stemler and Sternberg (chap. 6) offer many provocative suggestions for future research, but both approaches also require a more fine-grained analysis than what is typical in SJT development.

## NEED FOR MORE THEORY AND THEORETICAL DEVELOPMENT

One salient theme throughout this book is a need for greater theory in SJT research and practice. Perhaps this theory has been lacking because of the applied nature of early SJT research. But we are now at a point where such theory should be part of the initial test plan, just as it should for any good test and predictor development. In this regard, every chapter in this book offers theoretical advice and suggestions for enhancing theory in SJT research. Adopting a more theory-driven approach will hopefully also link SJT research back into mainstream industrial and organizational psychology and psychological research more generally. Among other things, this may help promote the visibility of our profession to our scientist peers.

Theory in other areas of psychology should find wider application in the study of SJTs. Theory on situation perception (see Gessner & Klimoski, chap. 2), for example, will not only guide developments in the presentation of stimuli (i.e., the situations), but should help ensure that these situations are perceived as intended. Similarly, the relevance of theory in judgment and decision making has already been pointed out (Brooks & Highhouse, chap. 3). More thorough integration of these literatures into the SJT arena will offer up new and better insights into what we are measuring and how we might do it better.

## NEED TO KNOW THE LIMITS OF SJTs

We must move beyond simply examining criterion-related validity to examine the boundary conditions of operational SJTs. These include issues of faking and coaching (Hooper, Cullen, & Sackett, chap. 10), user reactions to SJTs (Bauer & Truxillo, chap. 11), multimedia SJTs (Olson-Buchanan & Drasgow, chap. 12), and international use of SJTs (Lievens, chap. 13). Simply put, we don't know a great deal about SJTs in actual applicant contexts, and therefore we need to know the extent to which SJTs are fakable and coachable; how applicants perceive their use; and how we can best administer them in the most efficient manner possible. It is interesting to note that these are often primary concerns to practitioners, so while our focus on criterion-related validity has been useful it is also limited in promoting SJT use in practice.

Likewise, as organizations continue to become global and international, it is incumbent on researchers to identify the cross-cultural generalizability—and limits—of SJTs. For example, a consulting organization in the United States may wish to export its SJT to clients around the world. Will the test be acceptable, will it predict performance, and will the scoring keys be the same? Lievens (chap. 13) presents many reasons to expect similarities and differences across cultures in how applicants complete a SJT. We should be cautious at this point about assuming SJTs will work equivalently in countries other than the one it is developed in. Alternatively, one might ask whether it is possible to create a SJT that generalizes across cultures. Given the highly contextual nature of SJTs, that poses a very interesting question.

## NEED TO EXPAND SJTs TO NEW ORGANIZATIONAL CONTEXTS

To date, nearly all SJT research has been conducted in staffing contexts, yet chapters by Fritzsche, Stagl, Salas, and Burke (chap. 14) and Mumford, Campion, and Morgeson (chap. 15) provide exciting new uses for SJTs that have scarcely been considered. Given the highly contextual and problem-solving nature of SJTs, coupled with their relatively low cost, it is surprising they have not been more widely used for training and development purposes. We suspect this situation will change dramatically in years to come, and Fritzsche et al. (chap. 14) will help direct this future research.

Likewise, the use of SJTs in group and team research remains practically nonexistent, but we can see many possibilities for staffing teams, team building exercises, and preparation/training for teamwork. The chapter by Mumford et al. (chap. 15) certainly offers a number of innovative approaches and connections that should stimulate the use of SJTs in team contexts. We believe SJTs will find other new applications in some fairly novel situations. For example, they may prove useful for individual assessment or top executive selection, primarily because of their ability to tap judgment (something critical for senior management positions). Likewise, to the extent SJTs are useful measures of knowledge, they may prove to be among the best predictors for jobs that are primarily knowledge-based. If we are truly moving to a knowledge-based economy, the SJT may find itself to be in a league of its own.

## CONCLUSION

We know SJTs tend to do a good job predicting performance, but our attention must now turn to why and how. For years, we lamented the poor construct validity of assessment centers, yet continued to use them because they were highly predictive. Should SJTs live a similar fate? We think not because the chapters in this book offer a rich theoretical network that can be applied to answer these questions. SJTs will continue to be used in practice, and it is time researchers start addressing these practical questions with a stronger theoretical approach. This movement has already started as the chapters in this book attest.

# Author Index

# Subject Index